Engraved by I.Barber from a Drawing by I.Addis for the Excursions through Ireland.

MAYNOOTH COLLEGE.

Maynooth
And
Georgian
Ireland

by
Jeremiah Newman

1979

First published 1979
Kenny's Bookshops and Art Galleries Ltd.,
Galway, Ireland.

Cloth   — ISBN 0 906312 18 3
¼ morocco — ISBN 0 906312 19 1
fine binding — ISBN 0 906312 20 5

Decorations by: Thomas Ryan R.H.A.
Binding: Kenny Galway Fine Binding Ltd.
Typeset and Printed in the Republic of Ireland
by Standard Printed Products, Galway.

Contents

Preface

The present book was unconsciously begun about twenty three years ago when, as a young Professor at Maynooth, I started the hobby of taking notes, every time I got the chance, about the history of the College from its beginnings to the end of the last century.

The more this proceeded and the years went by, the more I realised that there was room and need for the publication of the material. In fact that material is now so vast that it would take many volumes to record fully, but being neither a professional historian nor anxious to produce a heavy study, I have avoided the temptation to even try to do this. In any case time alone would not permit it. I should mention, however, that, even though I have omitted all footnotes, for reasons of space-saving and readability, practically everything that is said in the book could be annotated if necessary.

Needless to say, during a period of over twenty years, my research has taken me into every major library and archives in Europe, America and Australia that I am aware has any source material concerning Maynooth College. I can only thank collectively here all who helped me in any way over the years. While President of Maynooth, from 1968 to 1974, I was particularly fortunate in having access to special sources in the College and Presidential Archives. It is, of course, likely that further material will continue to turn up in the future but there is a law of diminishing returns in such matters and it is better not to seek perfection.

I hope that, unusual in its approach though it may be, this book will succeed in conveying a picture of Maynooth College during its early days that is not very familiar either in Ireland or abroad and, in its own way, add to the distinction of a place that I have loved.

JEREMIAH NEWMAN

Kilmoyle
19 August 1979.

Introduction

In 1945 Neil Kevin, author of the immortal *I Remember Maynooth,* wrote as follows: "After one hundred and fifty years, Maynooth College begins to grow old. One of the signs of age, a failing memory,begins to be noticeable here. Already clues are missing, and when conversation turns to reminiscences, there are doubts and gaps. Healy, in his history of the first hundred years, did one man's best, reaching out to nearly eight hundred folio pages, proceeding in his narrative with exactness, very faithful to what we might call an ecclesiastical sense of what was important. It was inevitable that he (or any other historian) should leave unanswered many questions of the kind that age makes more interesting. What is lacking is not a historian, but a diarist who would have written for us between the lines of history" *(The Dublin Review,* vol. 217. p. 57).

In a sense that is what this book tries to do. It is certainly not intended as a definitive history of Maynooth College during the Georgian period, even though at times perhaps it does shed light on some unknown or misinterpreted aspects of that history. It has tried, as far as possible, to omit material that has already been covered in depth by Healy's *Centenary History (1895)* or Meehan's *Window on Maynooth* (1947), but obviously for the sake of completeness it has not been possible to adhere to this totally. But what it is hoped the book has succeeded in doing is to treat of its subject matter in a new way — concentrating not on the bare bones of events relating to professorships or buildings or students but seeking rather to give a human slant to them. And if this sometimes means that the disedifying and even scandalous facets of College history come to the fore, it is hoped that the College is by now certainly old enough to take this, and to laugh at the more humorous episodes.

Indeed a recalling of some of these incidents after a period when Maynooth has seen rapid change, controversy about its teaching, student unrest and scandal amongst the staff, should be of help in making the public aware of the fact that such things took place there before, and that the great College and all it represents for the Irish Church survived. From that point of view the book should have a special interest in showing the almost uncanny way in which history is seen to repeat itself.

It will be appreciated that the everyday work of any institution is never re-counted. It is the unusual, the sensational that always captures the imagination. It has always been so. For that reason the great work for which Maynooth College is owed the thanks of the Church in so many countries — namely the education of solid and devoted priests — gets little coverage here. That has been done elsewhere and in any case, as has been mentioned, is but little documented.

If what is recounted here tends towards the unusual or the unexpected, it is both because of this lack of source material for the other as well as the desire to produce a readable narrative in keeping with the times which it covers. An attempt is also made to catch glimpses of Georgian Ireland through the eyes of the Maynooth of the time. And throughout the method of allowing the sources to speak for themselves has, where at all feasible, been adopted, partly because of a desire to provide authentication in the text and partly a desire to retain the quaint language of Georgian days. The whole may contribute to a better understanding of that fascinating but relatively little known period in Ireland.

Chapter I

Ye Royal Catholick College

When, in 1845, the architect of the Gothic revival Augustus Welby Pugin spoke of 'Ye Royal' College at Maynooth, his archaic diction fitted its subject. Maynooth College or, as it has been commonly called for the last century and a half, St. Patrick's College, Maynooth, is old by Irish Catholic standards. It was founded in 1795 by an Act of George III.

From its early days even to the present the College is frequently linked with a much earlier educational establishment. In 1827 *Leigh's New Pocket Book of Ireland* says that "there had for some centuries previously existed a College at Maynooth, consisting of a Provost and six Priests, on the foundation of Gerald, Earl of Kildare", while nearly one hundred and fifty years afterwards another English writer on Ireland records that "in 1795 Maynooth College, the Geraldine foundation, was reopened".

While it is nice to think that the present College is directly linked with the older one, its origins are Georgian rather than Geraldine. Even at that it is now quite a venerable institution, one of the oldest of its kind in these islands. On the reasons for its establishment there is general agreement. Plowden, who wrote about this soon after, summed it up as follows:

"It is well known, that a principal inducement to establish the Catholic College at Maynooth, was to prevent the mischief of young men destined for the gospel ministry being sent abroad for that education which the impolicy of the laws had so long prevented them from receiving in their own country. The complaint formerly was that they brought back with them the unconstitutional principles of absolute monarchy and arbitary government: the latter dread has been that they would return to their native land infected with the licentious poison of modern democracy, and hostility to all establishments.,

Cusack, O'Connell's biographer, gives the same reason only much more pointedly: "As the Government had some apprehensions lest the Catholics should avenge themselves in any way for the duplicity with which they had been treated, it was proposed to establish the College of Maynooth . . . . It was moreover believed that if Government endowed Maynooth the Irish hierarchy would feel bound in return to support Government. It was at least certain to all but the most obtuse, that a rebellion was imminent in Ireland, and this seemed a probable means of enlisting the Catholic clergy on the side of England".

A WIND FROM FRANCE '89

As if to indicate their awareness of the happenings on the Continent, the Revolution in France had scarcely begun when a petition was made to the Irish Parliament by the Catholic Committee for relief from disabilities. Education was high on the list of items for which remedies were sought. It was the culmination of a long campaign.

As early as 1782 a Bill had been passed which permitted some measure of Catholic education. It opened up debate on what came to be called 'The Catholic Education Question'. That was the year of the Declaration of Independence in which Ireland had secured a Constitution. But Catholics continued under all sorts of handicaps. Hence it was that the Catholic Committee — an association in existence since 1759 — became more active towards the end of the century.

Its remonstrances were not lost on the Government, particularly after the launching in 1791 of the Society of United Irishmen. So it was that in 1792 a further Repeal Act removed most of the remaining restrictions on Catholic education. Carlow College was opened in 1793 with the help of private Catholic resources for the purpose of providing "for the education of Roman Catholic youth". It is therefore not surprising to find the Catholic Committee going into voluntary dissolution in April of that year after having set up a special group to seek to further the improvement of the system of education for Irish Catholics, both lay and clerical. In the circumstances, neither is it surprising that at the same time the Committee should have sent an Address of Loyalty to His Majesty the King.

In Rome the Pope's men were watching. Early in 1793 Cardinal Antonelli, the then Prefect of Propaganda, was writing to the Archbishop of Dublin, Dr. Troy, to the effect that when the Irish Archbishops held their next meeting they should consider carefully how to educate young men for the priesthood now that the French colleges had been closed.

His Grace of Dublin took his time about the matter. He had his reasons. In November, 1793, we find him preparing to consult the King's Attorney General in Ireland with a view to ascertaining whether under the new Repeal Act Catholics were empowered to bequeath, grant or supply money for seminaries. After all, Carlow could scarcely be regarded as having set a precedent in this respect as, technically at least, it catered for the general education of youth rather than specifically priestly training. Dr. Troy had drawn up a document — to be signed by the four Archbishops and a number of Bishops — binding each to contribute at least ten guineas, and each parish priest at least one guinea towards the establishment of a central fund for the setting up of seminaries. Monies received from Rome and the laity should also be devoted to this purpose.

At the end of November Dr. Troy wrote to Lord Hobart, the Chief Secretary, setting out the difficulties in the way of educating priests following the French Revolution and quoting Edmund Burke to the effect that a Protestant University was not a suitable place for this. The Bishops, he said, were awaiting the authority of the legislature before setting up seminaries. They would also need financial help.

With Burke, there entered into the picture one of the most influential personalities associated with the beginnings of Maynooth College. As early as December, 1793, Burke was writing to the Bishop of Cork, Dr. Moylan, suggesting that his son Richard Burke (former agent of the Irish Catholic Committee, although himself a Protestant) and the Reverend Dr. Thomas Hussey (former chaplain to the Spanish Embassy in London and diplomatic envoy of George III) be appointed as negotiators in London on behalf of the Irish Bishops' seminary interests, Moylan was quick to reply that this idea had the backing of the Irish prelates.

Burke the elder was to prove a valuable advisor. in his letter to Moylan he recommended "that you consult as little as possible, in the first digestion, with those who are not convinced that the whole ought to be under the exclusive management of the Bishops", by which he meant that the Irish Government, in the person of the Lord Chancellor (Fitzgibbon, the Earl of Clare), the Catholic laity of the more liberal kind and Trinity College, Dublin, should be kept in the dark at least for the present.

Meanwhile, the Irish Bishops prepared for an offensive. It was prefaced, appropriately, at the close of 1793 by an address of loyalty to the Lord Lieutenant, Earl Westmoreland, to be presented to the King. Hard on the heels of this came a memorial to the Lord Lieutenant — from Dr. Troy on behalf of all the Bishops — asking him to recommend to the King the granting of a royal licence to enable endowments for seminaries to be received. Due emphasis was laid upon the danger of "contagion by sedition and infidelity" owing to the "pernicious maxims of a licentious philosophy" to which students were exposed abroad, the unsuitability of the education provided in Dublin University, and the usefulness to the State of a home trained clergy in "assiduously instructing their respective flocks in the sacred precepts of Christianity, and for inculcating obedience to the Laws and veneration for His Majesty's Royal Person and Government".

On foot of this their Lordships sought royal support for the endowment of "Academies or Seminaries for educating or preparing young persons to discharge the duties of Roman Catholic clergymen in the Kingdom, under Ecclesiastical Supervisors of their own Communion". A copy of the petition was immediately dispatched to Cardinal Antonelli who acknowledged its receipt at once, and wished the petitioners every success. The Cardinal was sufficiently optimistic about its likely outcome as to outline the care which would have to be exercised in the choosing of Professors. Rome was certainly not being kept in the dark nor refraining from throwing its own light on the situation.

At home episcopal caution prevailed. In April, 1794, the Archbishop of Dublin writes to the Archbishop of Cashel, Dr. Bray, telling him that the Crown lawyers, to whom the Bishops' memorial had been sent, would be meeting in Dublin the following week. From a report to him by the Lord Chancellor he has reason to think that their verdict will be favourable. Clearly the Earl was at least pretending not to be in the dark.

Not for the first time was his advice somewhat misleading. During 1794 discussions took place in London, of which no record has survived, between the English Home Secretary, at that time the Duke of Portland, Earl Fitzwilliam, Richard Burke, Dr. Hussey and others, which are said to have revealed certain reservations on the part of Portland and Fitzwilliam about the endowment of seminaries for the exclusive education of the clergy. The problem may have been linked with the legality of such endowment within the existing statutory system. It was now the Government's turn to pose a question similar to that which had been asked earlier by Dr. Troy. In October Lord Westmoreland got in touch with the Prime Sergeant, the Attorney General and the Solicitor General, enclosing the Bishops' petition and asking opinion as to what might properly and legally be done.

In the meantime mid-November saw the delivery to Dr. Troy of a letter from Dublin Castle stating that the Bishops' address of loyalty had been presented to His Majesty and was graciously received.

But another headache now afflicted the Bishops, this time caused by Roman reservations. Already in September, 1794, Dr. Bray of Cashel wrote to Dr. Young, Bishop of Limerick, as follows: "I understand that Cardinal Antonelli and other Round Heads in the City do not relish the Oath and Declarations annexed to the last Act of Parliament in our favour. I hope . . . that Dr. Troy will not call a general meeting of our Prelates until his Grace has submitted to their consideration the answer he expects to our Memorial".

Nevertheless, November brought a communication from Cardinal Livizzani in Rome to Dr. Troy thanking him for his letter of congratulations on the former's appointment as Cardinal Protector for Ireland and commending him for his efforts to provide seminaries, adding that he, Livizzani, was glad to hear of the recent measures which had been taken to that end. Late December brought a further assurance from Cardinal Antonelli, congratulating the Irish Bishops on their efforts to found seminaries, stressing how desirable it was that these be independent of the Protestant University of Dublin and wishing to know whether the Government proposed to subsidise them.

It was back again to the home front, in particular the Irish Parliament. During September and October Grattan had been in contact with Burke on the subject of seminaries. Or rather should one now say 'seminary' for the singular has come to replace the plural for the first time. Grattan had seen Hussey who had mentioned the question of "the College". Burke's views would be welcome. Grattan himself was convinced that "it is absolutely necessary to allow the Catholic clergy a Catholic education at home. If they cannot have a Catholic education at home, they can have none at all, or none that is not dangerous".

13

On 23 December Troy wrote to Bray, inviting him and a dozen other prelates to come to Dublin before or for Thursday, 15 January, 1795, to prepare for the seminaries' business which, he said, would shortly be coming up before Parliament. he intimated further that an address to Earl Fitzwilliam and a petition to Parliament were being prepared and expected that the Bishops would sign them. In addition he informed Bray that "Mr. Hussey wrote to me on the 17 instant that Lord Fitzwilliam wished his presence here during the progress of our business" and that he had replied urging Hussey to come as he could "render us splendid service at the Castle".

Behind the scenes the die was cast although Dr. Troy does not yet seem to have been aware of it. Amongst his papers is to found a copy, dated 24 December, 1794, of the reply from the Attorney General and other lawyers to the Lord Lieutenant, giving their opinion that under the law as it stood — in particular the Act of the 33rd year of the reign of George III — the Bishops' petition could not legally be granted. It would appear that (possibly because of the Christmas season) Dr. Troy did not know about this until the New Year, for on St. Stephen's Day he was writing to the Bishop of Limerick to the effect that on that very morning he had had a conference on the subject with the Lord Chancellor "who appeared very well disposed". He concluded: "The Prospect continues favourable". This time Lord Clare seems definitely to have been in the dark and not at the Bishops' doing.

Early January brought the bad news, a negative reply from Westmoreland to the memorial of 1793. Fate, however, held other cards. Two days later, on 4 January, Fitzwilliam arrived as new Lord Lieutenant and on 5 January Westmoreland took his departure. Soon afterwards, in his speech from the throne in the Irish Parliament, the new Viceroy again raised hopes by presaging "some new arrangements" in the field of education. Grattan followed up by announcing that a plan for the education of the Catholic clergy would soon be submitted.

The Irish Bishops were quick on the uptake. On 2 February, 1795, they wrote to Grattan (or at least eighteen of them did) explaining their project more clearly, and expressing their reliance on his brilliant exertions to promote the measure.

This letter was of very great significance and thereby was to hang a tale. For in it they substantially changed their position. Whereas, they said, in 1794 they had only contemplated a College for clerical education, now in deference to the views of the Duke of Portland, Earl Fitzwilliam and Mr. Burke, they were prepared to extend their plan to general instruction, as these statesmen did not wish to see the Catholic laity excluded from the proposed changes. They sought four Colleges endowed equally by Parliament.

One is forced to wonder whether this broadening of scope was not intended at least by the Bishops simply as a formula to get over the legal barriers that had

14

been pointed out, rather than a commitment to a new lay dimension to Irish Catholic education. This puzzlement is deepened when one finds a second letter from the Bishops, of 11 February, this time to the Lord Lieutenant, conveying their hope that the measure for "clerical education" will get through, and hoping also that the choice of the Professors will be left to the Bishops themselves.

Fate was to play its cards again. Came the sudden recall of Fitzwilliam, quite likely for one thing because it was feared that he would give too much to the Irish Catholics. He was followed as Viceroy by Lord Camden.

Dr. Hussey had just arrived in Dublin, whither he had been sent also by Portland to help in the promotion of the education issue. He wrote to Portland inquiring whether he should remain. The reply came fast and clear. Yes, he should remain as Portland hoped to have a Bill introduced shortly. The time was the Spring of 1795 and a new phase had begun.

SCHEMES AT THE COURT OF ST JAMES

Dr. Hussey and Edmund Burke were now to become the centre of complex negotiations in London. Hussey had the ear of both Government and Bishops while Burke had sagacious advice to offer on how best to prosecute affairs.

As Hussey informed Burke in January, before their letter of 2 February to Grattan, the Irish Bishops were in Dublin to confer with him, Hussey, at his request, "on what might be most useful in so important a case". It was the start of a long correspondence with Burke right up to the establishment of the College. In view of the recent set-back and the innumerable pitfalls which surrounded the issue, one can only marvel at the rapidity with which this proceeded.

In late February Hussey wrote again to Burke: "From some expressions of the Duke of Portlands dispatches, he insinuates that the matter of Catholic clergy education must go on. I will not desist that object, however personally expensive my stay is . . . . I dare not give you more of my opinions through the suspected channels of a post-office . . . ."

Ireland, said Hussey in another letter to Burke around the same time, was on the brink of civil war because of the recall of Fitzwilliam, a sentiment that was reinforced during a debate in the House of Commons on 2 March when Sir Lawrence Parsons declared that owing to the pattern events were taking every gentleman in Ireland would be under the necessity of keeping five or six dragoons in his house for his protection, which Sir Richard Musgrave, the historian of the impending rebellion was later to say turned out to be "prophetick truth".

Portland's commission to Hussey to remain in Dublin, so as to be in a position to help with the putting through of a new education Bill, arrived in March, following intimation of which by Hussey to Burke came an important message from the latter to the former.

Burke was unswervingly emphatic in his advice that neither the Government nor the Protestant Church in Ireland nor the University of Dublin should be given

15

control of any new College for the education of the Catholic clergy. Writing to Hussey on St. Patrick's Day, 1795, he asked: To whom are you going to submit the seminary for the education of your priesthood'? Is it to be Dr. Duigenan (of Trinity College)? Is it to be the Speaker of the House of Commons? Is it to be the Lord Archbishop of Cashel? "In a word, and to sum up all, is it to be Lord Fitzgibbon?"

He continued: "You are to judge their plans ands views by the Act of Parliament which they passed a year or two ago, when they took off the penalties on your keeping schools. They put any new schools you might have in future under the direction of the College of Dublin. Probably a more contumelious insult was never added to a cruel injury, from the beginning of the world to this hour''.

Burke's advice was the pursue the negotiations by all means but to beware of undue control by those mentioned. He would, he said,

> "much rather trust to God's good providence, and the contributions of your own people, for the education of your clergy, than to put into the hands of your known, avowed and implacable enemies . . . the very fountains of your morals and your religion . . . the scheme of these colleges, as you are aware, did not originate from them. But they will endeavour to pervert the benevolence and liberality of others into an instrument of their own evil purposes . . . If you consent to put your clerical education, or any other part of your education, under their direction or control, then you will have sold your religion for their money . . . There has been for certain, amongst your Irish politicians, a scheme . . . for dividing the clergy from the laity, and the lower classes of Catholic laity from the higher. I know that . . . they hope that the Catholic clergy will be brought by management to act their part in this design."

With hindsight we can see running through this not only a solicitude on the part of the Protestant Burke for Irish Catholic interests, but also a reflection of the internecine rivalry between Tories and Whigs that marked the period. Indeed it is now clear that one of the reasons for the recall of Fitzwilliam was his over abrupt clearing out of Tories in favour of Whigs in the Dublin administration. Fitzgibbon was next on the list. In fact from the beginning of the seminary project it is pretty clear that it was under Whig rather than Tory sponsorship, which helps to explain why Fitzgibbon was often in the dark as regards what was happening. It was Whigs like Portland, Fitzwilliam and Burke who carried on quietly, so much so that it is doubtful whether Pitt and the other Tory leaders in the coalition Cabinet in London knew much if anything about it until it had reached a point of no return.

That point was very near when, on 31 March, 1795, the new Viceroy, Lord Camden, arrived in the afternoon at Kingstown. He presented himself at the Castle around 7 p.m. To the public in general it must have appeared that their hopes from Whig liberalism were now dashed, something which later that evening the

16

populace of Dublin took out on Fitzgibbon when, as he was returning home from the Castle function, his carriage was attacked by a mob and he himself received a stone in the face.

Unknown but to a few, the Whig interest in the seminary project continued. Portland was still Home Secretary in England, with responsibility in that capacity for Irish affairs, while the new Chief Secretary in Ireland, Thomas Pelham, was also a Whig. Portland had decided that a Bill must be produced while Camden, despite his Tory leanings, was well aware that, like it or not, something had to be granted to the Catholics. It was a matter of making the best of things.

Hence it was that just a fortnight after his arrival in Ireland Camden, in true Tory fashion, reported to Portland:

"The Bill to allow and establish Seminaries for the education of Priests of the Roman Catholic persuasion is that upon which I have chiefly to trouble your Grace at present. It had been proposed by Dr. Hussey to found a College for this purpose by Charter from His Majesty, and as it was intended (if that mode had been adopted) to enact that the superintendence and visitation of this College should not be under the authority of any Diocesan or Ordinary of the Protestant Establishment, but that a person amongst the Highest Orders of the Clergy of the R.C. persuasion should enjoy such authority, it was objected that a Charter so drawn would give too much encouragement to the idea of an Establishment for the Clergy of that Religion. It has therefore been proposed to remedy this objection that a Bill should be drawn to empower certain persons to act as Trustees for the money to be applied to the establishment of a College for the education of a certain number of persons of the R.C. persuasion. The Trustees are to be empowered to make such Bye Laws and Statutes as are necessary for the interior Discipline of the College and are to elect in case of a vacancy, but the Chancellor and the three Chief Judges for the time being are all to be Trustees officially and as founders of the College will be its Visitors.

By this measure there will always be the most respectable and the fittest persons of the Protestant Establishment to examine and superintend this Seminary, and the rest of the Trustees, who should be of the R.C. persuasion, may be named as individuals, and not as enjoying any titular Rank or Dignity. I enclose your Grace a list of those whom it is intended to name in the first place, and I beg also to add that this alteration in the original mode of bringing this business forward, was upon the suggestion of the Lord Chancellor and the Lord Chief Baron, and I must do Mr. Hussey and Dr. Troy (titular Archbishop of Dublin) the justice to say that they immediately acceded to the proposal, and I send your Grace a Copy of the Bill which Mr. Attorney General has been directed to prepare".

17

This report is highly interesting for by and large it represents what was eventually to go through. One is somewhat surprised to find Hussey and Troy in such agreement on it, for we know that Burke was strongly opposed to the inclusion of the Judges and especially the Lord Chancellor among the Trustees. Had he not written to Hussey: "Do not be misled by childish discussion about the rights of states and governments to control education. The real question is who are the men and who would exercise this power. Know the men you have to deal with in their concretes and then you will judge what trust you are to put in them when they are presented to you in their abstracts". In other words — the Lord Chancellor in the abstract, yes, Lord Fitzgibbon in the concrete, no.

Camden's report, dated 14 April, together with Portland's reply, dated 20 April, are to be found amongst the *Secret Ministerial Correspondence* in the manuscript room of Trinity College, Dublin.

Portland's reply was by return of post: "The Bill your Excellency sent me over last night for the establishment of Catholic Seminaries of Education seems very well intended to answer that purpose, and I hope you will not object to my having directed a copy of it to be sent to the Archbishop of Canterbury, because upon a subject of this kind there cannot be too much consideration".

Concerning Drs. Troy and Hussey, Portland directed Camden to "take such notice, either in the King's name, or that of His Majesty's Confidential Servants, as you shall judge most proper and most conducive to the success of the source in which you may find it expedient to employ them".

Thus, in one form or another, Whig hopes for political benefit from the appeasement of Catholics and a package deal, acceptable to both parties as well as to the Irish Bishops, was on the way.

KING AND POPE CONCUR

Now developments took place even more rapidly. On 23rd April leave was given for the introduction of a "Bill for establishing a College for the better Education of Persons professing the Popish or Roman Catholic Religion and intended for the Clerical Ministry thereof". The following day Pelham presented to the Irish House of Commons a "Bill for the better education of Persons professing the Popish or Roman Catholic Religion". There was question of "one academy" only, whose scope, at least as implied by the title of the Bill as actually presented, seemed fairly broad.

The speeches on the occasion are not reported but one gathers that the Bill passed through the House without serious opposition. Warburton quotes somebody as having said that it was only fitting to "give these the means of education at home who formerly gave it to all the world". The more immediate reason for the measure, relating to the current pragmatic interests of both the Government and the Bishops, was voiced by Pelham who is reported by the *Cork*

Evening Post of 27 April as saying that "the question of providing for the education of the Catholic clergy was most urgent, considering the situation of Europe at present".

Here it will be noticed, the scope of the institution is again restricted to clerical education. This may well have been the reason why, when the Bill came up for a second reading on 28 April, we find Grattan presenting a petition from quite a number of Irish Catholics against it on the ground that appointments to the staff should be made not by the Trustees but by the teaching body of Trinity College. It may have been that the petitioners wished that Catholic laity should be free to be educated in the College. On the other hand, it may equally have been that these liberal Catholics were afraid that because of the title of the Bill, the new institution would be open only to Catholics, whether clerical or lay, and thus serve to "perpetuate that line of Separation between His Majesty's Subjects of different Religions" *(Commons Journal).* This could indicate the growing ethos of the United Irishmen.

In any case the Bill was carried practically unanimously, Grattan himself supporting it. Dr. Troy was caustic in his remarks concerning those Catholics who had petitioned against it: "God forgive and mend them. I believe not one of them would be appointed trustee . . . They have excluded themselves by signing the petition against the Bill".

However, in spite of the easy passage of the Bill during its first and second readings, a hornet's nest had been disturbed by the liberal Catholic petition. The question was what exactly was the scope of the College? At the Committee stage, on 1 May, Pelham said in reply to a question that whereas provision had been made originally in the Bill for the education of the laity, this had been dropped at the request of the clergy and the proposed College was intended solely for clerical students.

There was a moment of drama when, following this revelation, notice was given that the title differed from that for which leave to introduce the Bill had been given. The Bill was therefore formally withdrawn, leave given to introduce a new one and this given its first and second readings, all on that same day, 1 May, 1795.

The *Dublin Evening Post* of 2 May was at pains to explain that the whole affair was due to a technical error, so that in all probability the phase "intended for the Clerical Ministry thereof" was not designed ever to have appeared — even though it accorded with the nature of the Bill — in order to allay fears concerning an Establishment of the Catholic Clergy.

Whatever about its title, whether of the first or second instance, it emerges without doubt that the Bill was designed for the establishment of a College solely for the training of those called to the priesthood. This was confirmed some years afterwards in the letters of Lord Kilwarden who himself had earlier proposed to Pelham "the fitness of founding a College, contiguous to Trinity College and to be a member of the University of Dublin" in which the Fellows should be Roman

19

Catholics and the education of students for orders might be carried on". In short, the Bill of 1795, irrespective of title or of any seemingly contrary stance on the part of anybody, including the Bishops, at any time beforehand, was a Bill for the education of the Catholic Clergy.

It passed its third reading on 8 May, on which day it was also given a first reading in the House of Lords, where it was passed five days later. Royal assent to it was received on 5 June.

Speaking to both Houses of Parliament, at the close of the Parliamentary session on that day, the Viceroy, Lord Camden congratulated the Lords and Commons saying: "A wise foundation has been made for educating at home the Roman Catholic clergy".

There were to be twenty-one Trustees of the new College. These included four Protestants (the Lord Chancellor and three Chief Judges), six lay Catholics (Lords Fingall, Kenmare and Gormanston, Sir Edward Bellew, Sir Thomas French and Mr. Richard Strange), the four Catholic Archbishops, six other Bishops, and Dr. Hussey, the last named eleven being designated as individual clergymen. All the Trustees and students would have to take the Oath of Allegiance prescribed for Catholics by the 13th and 14th of George III and no Protestant or son of a Protestant was to be admitted.

EARL FINGALL

Engraved for the Hibernian Magazine

20

If Government had acted swiftly, the Bishops continued to do so. There was no question of a Summer recess. At a meeting of the Hierarchy as a whole on 9 June, it was decided that each Bishop should be invited to assist at the deliberations of the Episcopal Trustees prior to the general meetings of the whole Trustee Board. Thereby was a custom started that still continues even in very changed conditions.

The first meeting of the Board of Trustees took place on 24 June in the Lord Chancellor's Chambers in the House of Lords: Earl Fitzgibbon was now well in the picture. It did little more than announce that the College was started although it emerges from a advertisement which the papers carried shortly after, that an establishment for both clerical and lay students was envisaged. Lord Clare had got things moving in the way he wanted, or at least he thought he had. The second meeting next day really got down to business. It was held in John's Lane Chapel House and was attended by none of the ex officio Protestant Trustees, who thereafter attended only once more ever at a meeting on 28 July of that year. Whether this abstention on their part was by accident or design is not known. Perhaps they felt that they could exercise adequate control through their visitorial powers. In any case it left Lord Clare again in the dark with consequences that later caused difficulties.

At the second meeting Lord Fingal was in the Chair. Dr. Hussey was appointed President of the College and a Vice-President and Procurator were deemed necessary. Ten Professorships were also deemed necessary, including — to the credit of the Trustees — a Professorship of the Irish language. For the present two hundred students were to be admitted to the College.

At the third meeting of the Trustees, also held in John's Lane Chapel House, on 26 June, a Committee consisting of Archbishop Troy, Mr. Strange and Dr. Hussey was set up to further the entire matter, and to call a Trustee meeting whenever they thought necessary. Shortly after this Dr. Hussey seems to have left Ireland for England and not to have returned until the following year.

His absence meant undoubtedly that Westminster was satisfied. What, one asks, of Rome? That Rome had been kept informed and was also satisfied is clear from a letter of 9 July from Propaganda to the Irish Bishops expressing congratulations on the foundation of a College for the training of the Catholic clergy of Ireland, urging loyalty to the Crown and vigilance concerning sound doctrine. Should any controversy arise, the Bishops should have recourse to Rome.

As for Burke, his feelings continued to be mixed. He was happy up to a point but found it difficult to be entirely satisfied. In an undated letter to Hussey, written probably in June or July of 1795, he gave expression to his views at length:

"... I hope you will not think me inattentive to you, or your most important pursuit. If that business is conducted as it ought to be, and as surely it will be (if the hands of jobbers are kept out of it), I expect more good from it than from anything which has happened in our age. I hear, and am extremely alarmed at hearing, that the chancellor and the chiefs of the benches are amongst your trustees. If this be the case, so as to give them the power of intermeddling, I must fairly say that I consider not only all the benefit of the institution to be wholly lost, but that a more mischevious project never was set on foot. I should much sooner make your college . . . a subordinate department of our Protestant university — absurd as I always thought that plan to be — than make you the instrument of the jobbing system. I am sure that the constant meddling of the bishops and clergy with the Castle, and of the Castle with them, will infallibly set them ill with their own body. All the weight which hitherto the clergy have had in keeping the people quiet will be lost, if once this should happen. At best, you will have a marked schism, and more than one kind; and I am very much mistaken if this thing is not intended, and diligently and systematically pursued. I am steadily of my old opinion, that this affair had better be wholly dropped, and the government boon, with civility and acknowledgement declined, than to subject yourselves and your religion to your known and avowed enemies, who connect their very interest to your humiliation, and found their own reputation on the destruction of yours. I have said so much on this point already, that I shall trouble you no more about it''.

In spite of his forebodings Burke went on to say that he had just given instructions for the despatch of some books which had belonged to his son Richard, recently deceased, for the library of the new College. They are still amongst its prized possessions.

On 30 June the College opened for the matriculation of students and the first student was inscribed that day, but it was not until November that a formal notice of the opening of the College was posted in *The Dublin Journal.*

There was much to be thankful for if all went well in the future. And so in November the Trustees wrote to Propaganda thanking it for its letter of congratulations on the founding of the College and assuring the Prefect, Cardinal Gerdil, that they would be assiduous in carrying out Rome's instructions. It only remained to thank the Government and this too was duly done. In early December Dr. Troy wrote to Pelham, the Chief Secretary, thanking him for his help in regard to the College, significantly adding that the estimates in respect of it would be ready shortly and it was hoped that Parliament would grant them. In different ways, albeit very different, King and Pope had concurred in a novel and exciting venture.

GETTING UNDERWAY

We have already spoken much of the Reverend Thomas Hussey, appointed first President of Maynooth College on 25 June, 1975. In view of his services to date to both Government and Bishops, it would almost be an understatement to say that his appointment was a foregone conclusion. Musgrave tells us that he was recommended by Edmund Burke to Lord Fitzwilliam when he was coming to Ireland "as a person well qualified to superintend that institution" while Healy, the official historian of the College, has no hesitation in assuming that, in view of his connections with them it was no doubt at the suggestion of Burke, Portland and other statesmen that Hussey was chosen to be the first President. He certainly had helped a lot and the Bishops must surely have felt bound by both honour and prudence to offer him the Presidency.

One wonders in fact whether they had much option. *The Black Book of Edgeworthstown* has it that the Abbé Edgeworth (a distinguished figure in the France of Louis XVI who now lived with the French emigrés in London with an offer of a pension from Pitt) was invited to accept the Presidency but refused it. There is no evidence for or against this of which we are aware but it would appear to be unlikely in view of Hussey's preeminence.

The said Thomas Hussey had had a remarkable career heretofore. Born about 1745, he had studied at Salamance and spent some years as a Trappist monk. Ordained secular priest by Papal mandate because of his ability, he was appointed Chaplain to the Spanish Embassy in London, in which capacity he came to enjoy the friendship of the English Monarch and his Ministers. George III placed so much reliance on him that he sent him on a special secret mission to Madrid during the American Civil War.

GEORGE III

He was also involved in diplomatic circles in Vienna. Against this background it is not surprising that Westminster should have looked upon him as entirely suitable for the purpose of nursing the fledgling College into loyal maturity.

At the same time there was no question of the Irish Bishops accepting a system whereby the Government was given a formal say in College appointments. Just at that time a questionaire was sent round to them by Drs Troy of Dublin, O'Reilly of Armagh and Plunkett of Meath, asking about the possibility of their approving a procedure by which "the Government could be allowed the appointment of the President or Professors of Maynooth?" The reply was: "Negative; No interference is admissible". Of course bowing circumspectly to Government wishes, if it suited in individual cases, was a completely different thing.

As it happened, the King of Spain refused to release Hussey immediately and, after his appointment as President, he continued nominally in his post at the Spanish Embassy. Neither does he appear to have contributed a great deal to getting the infant College off the ground.

Whoever was responsible for this it was a remarkable *tour de force*. Staffing was the first problem. The ten Professorships instituted at the Trustees meeting of 25 June were: Dogmatical Divinity and Ecclesiastical History; Moral Divinity and Canon Law; Sacred Scripture and Hebrew; Natural and Experimental Philosophy; Logick, Ethics and Metaphysics; Mathematics; one each in Greek and Latin; English Elocution; Irish Language.

The 25 June meeting also fixed the stipend to be allowed to the two hundred free scholars who were to be admitted on the establishment — £20 per annum for board. It further specified "that neither the President, Vice-President nor any other person shall derive any benefit from the savings or profits, if there be any, but that such savings be applied to the general funds of the College — and it is hereby strictly ordered that any person entrusted with payments for the use of the College, having ready money in his hands, who shall presume to substitute his own or any other notes payable at a future date, be instantly dismissed by the President from his employment in the College". Even as early as their first business meeting, the Trustees were taking no chances in the field of finance.

This meeting also decided that annual meetings of the Trustees were to be held in January and three quarterly meetings in May, August and November, while in case of urgent business the President was empowered to call meetings on giving twenty one days notice.

It says a lot for the amount of backstage work that must have gone on for months before then that the Trustees were able at their fourth meeting, held on 27 June, 1795, not only to appoint a Vice-President but also to fill nine of the ten Chairs that had been set up two days previously.

As might be expected, practically all the appointees were from abroad, from the ranks of able Irish ecclesiastics who had gained distinction overseas, English Catholics of distinction or expatriate French clerical scholars who had fled the Revolution. To the Vice-Presidency was appointed the Reverend Francis Power of the Diocese of Cloyne, a native of Waterford who had become Canon and Archdeacon of Avignon. He took possession at Maynooth in December. The Chair of Dogmatic Theology went to the Reverend Maurice Aherne, priest of the Diocese of Kerry. The *College Records* describe him further as "Licentiate of Divinity, formerly Professor of Philosophy in the University of Paris, Fellow of the Royal Society of Navarre, Canon and Vicar General of Chartres in France". He took possession in October. Then there was the Reverend Thomas Clancy who was appointed to the Chair of Sacred Scripture. He was a priest originally from the Diocese of Tuam who had achieved position as a Franciscan as far afield as Prague where the Irish Province had a College until suppressed by the Emperor, Joseph II. He did not take possession until the following year and did not remain long on the staff.

To the Chair of Mathematics and Natural Philosophy and that of Logic, Metaphysics and Ethics were appointed the first of the French Professors who were to play a prominent part in the history of the College. To the former Chair came the Reverend Pierre Justin Delort, a priest of the Diocee of Bordeaux (or 'Bourdeaux' as the *College Records* have it), Doctor of Laws in the University of that city, while to the latter came the Reverend Andre Darré of the Diocese of Auch, France. Delort took possession in October, Darre not until May, 1797.

The Chair of Rhetoric was filled by the Reverend John Chetwoode Eustace, a man of Irish birth educated at Douai who had become very Anglicised and a tutor to English and Anglo-Irish noblemen, later to become celebrated for an accomplished work entitled *The Classical Tour in Italy*. Another Irishman, although this time much more of the soil, went to the first Chair of Humanity.

MR. WALKER

This was the celebrated James Bernard Clinch, Master of Arts and Fellow of the Royal Irish Academy and loyal Catholic layman if ever there was one. Yet another Irishman, the Reverend Charles Lovelock of the Diocese of Tuam, and Master of Arts, was appointed to the second Chair of Humanity, although he does not appear to have ever taken possession of it.

The sole native-born Englishman to be appointed to the College staff on that historic day of 27 June, 1795, was Mr. John Walker — in the Chair of English Elocution. Actor, schoolmaster, philologist, and lexicographer, Walker was the friend of Dr. Johnson, David Garrick, Oliver Goldsmith, Edmund Burke and Dr. Hussy. He had come to Ireland in the middle of the 18th Century and become a Catholic in 1768. In succeeding years he lectured in elocution in various places including Oxford University, and was the author of a series of works including *A General Idea of a Pronouncing Dictionary of the English Language on a Plan entirely new* (1774). He was recommended for the Chair at Maynooth by Burke. It is a pity that this talented man never seems to have taken possession of his chair. His lectures may have been given by Mr. Mark Ussher from Cork who was later appointed Professor. Finally, on that 27 June, the Chair of Irish Language — one of the first in the country — was assigned to the Reverend John McLoughlin. He too does not appear to have taken possession of his chair, for what reason we do not know.

The meeting also decided that teachers of modern languages might be admitted at the discretion of the President and paid by their respective pupils, after the manner of the *'Privatdozents'* of the German Universities of the time.

More appointments were to follow before long. Yet even then there were disappointed candidates, some of them very distinguished. Among these we find the Reverend Dr. Lanigan of Cashel, Professor of Divinity, Hebrew and Ecclesiastical History at Pavia. He had to leave there when the University was broken up for a while after Napoleon entered the city. He sought refuge in his native land and wrote from Pavia during the Summer of 1795 to his Bishop, Dr. Bray, in his capacity as one of the Trustees of Maynooth, seeking appointment. He never got it. One wonders whether the fact that he was the fellow-student and possibly the friend in the Irish College, Rome of Dr. Charles O'Conor (the later 'Columbanus' who clashed with the Bishops) had anything to do with it. Anyhow it appears that Dr. Lanigan did not enjoy great health.

Whatever about this, on 11 November, 1795, the Secretary to the Trustees, Dr. Dunn, was able to report that the Seminary course was now under way, with four Professors and thirty seven scholars and that some kind of accommodation was available for thirteen more to complete the number of fifty who were daily expected.

It was high time to go public. Hence, on 25 November, 1795, the *Dublin Evening Post* carried the following notice:

"The trustees of the Roman Catholic College, wishing to give the benevolent intentions of his majesty, and both Houses of Parliament, all the effect which the present circumstances of the institution will admit, inform the public, that Professors have been appointed to teach the different branches of science and *belles lettres,* which usually constitute a College course. For want of a more ample accommodation at present, it has been found necessary to confine the studies of the current academic year to a course of moral theology, of the first part of mathematics and philosophy, of rhetoric and *belles letters,* and of the first class of humanity; Professors in each of these departments are now resident at Maynooth. Lectures on the two first branches have already commenced; and the Professors of rhetoric and humanity will proceed to lecture, as soon as the scholars qualified to each class will be given on the establishment. The trustees have agreed to let certain lots of ground belonging to the College for the building of houses, designed to accommodate boarders. Each lot will be sufficiently large to allow a suitable garden to each house. As the object of the trustees is to provide the public with the most expedious means of deriving from the institution the important and extensive advantages justly expected from it, they have given direction that a very small ground rent be reserved, and such other encouragement given as will secure to those who may be disposed to treat, a profitable return for the expenditure of their money".

How very like the more recent hostel development is this! It is fascinating too to note that there is no word here about a seminary for the training solely of students for the priesthood, whether or not this has any significance.

There is an addendum to the effect that "proposals will be received at the College for quarrying stone, and burning brick, in the vicinity of Maynooth. Large quantities of these materials will be wanting in the course of next Spring, for the erection of halls, and other necessary buildings which it is intended to complete with all possible expedition".

But this is to jump the gun. The story must first be told as to how the Royal Catholic College came to find habitation as well as a name at Maynooth.

Chapter II

For Clerk and Layman Both

Following the first meeting of the Trustees, held in the Lord Channcellor's Chambers, House of Lords, on 24 June, 1795, it was ordered: "That notices be published in the papers that the Trustees will receive proposals for lands and buildings in the vicinity of Dublin for the new Seminary and that applications for that purpose be made to Mr. Strange, Dr. Troy or Dr. Hussey".

In accordance with this, the *Dublin Evening Post* of the next day carried the advertisement: "Roman Catholic College. Wanted, in the vicinity of Dublin, a large building, with some acres of ground, for the establishment of the Roman Catholic College, lately endowed by Act of Parliament. Proposals in writing will be received by the Most Rev. Dr. Troy, Richard Strange, Esq., Eccles Street and the Rev. Dr. Hussey, No. 12, Usher's Quay".

On the 2 July the same newspaper reported: "Monday (29th) there was a full meeting of the heads of the Roman Catholic clergy in Ireland, at the episcopal chapel in Francis Street, when a solemn High Mass was celebrated and a very excellent sermon preached by Rev. Dr. Hussey, on the inauguration of the Catholic College. The trustees of the Catholic College have not yet been accommodated with a situation to their liking for the establishment of their seminary. Several situations have been mentioned for their choice; and amongst them Stillorgan house and demesne, the house of Mr. Mitchell, near Glassnaeven (sic.), the house and concerns of the late Judge Helen at Mespil bank, corner of Donnybrook road. Their object is a situation so contiguous to town as to facilitate the accommodation of day students of the laity".

How easily this could have been transposed to fit the late 20th century! And how ironical that one of the areas mentioned should have been chosen in the 20th century as the new site for University College, Dublin. Even more astonishing is the clear implication — despite all that had gone on whilst the Bill was in passage

— that the scope of the Royal Catholic College was to extend to education of the laity. It is also surprising that there is no mention of an offer of the house at Maynooth owned by Mr. Stoyte, the agent of the Duke of Leinster.

By 28th July — at the second and last meeting of Trustees to be attended by the ex officio Protestant members — the matter of location was decided. Dr. Plunkett of Meath records in his diary: "I came to Dublin to attend in quality of trustee, at a board of the trustees of the Roman Catholic College, held at Dr. Troy's, and, on the 28th, at the Lord Chancellor's chambers, in the House of Lords, when it was decided that Maynooth should be the place for establishing the Catholic College.

The resolution of the Trustees on that day, as recorded in the *Journal of the Trustees* reads: "Resolved, that the proposal of Mr. John Stoyte for his ground and buildings in Maynooth ought to have the preference and it was accordingly ordered that measures be forthwith taken to close with said Mr. Stoyte on the basis of his proposal".

By way of reporting this a rather strangely worded piece appeared in the *Dublin Evening Post* of 30 July: "We can assure the public from undoubted authority that the Catholic committee (sic.) have taken Mr. Stoyte's elegant house at Maynooth, with the castle, for a seminary for their clergy". How out of touch with events one of the trustees, Lord Kenmare was, may be judged from his letter to the Archbishop of Cashel dated 31 July in which he declared that "our College is like to be establish'd at Maynooth or Leixlip".

FOUNDATIONS ARE LAID

Perhaps the fullest and most accurate account extant of what was taking place is contained in a letter of the said Archbishop to the co-adjuter Bishop of Limerick, Dr. Young, sent on the very day that Kenmare penned his outdated information. Dr. Bray writes:

"My very dear and hon'd Lord — The following is a copy of a letter which I rec'd by the last post from Doctor Troy: I sit down to inform your Grace that at a meeting this day of the College Board in the house of Lords, composed of Lords Clare, Clonmell, Yelverton, Gormanstown, Mr. Strange, Dr. Plunkett and myself, Mr. Stoyte's proposal about his concerns at Maynooth was unanimously preferred to all others. The terms are three thousand guineas, and thirty pounds yearly rent, with a peppercorn on the demise of every life or lives, which are renewable forever. It was resolved also to purchase Chamberlaine's interest in the adjoining land, for the difference between three thousand guineas and four thousand pounds; which is the total sum to be expended, in order to derive immediately under the Duke of Leinster, who has promised to grant a lease forever on moderate terms, not to exceed one guinea per acre. Possession is to be given on the first of September next, and rent to commence from the first of November. If we don't build pension houses on the land, we can let a great part of, at a considerable profit-rent. This Bargain when effected is considered a very good one. Le Faure insisted on a bargain having been concluded with him, and published it in the newspapers, without any foundation but his own desire to force an agreement — his conduct was condemned by the judges. My mind is now easy as our determination is so respectably positioned. The judges behaved with their usual politeness. Fifty students at most can be admitted into the College at the commencement; of which fifteen should be from Your Grace's province, on the principle of distribution agreed upon by the Prelates. The number from each Diocess (sic.) should be ascertained by their respective provincial Bishops — Dublin, 26 July, 1795. John Troy".

Dr. Bray goes on to ask Young to communicate this to other Munster Bishops. Each of them is to send two students for the moment, the Bishop of Kilfenora one. There is nothing whatsoever about lay students.

He then proceeds to describe the place in which the College is to be situated: "Maynooth is a little town built by the Duke of Leinster, separated from Carton house and demesne by a beautiful avenue of a quarter of a mile. The place taken for our College immediately adjoins the town of Maynooth — about twenty acres highly improved — and has an excellent house, never inhabited, completely finished and large enough to accommodate fifty or sixty subjects.

Chamberlaine's concern is the next, about twenty acres, and a roomy house. The whole concern is on the bank of the Grand Canal and about nine miles from Dublin and in the very centre of a beautiful, healthy and plentiful country". He himself and some other Bishops had spent almost two days around there "and received many great civilties from the Duchess of Leinster and from Lady Louisa Conolly of Castletown — neither the Duke nor Mr. Conolly were at home".

The legal trouble referred to in the foregoing arose in connection with Stillorgan site, as we learn from a notice in the *Dublin Evening Post* of 4 August: "Some of the newspapers having announced that the trustees of the Roman Catholic College, receding from their bargain for the house and demesne of Stillorgan, had actually agreed for a situation at Maynooth, and report to the like effect being current, the Proprietor of Stillorgan feels it necessary for the satisfaction of the public, to give a recital of the several particulars of the bargain of the sale of Stillorgan, on the 8th July last, closed with him by the Rev. Dr. Troy, the Rev. Dr. Hussey, and Richard Strange, Esq., which will be published in a few days. This recital of facts was carefully perused and noted by the Rev. Dr. Troy, at No. 101 Grafton Street, on Saturday last, the 18th July, in the presence of the gentleman of the first character. To this recital will be added a statement of the conduct of the Rev. Dr. Troy, in relation to this business from the aforesaid 8th to the 29th July; and also the letters of correspondence relating to the bargain, and the detail of circumstances which induced the proprietor, at the time of the closing the bargain, to place a full reliance on the honour of the parties."

Despite all this recital, statement and detail Maynooth and not Stillorgan was to be the site of the new College. It would seem that the dispute went to law in some form and that the College Trustees were vindicated. Shades of University College, Dublin!

Powerful interests had favoured the choice of Maynooth. Writing to Bray of Cashel, Dr. Troy tells of how he had thanked the Duchess of Leinster and Lady Louisa Conolly who had interested themselves in the matter and Healy tells us that it was the belief of a later President, Dr. Crotty, that Maynooth was chosen because the Duke of Leinster was very anxious to have the College there and also because it was considered more favourable to the morals and studies of the students than the immediate neighbourhood of a great city. Does the last point not also hold for later?

And so it was that on 1 October the College at Maynooth opened formally and lectures began on the 6th, with nearly forty students under Professors Ahearne, Delort, Eustace and Clinch. In spite of the praise lavished on Stoyte House by the purchasers, accommodation was now the big problem. In November the *Dublin Journal* carried a notice inviting prospective tenants to rent lots of land for the building of student residences but it would appear that there were no takers. The first break came in December when Pelham informed Troy that Parliament expected a plan of building with a view to voting money for it. It would be better, he thought, to begin with the chapel, the hall and lecture room and to leave dormitories, etc. for later — a typically Georgian approach. He thanked the Trustees for having expressed themselves well pleased with his efforts to date for the College.

At their January meeting the Trustees commissioned plans from architects and builders and at a further meeting on 3 February those of the well-known architect Michael Stapleton were accepted. Parliament was duly petitioned for the funds necessary as well as for running costs for one year ending March, 1797. It was further decided that for three years students already in Holy Orders would be admitted for better training. They were exempted from the payment of "caution money" on admission!

That the Trustees were under great pressure from Bishops to take students is evident from a letter of Troy to Young the same January: "It was with great difficulty that only two could procure lodgings at Maynooth in order to attend the Lectures in the College. They are both Priests, one of Tuam and the other of Meath. The students on the foundation are crowded in the College. To remedy this inconveniency it is in contemplation to take a large adjoining house, or to build some houses on the College ground for their accommodations, till the College is enlarged, after which they are to serve for Pensioners".

A pattern was beginning to emerge — that of scholars resident in the College "on the establishment", that is free scholars, and non-resident students, whether in hostel accommodation or local boarding, who paid for themselves. The trouble was to find adequate accommodation for either category.

As regards the resident students Troy was optimistic when writing again to Young on 1 March, 1796: "From what has been saved of last year's parliamentary grant, and likely to be saved from that of the present session, the College Trustees will be enabled to expend £6,000 on the erection of the front side of an intended new square, which will accommodate two hundred students, besides a temporary chapel, refectory and necessary halls". This was the start of what was later called Long Corridor.

In like vein Bray of Cashel reported to Conway of Limerick the following day: "Stapleton's improved plan was preferred, and presented to Parliament and Government with the Amounts and Estimates. We have also in hands £500 to be expended in building, or renting if possible, lodging houses, for the immediate accommodation of additional students, particularly lay pensioners, to render the institution more general, useful and palatable to the Public".

There we have it — the entire unfolding of the pattern: resident scholars for priestly training on the establishment, with other students, both clerical and lay, in a non-resident and paying capacity. How very like the pattern of the late 20th century, financial aspects excluded!

As before, things moved quickly in the matter of building. On 20 April, 1796, the *Freeman's Journal* was able to report that "This day his Excellency the Lord Lieutenant will lay the first stone of the additional buildings to the Royal College of St. Patrick at Maynooth". Afterwards it gave a full account of the event:

"This day his excellency the Lord Lieutenant, accompanied by the Lord Chancellor, and other chief judges, etc., etc., came to lay the first stone of the new Roman Catholic seminary. His excellency was received by the President, professors, and students at the gate; the Duke of Leinster, and the principal nobility and gentry in the neighbourhood besides the trustees of the College being present. The band of the Londonderry militia, as soon as his excellency alighted, played 'God save the King'; as soon as he was seated he was addressed in odes in Latin and English. He then proceeded to lay the first stone — during which ceremony the band played 'God save the King' — to which the students, and an immense concourse of people joined in the chorus. Afterwards his excellency partook of some refreshments, and returned to the Castle, where the trustees of the seminary had the honour of dining with him".

In actual fact odes in Greek, Latin and English were recited and, as we are told by *Walker's Hibernian Magazine* for the following May, lines were also inscribed on a plate fixed to the foundation stone and dedicated to Lord Camden, on a silver trowel presented to Camden and on a gold box presented to Pelham. Professor Eustace had composed the ode in English.

Another account of the day was given by *The Hibernian Journal* for Friday, 22 April:

"At the entrance of the town of Maynooth, his Excellency was met by the students of the College, with a grand band of music, who after a most respectful salutation, preceded his Excellency in procession to the place where the building is to be erected, playing 'God Save the King', amid the acclamation of myriads of spectators. His Excellency was accompanied by His Grace the Duke of Leinster, the Earl of Clonmell, the Right Hon. Thomas Conolly, several other dignified characters and gentlemen, who countenances bespoke the most pleasing sensations of the mind, at seeing this testimonial of liberality in the legislature and government of Ireland demonstrated to their Roman Catholic brethren".

Clonmel was one of those who dined that evening at the Castle with, as his diary records, "the Chancellor and two other chief judges and ... several Popish bishops and other trustees". He adds: "A very new scene in this kingdom, and important in its consequences". How new was the scene can be gauged from the entry in Dr. Plunkett's diary for that day which records that he, together with Drs. O'Reilly and Troy, and Dr. Hussey, travelled from Maynooth to the Castle with Camden in his own carriage. We know too that Dr. Troy was asked to say Grace at the Castle dinner. To quote a Catholic pamphlet of that year: "This was the first time since the Reformation that a Catholic Bishop was permitted to dine or sit in company with a Lord Lieutenant of Ireland".

In July of the following year Camden very graciously sent a present of books for those gentle men who had made the addresses to him on the occasion of his visit to lay the stone. The Vice-President thanked him and assured him that this would be done with all due solemnity. The books consisted of the works of Homer, Virgil and Milton, the three sets being bound in "Turkey leather".

That year too we are told by one of the newspapers "His Grace the Duke of Leinster made a present to the College of a capital pedestal of Portland stone, four feet high, to serve as a stand for a horizontal Sun Dial, to be placed in the area in front of the new College, as it required a dial of a size never yet seen in this Kingdom, the trustees gave their direction to an Irish artist to execute one in Dublin. It is now completed in such a manner as to give satisfaction to all who have seen it, and, as we are always happy to have an opportunity of recording every Irish work of art, we shall lay before our readers a description thereof". A detailed description follows. "The whole of this elegant piece of work was executed by Mr. Thomas Saunders".

As for 1796, it closed quietly. In August the Trustees approved a contract with the builder Samuel Parker for a house to lodge the scholars until the large buildings were ready and which afterwards could "serve for the reception of Pupils not designed for the Ecclesiastical State".

When an attempt was made on the life of George III the Trustees drafted a message to the Lord Lieutenant expressing their abhorrence at the crime but for some reason never sent it. There were portents for the future at the end of the year when a French fleet appeared for a week off Bantry Bay.

'SERVICE AT THE CASTLE'

In late 1796 Dr. Hussey, the President of the College, returned to Ireland at the express wish of the Duke of Portland, to be an intermediary between the Castle and the Bishops. He now held two positions — without emolument for either — the Presidency of Maynooth and Chaplaincy General to the forces in Ireland, "a sort of superintendent to the Regimental Chaplains" was how Burke described it. At this time he was probably the only formal contact between the State and the Catholic Church in Ireland.

In many ways he remains somewhat of an obscure figure. Flagg Bemis in his *The Hussey — Cumberland Mission and American Independence* accuses him of spying for Spain. He suggests in fact that Hussey was a double agent but was tricked by the Home Office which supplied false information for transmission to the Spaniards. *The Gentleman's Magazine* for September, 1803 wrote: "The enemies of the administration said he was employed by the Government to sow the seeds of dissension with a view to bring about the union; others considered him an agent of France".

Some British connection is certainly indisputable, as witness the thanks tendered to him by Government, the large monetary reward for services and the

34

guard of honour when he became Bishop of Waterford in 1797. And yet there are unresolved questions. It is true that W. J. Fitzpatrick, in his *Secret Service under Pitt,* says plainly that "in 1796 Dr. Hussey, afterwards Bishop of Waterford, seems to have accepted the post of secret agent". However, he quickly adds that "it cannot be said that this agency was of a base character" but was rather an above-board one for the purpose of negotiating with the Irish Catholics.

The pension would have been quite in order because Hussey did engage in much negotiation. The guard of honour could be explained by his post with the forces. And as regards this itself, a letter of Portland in November, 1796, shows that the Government wished to pre-empt the Pope's appointment of Hussey as Vicar Apostolic to The Catholic Military of Ireland by Pitt's appointing him over the chaplains. It was also hoped that his well-known anti-Jacobinism would help to stamp out disaffection in the army.

The British, at the same time, never trusted Hussey completely. Even though Fitzpatrick is at a loss to explain "what was the precise nature of the hold which Hussey, originally a Carthusian monk, acquired over the Court of England", he has to admit as probable that the Reverend Arthur O'Leary was "forced on Hussey as colleague in London against his will", obviously for the purpose of spying on him for Pitt. It is true that O'Leary became attached to the Spanish Embassy while Hussey was there and that the two did not agree: "Two of a trade never agree" remarks Fitzpatrick.

Dr. Hussey was in London for most of 1796, not so much as Chaplain to the Spanish Embassy, although he retained a salary from same, as for the purpose of selecting Professors for Maynooth from among the many and learned Continental refugee scholars who then thronged the City. In June he dined one evening with the Duke of Portland, having spent an hour earlier in the day with Lord Fitzwilliam. That same month Camden wrote to Portland from Dublin Castle:

> "I have great satisfaction in being able to state to your grace that I hope the Government in Ireland possesses the good opinion of the more respectable part of the Catholic persuasion in a higher degree than I could have ventured to hope or expect some months since. I am convinced at the same time that the activity and zeal, as well as good temper, which has been manifested by Dr. Hussey, have contributed very much to this event, as I have great pleasure in assuring your Grace that I think his presence in Ireland has been materially useful, not only in the establishment of the Roman Catholic College, but in contributing to the moderate conduct, which has lately been exhibited by his Brethren of that persuasion".

In September Camden was writing to Portland to the effect that Hussey should return to Ireland as it was desirable to communicate with the principal Catholics both clergy and laity "and I do not know so proper a person through whom to communicate, as Dr. Hussey. I should therefore be desirous that Your Grace would have the goodness to signify my wishes that Dr. Hussey should come over to this Kingdom, unless he is employed in any business which Your Grace may consider as more important''. By 30 November Hussey was back in Ireland, in Maynooth.

"I hastened down to the favourite spot, this *punctum saliens* of the salvation of Ireland from Jacobinism and anarchy. I found it advancing, in every respect, even beyond my expectations" — in this vein he wrote to Burke after getting there. But then there comes an alert about "the men who are Jacobinizing this country . . . . under the name of 'United Irishmen' . . . I am terrified at what I foresee, regarding my own unfortunate native country. To pass by parliament, and break the connexion with Great Britain, is, I am informed, the plan of the United Irishmen. The wretches never consider that their grievances are not from England, but from a junto of their own countrymen; and that Camden, Pelham, and Elliot (whom, notwithstanding my difference with them, I think the three most honest men in office here) are as completely junto-ridden as my former patron, the King of Spain, is convention-ridden. At any rate I am shut out from all conversation with the Castle''.

Burke, while passing on this letter to Fitzwilliam, informed him also that he was going to tell Hussey to stay close to Maynooth and forget for a while that he had gone to Ireland at the express wish of Government.

One can only surmise that the reason for the sudden change of attitude of the Castle towards Hussey was because he had begun to interest himself actively in the welfare of the Catholic soldiers who, as he told Burke, were being subjected to violence in order to force them to attend the services of the Established Church. By the end of December he had been appointed Bishop of Waterford.

The signs of the times were ominous. At that December's end, according to Camden, "the deep snow has prevented the Mail or any Messenger arriving from Cork''. If they had arrived they would have had an alarm to convey: the French were on the sea! Still, calm prevailed. Writing to Burke in January Hussey opined: "As for an invasion from the French, it cannot be dreaded. There are not five Catholics in the Kingdom, worth ten pounds, that would not spill their blood to resist it''. Was Hussey's intelligence slipping? Probably not, for we are told elsewhere that this view was verified by the conduct of the peasantry in the South of Ireland on the appearance of the French fleet.

On 20 January, 1797, Dr. Hussey attended the last meeting of the Maynooth Trustees before his consecration as Bishop of Waterford., He did not resign the Presidency. Earlier he had told Burke that he would continue as President of Maynooth and Chaplain General to the Forces as well as being Bishop of Waterford. That the Trustees thought otehwise emerges from a letter of Archbishop

36

Troy to Archbishop Bray in late December, 1796, pointing out that the Presidency was likely to fall vacant by the probable resignation of Dr. Hussey and stressing that the episcopal rather than the lay trustees should be the ones to determine the weighty matter of replacing him. But Hussey continued obdurate. As late as 2 April, 1797, he writes to Burke: "I have not, nor will I ever resign the Presidency of Maynooth. As I receive neither salary nor emolument from it, I feel no dishonesty and I see the necessity of holding it till the plan be finally settled".

The publication of his famous Pastoral shortly afterwards, in which he castigated the authorities for their attitudes towards the Catholic military, rendered him absolutely *persona non grata* to the Castle. Camden wrote to Portland: "I enclose your Grace a publication of Doctor Hussey's, lately made titular Bishop of Waterford. He had enjoyed your Grace's good opinion, and *I* was much disposed, till lately, to think well of him. The perusal of his address will convince your Grace of its dangerous tendency, and I wish to suggest to you whether the pope might be requested to recall so dangerous a man from this Kingdom".

Camden was only conveying an outburst of hostility against Hussey on the part of the régime in Ireland. In the Spring of 1797 there appeared a pamphlet by an anonymous author entitled *Strictures and remarks on Dr. Hussey's late pastoral,* which suggested that the government should remove him from the Presidency of Maynooth and "place a gentleman of more prudence, more moderation, and more Christian charity at the head of that learned seminary".

Burke hastened to console him, telling him not to worry about the rumours concerning his disloyalty, that there were also rumours about Dr. Troy, even to the extent that he had taken the oath of the United Irishmen. But he did hint also that Government had called for Hussey's dismissal from the Presidency. By May, Troy was conveying to Plunkett that he had written to Hussey, presumably from the Maynooth Trustees, "assuring him that everybody present here considered the Presidency as incompatible with the duties of a Bishop. I was silent about any desire or wish of the Castle that he should resign, because, from my opinion of his temper, I apprehend that very circumstances would determine him to retain the Presidency. *Non est sicut ceteri hominum,* although he is no Pharisee". But the hard fact remained that Pelham regarded the pastoral as "intemperate and inflammatory". Six months later Troy wrote to Bray that Dr. Hussey, who is presently recovering from the bursting of a blood vessel,"may be prevailed on to resign the Presidency". If not, the next meeting of Trustees would declare the duties of President and Bishop incompatible. Drs. Flood and Everard were mentioned at the last meeting as possible successors.

Dr. Flood was appointed President of Maynooth on 17th January, 1798. Hussey made no reply to the Board's letter telling him of this but he did write to Dr. Flood to congratulate him. What are we to think about the whole thing? The Protestant Bishop of Meath in a letter to Lord Castlereagh in 1799 spoke of Dr. Hussey's removal from the College following a call from the Government linked with the alienation of his brother Bishops and Pelham wrote to Duigenan of Trinity in February, 1799 declaring that the Board of Maynooth had displaced their President for non-residence. The unfortunate Hussey seems to have alienated everybody for we are told too that, when he approached his old friend Portland in the graveyard after the funeral of Burke, the Duke turned abruptly away. What of Burke himself? Well, for what it is worth, Cox's *Irish Magazine* for February, 1808, relates that he was "attended spiritually in his last illness by Dr. Hussey". Whether Burke, the son of a Catholic mother, ever became a Catholic we will never know for certain. But it is surely a tribute to Dr. Hussey that Burke should have had him minister to him at the end.

THE ENIGMATIC EARL OF CLARE

It has been already noted as strange that, in view of the acknowledged purpose of the 1795 Act, the Trustees had decided to establish a lay college at Maynooth. That they did so is unquestionable. Explanation is required. The Bishops, in their letter to Grattan on 2 February, 1795, had said at that time that since Burke, Lord Fitzwilliam, the Duke of Portland and others were anxious that the laity should be included in the general scheme, they, the Bishops, were agreeable to this. And Dr. Hogan, former President of Maynooth, in his book *Maynooth College and the Laity*, suggests that it was decided deliberately that the Bill should be drafted on general lines, so that provision for the laity could subsequently be made if the Government agreed to it.

There is certainly reason for believing that Portland and the others were in favour of such a scheme originally, and it may well be the case, as Hogan maintains, that in the course of a very few years the Bishops decided to take advantage of what they regarded as the legal position enshrined in the general terms of the Act of Foundation, and to devote part of their income to the education of the laity.

They could easily have been tempted to erect a lay academy under the aegis of the clerical one at a time when the running of exclusively Catholic schools still suffered from severe disabilities.

The suggestion has also been made, however, that they may have been led into it by the Chancellor, Lord Clare, who misguided the Trustees as to the Government's intentions. This is something which deserves attention. Indeed it opens up an episode of absorbing interest.

John Fitzgibbon (1747-1802) was the son of a man originally destined for the Catholic priesthood but who had conformed. In 1786 he married the daughter of a vehement anti-Catholic known as 'Burn-Chapel' Whaley because of his fondness for destroying Catholic houses of worship whenever he got the chance. He became Attorney General in 1783. Six years later he was elevated to the Peerage as Baron Fitzgibbon and, as a reward for his unflinching loyalty to the Castle, achieved a distinction never before conferred upon an Irishman by being made Lord Chancellor of Ireland. In 1795 he was advanced to the dignity of Earl of Clare.

Clare lived at No. 6 Ely Place, in much state and splendour, although he might well have adopted the precaution taken by his neighbour John La Touche who, apprehensive of mob violence, put up a strong iron gate at the top of the stairs at No. 5 and had orifices in the stairs themselves for firing through in order to command the approach therefrom. For if La Touche had reason to fear, Fitzgibbon had even more. His bitter anti-Catholicism and Tory illiberality led to an attempt to break into his house on the famous evening that he returned from the Castle after Fitzwilliam's recall. Later his role in the Union was to lead to most unruly scenes at his funeral, when a dead cat was thrown at his coffin. It is significant that his papers were destroyed in 1802 by orders of his will.

It is very likely also significant that the first notice to appear indicating the intention of the Maynooth students came after their inaugural meeting held in the Lord Chancellor's chamber on 24 June, 1795. There is no evidence that any such students were received for quite some time, and although it is possible that some might have been boarded in the town as pensioners, not on the establishment, what indications there are suggest that this did not occur until about 1800.

In that year, a meeting of the Trustees which dealt mainly with affairs of the Lay College resolved "that Lord Fingall, the President and Secretary may purchase Mr. McManus's interest in the Cabins contiguous to the College" — possibly for the accommodation of lay students as well as other externs. Fingall had a son in the Lay College.

On 10 August, 1796, a contract for a building for the Lay College was approved in that it was decided that the new building commissioned from Samuel Parker to lodge the scholars of the establishment until Stapleton's buildings were finished should than serve for the accommodation of the lay students. It was completed in 1798. In the interval the Lay College continued to take root. Five months after the building had been agreed upon the Trustees decided that the uniform of its students was to be the College cap and gown "with light or sky-blue tassels", also that "each room shall be provided with a good bed, bed-clothes and linen excepted . . . . The furniture of each room shall consist of a table, two chairs, and a wash-hand basin and stand". The students were to dine in the refectory of the clerical College and breakfast and sup in the parlours of the building they inhabited.

By 1800 things were definitely in full swing. In January the Reverend P. Coleman was appointed Principal and on 8 April the *Dublin Evening Post* announced that the Trustees wished to inform the public that, as from 1 May, "a separate building will be opened upon the College ground, for the reception of Lay Students", under his "inspection". The President of the main College was shortly afterwards also given a function of superintence over the Lay College, particularly as regards ensuring that each person in it would take the Oath of Allegiance. One thousand pounds was to be spent on the improvement of that College.

Trouble, however, was imminent. During the Summer of 1801, in the course of a visitation of the Royal College by Lords Kilwarden, Norbury and Avonmore, the President, Dr. Flood, casually drew the attention of the visitors, while walking through the College grounds, to the building, on the grounds although a field or two from the College proper, in which lay students were put up. It was really a dormitory, containing no schoolrooms, from which Lord Kilwarden concluded that "the boys must go to the priests' College for their lessons". The Visitors expressed their surprise on finding this, calling it "a novelty", which seemed outside the purpose for which the College had been founded. Their fears were increased when the Duke of Leinster mentioned that it was intended to apply to Government for recognition of the Lay College.

All were very polite and inconsequential in attitude but consequences were to follow. On his return home from the Visitation, Lord Kilwarden informed the Lord Lieutenant, Lord Hardwicke, who in turn instructed the College agent Mr. Knox, (successor since 1799 to Marshall, Pelham's private secretary), "that in order to prevent any formal propositions to Government on the part of the College in favour of this Lay school, to which the Protestant Government might be under the necessity of giving a formal Negative, it was His Excellency's wish that the School should subside gradually and the matter end *sub silentio*". As if this kind of thing were ever possible: Lord Fingall was immediately apprehensive for the future of his son as well, possibly, about the property in the town of Maynooth which he was in the process of acquiring maybe for the school, when as rumour had it, he learned that there had been a peremptory order for the suppression of the Lay College. Immediately he went to Lord Clare, whose dispositions towards it were presumably well known and who in any case could be relied upon to combat Hardwicke on almost any matter.

Clare, true to form, bearded Hardwicke who explained to him that "as the Law now stood the Government would not interfere with the establishment of a school at Maynooth or anywhere else, but that it might be a question how far it was eligible to suffer a Lay school to be added to the Institution and that without insisting upon any sudden or immediate dissolution of the school, it seemed to me better that it should subside". Clare ranted about the desirability of a system of mixed education and, says Hardwicke, upon being asked "whether he meant a system upon the plan of Eton or Westminster, where the Collegers and Oppidans are educated together in the same classes without distinction of Order, he assented to the comparison".

Whatever of this, although the intention of Government to let the Lay College gradually subside was clear to Fingall who decided to remove his son the following year to a school in England, Fitzgibbon did not relinquish his ideas. On 4 December he sent for Archbishop Troy and informed him that there was no question of Kilwarden's being dissatisfied with the school and that he had not at all complained about it. At least that is the tenor of the memorandum on the interview which was later made at Hardiwicke's request. For when the latter heard about this interview shortly afterwards through the Civil Undersecretary, Samuel Marsden, on whom he relied a good deal, all hell broke loose — he was not going to have Fitzgibbon countermanding his orders.

Straight away Marsden was asked to secure from Troy an account of what transpired, which was communicated to Clare for his comments. Again the two met at the Castle for a conversation which Hardwicke got minuted also by one of his Chief Secretaries, Charles Abbot, subsequently Baron Colchester. Fitzgibbon protested that Dr. Troy's account of what had taken place had greatly misrepresented the real facts, that he and "the old gentleman" had only spoken of Maynooth for three minutes and that he honestly had in no way intended to countermand Hardwicke's order. in fact, he said, he had only told Dr. Troy that the boys were not to be taken away, that they were to go on as they were but that no public money was to be laid out until they heard further from Government on the subject. He claimed that it had been the understanding of Lord Cornwallis that Maynooth College should be a place for the joint education of students for the priesthood and lay boys.

Even though what Fitzgibbon admitted having conveyed to Troy was obviously enough not at all what Hardwicke had intended, the Lord Lieutenant felt it necessary to ask him for his observations in writing as it might be necessary to have them considered by the King's ministers. But he was highly critical of Clare, although not to his face. He wrote to the British Prime Minister Henry Addington: "Whether Lord Clare has taken the part he has from spleen to the Government, or from a conviction that it was the right thing to do, I cannot pretend to determine. . . It would be very curious, after all that has passed, (if) Lord Clare should be attempting to acquire popularity with the Catholics at the expense of the Govt. He seems to me, with a great share of cleverness and vivacity, to be very deficient in consistency", for at the very time that he was defending the Catholic lay college he had also been talking about the need to control the Catholics, if necessary by the reintroduction of Penal Laws. Abbot, in an *aide memoire* for himself, was also critical of Clare.

Fitzgibbon sent on his observations on 28 December. They are of great interest. The 1795 Act, he said, was intended "for the education indiscriminately of persons of the Popish Religion". To guard against its getting out of hand, the Chancellor and the Chief Judges had been made Trustees but, reluctantly on their part because, as they had explained in late 1795, while they were always ready to help, their regular presence at meetings of the Trustees was incompatible with their judicial duties. Owing to this, he hints, abuses had crept into the running of the College. Dr. Troy and other titular Bishops had seized the opportunity to turn the place into a "Monastic Institution" devoted exclusively to the education of Popish Priests. This, when drawn to the attention of the House of Lords in 1799, had caused surprise and the following year he had been desired by Lord Cornwallis, after consultation with the bishops, to frame another Bill which "might subject their institution to some effectual controul (sic.) connected with the State.

41

One of the things to be cleared up was the scope of the College and:

"after a pretty long negociation with Dr. Troy, to which I submitted very reluctantly by Lord Cornwallis's desire, he consented to receive lay Papists for education according to the Original intention of the Institution, and he consented also to oblige the Ecclesiastical Papists to contribute in part to the expence of their maintenance and Education, whilst at College. Both points I consider to be essential to palliate the mischief of this institution, for I fear that the utmost we can do will be to palliate the mischief, after the strange precipitance and want of forethought which has hitherto marked every stage of its Progress. If the Irish Priesthood is to be educated at a Monastery at Maynooth, secluded from all intercourse with laymen, I cannot see what will be gained by reclaiming them from the foreign Popish Universities.

And if none but the lowest ranks in the community who are unable to contribute to the expence of their maintenance and education are received into the Irish College, I cannot see any one advantage to the State which can result from it. And I can see it will give a weight of patronage to some few popish ecclesiastics which they may use as a powerful engine to annoy the State. The great difficulty in correcting all this mischief is that we have most giddily made this establishment and have never looked to the necessity of making regulations to guard it from abuse.."

With this memorandum Fitzgibbon also forwarded to Hardwicke another memo from Dr. Troy about his conversation with him, one that was happily not substantially different from Troy's other account to Marsden. In a covering letter he concluded referring to Maynooth: "I am confident that of the many serious and important topicks which remain to be fully considered and finally arranged, for the settlement of this country, this institution will be found to be one of the most prominent".He received a courteous but curt acknowledgement from Hardwicke.

Hardwicke was not finished either. On 1 January he asked Kilwarden for a statement concerning the original intention and objects of Maynooth College and Kilwarden, who had discussed the matter fully with Abbot at Cork Abbey on Christmas Day, was quite categorical in his reply, dated 2 January, 1802: the College was founded "for educating young men for the priesthood in the Romish Church" and that is why he had raised a query about the Lay College when he first came across its existence. Nor is he aware that any change — tacit or otherwise — was made since the foundation by way of extending its legal scope to include lay students.

Hardwicke's final letter to Marsden for Troy's guidance ended the episode:

"The idea of a Lay boarding school being annexed to Maynooth College, the Intention of which was understood to be the education at home of a Sufficient number of persons for the Priesthood, appeared to present itself as a new Proposition, the Discussion of which I certainly thought it desirable to avoid. Upon this ground an Intimation was given to Mr. Knox in the most friendly manner, that it was the wish of Government that no further expense should be incurred and measures taken with a view to such an Establishment. It never was my wish or Intention that the day Pupils now at the College should be at once withdrawn from it, but that the Establishment should not be fixed as part of the College. When you see Dr. Troy, have the goodness to say further that it will tend greatly to prevent misapprehension upon such points, if when any doubt occurs, he will address himself directly to Government, as he may be assured that he will always be received with attention, and listened to with fairness and Candour''.

In other words — avoid consulting Fitzgibbon, whether directly or indirectly: spectre of Fingall. Hardwicke himself had certainly acted with fairness and candour even if he had ended with a compromise — the Lay College was never contemplated by Government, but it existed and should not be terminated abruptly, but equally it must not be a formal part of the royal foundation and no public funds should be spent on it.

The truth was that — irrespective of Fitzgibbon's delphic utterances — the Lay College had got a reprieve of a kind, which came in time to give satisfaction to Dr. Moylan, Bishop of Cork, who had just written to Pelham appealing on its behalf. No doubt he attributed the outcome to his own influence following his denunciation of the French while their fleet lay in Bantry Bay in 1797. In any case, the Lay College continued. In September, 1802, the *Dublin Evening Post* announced that ''the large and elegant house and demesne, which belonged to the late Dean Craddock, had been purchased as an appendage to the Roman Catholic College of Maynooth, being almost immediately adjoining it. This is to be appropriated for what is called 'a Lay College', where none will be educated but the sons of the Nobility and Gentry of the Catholic persuasion. The President was to be the Reverend William Russell and new Trustees were appointed. The only one of them who was a Trustee of the established College was our old friend the Earl of Fingall. The house in question is what was otherwise known as Riverstown Lodge. And according to later evidence it was then entirely separated from the Royal College by a wall.

Fitzgibbon's role remains enigmatic. Hogan has no hesitation in saying that he did what he did ''ostensibly in the interests of the laity, but in reality with the intention of wrecking the whole institution'' or at least with the hope of setting the laity against the clergy and ''by giving the laity a preponderance in the new institution, to bring it under the control of Trinity College and its Board''. Not even time has been able to tell . . . .

'COLLEGERS' and 'OPPIDANS'

While all this was going on between the men of politics, quite a diferent problem worried churchmen. It all arose from the decision of the Trustees in the Spring of 1796 against the sending of ordained priests for studies to Maynooth. In fact the decision was that no student exceeding the age of twenty years would be admitted after 1798. There was a flurry of excitement in the episcopal palaces for many Bishops had student priests in the house. Troy of Dublin was writing to Bray of Cashel, Bray to Young of Limerick and so on. Some of the prelates were particularly annoyed because it had earlier been decided in 1795 to admit student priests for three years. In order to try to clear up the confusion the Trustees explained at their meeting of 12 May, 1796, "that the permission to admit Priests into the College for three years, from the Spring of 1795, was and is meant to include those only who had been on the Continent, and were interrupted in their studies — and that in future none be admitted but persons of that description, except such as are now at Maynooth, or who have been ordained before Autumn, 1795".

Actually the hand of the Government was also in the matter for, as Troy writes to Bray two days later: "So far is it from the intention of Government that Priests be admitted as students into the College, that the Lord Lieutenant and the Chief Judges expressed surprise on observing so many grown up young men there, on the 20th ultimo. Explanation of disturbances on the Continent and of other present circumstances was necessary to satisfy them". He adds too though that the President and Professors were also against admitting priests. The academic world . . . .! Bishop Young of Limerick was particularly peeved and exercised. His expostulations to Archbishop Bray made it necessary for the latter to write more than once to Archbishop Troy protesting as strongly as possible. Young had the backing of "their Lordships in Limerick", Dr. McMahon of Killaloe who lived in Limerick at that time and Dr. Conway the aged Bishop of the Diocese. He wrote to Power, the Vice-President of the College, outlining his difficulties, but the latter was in little position to do much as he was not in great health that year.

Young's pressure was so great that at the end of October Dr. Hussey sent him a palliative:

"I take this early mode, by post, of informing you that an explanation took place in the board of Trustees at our last meeting, which enables you to send, either to fill the vacancies you may have upon the establishment, or as externs, this year, persons already ordained, tho not interrupted in their studies on the Continent. I am happy to think that this will solve some difficulties you mention in your letter to the Vice-President. The next meeting of the Trustees will be on 11th November; when I should wish you would permit us the honour of receiving you and I hope your pastoral duties will be no obstacle to it. I am particularly interested in it as it may be the only opportunity I may have of presenting my respects to you in person before my return to London".

Almost the same post brought another letter from one of Young's students at Maynooth, Mr. Shea, confirming that additional extern students would shortly be received which would obviously relieve the situation: "Doctor Hussey has taken a house to lodge 20 gentlemen, who (the Externs) can live cheaper perhaps than at home, for they are allowed potatoes and other vegetables from the College . . . . there are many who come on the same condition, 4 from Cork, 4 from Kerry, etc., and as an additional encouragement, Dr. Clancy, Professor of Morality, has offered himself to teach a course of Logics this year. The Courses will begin on Monday next; every step will be taken to make things as comfortable as possible. They are to mess in a Lodge within the precincts of the College, to provide themselves with such little necessaries as are wanting". This is not at all unlike the arrangement made for canteen facilities when the College opened to extern students in the 20th century.

Young was not satisfied, however, and wrote to Bray to that effect. That priests were to be accepted for this year, as externs, was not good enough. He made it very clear that he did not accept as satisfactory an arrangement, whether for long or short, which relegated Priest students to the category — to use Hardwicke's language — of 'Oppidans' rather than 'Collegers'. His fulmination on this to Bray is full of interest. Much inconvenience, says Young, can result "from converting the College into a meer (sic.) community for Boys". He gives an example relating to some of Dr. McMahon's students:

"He sent two who were not in orders to occupy his places there, who after eating the bread of his Diocess for a year, took a Vocation for the matrimonial instead of the ecclesiastical state. This instance cannot fail of leaving a dangerous impression on the minds of the other youths of that house, and I must point out to the Trustees who wish to make a Community out of it, the mischief of the measure to the Mission. Our College at Louvain was a mixed house, and others in the same university. Boys and Priests studied there, together, and during the ten years I was in it, nothing occur'd that could make either wish for a separation. The experiment of mix'd Colleges has been tried, and I am bold to say the Mission of this Country derived more advantage from the former than the latter, the former sent home more Labourers, and who in general have been as conspicuous for zeal and regularity of Conduct as any Communisterians".

How fascinating it is that at a time when some people should have been concerned about the admission of lay students to Maynooth, others were concerned about the exclusion of priests. And how relevant the arguments of both to the 20th century developments which saw the College catering for layman and cleric, both young and old, in various types of courses.

Young got his way at least for a while, as Hussey wrote in late November to tell him that the Board of Trustees had prolonged the time for admitting priests into the house. Twenty prospective students are to be subjected to a public examination next Monday but he fears that some of them will be refused due to ignorance

45

of the Latin language. "The Professors give their decision *per vota secreta,* to avoid cabals, and partialities, should there happen to be any such among them". Bray wrote simultaneously indicating that the extension was until the year 1802:

> "and the same indulgence is to be afterwards continued, if found expedient . . . . The building is greatly advanced and very solid. The students made a very decent appearance and the house is under the strictest discipline — everything contributed to give us real satisfaction. Dr. Hussey, by his Oeconomical arrangements, and by the approbation of the Prelates who met at Maynooth, will provide 26 places for extern Students, one at the disposal of each Bishop, besides those already on the establishment . . . . Doctor McMahon and Your Lordship can send a subject on this footing, whether priested or not, but each subject must bring ten pounds, to buy bed, furniture, etc. Under this arrangement, the College is to provide those Extern students with lodging, half a pound of meat to each per day and a sufficiency of necessary vegetables".

This new arrangement about priest students was to last longer than expected for, in May, 1804, we found a resolution of the Trustees emphasizing "that it is the opinion of this Board that the students, who have finished their Course of Divinity, and shall have received Priests' Orders, shall be considered as vacating their places in College, and that their places be occupied by other students". Apparently some of them, at least, regarded their position as students in the College as 'more eligible' — to use an old phrase — than appointment outside in the Ministry!! That year, by the way, twenty four priests, thirty deacons, forty one sub deacons and thirty one 'Minorists' were ordained and fifty nine students tonsured. (Not that things were perfect in the College in every respect, although between 1800 and 1804, some 123 priests had been sent out on the mission. The problem was more physical than spiritual).

That there was a serious health problem there at the beginning emerges from a letter from the Vice President to Dr. Young that December of 1796: "The numbers already wrested from their studies here, thro want of health, since the last vacation, is alarming, and calls upon our Prelates to have a strict regard, in their choice, to the health and frame of the subjects they send". He is glad however, to be able to inform him that his candidate "has gone thru the fiery ordeal of examination with much credit . . . Mr. Shea can inform you how fatal that Test has proved to several unfortunate candidates, tho' indeed I never witnessed more impartiality".

Some years later the Archbishop of Armagh was to say to the Archbishop of Dublin that his curates are zealous and proper "but like all coming from Maynooth, they cannot bear much fatigue".

The College went on. On 18 January, 1797, the Trustees resolved that the Vice President, Prefect and Professors of Divinity should wear "a clerical sutane or camaille edged with ermine and white Tassell in the cap". The other Professors were to sport "a clerical sutane and camaille edged with green silk fringe and green tassel in the cap", while for those Professors who were not in orders the regulation was for "the College gown to be worn in place of the sutane".

The year had seen many changes in the staff. In April Dr. Clancy had left and returned to Prague. Some thought he had been dismissed, notably Fr. Luke Bellew, relative of Sir Edward Bellew, who declared himself "both affected and surprised to hear of Dr. Clancy's removal from Maynooth . . . . Perhaps Dr. Clancy had the misfortune to differ in opinion with one or other of the French doctors on the pope's infallibility or some other of their four famous articles". Fr. James McCormick, Franciscan of St. Isidore's, Rome, supplied the information that "the reasons Mr. Clancy advances to me for having quitted Maynooth is that the noble family of the Countess of Thunn in Prague has so much importuned the provincial of Ireland, the Archbishop of Dublin and others concerned in the interests of the said Catholic college, to permit Abbe Clancy to return to Prague to act as Professor to the son and heir of the family, that he at length obtained permission to quit said college". In any case the Irish climate does not seem to have agreed very well with Dr, Clancy, who suffered from arthritis in the hands and feet. Indeed he used to go every Summer to Saxony to benefit from the baths there. Hence, in spite, according to McCormick, of having been pressed to stay on in Ireland and "stand candidate for the vacant mitres of Ireland", Dr. Clancy left for Prague. He died in 1814 of gangrene caused by a bruise on his heel from his boot. So we are told by Charles Maguire, O.F.M., writing to McCormick from Chlumetz.   Dr. Lanigan is thought by some to have been offered the Chair left vacant by Dr. Clancy but in a pique declined the offer. According to Fitzpatrick, in his *Irish Wits and Worthies,* he did so because he was "offended at some remarks by one of the Trustees reflecting on the character of Tamburini, under whom Dr. Lanigan studied . . . . as it seemed to throw suspicion on himself". A fuller story is given by Dr. Matthew Kelly, later Professor of Ecclesiastical History at Maynooth. According to him, Lanigan was elected to one of the professor's chairs at Maynooth but difficulties arose about an anti-Jansenistical formula, drawn up by some French refugee clergy and proposed to him for signing by Dr. Moylan of Cork, which he refused to do as he was hurt at the suspicion about him. Brennan, in his *Ecclesiastical History* maintains that the motion of the Bishop of Cork was overruled, but, if so, Lanigan still declined the Chair. Fitzpatrick says that "he seems not to have recovered his equanimity for the rest of the day and henceforth received on the defensive all overtures. He left the hall, but ere he had crossed the threshold of the college gate, word reached him that Dr. Moylan had offered to withdraw his motion, provided Dr. Lanigan would sign another document, we believe the Bull *Auctorem Fidei"* — but to no avail. He was not the only distinguished historian to decline a Maynooth chair in those days. Dr. Lingard, the famous author of the History of England did so a little over a decade later. As regards the Lanigan case, letters of Archbishops Troy and Bray leave no doubt but that their Lordships, as also the President Dr. Hussey, had grave doubts abot his doctrinal orthodoxy.

The year continued. In November, John Chetwoode Eustace returned to England and resigned shortly afterwards. Whether or not these events had any relevance we know not but at the beginning of 1798 the salaries of all the Staff were raised, ranging now from £113.15 per annum in the case of the President, to £91 in the case of the Senior Professor of Divinity, to £60 in that of the Professor of Experimental Philosophy and £30 in that of the Sacristan. The Agent, whose office was largely a sincecure, was in receipt of £300 p.a. The subsistence of the eighteen Masters was fixed at £40 each p.a. and that of the two hundred resident students at £25 per head.

Dr. Ferris of the Diocese of Kerry was appointed the first Dean and, as already mentioned, Dr. Peter Flood, former Professor in the University of Paris, was elected President.

Preparations were being made for the appointment of the great French Professors, Drs. Delahogue and Anglade. Delahogue was appointed in May, 1798. Former Professor of Divinity at the Sorbonne, he had fled the Revolution in 1792 for London, as also had Anglade where they met again. Indeed there is evidence of the existence of a European network of such emigrés, who kept in close touch with one another.

The papers of Delahogue and Anglade are to be found in the *Archives of the Diocese of Clogher,* whither they went during the 19th century when Dr. Charles McNally of the Maynooth staff became Bishop there. McNally had been executor to Anglade who before him had been executor to Delahogue. The papers show how the latter, before leaving France, received a certificate from the District of Corbeil, having made a *contribution patriotique* in the 1st *arrondissement* of Paris, in conformity with the Decree of the National Assembly of October, 1789. He got a Passport from the Municipality of Paris on 4 July in "the 4th year of Liberty", that is, 1792. He is described as aged fifty two at the time, height 5' and 2", with details about eyes and hair. He would have been about fifty eight when appointed to Maynooth. The man must have been dismayed when, on the very month of that appointment, he who had run from the Revolution in France found himself faced with revolution in Ireland.

Chapter III

'Political Delirium'

The new President, Dr. Flood, was a diligent man, and if he was a worrier few could blame him in the times that were in it. As President he made a practice of calling on the students every Saturday to see that they had memorised a portion of the New Tstament. Each Sunday evening he attended at the public hall where the students were wont to preach and offered his criticism of the sermons. He was introduced to the students in the presence of Dr. Troy, on 14 march, 1798.

Little did he know what was in store for him. To some extent he should have been apprehensive. It is a coincidence that he was Parish Priest of Edgeworthstown for some time before his appointment — a place connected with the Abbé Edgeworth — and must have heard of the arrival from Brest of the French fleet of forty-three ships and fifteen thousand men under General Hoche in December, 1796.

At the time Lady Louisa Conolly had been full of apprehension especially for her niece, Lady Lucy Fitzgerald, then staying in Kildare with her brother Lord Edward Fitzgerald and in love with Arthur O'Connor, the United Irishman. The following Christmas there had been another "alarm", recorded in her diary by Emily, Duchess of Leinster, "of the French being off the coast of Ireland". Truly, the indications were getting grim. In July of 1797 a bandit entered the country residence of the Prime Sergeant at Hermitage near Lucan and robbed it of a blunderbuss, two pistols and a fowling piece — for what purpose one need only imagine. Dr. Flood could scarcely have been blind to these and other happenings of a disturbing nature, from Athy to Monastereven, Dunlavin and Castledermot.

Then too, just before he took office, the College had been attacked in the House of Commons by Dr. Duigenan, member for Trinity College, on the grounds of the political unreliability of his predecessor, Dr. Hussey, and also the charge that "although Parliament had given them leave, not one Roman Catholic had yet subscribed six-pence to the endowment of the College". Even though the grant was carried — the College having been defended by Pelham and Sir Hercules Langrishe — it was evident that lively times were in store for the new President.

The vicinity of Maynooth itself was in ferment. A local corps, the 'Maynooth Cavalry', had been formed the previous November, with His Grace the Duke of Leinster as Captain, also the Clane Rangers. They had their marching song:

> *"Let us then, my boys, to the Vicar's repair,*
> *There we're sure of good claret and sure of good cheer,*
> *Tho' the Chaplain can't fight, we are sure of his prayers,*
> *For long life to the Duke and his Clane Volunteers".*

The Maynooth Corps, Rangers, or Volunteers seem to have been the same as the Carton Union, which consisted of Infantry and Cavalry under Colonel Hugh Cane of Dowdstown, near Maynooth. F. McManus was Captain-Lieutenant, Langrish Cavanagh Lieutenant and Richard Cane Chaplain. Their origin went back as far as 1779.

Now one and all got ready for action.

Musgrave writes of the scene:

"The following symptoms of the approaching rebellion appeared in the county of Kildare in the years 1797 and 1798: Constant nightly meetings which the utmost vigilance of the magistrates could not prevent: the abstinence of the lower class of people from spiritous liquors, to a degree of sobriety too unusual and general not to be systematick: the infrequent application to magistrates in matters of dispute: the declining to pay rent or any debts whatever, by those who had the means to do so, and who had been before very regular: the constant resort of the popish multitude to the confession-boxes of their clergy: the refusal to take bank notes, from an idea that the approaching convulsion by subverting the Government would put an end to the currency: the eagerness of the people to take oaths of allegiance to lull the magistrates".

On Sunday 25 March, 1798, the Redcoats came to Castletown, searched the house for arms and took them away so that they would not fall into the hands of the "disaffected". Next morning they were refused entry for the same purpose by Lady Sarah Napier at Celbridge. On 3 April came an Order from Military Headquarters, Kildare, "to the inhabitants of Co. Kildare" requiring the surrender of all arms within ten days.

JACOBINS IN THE HOUSE!

Dr. Flood had much to claim his attention. In April the Archbishop of Dublin was alerting Cashel to the rumour that during the late visitation of Trinity College "a great Law Lord" (could it have been Fitzgibbon?) had signified his intention of investigating Maynooth. The very existence of the College could be endangered — particularly, of course, if seditious elements were found therein. A meeting of the Trustees, to which as many as possible were urged to come, was called for 9 May. It was to be Dr. Flood's baptism of fire.

He describes what occurred fully in a pamphlet published two years later.

> First Resolve: "The Trustees, considering with grief the unhappy spirit of political delirium, which, after having marked its progress, through some of the most cultivated parts of Christendom, by the destruction of order, morality and religion, appears to have made such strides in this Kingdom as menace ruin to everything we should venerate and esteem as Christians and as men; and deeply sensible of the perfect opposition between every part of such pernicious system, and the beneficient objects of the institution over which they preside, think it expedient to order that the President be directed to maintain the most vigilant inspection over the conduct of every individual in any manner to a participation of the benefits of the College; that he be impowered, and is hereby impowered, to punish by expulsion such person or persons as may be their actions or discourse support or abet any doctrines tending to subvert a due regard to the established authorities, and that the Scholars and Students be instructed that on those topics and in these critical times, a conduct not only free from crime, but even from suspicion, is expected from their gratitude, attested allegiance and sacred professional character"
>
> Second Resolve: "The Trustees, alarmed by the public reports charging some individuals of the College with principles of disaffection to the established Government, do hereby order that the President do proceed tomorrow to Maynooth; that he there interrogate in the most solemn manner each individiual relative to said charge, and that he immediately expel every such person, as, on said inquiry, shall not have given every satisfaction respecting the purity of his principles".

The smoke was not without fire for, as Flood continues:

> "Pursuant to these orders the President returned to Maynooth on the day following, and there interrogated, separately and individually, all and each of the Scholars on the establishment, in number 69. Fifty-nine gave every satisfaction respecting the purity of their political principles. They all and each made oath that they had never been at any meeting of United Irishmen, nor any other private or illegal oath; knew nothing of their principles except from public report. Of the remaining ten, eight candidly owned they had thro' ignorance, and want of foresight, been induced to make that illegal oath; some at so early a period as 1793, some in '95, and others so late as August '96; none later: but never had fre-

quented any illegal meeting. All had repented of their errors before the month of November '97, and taken the oaths of fidelity and allegiance to his Majesty:The two others refused to answer to the interrogateries. These ten were indiscriminately expelled on same day.

The schools, in particular, those of Belles Lettres and Rhetoric, were at that time frequented by many students, who lodged and boarded in the town; their only connection with the inmates was their attendance at the public lectures; they, however, underwent the same interrogatories. All, save seven, gave the most satisfactory proofs of untainted loyalty; of the latter, six were in the same predicament with the eight scholars above mentioned; the seventh, though he repeatedly disclaimed every sentiment of disaffection to Government, refused all further satisfaction. It was immediately signified to those seven, that their further abode in the town was to no purpose, the schools should be shut to them on the day following''.

After the expulsions, Dr. Troy, Lord Fingall and Lord Kenmare expressed the opinion that none of those ordered out should be readmitted for the present. The poor fellows found themselves blocked on every side. On the inside of the cover of the *Liber Matriculationis in Scholam Medicinae* of Trinity College for the period one finds their names inscribed, to bar them from entry there too. Of one of them — O'Hearne of the Diocese of Waterford and Lismore — we shall be hearing again later. A note from the Registrar of the Medical School says: "The above I recd. when Sr. Lectr. in May, 1798, from the present Provost, as I understand by the Chancellor's orders, that in case any of the above expelled persons were candidates for admission to the College I might not permit them to enter."

In the circumstances it was droll that a meeting of the Trustees on the day on which the expulsions were taking place should concern itself with resolving that "no wine, tea or sugar be allowed at the expense of the Seminary to any Master or Professor" but a yearly monetary allowance made to them instead. It surely was not a time for sugar. On 19 May Lord Edward Fitzgerald, near neighbour to the collegians, received his uniform in Dublin — a green military outfit, edged with red, with a cap of conical form. Later that day he was arrested. On the nights of 20th, 21st and 22nd fires could be seen on the Wicklow mountains, affecting all the adjacent country. One is reminded of Easter 1916 when the glare in the sky from the fires in Dublin ignited the national spirit of many of the students at Maynooth.

INSURRECTION '98

The 1798 Rebellion broke out on the night of 23-24 May of that year. According to the prearranged plan, the signal for it to the more remote parts of the country was to be the failure of the daily mail coaches to arrive in Dublin — the

52

Belfast coach was to be intercepted at Santry, the Cork coach at Naas, the Limerick coach at the Curragh and the Athlone coach at Lucan.

At the time appointed the Athlone Mail was duly stopped at Lucan, robbed and burned. The Maynooth Post Office contacted the Castle, reporting the incident at "Lukin", with the information given by the guard to the Company of foot, part of the Regiment of Highlanders who had been called from Maynooth to the scene. Already the whole place was up in arms: "All is confusion in this country". Four men had been shot during the night at Dunboyne and there were "dreadful accounts" from Naas, Clane and Prosperous.

On the night of 23rd Naas had been attacked by the rebels who, it was reported, were repulsed with the loss of two hundred men, while on the morning of the 24th, a body of rebels seized Dunboyne. About the middle of the same day, a party of the North Cork Militia stationed at Prosperous were attacked. At the same time Clane was successfully attacked although the attackers were later dislodged. An engagement took place at Rathangan in which the rebels were forced out of the town. The leader of the insurgents in Co. Kildare was William Aylmer, who had taken the place of the imprisoned Lord Edward Fitzgerald.

The events of these stirring days were commemorated in song. One of the ballads was entitled 'Captain Doorly':

"Prosperous town we then did take, Kilcock and famed Maynooth,
When horse and foot came dashing on with their bold undaunted youths;
We set fire to the town and to rout put them all,
In search of Colonel Saunders and we can't find him at all".

Captain Doorly had commanded the United Irishmen at Rathangan.

"The Song of Prosperous' was in like vein to 'Captain Doorly':

"The boys we have forsaken, Kilcock town have taken,
Leixlip, Johnstown and Maynooth, with all its cavalry,
And home we have returned, Sparke's house we burned,
In recompense for Kennedy that died there on a tree".

At the outset of the rebellion an Address of Loyalty by a number of prominent Roman Catholics was published in the *Dublin Journal* and presented to the Lord Lieutenant on 30 May. On 27 May the Archbishop of Dublin, Dr. Troy, issued a letter to his clergy condemning the rebellion. What of the Catholic College at Maynooth? Musgrave writes:

"From the supposed sanctity of this town, as a college had been recently erected there, and endowed at a very great expence by the protestant state for the education of popish priests, it was hoped that it would not have been molested by the rebels . . . . About twenty of the Carton cavalry, of which his grace the Duke of Leinster was captain . . . . did permanent duty there, for some time previous and subsequent to the twenty-fourth of May; and ten of them were constantly stationed on the different avenues leading to the town: the duke was absent at that time in England".

Some of his daughters, however, were at home and, immediately after the rising had occurred, a regiment of Scottish fusiliers was sent from Dublin to occupy the house. We are told that they piled their arms in the colonnades but that, on

Lady Fitzgerald's writing to the Chief Secretary — then Lord Castlereagh — the troops were withdrawn to the town of Maynooth "and the anxiety of the ladies relieved". Nevertheless, the Fitzgerald girls decided to go to Dublin for safety and the Steward, Mr. Stoyte, stowed away the family plate as a precaution, bricking it up in a wall near the Duke's room. The ladies had to go to Leixlip to get passes from the officers in command there. On their way they saw the hanging body of a man, decorated with green ribands and, in the distance, the flames at Dunboyne.

At Castletown things were no better. Lady Louisa Conolly wrote from there:

"This last week has been a most painful one to us. Maynooth, Kilcock, Leixlip and Celbridge, have had part of a Scotch regiment quartered at each place, living upon free quarters and every day threatening to burn the towns. I have spent days in entreaties and threats, to give up the horrid pikes. Some houses burnt at Kilcock yesterday produced the effect. Maynooth held out yesterday, though some houses were burnt and some people punished. This morning the people of Leixlip are bringing in their arms. Celbridge as yet holds out, though five houses are now burning. Whether obstinacy, or that they have them not, I cannot say, but you may imagine what Mr. Conolly and I suffer. He goes about entreating to the last — spent all day yesterday out among them, and today is gone again. He goes from Maynooth to Leixlip and Celbridge and begins again and again to go round them. We have fortunately two most humane officers, that do not more than is absolutely necessary for their orders. At present I feel most prodigiously sunk with all the surrounding distress".

On 4 June Lord Edward Fitzgerald died in Newgate Prison, having been deprived of visitors until too late. He was interred in St. Werburgh's church, until a suitable opportunity could be found to permit of his remains being transferred to the family vault at Maynooth. The cortege "of the exalted ladies and the adoring people" was jeered at by the "satraps" of Government. His will, made on 27 May, left his estates to his wife and children but they were attained and seized by the Government.

His brother, Lord Henry Fitzgerald, who had come to Ireland to see him, sent a scathing letter to Lord Camden: "Your ill-treatment has murdered my brother, as much as if you put a pistol to his head". Camden was to resign shortly afterwards, to be succeeded by Cornwallis. The Maynooth area was naturally in uproar. On the same 27 May Richard Cane appealed to Pelham: "Sir — I had the honour of requesting some time ago that you might be so good as to send here as many of the army as could be spared conveniently from Dublin duty. Since that time a great deal of mischief has been done that might have been prevented. Perhaps there is not in the Kingdom a town more seditious, and disloyal than that from which I date my letter". On 1 June Lady Louisa Conolly wrote:

"There have been several skirmishes in this neighbourhood. Two hundred of them (the Rebels) forced through our gates and passed across the front lawn at three o'clock on Saturday morning last, the 26th, when I saw them. But they went through quietly. However, it is thought prudent to put our house into a state of defence. We are about it now and we shall remain in it . . . . But to return to the rebels. They have a camp at Blackmore hill near Russborough . . . At Dunboyne, the first breaking out appeared; and the town is burnt down all to a few houses. Mr. Conolly tells that the destruction in the country, from Sallins to Kilcullen bridge, made him sick and that many years cannot restore the mischief".

The main thrust of the rebellion in Co. Kildare fizzled out within a week or so of its launching. On Sunday, 27 May, Major General Sir James Duff marched from Limerick with six hundred men of the Dublin Militia and some field pieces to surround the town of Kildare. He found the rebels withdrawing and put them to flight. Yet the 2nd of June saw a large body of them entering Kilcock, who, according to the *Dublin Evening Post*, "forced along with them every man they could lay hold of". But the 3rd saw a reverse for them at Gibbet Rath, where over two hundred were massacred by Duff.

Aylmer, the rebel leader, therefrom began a guerilla campaign. Still the time for more daring action had not entirely passed. On 10 June five hundred men under his command overwhelmed the small garrison in Maynooth town. To quote Musgrave's account:

"About one o'clock in the morning of the tenth of June, 1798, two men approached the town and addressed one of the corps, who was at an outpost; and pretending to be travellers, and that they had lost their way, begged admittance into the town, to get a lodging, but on being refused, they drew back a few paces and both fired at the sentinel at the same time: on which he galloped with the utmost speed to the guard-room and alarmed his fellow-soldiers, and was pursued by about five hundred rebels, headed by William Aylmer their commander".

Due to "disaffection" only seven of the Maynooth Corps mounted their horses and only four fired on the rebels. The Corps retreated, many joining the rebels, the rest the yeomanry at Leixlip.

On the 18th came disaster — the routing of Aylmer's forces (said to number over three thousand) at the battle of Ovidstown near Kilcock.

Where were the Maynooth students the while? Well, the *Dublin Journal* was quick to imply that the College was "a nursery of traitors". Dr. Troy demanded a withdrawal of this but only got it in a half-hearted way. Later on Musgrave was to put on record that "sixteen or seventeen (students) were expelled on account of being concerned in the rebellion. Some of them were slain in fighting against the king's troops, and others fled to escape the punishment which their guilt merited. I have been assured that between thirty and forty of them fought against the king's army".

In a later pamphlet Dr. Duigenan of Trinity College maintained that about thirty six students from "that Monastery" were reported to have joined the insurgents and fought at Kilcock and other places against the King's forces.

There certainly was plenty of suspicion about the College. The *State of the Country Papers* in Dublin Castle contain a letter from Lord Altamont to the Castle: "My brother desired me to acquaint you that he had received *private* information that a man of the name of Sharkey, a student or professor at Maynooth College and now residing there, had some confidential employment from the Dublin Directory and ought to be carefully looked after". Around the same time a Mr. Clements was writing to same about one Michael Brady "mentioned to me as a teacher in the College of Maynooth" who "had made his escape from that place with much difficulty principally by the assistance of a Lady of that country. He is now I am informed with his relations, who I know to be as disaffected a set as any in Ireland, in a mountainous part of this country. He talks much of the French invasion".

The President, Dr. Flood, was doing his best. He had associated himself and his students with an appeal 'To such of the Deluded People, now in rebellion again His Majesty's Government in this Kingdom, as profess the Roman Catholic Religion' which had been issued on 26 May and reported by *Faulkner's Dublin Journal,* the *London Gazette* and the *Dublin Evening Post.* He had also signed the Address of Loyalty of 30 May to the Lord Lieutenant, which was carried by the *Freeman's Journal* for a week.

The Maynooth area continued to be disturbed. *Faulkner's* for Thursday, 14 June, carried a piece about "an ill-fated report which reached the town on Tuesday evening", to wit, that Castletown, the seat of Mr. Conolly, had been attacked by the rebels in force. "A detachment of Captain's Beresford's Cavalry instantly proceeded to the place — and found it was only a rumour".

June 24 saw the commencement of the Summer vacation in the College and a welcome respite for Dr. Flood. On that day he wrote to Plunkett, Bishop of Meath:

"We commence vacation that day. Prudence prevents me from entering into any details. Give me leave to refer your Lordship to the bearer, Mr. Keegan, or Mr. Roe, for particulars. I hope ere long to see you in person, and, *os ad os loqui.* I shall only tell you at present that I act under the instructions and advice of Lord Castlereagh, Secretary Cooke, Dr. Troy, and Lord Kenmare. I waited on Lord Castlereagh twice last week, and I am happy to inform you that he has repeatedly assured me that the College should continue to enjoy the fullest protection from Government. We received, a few days ago, from the Treasury — without solicitation — £750. We expect, *Deo juvente,* to resume studies on the 24th or 25th August, but I fear it will not be in our power to receive additional students; *pendent opera interrupta:* all our carpenters, slaters, joiners, etc., have been forced away by the insurgents. Some of these miscreants have repeatedly threatened to make the students march in their ranks . . .

The Lord knows I have scarce enjoyed a day's peace or quiet since I came here — from one embarrassment into another. I owe you that I am heartily tired of the Presidency":

a sentiment that was not unknown at times to a much later successor in the post .

58

Despite it all, on 4 July, 1798, Dr. Young, Bishop of Limerick, was enquiring of the Archbishop of Cashel just to know "whether the classicks are taught at Maynooth". He complains that he has asked about this of both the President and the Vice-President but neither have replied to him. Would anybody blame them for not having done so?

AFTERMATH

By the end of June the rebellion was petering out. But the aftermath was to be terrible. Lady Sarah Napier writes from Celbridge concerning the Duke of Leinster's tenants: "The county of Kildare, in which is all his property, is almost desolate, and growing worse every day. The peculiar marked object has been to ruin his tenants and the insurgents will now finish it; for although personal attachment to him make them very anxious to avoid it, yet necessity forces them to take what they can".

She has to agree that the stupidities of the régime had caused many of the tenants to join the insurgents: "The cruel hardship put on his tenants, preferably to all others, has driven them to despair, and they join the insurgents saying 'It is better to die with a pike in my hand than be shot like a dog at my work, or see my children faint for want of food before my eyes". One of these very pikes came into the possession of the President of the College in the 1960's.

Of Castletown itself Lady Louisa Conolly writes in early July: "Our house is a perfect garrison. Eighteen soldiers sleep in our salon and we are all blocked up, and shut up, except the hall-door, and one door to the kitchen-yard, and are frequently ordered all into the house upon the alarm being given of the rebels being near Celbridge".

On 12 July Castlereagh sent a letter to the leaders of the rebels in Kildare offering good terms if they surrendered within forty-eight hours. They would not be sent to Botany Bay but must be banished from the Kingdom for life. The following Sunday morning, 15 July, a reply was received at Maynooth — the leaders are not sure of Castlereagh's meaning. Does it mean that they should go to America? If so they will try to get their men to agree for these are afraid of deception. They have been prevented by their leaders from engaging in greater robbery and burning. The forty-eight hours passed. Again came a note from the victors stationed at Maynooth, ironically signed by Sir Fenton Aylmer, namesake of the rebel leader, extending the time allowed for surrender, but it should not be prolonged. A great army is on the way. The rebels are to lay down their arms on the Hill of Ballygordon "where the army from Maynooth will also march but keep a certain distance from them". It is desirable that this should take place before tomorrow evening. So run the *Rebellion Papers* in Dublin Castle. They show that even though Sir Fenton Aylmer had sent his reply to the rebels, he was at all sure of what was the right thing to do. In another note he conveyed as much to Castlereagh. In the meantime, he promised that there would be no relaxation by His Majesty's troops under his command.

The 24th of July saw Lord Cornwallis reporting that the principal leaders in Kildare had surrendered.

William Aylmer was kept in custody for a while, after which he went to England and later to Austria where he enlisted in the army of the Archduke Franz Joseph. He ended up in South America, where he was killed while serving with an Irish contingent on the side of Simon Bolivar.

What was happening in the College during this eventful period? For one thing, even though it had been decided previously that the students on the establishment should remain in College during the Summer, they were ordered home. Unperturbably, as is their wont, the Trustees met on 27 July, although only four were present. The Duke of Leinster, brother of Lord Edward, now back from England, dined in the College with them and afterwards invited them to dine at Carton. Eighteenth century life had not collapsed. But poor Dr. Flood, the President, had his worries. He was writing to various Irish Bishops that the new building would not be ready for next year and the houses which were rented by the College had been requisitioned by the military. To Dr. Plunkett of Meath on 21 August from Maynooth:

"I arrived last night here, firmly resolved to set out for Navan tomorrow — man proposes but God disposes. On my arrival here, I found my favourite mare sprained in her back. The servant tells me she leaped a ditch and fell. She cost me 22 guineas. . . I must travel in the lay coach . .

Tis with regret I must inform you that our works have been almost stationery here these three months past. Under the pressure of the times, little or nothing could have been done. We have about 450 of the military quartered in this little town. The houses tenanted by the college last year are full of soldiers, and hence I fear we can have few or no externs. I am preparing, with all possible expedition, rooms in the new building for the 50 students on the present establishment, and I think I shall be able to accommodate one additional subject from each diocese. We shall then be 75 on the 17th of next month; 50 more will be received before Christmas, and I flatter myself we shall have accommodation for the stated number, 200, before the 1st March, 1799. Each student, previous to his admission, must produce a certificate in due form, of his having taken the Oath of Allegiance, pay seven pounds for a bed, which is to remain his own property, and if not in Holy Orders, deposit 20 pounds to be forfeited to the College, in the case of Expulsion or non-admission to Orders.

It was moreover resolved by the Board of Trustees at the General Meeting in May last, that each student henceforward admitted to the Establishment should pay six guineas entrance to be applied to the general exigencies of the College. The above, My Lord, are indispensable pre-requisites, no admission without them. We continue here to experience the fullest protection from Government".

He did meet Dr. Plunkett sometime afterwards and "lamented" the lack of Spiritual Directors for the students. Plunkett agreed that it was a serious drawback.

The "protection from Government" which the College enjoyed was to have its lighter moments. One was the incident when one of the Professors, the French anti-revolutionary Abbé Darre, and an Irish priest called Fr. Luke Mooney (possibly a priest-student, for the only Luke Mooney on the *College Register* did not matriculate until 1808) were stopped by a sentry between Carton and the College. The story is told in the novel *Harry Lorrequer* by Charles Lever. Its theme derives from the Winter of 1798 and is very likely to be historical as Lever's father was employed as contractor for work on the new College buildings. We are told that old Mr. Lever used to tell the story a hundred times. He was friendly with a number of the Professors. His son could not have but lived the thing. As in his other novel *Jack Hinton* the preface to which tells us that all of the characters are from real life, so too the preface to *Harry Lorrequer* says: "In sketching Harry Lorrequer I was in a great measure depicting myself, and becoming allegorically an autobiographist".

We can take it, therefore, that the story from the Winter of 1798 is historical. It is about a visit of Frs. Darre and Luke Mooney to Carton which concluded with a postscript. A later writer says that "many of the professors were good fellows that liked grog fully as well as Greek, and understood short whist, and five-and-ten as intimately as they knew the Vulgate of the Confessions of St. Augustine. They made no ostentatious display of their pious zeal, but whenever they were not fasting or praying, or something of that kind, they were always pleasant and agreeable; and, to do them justice never refused by any chance an invitation to dinner — no matter at what inconvenience." There certainly was inconvenience on that winter night in 1798.

"It was towards the latter end of the year '98 — the year of the troubles — that the North Cork was ordered, 'for their sins', I believe, to march from their snug quarters in Fermoy and take up a position in the town of Maynooth — a very considerable reverse of fortune to a set of gentlemen extremely addicted to dining out, and living at large upon a very pleasant neighbourhood. Fermoy abounded in gentry; Maynooth, at that time, had few, excepting his Grace of Leinster, and he lived very privately, and saw no company. Maynooth was stupid and dull — there were neither belles nor balls; Fermoy (to use the doctor's well rememberd words) had "great feeding" and "very genteel young ladies, that carried their handkerchiefs in bags and danced with the officers."

They had not been many weeks in their new quarters when they began to pine over their altered fortunes, and it was with a sense of delight, which a few months before would have been incomprehensible to them, they discovered that one of their officers had a brother, a young priest in the college; he introduced him to some of his confreres, and the natural result followed. A visiting acquaintance began between the regiment and such of the members of the college as had liberty to leave the precincts: who, as time ripened the acquaintance into intimacy, very naturally preferred the mess of the North Cork to the meagre fare of "the refectory". At last, seldom a day went by without one or two of their reverences finding themselves guests at the mess. The North Corkians were of a most hospitable turn, and the fathers were determined the virtue should not rust for want of being exercised; they would just drop in to say a word to "Captain O'Flaherty about leave to shoot in the demesne", as Carton was styled; or, they had a "frank from the Duke for the Colonel", or some other equally pressing reason; and they would contrive to be caught in the middle of a very droll story just as the "roast beef" was playing. Very little entreaty then sufficed — a short apology for the "derangements" of dress, and a few minutes more found them seated at table without further ceremony on either side.

Among the favourite guests from the college, two were peculiarly in estimation — 'the Professor of the Humanities', Father Luke Mooney; and the Abbé d'Array, 'the Lecturer on Moral Philosophy and Belles Lettres'; and certain it is, pleasanter fellows, or more gifted with the 'convivial bump', there never existed. He of the Humanities was a droll dog — a member of the Curran Club, the 'monks of the screw', told an excellent story, and sang the 'Cruiskeen Lawn' better than did any before or since him; — the Moral Philosopher, though of a different genre, was also a most agreeable companion, an Irishman transplanted in his youth to St. Omer, and who had grafted upon his native humour a considerable share of French smartness and repartee — such were the two, who ruled supreme in all the festive arrangements of this jovial regiment, and were at last as regularly at table as the adjutant and the paymaster, and so might they have continued. had not prosperity, that, in its blighting influence upon the heart, spares neither priests nor laymen, and is equally severe upon mice (see Aesop's Fable) and moral philosophers, actually deprived then, for the 'nonce', of reason, and tempted them to their ruin. You naturally ask, what did they do? Did they venture upon allusions to the retreat upon Ross? Nothing of the kind. Did they, in that vanity which wine inspires, refer by word, act, or innuendo, to the well-known order of their Colonel when reviewing his regiment in 'the Phoenix', to 'advance two steps two steps backwards and dress by the gutter?' Far be it from them? though; indeed either of these had been esteemed light in the balance with their real crime. 'Then, what was their failing — come, tell it, and burn ye?' They actually, I dread to say it, quizzed the Major coram the whole mess! Now, Major John Jones had only lately exchanged into the North Cork from the 'Darry Ragement', as he called it. He was a red-hot Orangeman, a deputy-grand something, and vice-chairman of the 'Prentice Boys' besides. He broke his leg when a schoolboy, by a fall incurred in tying an orange handkerchief around King William's august neck in College-green on one 12th July, and three several times had closed the gates of Derry with his own loyal hands, on the famed anniversary; in a word, he was one that, if his Church had enjoined penance as an expiation for sin, would have looked upon a trip to Jerusalem on his bare knees as a very light punishment for the crime on his conscience, that he sat at table with two buck priests from Maynooth, and carved for them, like the rest of the company!

Poor Major Jones, however, had no such solace, and the cankerworm eat daily deeper and deeper into his pining heart. During the three or four weeks of their intimacy with his regiment, his martyrdom was awful. His figure wasted, and his colour became a deeper tinge of orange, and all around averred that there would soon be a 'move up' in the corps, for the major had evidently 'got his notice to quit' this world and its pomps and vanities. He felt 'that he was dying', to use Haynes Bayley's beautiful and apposite words, and meditated an exchange; but that, from circumstances, was out of the question. At last, subdued by grief, and probably his spirit having chafed itself smooth by such constant attrition, he became, to all seeming, calmer; but it was only the calm of a broken and weary heart. Such was Major Jones at the time when, *'suadente diabolo'*, it seemed meet to Father Mooney and D'Array to make him the butt of their raillery. At first, he could not believe it; the thing was incredible — impossible; but when he looked around the table, when he heard the roars of laughter, long, loud and vociferous; when he heard his name bandied from one to the other across the table, with some vile jest tacked to it 'like a tin kettle to a dog's tail', he awoke to the full measure of his misery — the cup was full. Fate had done her worst, and he might have exclaimed with Lear, 'Spit, fire — Spout, rain'; there was nothing in store for him of further misfortune.

A drum-head court-martial — a hint to 'sell out' — ay, a sentence of 'dismissed the service', had been mortal calamities, and, like a man, he would have borne them; but that he, Major John Jones,D.G.S.C.P.B., &c. &c, who had drunk the 'pious, glorious and immortal', sitting astride of 'the great gun of Athlone', should come to this! Alas, and alas! He retired that night to his chamber a 'sadder if not a wiser man'; he dreamed that the 'statue' had given place to the unshapely figure of Leo X., and that 'Lundy now stood where Walker stood before'. He jumped from his bed in a moment of enthusiasm, he vowed his revenge, and he kept his vow.

That day the major was 'acting field officer'. The various patrols, sentries, pickets and outposts, were all under his especial control; and it was remarked that he took peculiar pains in selecting the men for night duty, which, in the prevailing quietness and peace of that time, seemed scarcely warrantable.

Evening drew near, and Major Jones, summoned by the 'oft-heard beat', wended his way to the mess. The officers were dropping in, and true as 'the needle to the pole', came Father Mooney and the Abbé. They were welcomed with the usual warmth, and, strange to say, by none more than the major himself, whose hilarity knew no bounds.

How the evening passed, I shall not stop to relate; suffice it to say, that a more brilliant feast of wit and jollification not even the North Cork ever enjoyed. Father Luke's drollest stories, his very quaintest humour, shone forth, and the Abbé sang a new *chanson à boire,* that Beranger might have envied.

"What are you about, my dear Father D'Array?" said the Colonel:

"you are surely not rising yet; here's a fresh cooper of port just come in; sit down, I entreat".

"I say it with grief, my dear colonel, we must away; the half hour has just chimed, and we must be within 'the gates' before twelve. The truth is, the Superior has been making himself very troublesome about our 'carnal amusements', as he calls our innocent mirth, and we must therefore be upon our guard".

"Well, if it must be so, we shall not risk losing your society altogether for an hour or so now; so, one bumper to our next meeting — tomorrow, mind, and now, Monsieur l'Abbé, *au revoir*".

The worthy fathers finished their glasses, and taking a most affectionate leave of their kind entertainers, sallied forth under the guidance of Major Jones, who insisted upon accompanying them part of the way, as, from information he had received, the sentries were doubled in some places, and the usual precautions against surprise all taken. Much as this polite attention surprised the objects of it, his brother officers wondered still more, and no sooner did they perceive the major and his companions issue forth, than they set out in a body to watch where this most novel and unexpected complaisance would terminate.

When the priests reached the door of the barrack-yard, they again turned to utter their thanks to the major, and entreat him once more not to come a step farther. 'There now, major, we know the path well, so just give us the pass, and don't stay out in the night air'.

"Ah, oui, Monsieur Jones", said the Abbé, *"retournez, je vous prie.* We are, I may say, *chez nous. Ces braves gens, les North Cork,* know us by this time".

The major smiled, while he still pressed his services to see them past the pickets, but they were resolved, and would not be denied.

"With the word for the night we want nothing more," said Father Luke.

"Well, then" said the major, in the gravest tone — and he was naturally grave — "you shall have your way; but remember to call out loud, for the first sentry is a little deaf, and a very passionate, ill-tempered fellow to boot."

"Never fear," said Father Mooney, laughing. "I'll go bail he'll hear me".

"Well — the word for the night is — 'Bloody end to the Pope', — don't forget now, ('Bloody end to the Pope'). And with these words he banged the door between him and unfortunate priests; and, as bolt was fastened after bolt, they heard him laughing to himself like a fiend over his vengeance.

"And big bad luck to ye, Major Jones, for the same, every day ye see a paving-stone", was the faint sub-audible ejaculation of Father Luke, when he was recovered enough to speak.

"Sacristi! Que nous sommes attrapés," said the Abbé, scarcely able to avoid laughing at the situation in which they were placed.

"Well, there's the quarter chiming now; we've no time to lose. Major Jones! Major darling: don't now, ah, don't'. Sure ye know we'll be ruined entirely — there now, just change it, like a dacent fellow — the devil's luck to him, he's gone. Well, we can't stay here in the rain all night, and be expelled in the morning afterwards — so come along."

They jogged along for a few minutes in silence, till they came to that part of the 'Duke's' demesne wall, where the first sentry was stationed. By this time the officers, headed by the major, had quietly slipped out of the gate, and were following their steps at a convenient distance.

The fathers had stopped to consult together what they should do in this trying emergency — when their whisper being overheard,. the sentinel called out gruffly, in the genuine dialect of his country, 'Who goes that?'

"Father Luke Mooney and the Abbé D'Array", said the former, in his most bland and insinuating tone of voice, a quality he most eminently possessed.

"Stand and give the countersign".

"We are coming from the mess, and going home to the college," said Father Mooney, evading the question, and gradually advancing as he spoke.

"Stand, or I'll shoot ye," said the North Corkian.

The Sentry challenging ye Fathers Luke and the Abbé

Father Luke halted, while a muttered 'Blessed Virgin!' announced his state of fear and trepidation.

"D'Array, I say, what are we to do?"

"The countersign," said the sentry, whose figure they could perceive in the dim distance of about thirty yards.

"Sure ye'll let us pass, my good lad, and ye'll have a friend in Father Luke the longest day ye live, and ye might have a worse in time of need; ye understand."

Whether he did understand or not, he certainly did not heed, for his only reply was the short click of a gun-lock, that bespoke a preparation to fire.

"There's no help now", said Father Luke; "I see he's a haythen; and bad luck to the major, I say again." And this, in the fulness of his heart, he uttered aloud.

"That's not the countersign," said the inexorable sentry, striking the butt-end of his musket on the ground with a crash that smote terror into the hearts of the priests.

"Mumble — mumble 'to the Pope', said Father Luke, pronouncing the last words distinctly, after the approved practice of a Dublin watchman, on being awoke from his dreams of row and riot by the last toll of the Post-office, and not knowing whether it has struck 'twelve' or 'three', sings out the word 'o'clock' in a long sonorous drawl, that wakes every sleeping citizen, and yet tells nothing how 'Time speeds on his flight.'

"Louder", said the sentry, in a voice of impatience.

"— to the Pope",

"I don't hear the first part."

"Oh, then, said the priest, with a sigh that might have melted the heart of anything but a sentry, 'Bloody end to the Pope; and may the saints in heaven forgive me for saying it.'

"Again," called out the soldier; "and no mutterings."

"Bloody end to the Pope," cried Father Luke, in bitter desperation.

"Pass, Bloody end to the Pope, and good night," said the sentry, resuming his rounds, while a loud and uproarious peal of laughter behind told the unlucky priests they were overheard by others, and that the story would be over the whole town in the morning.

Whether it was that the penance for their heresy took long in accomplishing, or that they never could summon courage sufficient to face their persecutor, certain it is that the North Cork saw them no more, nor were they ever observed to pass the precincts of the college while that regiment occupied Maynooth

Major Jones himself, and his confederates, could not have more heartily relished this story, than did the party to whom the Doctor related it. Much, if not all the amusement it afforded, however, resulted from his

inimitable mode of telling, and the power of mimicry with which he conveyed the dialogue with the sentry; and this, alas, must be lost to my
readers — at least to that portion of them not fortunate enough to
possess Dr. Finucane's acquaintance.''

As for Dr. Finucane, he too was the subject of a story by Lever, in the same
novel, but we have enough of the stories about the North Cork Militia during that
Winter of 1798 in Maynooth.

The College itself at the time was under the necessity of proving its allegiance to
Government. In October, 1799 Dr. Troy of Dublin wrote:

"If upon enquiry it be found that any United Irishman or abettor of their
irreligious and revolutionary system has been clandestinely introduced
into the College, it is my wish and that of every other Trustees that he be
punished, but if none such be discovered there, I hope you will vindicate
the College from any aspersion or unfavourable suspicion which may be
occasioned by the apprehension and confinement of Thomas Power one
of the scholars, by ordering his discharge and declaring the information
against him unfounded''.

The Vice-President of the College, the Reverend Mr. Power, had made in-
tercession on behalf of the same Thomas Power who may well have been a
relative of his. It was on his calling that Dr. Troy had written this letter. The Vice-
President had supplied him with the following:

"There exist no such persons in Maynooth College as Francis Hearn or
John Power. The only student bearing the last surname is called Thomas
. . . One Maurice Power who resided in said College for upwards of two
years was obliged to quit in October, 1797, not feeling himself disposed
to enter Holy Orders, as the College is founded solely for such as are to
receive Priesthood. His unguarded behaviour, as I understand, has
betrayed him into many *faux pas* for which he is said to be still smarting,
but where or how I am utterly ignorant. In May, 1798, Mr. Francis
Hearn, from Waterford, who was also out of Orders, was dismissed the
College for being concerned in the business of United irishmen, and has
never since appeared there, nor, as I could learn, had any connection or
correspondence with any of its members since that period. To every article of this declaration I am ready to make a legal deposition if required,
and have in consequence subscribed, after observing that Thomas
Power, now a scholar in the College, seems to be an inoffensive,
harmless young man''.

The unfortunate Francis Hearn or, more properly, Hearne, came of a
distinguished Waterford family. An uncle of his was Professor in the University
of Louvain and another relative built Waterford Cathedral. It is pretty clear from
the foregoing that the civil authorities were in search of all those connected with

the United Irishmen, including the former students of Maynooth College. Whatever about Power, Hearne was apprehended and sentenced to death. Faulkner's *Dublin Journal* of 9 November, 1799 stated that "great exertions were made by the Roman Catholic clergy of this city, to save the life of Hearn, a student of Maynooth College, who was lately tried by Court-Martial at Waterford and pleaded guilty. The obstinate refusal of the culprit to make atonements for his guilt by revealing the extent of the treasons in which he was concerned, very properly excluded him from that mercy which might have been otherwise extended to him". In reply to the newspaper Dr. Troy said that

> "the direct tendency of this misrepresentation is to indispose every loyal man against me and the R.C. Clergy of this City, and to asperse the reputation of Maynooth College. I appeal to yourself whether I or any of my clergy in this City, interfered with Government on behalf of Hearne? I can add that I absolutely refused to go or to write to you in his favour, tho' ernestly pressed to do either. Hearne was a student of Maynooth College, but expelled from thence before the Rebellion: at the same time some students were expelled from Trinity College for the same reasons. An impartial observer of these occurrences would rather command the zeal of the Visitors in purging these establishments from suspected persons, than insinuate anything to the discredit of either. It is to be lamented that the *Dublin Journal* too frequently indulges, in similar party paragraphs, instead of endeavouring to allay the violence of parties. If you have any influence on the Editors of that print, I request you will have the goodness to exert it in inducing them to explain away in a future publication the mischievous tendency of the paragraph I have copied and do justice to the College of Maynooth . . . ."

— a sentiment the like of which could well have been expressed in the latter part of the 20th century.

Dr. Troy was naturally very concerned about reports that would give the impression that the College was "a nursery of traitors". There were some who were very ready to make the accusation. In December, 1799 a Mr. Luke Fox wrote to Castlereagh:

> "The avowed principle of that institution is to educate for the Romish priesthood a class of men separated from their fellow-subjects, of every religious persuasion, as well Romish as Protestant . . . . It is, in fact, to a certain degree, supplying the whole of your parochial clergy from a Monastery, training in the deepest prejudices of the most dangerous political and religious sophistry . . . . There is nothing, notwithstanding the honest ravings of Doctor Patrick Duigenan, that disqualifies men from becoming peacable and loyal subjects. But there is a deadly princi-

ple in the Spanish leaven, imported to Maynooth, which is uniform in perversion . . . . This, seminary is to be abolished: No separate place of education is to be allowed to Catholic Priests. Let them mix and converse with their fellow subjects''.

Poor Hearne died for his principles. There is a long letter in the *Dublin Diocesan Archives* to the Archbishop, Dr. Troy, from Father William Power — again that Waterford name — Vicar General of the Diocese of Waterford, which tells about his execution. After being expelled from Maynooth he had gone to Carlow, still as a student for the priesthood, but the Government had pursued and indicted him: he had been sworn in as a United Irishman by no less a person than Dr. Drennan. His execution must have been macabre. Fr. Power's letter tells of how, as he was about to die, he was posed questions by some of the attendant army officers who tried to inculpate Maynooth. Hearne stood on the scaffold. Father Power intervened. The result was that the condemned man attributed his downfall to drink and the company he kept, also the French revolutionary pamphlets which he had read while studying at Louvain before coming to Maynooth. It was the end of the rebellion of 1798 insofar as it affected Maynooth College.

Chapter IV

Of Bishops and the Government

For all its ostentation the eighteenth century ended quietly enough in Ireland. That it should have done so was probably inevitable after the cataclysm of the '98 rebellion.

In Maynooth College life not so much went on as began to get under way in peace. Its texture at that time has been transmitted to us in the letters of the Armagh student, Eugene Conwell. He had arrived in College during the Spring of 1798, found no accommodation awaiting him and was only allowed to stay at all "as a great favour". In addition the change of diet made him ill. In September he is writing home to send him his "old black coat and waist coat, one pair of coarse twilled sheets — a couple of nightcaps". He complains that the last letter from his sister cost him "double postage on account of the mode it was folded up in" and wishes that they would pay the postage of their letters to him "as money is not too plenty".

Fin de Siècle

At the opening of term in October, Conwell had to make a deposit of six guineas — "My bed will cost me as much more, tho' I only paid a part of it, and I must also furnish my room and buy a Cloak and Cap". His first lecture was from the Frenchman Darre, on "the nature of Logics". He found Darre "an agreeable, sweet little man, but his pronounciation is not easily understood in giving the dictate". The building in which he lived was "about 40 perches from the College". It had thirty students in it. It was a cold house, he says, having only just been finished. "We are obliged to provide the candles for our rooms. In short we have nothing from the House but diet and lodging".

He awaited the return of the general student body who had been sent away on the outbreak of the rebellion: "The gentlemen students of this college were very dilatory returning here after vacation. They are coming in every day yet". This was 28 October, 1798. But "the Duke of Leinster often visits us . . . . Every Wednesday almost we visit his Demesne which is most spacious and beautiful, and of endless variety". He had also visited Celbridge House, the residence of Mr. and Mrs. Conolly. Early in the term though it was, Conwell wrote to his granduncle on 1 November: "I sustained a Thesis a few days ago on abstract ideas in general, and I assure I considered it the most glorious day of my life". In January he visited Dublin; it cost nearly half a guinea to go and come. In truth he did the journey economically because we know that in 1795 the journey from Maynooth to Dublin by carriage for three persons cost £1-14-1½. By 15 February he had preached in the chapel of the town the previous Sunday.

For their part the Bishops were preparing for a new chapter in the life of the institution as the Government was for the country. In October, 1798, the Archbishop of Cashel reported to the Bishop of Limerick that the Archbishop of Dublin wished to consult the bishops as a whole about it. There was question too, he understood, of Lord Castlereagh's wishing to grant an annual stipend to each of the Catholic clergy. Troy had remarked that while he would have opposed such a measure some years ago, circumstances had changed. He would now be prepared to settle for a compromise — acceptance of an annual sum for the poorest clergy. The Bishop of Limerick appended a note in his own handwriting to Cashel's letter: "I gave a decided Negative to the affair in my answer to this, and concluded my letter thus — 'I never shall accept a bribe to acquiesce in the extinction of the Independance (sic.) of my Country'". Clearly he saw the Union foreshadowed and he did not resign himself to it. In December he writes to Dr. Bray listing many objection against accepting the Government's proposals for a clerical subsidy and on 31 of that month from "near Limerick" he writes again to same:

"My Dear and Honoured Lord . . . . We have a character to maintain, which next to the grace of God is the basis on which the Catholick Religion rests in this Country and from the exalted station God has rais-

72

ed us to, is more exposed to microscopick observations and critical censure than any other, and we ought not to give the present generation nor posterity either any occasion to cast a shade on our good name: for my individual part I always reprobated the conduct of the Scotch who betrayed the interests of King Charles the 1st for money, and of their posterity who sold the independance of their Country to England for £20,000.

The cards are shuffled for playing a similar Game with Ireland, and it does not become us to expose ourselves to the reproach of being venal, which will unavoidably be cast on us if we accept the offers that have been made. If the union can promote the glory of God in any degree I rejoice in it. At the same time I declare that as a Citizen I am satisfied with the constitution of our country in its *present* form, but shall accept no bribe to acquiesce in the annihilation of its independance''.

At Maynooth things were what might be described as ''idling''. The accounts for the year show the salary scales as already outlined, with £100 for ten servants and another £240 for twelve more. The grant sought amounted to a total of £8,000. In October, Delahogue, not long in the place, sent a copy of his new book to Troy who read it with great interest and wrote back: ''Nothing can be more applicable to the information and instruction of the French Constitutional Clergy while every orthodox reader must benefit by the attentive perusal of it and admire your zeal and diligence in supporting the authority of the Catholic Church''. Authority, whether secular or ecclesiastical, was still very much under siege. That December the *Hibernian Journal* reported that a house near Dunboyne was broken into by a party of ''rebels'' with their faces blackened, despite the presence of a strong military guard there. There had appeared also Dr. Duigenan's pamphlet entitled *A Fair Representation of the Political State of Ireland,* which described Maynooth as ''a noxious and unconstitutional weed'', ''a glaring effect of the spirit of Burkism, diffused among our rulers both in Great Britain and Ireland''.

Castlereagh was wasting no time. He had approached the four Archbishops and six Bishops who were the clerical trustees of Maynooth to try, at their forthcoming meeting (January, 1799), to put forward some scheme whereby the Government might be satisfied about the loyalty of anybody proposed to fill a vacant See before his name was sent to Rome. The Veto controversy had begun. These Bishops in reply were prepared to accord to the Irish Viceroy a certain right of objection to a proposed name but reserved to themselves — or at least to the prelates of the ecclesiastical province concerned — the right of final judgement.
In so replying the Maynooth Trustees spoke only for themselves. In shame indeed it must be said that they seemed to echo the wishes of Government. Was the grant to the College talking? The answer is probably 'Yes' and 'No', for they did hedge round their agreement. They were also careful to point out that no change in the present mode of proceeding could be made without the consent of the Pope.

Later, in 1808, the Bishops were to say that there should be no change at all in the system, whether as regards episcopal appointments or the clergy living by the voluntary offerings of the people. in 1813 came a Catholic Relief Bill containing a veto clause and in 1814 the Quarrantotti Rescript accepting it. In 1815 Pope Pius VII disavowed this, leaving the Bishops free to reject it. Came another Bill in 1821 with a similar clause but it was rejected by the House of Lords. In 1829 Catholic Emancipation was to be granted without any attempt at a veto.

But in 1799 the 'Maynooth Resolutions' as they were called, held the field, even though Dr. Young of Limerick observed that they were framed by "no other than the Trustees of Maynooth College, whose number if all were present, was only eleven". It was not Maynooth's greatest hour. As things happened, the Trustees' agreement to the veto remained confidential in that it did not appear in the Press or come before Parliament. Not until 1805 was the veto question really discussed. It was to die for a while in 1808, when Grattan revealed the 1799 resolution to the House and Mr. Ponsonby, though friendly, killed it when he said that its meaning was that there was no objection to making the King the virtual head of the Roman Catholic Church in Ireland. At their General Meeting on 14 September, 1808, the Irish Hierarchy threw out the measure.

In early 1799 things were more fluid. Cashel, writing to Limerick in February, expresses the belief that the Government intended to make a subsidy only, and not a permanent subsistence for the Catholic clergy. In the event, of course, Government would "certainly expect some degree of patronage. But we are firmly resolved it shall not be to the prejudice of Religion or Discipline. Your Lordship's remark appears to me well founded, that the proposal of such a subsidy is an appendage of an intended Union, or a *douceour,* not to say a specious deceitful Bait, to render that Business more palatable to the Catholic Body".

On 23 February Troy wrote from Dublin to Young, who was clearly a man to be reckoned with:

"As the measure of provision for our Clergy seemed connected with that of an incorporating Union of this Kingdom with Great Britain, it must share its fate and consequently remains in a state of suspense. I enclose the resolutions of the Prelates lately assembled here on the Subject. They have been handed to Lord Castlereagh, who has probably transmitted them to the Duke of Portland, but are not to be made public until something be concluded".

A postscript says that the prelates present "adopted the resolutions in consequence of communications from Lord Castlereagh concerning the determination and wishes of Government, which suspects the Loyalty of many of our Clergy since the late Rebellion. More of them I hope have been rather imprudent than criminal". It is obvious that Troy was a master of the art of negotiation in a difficult period. He had got agreement from many of the Bishops to the measures. Dr. Moylan of Cork was prominent in agreeing but Dr. McMahon of Killaloe was silent. Young of Limerick was firmly opposed: ".... nor did I commission the Archbishop to dispose of my suffrage in this affair, which I look upon to be productive of dangerous consequences to the cause of Religion in this Country. God grant I may be out of my opinion".

At the College in March the President was finding the going hard:

> "I am so weak and my sight is so dim, that I can scarce hold the pen or see what I write .... Though ill prepared for an augmentation or increase of our numbers, 'tis, nevertheless, thought not only expedient but necessary, it should take place about the 20th of next month. We shall then, God willing, have about 150 students on the establishment before the end of April .... We intend to complete our full number of 200 about the end of June. We are threatened, in case of non-compliance, with a subtraction of a considerable part of the grant."

The new Dean, Fr. Ferris, had not yet arrived. He was in fact in Rome impatiently awaiting money to enable him to set out for Maynooth. Father Luke Concannon wrote from there to Dr. Troy telling him that Ferris had even no lodging. Still, "Everyone advises him against going home; armies are on the roads and privateers on the sea". In spite of all he is determined to go "but I greatly fear Ferris will be robbed of everything he carries on him".

In late March Dr. Troy was writing to Dr. McMahon, explaining how the Metropolitans had acted for their Suffragans — although no one had answered for him (Dr. McMahon) who had remained silent or Dr. Young who had objected to the subsidy-veto-union measure. Troy tried to be insistent with McMahon, saying that they had no option but to face the question due to the circumstances of the times, especially in view of the disloyalty of many of the clergy during the rebellion. There is question simply of a veto in respect of episcopal appointments: "The plan for providing for our Clergy is not spoken of and I am certain the Bishops will not revive the discussion of it. They could not avoid it on the last occasion without prejudicing the Government against us, and increasing the number of our Enemies, become almost innumerable since the Rebellion. We would likewise offend His Holiness, who is inclined to go as far as possible to gratify His Majesty, to whom he considers himself under many obligations".

During the same month the President of Maynooth was writing to the Bishop of Limerick, concerned with more immediate affairs. Despite the state of the buildings, it is thought necessary that 75 more students should be received between April and May next. Then the College would have 150 students (and be well on the way to its quota of 200) — Dublin 30, Tuam 30, Armagh 45 and Cashel 45. Thus was the provincial allocation. "Should we fail in this respect we are threatened with a subtraction of part of the intended grant for the present year; I say intended, for it has not as yet passed the house of Lords; this we owe to the well known friendship of a certain Lord . . . ." There is little doubt that the reference here is to the Earl of Clare, Black Jack Fitzgibbon. At this stage Dr. Flood was so indisposed that the letter was written for him by a student. He was recovering slowly from illness: "My sight is as yet so dim that I can neither read nor write without experiencing an extraordinary degree of megrim and giddiness in the head".

It was around this time that Lord Clare began his scheming to the detriment of the College. In April, when the Bill for the annual grant came up to the Lords from the Commons, he complained that grave abuses had crept into the establishment and that the money granted by Parliament had been misappropriated. We have followed the course of his misadventure. At the same time the Protestant Bishop of Meath was writing to Castlereagh claiming the right to exercise vigilance over Maynooth by reason of its being on the borders of his diocese! Cornwallis wrote to Portland on 18 April telling him of Fitzgibbon's attack, made in the House of Lords, the previous Thursday. The Lord Chancellor had been all too successful as the Bill for the grant was rejected by twenty-five votes to one. Cornwallis said that both he and Castlereagh were surprised by "such an extreme". But the latter is to introduce a new Bill right away — for fewer students than the envisaged two hundred. There should be no inconvenience as there are only sixty-one in the College at present. Lord Clare's attack was reported in full by the *Dublin Evening Post* of 22 April, 1799:

"The Lord Chancellor entered at some length into observations upon the seminary of Maynooth. He considered it inadequate to the purpose for which it was established, and therefore not entitled to the bounty which it claimed from Parliament. The school was merely calculated for the education of youth of a middle class, the consequence of which was, the parents of those of a higher distinction would not send their children there — His Lordship noticed several abuses which had taken place in forming this establishment, one of which was, the appointment of a collector at a large salary, for whom there was no business. He entered into an examination of the conduct of the Roman Catholic clergy of this seminary, in the course of which he depicted in very reprehensible terms the seditions of Dr. Hussey, who instead of being a Minister of the Gospel, and a preacher of peace, had been the author of a diabolical pamphlet, that went to commit Catholics against Protestants and to create rebellion in the country. When the persons in the management of this College came forward to ask a boon of Parliament, they should shew themselves deserving of it, and that they were useful to the State. But that they could not do. Had they shewn themselves active among the lower classes, during the late disturbances, in rescuing the unhappy people from fatal delusions, and in extinguishing the flame of rebellion? They had not — though they might have prevented such a mischief, had they done their duty. Some Roman Catholic clergymen were found at the head of the rebels, encouraging and deluding them to outrage, and others were silent observers of crimes, sanctioning them by not timely expressing their abhorrence of the enormities, and exhorting their flock against the treasons of the day. His Lordship, after many pointed remarks upon the institution of Maynooth College, as being a useless expense to the public, moved that the Bill should be committed for 1st August''.

Lord Glentworth suggested that ''alterations might be made in the Bill, to give a better plan to the institution''. The question was put ''for the Bill being committed on the 1st August — contents 25, not contents 1''.

The Bishops were not amused. A letter in the *Cashel Archives* reads: ''God send that what the Chancellor has done lately does not defeat the Institution *in toto,* his conduct looks as if he intended its annihilation and the zeal which the ecclesiastical Trustees have hitherto displayed in strenuously inculcating the principles of Loyalty and subordination in their Dioceses instead of being the subjects of his approbation . . . . The speech which appeared as his in the last *Evening Post* has excited the general indignation of the R.C. here''. At Maynooth itself Professor Delahogue did not take the matter lying down. He was not that kind of man. Writing to him Dr. Troy conveyed the thanks of the Trustees for his ''communications'' concerning the College. These ''were received by them with thanks and considered as signal proof of your zeal and attention to the reputation of the Establishment. They remarked that many are already provided for by the Constitutions, and they will avail themselves of the others in the formation of such additional regulations as they shall deem necessary for the good government of the College in Spirituals and Temporals''. J. C. Hippseley hoped for a favourable outcome to all that was occurring. It would be a pleasure for him to be able to show that the ''wild theories'' of some of the Jesuit writers were not held by ''the most considerable Seminary of Catholic Education in His Majesty's Dominions''.

The Trustees thought it necessary to issue a statement, as a result of the misrepresentations in the ''public prints''. They protested that no part of the Parliamentary grant remained unaccounted for. They recounted ''that scholars were admitted in the year 1795, and lodged in the house purchased from Mr. John Stoyte, and in others at Maynooth, where they were maintained six months before the foundation stone of the new building was laid by Earl Camden in April, 1796. It has therefore been erroneously insinuated in the prints that the Trustees charged for the subsistence of scholars before there was a house for their reception.'' They added ''that, so far from promoting or abetting the late wicked Rebellion, the president, masters and others of the Seminary exerted themselves in suppressing it in the neighbourhood of Maynooth. Captain Irwin and officers of the Duke of York's Highlanders witnessed and commended their loyal exertions''.

As far as the students were concerned, the Trustees added "that well-grounded apprehensions had been entertained that the rebels intended to force such of the scholars as were not in orders to join them. To prevent this, they were sent to their respective homes with the approbation of the Lord Lieutenant, who granted them passports and protections".

The Archbishop of Cashel wrote to Limerick about this in May:

"The opposition in the house of peers to the Supply voted by the Commons was as unexpected as untimely, ill-grounded and disagreeable. The Trustees at an extraordinary meeting held here (i.e. Maynooth) on the 22 ultimo have fully justified themselves in a *Memoire* presented to Lord Castlereagh on the following day by Lord Fingall, Sir Edward Bellew and myself, in consequence of which Lord Castlereagh spoke so handsomely in the house of Commons on Wednesday 24th ultimo. The Lord Chancellor has since declared to myself and to many others, that he is friendly to our College and only wishes that an efficient internal government of it should be established somewhat similar to that in Trinity College, and subjected to a Visitational Controul of persons resident in Dublin or its Vicinity. He submitted this to my Consideration as it may come under discussion at the next Session of Parliament".

A postscript adds: "We are just now alarmed at the appearance of a French fleet, stated to be between Bantry and Lough Swilly, but hope Lord Bridport will give a good account of it". The reference here was to the Admiral of the Home Fleet. Earlier in the letter Cashel said: "On the measure of providing for our Clergy I can add nothing to what I have already mentioned to your Lordship . . . . The rumour of it has had no unpleasant effect here". In August Bishop Young's students wrote to him from Maynooth:

"My Lord — We your obedient Subjects, conscious of your ever being desirous to have us forwarded in our studies, as much as possible, take the liberty of acquainting you, that we, Mr. Lynch excepted, have been appointed to read Rhetorick during the course of next year. To this measure we did not concede, until we would know, whether it may meet the principal cause of our being appointed for Rhetorick, is because Mr. Clinch wishes to keep a few of his former Class for the ensuing year. We hope your Lordship will be pleased to write to the Vice-President, Dr. Power, as our reading Logicks, entirely depends on your determination: Your compliance, My Lord, will infinitely oblige your Lordship's most humble and obedient Subjects.

Dr. Young entered on the letter: "I complied with their Request and they were put to Logick".

Whatever of this, Clinch had been good to some students. One of them, James Caulfield, wrote to thank him for his defense of them after the '98 rebellion. He was, said Caulfield, a man

"who boldly stepped forward in vindication of truth and justice to rescue a set of poor, defenceless and innocent men from false villianous censures daily poured out on them, the wicked diabolical charges of treason and rebellion with which they were loaded, and the relentless menaces of destruction and death, whether by martial or civil law or assassination with which they were unceasingly terrified . . . I pray God long to preserve your life and health, with every desirable comfort and blessing, to be an ornament and support to religion, to vindicate its Ministers, to diffuse your rare stocks of science for the public good, and to do honour and give them celebrity to the College of Maynooth".

Pope Pius VI died in August, 1799. In September, Dr. Moylan of Cork wrote to Young of Limerick that "Lord Cornwallis's appointment to the Government of this Kingdom has been its Salvation. As soon as the Union is effected, as no doubt will be the case, we shall feel the advantages of it. Our College at Maynooth will have all the support of the Imperial Government. The Chancellor, who showed himself so inimical to it, is now its great advocate, and I have reason to hope that we shall have Provincial Schools established at the expense of Govt. to fit our youth for the College". Have your choice between milords of Clare and Cork . . . . In October Moylan again wrote to Young: "The General meeting of the Trustees of the College at Maynooth will be held about the beginning or middle of next month. It's probable that the final arrangement of that Establishment will then be made under Parliamentary sanction. The Prelates should therefore send up . . . . their remarks on what they might deem necessary to be changed in the former Regulations and their statements on what might appear to them advantageous to promote the great end of that establishment". The same October somebody wrote to Castlereagh (the signature is carefully erased) to the effect that only Maynooth educated people should be appointed to positions in the Roman Catholic Church in Ireland.

The College itself just went on as it has always done. In May, the Secretary to the Trustees conveyed their resolutions to the President, Dr. Flood. Each student on the establishment was to pay £8 per annum to the Apothecary; every person on it was to provide himself with "all linen for his private use and washing and mending thereof at his private expense". Then comes the nub or rub: "The President is authorized to receive Lay Scholars into Parker's Building, who shall pay thirty guineas per annum, half a year's Pension always in advance, and provide themselves with Furniture, etc." Young of Limerick was not impressed. To Bray he wrote: "As Government are so liberal to the establishment of Maynooth, the Board of Trustees have done well in my judgement not to confirm the Rule of demanding entrance money". He sought Bray's assistance as a Trustee in getting this back in the case of three Limerick students whom he had sent to Maynooth in September and who had paid it.

He was not the only Bishop to be disillusioned at the time. Sughrue of Kerry wrote to him: "As Maynooth does not promise to be productive soon, I must have recourse to shifts". He wondered whether some of his students might come to Limerick for lectures . . . .

EPISCOPAL STOCKTAKING

On 6 June, 1800 the first ordinations to the priesthood took place in Maynooth College. Two students from Meath were ordained by Dr. Troy. Many students remained on in the College during the Summer vacation although they were permitted to go home that year if they wished "on account of the extravagant price of bread etc. There are but two Pounds ten ounces of it for a shilling at present" (Troy to Bray, 14 August).

Not all Bishops were happy about the arrangement. One was Young of Limerick, another Dillon of Tuam and yet another Bray of Cashel. "I coincide perfectly with Your Grace in conceiving the great impropriety of sending the Maynooth students home every vacation. It was agreed at the general board last Jan. 7 that every Bishop should be at liberty to keep his students in the College during the vacation. Whether this resolution has been rescinded by any subsequent board, I know not, but my subjects were dismissed without enquiring whether it would be agreeable to me or not" (Dillon to Bray, 25 August). As the Summer passed Dillon's indignation mounted. "Notwithstanding this resolution (of 7 January) the superiors have thought proper to send the students adrift, indiscriminately, to the great detriment of their finances and, I fear, their morals. Most of the other regulations of last January were as little attended to. I hear that the half hour lessons of Philosophy still continue. Should the regulations made for that College by the Board continue to be thus overlooked I don't see for what purpose we should put ourselves to the trouble and expense of attending henceforward".

The unhappy authorities in the College — not for the last time — were being sniped at on more than one front. For just when the Bishops were making their complaints, Government was making its own.

We have already referred to Fitzgibbon's attack on the ground of abuses having crept into the place. But the Government's main hope just now was to secure the loyalty of the clergy by way of monetary subsidy to them. The Maynooth Trustees might be expected to help. In October it wanted to know particulars about the clergy in each diocese, particularly their average annual incomes. Troy to Bray that month:

"The College Trustees are to have a General Meeting here on 12th of next month. It will be the most Interesting One since the foundation of that Establishment, as not only the College but the proposed Provision for our Clergy must be considered. It will be fully attended. The Ecclesiastical Trustees, when assembled, will probably think it expedient to request the attendance of all their confrères, if they shall not, before the Meeting, instruct the Respective Metropolitans to act for them. No time is to be lost in demanding their instructions from the different Suffragans with an Injunction of *prudent secrecy".*

Bray sent a copy of this to Young and shortly afterwards a number of Castle queries concerning benefices, stipends and so on.

An Extraordinary Trustees' Meeting, held on 4 November, attended to the complaints of Dr. Dillon. It would seem that some of the Professors had been guilty of giving inadequate lectures, for the purpose of this meeting, as described by the *Journal of the Trustees* was "to take into consideration the conduct of some of the Professors relative to the observance of the hours of class regulated at the last general meeting". It was resolved "that the Rev. Messrs. Delort, Darre and Lovelock, by not having immediately complied with the orders of the Board, signified by the President, have conducted themselves in a manner incompatible with the discipline and welfare of the College and exhibiting to its members a very pernicious example of disobedience and therefore highly censurable". It was further resolved "that the Board, activated by a spirit of leniency, accepts the subsequent submission of the above Gentn. as an expression of regret for their past conduct and an earnest of their determination to observe in future all its regulations" And it was ordered that these resolutions "be communicated by the President to the said Gentlemen in presence of the other Professors". These were surely the days . . . ! Delort was probably angered for on the same day he applied for leave of absence from the Trustees, for six months, "on family business". He never returned to Maynooth.

Meanwhile, the Archbishop of Cashel had handed on to the Castle the requested details submitted by the Bishop of Limerick but did so in his own form for he said they could not have been presented to Secretary Cooke in the form submitted by Young. Bray had rewritten Young's submission in a way which the Bishops approved of, and had signed Young's name to this. But he was at pains to explain to the latter that "whatever may be the final issue of this measure, you may rest assured that the Catholic Prelates of Ireland will have chiefly in view the solid and permanent interests of our holy religion and of its Ministers, in every degree". To this reply Dr. Young added in his own hand: "The reason my letter was not given in at the Castle was that it disapproved of the measure *in toto;* in the words of Virgil *Timeo Daneas et dona ferentes.* See how this affair ended in the document that follows this letter and how soon it vanished like a Vapour before two Months elapsed". Young was quite right. The affair of the subsidy — and with it the Veto — did end soon afterwards. He had been the intrepid opponent of both.

Since April 1799 the Government had been considering a new approach to Maynooth College. That was the time when Lord Clare had made his famous attack on it in the House of Lords. He had been fully reported in the *Dublin Evening Post,* always liberal in tendency. Three days afterwards *Faulkner's Dublin Journal,* opposed politically to the Government, reported that it had been decided to refer the Maynooth case to a Committee of the House on 1 August. Both the friends and the enemies of the College got going. That year there appeared a vicious attack on the Maynooth grant, entitled *A Beacon Light: Maynooth Tried and Convicted.*

On the other side the Bishop of Cork, Francis Moylan, endeavoured to use his influence by writing to Pelham thanking him for his efforts on behalf of Maynooth from the beginning. The College President prepared a reply to Dr. Duigenan's slanders and published it early in 1800. And Grattan informed Clinch, the Maynooth Professor, that he was always ready to receive communications from the Bishops "on all political matters".

In January a Meeting of the Board of Trustees was held in Dublin. The *Diary of Dr. Plunkett,* R.C. Bishop of Meath, presents the scene to us: "The accounts were audited. The Lord Chancellor was waited upon, who expressed friendly dispositions towards the College of St. Patrick. Drs. Bray of Cashel, Dillon of Tuam, Plunkett of Meath and the Earl of Fingall, went as a deputation from the Board to visit the College of Maynooth and returned the same day".

In May the Protestant Bishop of Meath contacted Castlereagh about the new Bill for Maynooth which was in preparation. He offers some observations which have occurred to him. He differs widely with Fox for his condemnation of the institution. The problem is how to secure Government interests without clashing with religious prejudices. His proposal is that some of the *acting Trustees* should be Protestants, and hopes too that so will the majority of the Visitors. Some control needs to be exercised over the theological doctrines taught there, which should not be impossible for, having been educated in France, the President and Professors will remember the control exercised by the French Government and be ready to submit to an inspection of their dictated notes as in France. The Crown should have the exclusive appointment of the President. If so he might act as Censor of what was taught there. Given these changes, he is in entire agreement that promotion in the Irish Church should be conditional on an education at Maynooth, after the attainment of "a divinity degree and a testimony of good conduct and loyalty". For this purpose Parliament should grant Maynooth the power of conferring degrees. He would have no friaries, monasteries or other seminaries in the country and would give all Maynooth educated priests a stipend from the Treasury.

The question of university status for Maynooth was a moot point at the time. The previous Fall some money had been bequeathed by the late Protestant

Primate for the establishment of a university at Armagh but Whitehall thought that it would not be "of publick benefit to Ireland". Meath opined that Maynooth was a different matter. It was founded at a time when Roman Catholics were deprived of all means of having their clergy educated and also provided an advantage to Government in having these trained at home under its eyes. The case was entirely different therefore from that of the Dissenters.

The new Bill for Maynooth was going ahead and its content worried the Bishops a lot. Nevertheless, as the Summer approached they prepared to go ahead with sending there the full contingent of two hundred students between them for the next academic year. The terms of entrance were forwarded by the President: The Oath of Allegiance had to be taken, an entrance fee of eight guineas paid and each student to provide himself with a bed, a pair of sheets, six napkins and a silver spoon. Provisions in the College were both scarce and expensive. The new bill was the greatest worry. Flood confided to Young that

> "the new bill for the better regulation of this College, is I fear pregnant with much evil and may prove one day subversive of the establishment. All the Trustees, save three, are stript of the visitational powers, which are to be exclusively vested in the four Chief Judges, conjointly with Lord Fingall, Dr. O'Reilly and Troy, *sed quid hi tres contra tales actandus?* The Professors and students will be at liberty for the future to appeal from the Board to the Visitors: the consequences may prove fatal to both discipline and doctrine".

One wonders whether the Professors had a hand in this following the admonition of the previous November?

Duigenan's pamphlet, although entitled *A Fair Representation* was to cause particular worry in Catholic circles. It must have been felt that it might affect the Bill for Dr. Flood thought it worth while to reply to it. His publication was entitled *A Letter to the Hon . . . . M. P. London, relative to a Pamphlet by Patrick Duigenan.* It was brought out by Fitzpatricks of Dublin.

One of its main purposes was to refute Duigenan's accusation that many of the students had been involved in the rebellion of 1798. Not one student was killed in battle, not one fled from the gallows. Such of them as had been involved with the United Irishmen had been expelled before the rebellion began. None of them had been readmitted although some had sought this in 1799. There were similar replies to Duigenan, some of them stooping rather low in controversy by questioning his background and the manner of his obtaining a Fellowship at Trinity. Duigenan replied to Flood's pamphlet, going back again to his accusations about the College. Nineteen students had been expelled, he said, twelve intern and seven extern. He has proof of this from a document by one of the "Governors" of the College to the Provost of Trinity College aimed at excluding them from sizarships there. One of the twelve — O'Hearne of Waterford — had been hanged for high treason as also had one of the seven, named Power.

The same May of 1800 the British Parliament had agreed to the Act of Union. It was now virtually certain to go through. Hussey did not like it at all, as he plainly said to James Bernard Clinch: "As to your union . . . . I would prefer a union with the Beys and Mamelukes of Egypt to that of being under the iron rod of the Mamelukes of Ireland, but, alas, I fear that a union will not remedy the ills of poor Erin". He has been consulted about the salaries for the Catholic clergy. This too he does not like. The proposals are "directly hostile to the interests of religion"; they would turn the Church into "a mercantile, political speculation".

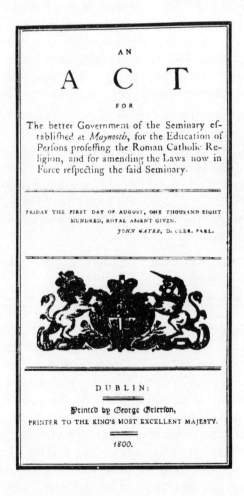

On Friday 1 August, 1800, royal assent was given to the new Act. Its full title was "An Act for the Better Government of the Seminary established at Maynooth, for the Education of Persons professing the Roman Catholic Religion, and for the amending of the Laws now in Force respecting the said Seminary". It certainly tightened the hold of the Government on the College, giving more power (although not over purely internal Church affairs which were to remain the concern of the Bishops) to the Protestant Visitors and laying down the formula of the Oath of Allegiance to be taken by the President who, in addition, would henceforward have to be approved by the Lord Lieutenant before taking up office.

He in turn was expected to see to it that the other members of the College swore loyalty to the King. The oath "To our most gracious Sovereign Lord King George the Third" renounced any belief "that the Pope of Rome, or any other foreign Prince, Prelate, State or Potentate, hath or ought to have any temporal or civil jurisdiction within this realm". Not that the aforesaid George III was then in a position to care very much. The taking of the oath was destined to remain until 31 July, 1868 when it was dropped on the recommendation of the *Report of Oaths Commission*. It was a year before the disestablishment of the College. In the intervening years those who took it were given a Certificate, costing one shilling, a photo-copy of which is to be seen in the *College Museum* today. It was taken by the Professors on their appointment and by the students in January, that is at the next quarter sessions after their admission to the College. In pursuance of it, in October, 1800, as the *College Records* show, Lord Cornwallis issued a decree from Dublin Castle, signed by the Secretary, Cooke, confirming Dr. Flood as President, even though he had been elected to that office on 7 January, 1798. And on 12 November Thomas Bourchier, Deputy Clerk of the Crown and Hanaper, testified that he had found, on search, that Flood had, in open court in the High Court of Chancery, taken the oath prescribed in the late Act.

Anno Regni quadragesimo

Georgii III. Regis.

C H A P. LXXXV.

An Act for the better Government of the Seminary established at *Maynooth*, for the Education of Persons professing the Roman Catholic Religion, and for amending the Laws now in Force respecting the said Seminary.

WHEREAS an Act passed in the Thirty-fifth Year of the Reign of His present Majesty, Entitled, An Act for the better Education of Persons professing the Popish or Roman Catholic Religion, and since

22 S 2   the

85

As we learn from *The Memoirs of Castlereagh,* on 29 January, 1801, Mr. Secretary Cooke wrote to Castlereagh, then the Chief Secretary to the Lord Lieutenant: "I dined yesterday with his Excellency, the titular Primate of All Ireland, and titular Primate of Ireland, and the President of the College of Maynooth, were there, and Lord Kilwarden, Lord Donoughmore, Hutchinson and Dr. Browne. We were cheerful and pleasant . . . "

The Government might be pardoned for thinking that it had sewn things up respecting the College. On 29 June, 1801 a "Proclamation" was issued "To the President, Masters, Profs., Fellows and Students of the Academy, College or Seminary at Maynooth" by the Visitors — Lords Kilwarden, Norbury and Avonmore, Lord Fingall, Dr. O'Reilly and Dr. Troy. Again in pursuance of the Act of 1800 they announce the holding of the first Visitation!

> *"Now Know Ye* that we will proceed, pursuant to the Powers duly in *Us* vested, on Thursday the sixteenth day of July next at Eleven O'Clock in the forenoon to visit the said Academy, College or Seminary, as well in the Head as all its members and We do strictly order and enjoin all Members of the said College and all its Ministers and Servants to attend Us at such proper Place as shall for Us be prepared for the purposes aforesaid within the said College".

In the College, life continued. A new horarium was approved: rising 5 o'clock, prayer 5.30 to 6, study 6 to 8, Mass 8, breakfast 8.30, study 9 to 10, class 10 to 11.30, recreation 11.30 to 12 noon. In the afternoon there was study again from 12 to 1, dinner and recreation 1 to 3, study 3 to 4.30, recreation 4.30 to 5, class 5 to 6.30, study 6.30 to 8, supper and recreation 8 to 9, prayers at 9, after which all retired in silence to bed. There were some variations on Wednesdays and Sundays. Vacation periods were fixed from Christmas Eve to 1 January; Easter Week; and from 1 August to 15 September. On 10 October Dr. Troy wrote from Dublin, in Latin, laying down regulations in respect of clerical dress. Each student is to equip himself with a soutanne and surplice and wear them during Mass and Vespers. Priests are forbidden under pain of censure to say Mass or distribute Holy Communion in the College or in the nearby "Lycaeum for Lay Adolescents" without being properly vested. For everyday wear all should cultivate a black garb, neither torn nor soiled. Clearly the Government was not going to have it all its own way — the Church too was making its institutional presence felt.

It was Spring, 1801. Through it all the students had survived. Eugene Conwell was thinking of the approaching vacation — a student preoccupation that did not end with him. Anyhow, economically minded as usual, he observes: "Those who remain here during Vacation must pay 5 Guineas for that liberty". He is presently reading the treatise "of the Church", in the "Class of Speculation". "Dr Troy of Dublin held an Ordination here last week. We had 5 Priests, 4 Deacons, and 7 Sub-Deacons ordained, besides a great number who received the Tonsure and Minor Orders. Some time ago we had an auction of old books belonging to a priest of this Diocese. They amounted to £28.14 and I am certain you would not give 2 Guineas for the two boxes. I could heartily wish you would purchase some of the unsold effects of Rev. Mr. Con — they would sell here readily for 6 or 7 Guineas''. This was in May to his uncle. A fortnight later he is advising against bringing the books ''until the students return to College after Vacation. At that time they will have plenty of money''. In November he dispatched a carman to Dublin for them and before the end of December had auctioned them successfully, hoping for some 9 or 10 pounds from them.

In that year the architect Michael Stapleton died and two formidable figures were appointed to the College staff, Dr. Thomas Coen of Clonfert (who had been the first student admitted in 1795) and Dr. Michael Montague of Armagh. It marked the beginning of a new period.

Chapter V

Of Masters and their Pupils

At the beginning of the new century the French Masters were consolidating their hold on Maynooth College. Delort left early on, it is true, but there were still Delahogue, Darre and Anglade, with support from other French-educated staff members.

Home products, such as Coen and Montague — they were quickly to increase in numbers — were only beginning to make themselves felt. Yet shortly the result was not unlike a 14th century Irish monastery, with Irish and Normans quarrelling openly. There were many Irishmen — some possibly hopeful of positions for themselves in the College — who had never been happy about the appointment of so many Frenchmen there. Luke Concannon O.P. wrote from Rome to Troy in 1798: "They're all the same — ungrateful. When the natives here were turned out of their religious communities and houses, French emigrants were put in by French command". It was true but somewhat harsh.

'LES SORBONNISTES'

At any rate, the ex-Sorbonne people had taken a firm grip. They constituted what Cardinal Maury, writing to Delahogue from Montefiascone in February, 1801, called a *"Societé d'emigrés"*, and many letters in the *Clogher Archives* attest to the way in which they kept in touch with each other and with constitutional developments in France. The letters usually came through London with the help of an intermediary, M. Lecointe. That from Cardinal Maury was transmitted by Lecointe at Devonshire Square, Bishops-gate Street, for delivery to *"M. l'Abbé De la Hogue, Docteur et Professeur da la Maison de Sorbonne a Maynooth,* near Dublin en Irlande"*. One wonders whether the French were simply tenaciously holding on to the titles of the Chairs from which they had been ousted, or whether they had come to regard Maynooth as an extension of the Sorbonne! A Mr. Mark Collison brought the letter to Delahogue, with a note that he had been overcharged ten pence. In it Cardinal Maury regrets that Delahogue has not come to Italy instead of having gone to Ireland. If affairs do not improve in the course of the New Year — through war or peace — so as to allow the emigrés to return to France, he exhorts Delahogue to join them in Italy. He would place him in his own Seminary, as Professor of Theology or Sacred Scripture with lodging: *"Vous serez echauffé et eclairé";* and with "500 *livres en argent"*. True, he would not be as rich as he is in Ireland but he would live longer in their little society which, although it is not Paris, is a coterie of his kind of people. The Sorbonnistes there are in solidarity one with the other. He sends his greetings to Ahearne, Flood and Ferris and is glad that the *"Seminaire de Dublin"* is in such good hands even though he would prefer them to be with him.

The Sorbonnistes were not doing badly at Maynooth and the Cardinal need not have worried about them: Delahogue lived to the ripe old age of eighty three. The years saw changes of course. Dr. Ahearne died on 7 February, 1801, but the following year brought the arrival of Dr. Anglade from Wales, where he had found employment for a time as gardener with a Protestant family after the granting of a licence to him by Portland to reside at liberty in Flintshire for a while. He regarded himself as still a Fellow of the Sorbonne during the years of his Professorship at Maynooth. He lived to be about seventy six, having been around fifty at the time of his appointment to Maynooth. Another Frenchman, the Reverend Francis Eloi was to be appointed in 1801 but did not remain for long, while another, the Abbé Feyton, was spoken of but never appointed.

The beginning of the year 1802 marked a new chapter of events. During the previous November the decks were cleared, as it were, by the Trustees conveying a resolution of thanks to Lord Pelham in gratitude for all that he had done for the College "which has already given proofs of its excellent tendency to diffuse throughout a numerous description of His Majesty's subjects a spirit of Civilization, Order and Loyalty". And, as if to preface the coming of a respite, on the same occasion the President was given sabbatical leave for a year, with expenses, to see after his affairs in Paris. Before he took it, however, he had to write the following March to Alexander Marsden, now Acting Secretary, explaining that the Revolution had robbed him of most of his property in France but that he had a certainty of recovering £4,000: "The sum in itself is trifling but of consequence to a person of my slender fortune"; says Dr. Flood in 1802! He needs a passport from Pelham before going: "I would not however presume to cross even the Irish channel, without giving intimation thereof to the government of this country". He got the passport and went about his business. Shortly afterwards, Eugene Conwell tells us, a letter from him was received at Maynooth in which he mentions "that the Catholic Religion is now perfectly established" in France "and that he assisted at High Mass with all the nobility of Paris on Easter Sunday". Nevertheless, about the same time another missive arrived in Dublin from Cardinal Maury for Delahogue, this time hoping that the latter has not yielded to the temptation to return to Paris. It is better to give the new régime six months trial. Those imprudent *emigrés* who have returned there are paying heavily. Delahogue should be content with the supply of wine from France, however mediocre it may be, and realise that there are more miserable people than he and M. Ferris. Truly Delahogue must have been complaining, and one would like to find his letters to Maury as those of Maury to him have been found.

That April a Proclamation of Peace with France was issued by the King, and in early May a ceremony to mark it took place in Dublin with much pageantry. The College was more on the brink of war. Lord Redsdale, the new Chancellor, was writing about the existence of two sets among the priests of the country, one favourable to the Government, the other bitterly hostile.
Many people began to contrast the mein of those coming out from Maynooth, especially their more nationalist stamp, with the more cosmopolitan outlook of those who had been educated abroad. The Sorbonnistes were at pains to remedy this in so far as in them lay. They were troubled too about matters, academic and disciplinary, in the College. Did they know what they wanted? In May, 1801, Delahogue was concerned about the reading of the *Code des Statuts* four times a year by the President, but grousing about the length of the vacation (he would like more). In 1803 he drew up observations on the discipline of the College and on the studies in Dogmatic Theology: the students absent themselves frequently from class. Not for the last time indeed, although Delahogue's own lectures must have been well prepared. Notes in Clogher dating from the time cover a dozen topics, ranging from Moral Principles to Ecclesiastical History, to Metaphysics. Further papers show his disquiet about the awarding of prizes, as well as about the time-table of classes, the election of Professors and the reading of the Rules. He is against the appointment of Junior Lecturers, although years after he was very glad to have the assistance of one himself in the person of John McHale.

The Trustees cannot but have had enough. Still they took Delahogue's representations seriously and set up a Committee to look into things in October, 1804. They were hampered by lack of adequate finances. Owing to the debts on

90

the new buildings, they found themselves unable to pay the salary of Dr. Eloi or that required in the case of the Abbé Feyton. In 1807 Dr. Eloi replied that he had sufficient personal means — as Vicar General of his Diocese — and wanted no salary. He would be happy to serve the Church in a teaching capacity at Maynooth. He would even pay for his pension. All that he wished was "a room with a fireplace", which he would fit at his own expense. Even this was not easy of attainment. Amongst the Conwell letters is one from John Archbold, a student, concerning a near riot in the College on 3 January, 1803, between students and a Professor's servant, about the use of "the" fire at breakfast time — the one wishing to make tea, the other to toast bread.

STUDENT UNREST

In 1800 there were sixty-nine students in residence with places on the establishment. Some had already come and gone, for example, Francis Hearne of Waterford, the spirited United Irishman. Others were to make names for themselves afterwards as Bishops, Professors or Pastoral Priests both at home and abroad. The future College Bursar and Dean, Michael Montague had matriculated in 1795. Kenrick of Dublin arrived in 1799, while Paul O'Brien, soon to be the first Professor of Irish, matriculated in 1801, as did Eugene Conwell of the "letters" that same year, together with Walter McEvilly of Tuam and William Crolly of Armagh, later to be Archbishops of their respective Dioceses. Mathias Crowley of Cork — of which more later — entered the College in 1804, John McHale of Tuam in 1806 and Theobald Matthew of temperance fame in 1807. In 1808 came Cornelius Denvir, afterwards to be Bishop of Down and Conor, in 1812 Thomas Feeney of Tuam and in 1817 Nicholas Callan of Armagh, who was destined to become a world-renowned scientist. The year 1818 saw the admission of Robert Ffrench Whitehead, who became the longest serving Vice-President the College has ever known. He was followed in 1821 by the famous theologian Patrick Murray and in 1822 by Joseph Dixon of Armagh, later to become Scripture Scholar and Primate. Charles W. Russell matriculated in 1821 — one of the greatest Presidents Maynooth was ever to produce — and three years after that George Crolly, the greatest Irish scholar in Moral Theology of the 19th century. There were many others and more to come.

These young men were clearly personalities. A great many of them were also people of substance. It was necessary to underline this early after the foundation of the College, in face of the charge that it only catered for poor peasants. On the contrary quite a number of its students came from classes with means, well to do for Irish Catholics at that time.

If Richard Kenrick, uncle of Francis Patrick Kenrick afterwards Bishop of Philadelphia and Peter Kenrick afterwards Archbishop of St. Louis, were of a relatively humble urban family, but decent, of scrivener's profession, the majority were of well-healed rural folk — John McHale of strong farmers in the West, and Theobald Matthew a member of the Matthew family of Thomastown Castle which, at the end of the century, had been fitted up as a hotel, with forty bedrooms, a large coffee room and a bar with waiters ("a detached tavern for the votaries of Bacchus" says the *Anthologia Hibernica* for 1793!), news rooms, billiard room and bowling green. One of the family was General Montague Matthew, M.P. for Tipperary and brother of Lord Llandaff. The family was also related to Lord Clonmel. Thomas Feeny (or Finney in the *College Calendar* reporting matriculations for 1812) was son of Daniel Feeny, a rich merchant and farmer at Crossboyne, who had got a good classical education at a Munster school (Munster was famous for such schools then) before going to Maynooth. He became President of St. Jarlath's College in 1818. Then there were Robert Ffrench Whitehead, born in Dublin and kinsman of Lord Ffrench, and Charles William Russell whose family, both on the side of father and mother, was one "of respectability and influence". He was a kinsman of Lord Russell of Killowen, and had received his early formation at Drogheda and Downpatrick under well-known teachers in formal schools.

Yet, in April, 1799, on the reading of the Roman Catholic Seminary Bill, providing the yearly grant to the College, the Lord Chancellor could enter at some length into observations upon the place, claiming that it was merely calculated for the education of youth of the middle classes, as a consequence of which parents of those of a higher distinction would not send their children there. Fitzgibbon once more. Lecky was more accurate when he said that the students were generally taken from the middle classes, although sometimes also from the higher and sometimes from the humbler classes of the people.

For his part, Castlereagh thought that the Maynooth situation was such that the less well off would not be inclined to frequent it but would go to Rome instead: "The benefits to be derived from the College instituted in Ireland, at Maynooth, cannot be sensibly experienced, but the foundation in Rome will always be viewed with partiality for the Clergy of the Roman Communion, as they conceive they derive some local advantages too material to be disregarded, and the only expense attending the education of the students is by their conveyance to and from thence, which is generally by sea". It is extraordinary to see how much the affairs of Maynooth College occupied the statesmen of the time.

Dr. Flood, the President, prepared for the new College year in the Summer of 1800 by again informing the Bishops of the conditions for entry. All who are to be admitted after 1 October are to pay an annual pension of £5. This measure is forced on the Trustees by a person "high in office" (was it possible Fitzgibbon?) but "tis calculated to do away the charge of beggary affixed on us by Dr. Duigenan". He suggests, writing to Dr. Young, that he should send up his "full contingent for Limerick before that fatal day". He himself has been "extremely ill". At this time the expense even of students "on the establishment" was quite high. These latter (or burse holders as they are sometimes incorrectly described) paid £50 for the first year and £12 a year afterwards, while pensioners paid £70 for the first year and £33 a year thereafter. There were many incidental expenses. Healy comments that it is evident that the poorer classes simply could not afford this kind of money and that the students were therefore "generally the sons of substantial farmers, or graziers, or shopkeepers and merchants in the towns".

They were the kind of students that could be expected to stand on their dignity betimes. They would not have been exactly disposed towards bearing with insults from either their Professors or fellow students. There was trouble among them because of some such incident early in 1803. The incident would appear to have been compounded of resentment against Dean Coen for his attitude to the students and ensuing differences among the students themselves.

It was very serious and culminated in a number of demands being made by them on the College authorities together with an appeal to the Visitors. A number of students got into trouble with their Bishops for refusing to pull out of the business, others with their fellow-students for doing so. In January his fellow student John Archbold wrote to Conwell, now left the College as a priest:

"I must conclude that Quinn blackened O'Beirne's and my character before Montague, as indeed, we did not confine ourselves in speaking of Montague never fearing the least danger.

"Next day or in two or three days Peddling Murphy, the Priest, retracted. He is seldom seen out now. Davy Synnot refused to sign because indeed he is Librarian, but was well hissed. Jos. Glynn has great effrontery. He was liked heretofore, but will be detested hereafter. He made Dick Kenrick retract, Matt Kelly etc.

"Doctor Troy wrote to Ennis ordering him to come to the College to make his subjects retract. Some of them were in Dublin and none retracted but Purcell and Kenrick. Judge Byrne, Wall and Tracy refused like men of spirit.

"In the meantime the four appointed Gentlemen (Wm. McMullan, Sheehan, Roche and Collins) drew up a Statement of the grievances: insult treatment in the refectory (which is nearly intolerable since our Procurator came) which is redressed if you speak by 'You're very impertinent. Hold your tongue. I'll expell you' and such language as this could not be endured by slaves, much less by those who aspire to Priesthood, and some of whom are Priests already; non-admittance into the Library; injustice in class; kneeling in the refrectory before servants — a punishment which Coen is bringing in fashion; being obliged to go out the Car Gate, whilst each Professor has a key for the Grand Gate — and some others which I don't recollect and which are of no great importance.

"Thus, between Meetings, Committees, etc., the week passed from Monday morning till Friday when Doctor Flood came home (who is now in a very poor state of health). The deputation went the next morning to him and then did he speak very much about his authority as President etc. and requested of them to return to class.

"In the evening Mr. Ferris came down to the Hall (no other man could venture to do it) to explain Doctor Flood's sentiments. He received a great deal of respect, but at last said that if they would not return to order that he would begin to separate them and left them thus. They told him that they only wanted to have their grievances redressed, and that his authority and that of the other Professors was suspended, as they had applied to a higher tribunal for that redress which their Professors refused them.

"They then agreed that the Deputation should go again to Doctor Flood and enquire what were his sentiments as they might not have understood him. They brought with them certain Articles which Doctor Flood should agree to with the other Professors:

1st. That none of the Professors should act in class in consequence of this business. 2nd. that Doctor Flood should not seek to punish any individual hereafter in consequence of it, or take any notice of those who were foremost in it. 3rd. that they should not endeavour to draw away any person from their cause, etc. and some others which are not of importance and which I forget,

but found something disagreeable in Doctor Flood . . . . for he told them that he would before twelve o'clock on Sunday expel every Man, and that whoever would refuse would be handed over to the Civil Power and lodged in Naas Gaol. These expressions exasperated them a little and they were resolved to persevere, but growing cool they agreed to come to some settlement. So the deputation went and everything was settled, that they should go to class, hold no more meetings until the meeting of the Trustees, when they are to be allowed to present and bring forward every charge they can allege, and are to get that redress which the Board shall decree.

"Thus all matters are settled till the meeting of the Trustees which will, as Dr. Flood says, be on the 5th Feb. . . .

"There are now the proceedings of one week — proceedings which will ever make memorable the 3rd January, to the honour of some and dishonour of others, but to the advantage, I hope, of all the students.

"Matters continue thus to be decided by the Board . . . . .

"As this subject is disagreeable it is time for me now to think of ending. There have happened some things since your departure which I have not room at present to mention on account of this long history. I send this by hand to Drogheda. I also send the 'Imitation of Christ' as you may want it. I expected to have a few more (letters?) written this Christmas but one thing or other intervening prevented me. In the Vacation the days were so cold that I could not write. I have more to say if I had room but as I have not I must conclude with every sentiment of affection."

These occurrences were referred by Bishop Plunkett of Meath to his Vicar General in January:

"Having been informed that the lawful authority of the president and immediate superiors in our College at Maynooth has lately been, and still continues to be, scandalously violated, by unjustifiable disobedience and resistance on the part of the students, I request you will, in the quality of Vicar-General of Meath, signify, in my name, to the gentlemen of this diocese, not only to withdraw from association inconsistent with the principles of religion and good government, but also to repair the scandal their participation in such unwarrantable proceedings has given by asking pardon for their transgression. Should they, contrary to my expectation, refuse to comply with this solemn injunction, let them know that I am determined to remove them from the college, and appoint in their room persons better qualified, by example and word, to preach to R. Catholics of this diocese the love or order and peace, and the reverence for lawful authority which the Gospel breathes. If grievances exist, they ought to be convinced that, in the meantime, dutiful submission to their superiors and respect for the statutes of the college must evidently tend to procure that just redress which never will be refused or delayed by the Trustees".

Later in the month Dr. Flood died, killed by the excesses of the recent rebellion and the present unrest among his students He was interred in the College Chapel, in the North Isle of the edifice near the Virgin's Altar. Plunkett again on 26 January: "This day, at ten o'clock at night, Rev. Dr. Flood, President of the College of St. Patrick, Maynooth, departed this life, after a lingering illness of some months". *Cox's Irish Magazine* was hard on him: "He was of a peevish, suspicious disposition, and though he was a promoter of learning, he rendered the students incapable of study by actually starving them". The poor man — as if any curtailment of their commons was due to anything other than necessity. But then Presidents afterwards as well have had to endure the hurtful and false invective of certain 'public prints'. Dr. Flood's death must have brought the students to their senses for the very next day we find Dr. Troy of Dublin informing Cashel that it was with satisfaction that he was able to sit down and write to him that peace had returned to the College. He had only just heard of Dr. Flood's death the previous night. Lord Fingall also wrote to Troy about the College but insisting that a meeting of the Trustees was required speedily and that Dr. O'Reilly of Armagh was of the same opinion. This would be for the purpose of appointing a new President. On the 28th Troy wrote to Bray saying that this should not be postponed because both Lord Fingall and Dr. Plunkett had told him that "the Spirit of insubordination (in the College) is only smothered and not extinguished".

The choice of President in the circumstances caused the Prelates much concern. The name of Dr. Andrew Dunn of Dublin, at the moment Secretary to the Trustees, was beginning to emerge. Troy regarded it as a sign from Heaven and so Dr. Dunn was appointed on 24 February, 1803. This was confirmed by the Lord Lieutenant, Earl Hardwicke, on 28 February and on 5 March the President took the prescribed Oath in Chancery. On 26th there had been a further meeting of the Trustees to investigate the resistance to authority which had broken out in January "under the pretext of grievances". Following on this, on 3 March both students and staff were assembled in the College Chapel and five students expelled, including two from Limerick, two from Cloyne and one from Down and Conor — all of whom were regarded as ringleaders. It had taken the Trustees three and a half days of deliberation and the sentence was pronounced in the presence of the Board.

Shortly afterwards, however, Troy was able to write to Young that the two Limerickmen, Hogan and Byrne, had shown "humiliated repentance" and that the Trustees recommended them to Young's benevolence. The Vice-President of the College wrote in like vein, saying that he was prepared to mediate for them if necessary: until the recent "universal delirium" they were model students. Let justice, he appeals, be succeeded by mercy, which will be good and fruitful for the Church as the opposite would be harmful. A few days afterwards the President himself interceded for the two students, while Dr. Ferris gave them individual testimonials in Latin, together with a plea for beneficence. The absence of authority in the College, which could have stopped the troubles at the start, should be remembered. All of these and related documents are carefully preserved in the *Diocesan Archives at Limerick*. They show that Young eventually relented. In fact Mr. Hogan in later life became Vicar General of the Diocese and distinguished Parish Priest of St. Michael's in Limerick City. But for a while Young forbade all exercise of orders, up to Sub-diaconate, received by his students at Maynooth (including Mr. Sheehan referred to by Archbold) without dismissorial letters from him, until absolved by his authority .Ferris wrote again on behalf of Shean (sic.):! "He was not present at the first act of disobedience to Mr. Coen's command, but signed the list (of demands) without knowing its object, which was subscribed by the whole number of the students then in the College, except two; this was the only active part he took in their proceedings; he was among the first to retract and make reparation". He had been advanced to ordination by mistake by the former President who thought that he had full powers from the Bishops in this matter. Young had certainly alerted his students to the fact that they were dealing basically with himself.

Another of them, a Mr. Murnane, wrote to him noting that it was the custom of the House to have students invited to different orders at the end of the year. Students, he said, sometimes do not know whether they will be advanced until the very day in question. He was worried that His Lordship "has interdicted us from the exercise of any office, or privilege, which our different orders afford" and worried too that he might not be called to further orders for "this day after Vespers I was told by the Revd. Dean that he would fire me for not officiating in the Choir as usuall; if I did so I thought that I would act contrary to my Bishop's orders". He was caught in a classical dilemma. Finally, on 19 May there was a letter from Sheehan, thanking the Bishop for having lifted the ban on them. Instant expulsion would, he says, have followed refusal on their part to take orders. The exigencies of everyday life at the time are mirrored in his adding that he has had to buy clothes, a surplice, a set of Collett, etc., and that he had gone to Dublin to see a Mr. Price who, he was informed, had some money for him but the latter "had set sail for London before I arrived in Dublin". Similar letters were passing between the President, other Bishops and their students.

In June the President, Dr. Dunn, was preparing for a meeting of Trustees in July which, he hoped, would tidy up things and "when some arrangements may be framed to obviate an evil which threatens the very existence of religion". Here there is undoubtedly an adumbration of the circumstances which surrounded, amongst other things, Emmett's rebellion. His own administration to date — despite Dr. Troy's hopes — had not proved exactly brilliant. The newspapers at the time were full of gossip about Maynooth affairs (though this was neither entirely new nor unknown much later in College history). Cox's Magazine was in the forefront and was asked for some proofs of its assertions. It declined a contest with an anonymous scribe but went ahead anonymously itself to castigate Dr. Dunn whose rule in the College had, it charged, "in ten months caused the expulsion of twenty-one students, and which lost to the Catholic hierarchy of Ireland, many young men, who might have been made perhaps, its ornamental members". In another issue Cox tells his readers that under Dr. Dunn two students had died for want of medical attention and that the President had been brought before the Trustees about it by the Physician.

BOLD ROBERT EMMETT

The times were indeed disturbed. When vacation time came round that 1803, difficulties in travel were experienced by the students due to the political condition of the country. William Crolly, later to be Primate, gave evidence about the situation to the Education Commissioners in 1826. Having set off on holidays, "when I arrived at Dundalk, I was told that unless we proceeded with very great rapidity, we might be apprehended, not being known in that part of the country. I recollect we hastened to Newry, as I was acquainted with some individuals there, who might be able to give an account of us, in case any person thought proper to call us to account. The first thing I heard was, that the French were supposed to be on the coast, and that there was a great alarm in the country". Emmett's rebellion broke out on 3 July. At the Maynooth Commission of 1826 another student of the epoch, then the Reverend John Cousins, gave a graphic account of the College at the time:

"There were two or three in the house that said they had a previous knowledge of it a few days or perhaps a week before it broke out, and accounted for their knowledge of it thus: that they had seen green uniforms making for the rebel leaders by the tailors of the College; and that they were bound to secrecy at the time. But the intended rebellion was not generally known in the house till about twelve o'clock of the day on which it broke out; it was Saturday, and the workmen at the College left their work at twelve o'clock. The general feeling then was that the fact should be communicated to Mr. Ashe, the rector of Maynooth, and a magistrate . . . . In general the students did not know what the object was, and the feeling that prevailed in the house was, that we might be taken out and forced into the ranks . . . . The whole population of Maynooth rose up; and when the students found that the rebels did not molest the College, and allowed them to pass and repass in security, they became more favourable to the rebels . . . The marauding parties remained about Maynooth for four or five days, eating and drinking at the farmers' houses, and there was no military party sent to scatter them; they remained for nearly a week in this way".

The Government did not have to wait on student information before learning of events in the town of Maynooth. The *Rebellion Papers, 1803* contain plenty of evidence to the effect that Connolly, a teacher in the town who was connected with the Lay College and a spy for the Government, sent word of it to Dublin. In his submission he outlines how already on Thursday, 11 July, he discovered that some ten people from the vicinity had been brought to Dublin by one Lyons, a shoemaker. Then on Saturday he noticed a greater crowd than usual in the place. Having business there, he "on going to the Lay College was stopped by Daniel Collison of Maynooth, son to the Post Office master of the place, who asked him whether he heard of the rebels turning out that night. On his return from the College he was stopped by several armed persons who in a compulsory manner obliged him to assist them in taking arms from several of the inhabitants of said place. After the mass of them were provided with arms Lyons and a man by the name of Frayne from Rathcoffey in the County of Kildare came on a determination of stopping the Mail Coach and disarming the guards which accordingly they attempted but failed in the attempt. Connolly was sent with four men to keep watch on the road from Maynooth to Kilcock and on his return was informed that the two Dragoons that came in with the Mail the night before were made prisoners by the Rebels and in a few moments saw them and they deprived of their arms and horses. The party proceeded to Celbridge where Connolly was detained for the space of two hours but saw no more of Lyons or Frayne until the hour of eleven o'clock. The party were then collected on the top of Windgate Hill in the Co. of Kildare where they were prevailed on by Conolly to lett (sic.) the Dragoons go but were severly repulsed by some and joined by others. However, they got their liberty. Conolly, Collison and others were then ordered to go take arms which they went on but did not succeed. They remained then at Windgate's until evening when the most of the Party through fatigue went to rest them. Conolly and Collison finding they had an opportunity of escaping returned to Maynooth. Conolly had then the arms which the rebels had given him, a Blunderbuss and sword which he delivered next morning with his information to his Grace and was informed that Collison made his escape to Dublin''. The document is signed 'Carter Conolly' and was confirmed upon oath.

Maynooth at the time was not short of confidential agents. Besides Conolly and Collison, there was William Lyon — also of the Lay College — as well as Michael Quigley, a bricklayer, who had returned from transportation after the '98 affair before the sentence of his banishment had expired. By all accounts the Government was not too alarmed. It was nothing like '98. True, soon after the arrival in June, 1803, of General Fox as Commander in Chief in Ireland, it was noted that Co. Kildare showed "strong signs of insurrection", as a result of which 12 July found the Lord Lieutenant recommending to Fox to send troops to three or four different places in that country "in order to keep down that mischevious spirit". General Fox therefore set out on a military expedition "into the interior".

If this were anything like Hardwicke's tour of the South of Ireland starting at the end of August, 1802, it has to be interesting. In Edward Brynn's *Castle and Crown* (British Rule in Ireland 1800-1830), published in Dublin, we are told that Hardwicke's trip was preceded by much deliberation as regards the route, the condition of the roads, the availability of horses and carriages and the like. Hardwicke went first to Kilkenny where he was joined by his wife, with her retinue and supplies. The party then moved on to Waterford, where he "bolstered the town's economy by purchasing some Waterford decanters". Then they went to Cork, the roughness of the roads making Lady Hardwicke ill, and in fact snapping the springs of their "postchaise', crippling two horses and leaving another near to death. From Cork they went to Bandon, and then to Killarney after a gruelling thirteen hour journey. After a day there, all started back to Dublin, which they reached at the end of September. We gather that Lady Hardwicke was ill again on her return, while the Viceroy, while expressing his delight at the state of the country, made it clear privately that he was very glad to be back 'in town'. In those days a journey 'into the interior' of Ireland was clearly not something to be undertaken lightly, least of all in the Summer of 1803 . . .

In Dublin just then things were not going well for the rebels. On 16 July their powder depot in Patrick Street blew up and they were in need of reinforcements. So on Thursday 23 July the leaders of the Co. Kildare rebels came into Dublin to see Emmett. They were disillusioned in their hopes. Their message was that only a few (mainly officers) had joined the rebellion in Co. Kildare. In Maynooth events were not great. On the 26th Daniel Collison supplied the Castle (again upon oath) with an account of what took place there on the 23rd:

99

"On the evening of Saturday the 23rd of July as Informant was in the House of his father in the town of Manooth (sic.) aforesaid a number of persons armed with Guns, Pistols, Pikes, etc. came to his said Father's House and obliged informant to take a Pistol and go with them to the main street of Maynooth where said party remained until the arrival of the Mail Coach and which time they had formed themselves into two Parties and upon the Mail Coach coming up Keraghan and his party fired first and as the coach passed the Inn yard of Maynooth aforesaid, Owen Lyons and his party fired: s-d Lyons being in uniform and armed with a Blunderbuss, and this Informant further saith there were a number of cars drawn across William Bridge in Maynooth aforesaid and s-d Bridge was guarded by a Body of Pikemen who threw down their pikes when the Coach had passed the Parties who fired. Saith that soon after s-d attack Lyons and Keraghan marched their Forces from Maynooth aforesaid to the Town of Celbridge where s-d Lyons went by Express to Rathcoole the Residence as this Informant believes, of Fox who acts as General to the Rebel Forces of the county of Kildare. Saith that s-d Keraghan and Connolly (who were both in uniform and wore a green jacket faced with green cockades), and s-d Keraghan and s-d Connolly marched their forces through the country disarming the inhabitants without distinction. And upon hearing of the Defeat of the Dublin Rebels they dispersed and went to their respective homes. Saith that the next day a woman came to informant and said that as the Boys had treated this Informant well, they expected that this Informant would send one of the Professors of the College to the Duke of Leinster to say that they were willing to do whatever he would advise and that if he required it they would lay down their arms provided he would protect them.

Saith that he this Informant did go to Abba Daré (sic.) of Maynooth College and Daré at Informant's request did go to the Duke of Leinster as Informant believes and returning brought for answer that all was granted, but that the Rebels should meet the Duke of Leinster at the Canal Bridge near Maynooth and on no account should they go to his House. This Informant went accordingly in quest of them and met a small party near Maynooth one of which Party offered and did accordingly bring Informant to the House of Thomas Frayne of Boreen near Maynooth, who had met the aforesaid Party in the town of Celbridge mounted and in uniform with a gold Epaulet and armed with a Blunderbuss and Pistol and saith that s-d Frane as this Informant heard and believes was to have headed and joined the Maynooth Rebels with Five Hundred Men for the purpose of attacking the City of Dublin. This Informant saith that he met the said Keraghan of the said Frane's House when Informt. with some Difficulty prevailed on s-d Keraghan to come in and put himself under his Grace's Protection. Sd. Keraghan gave this Informt. a gun with directives to give it to his Grace and this Informt. said that after this Informt. was forced from his Father's House as aforesaid, a servant of the Duke of Leinster's came Cooney came to Owen Lyons who commanded the Party of Rebels there assembled in this Informt's presence and hearing told s-d Lyons that the Duke's arms were left in the saloon, with refreshments for his Party and that the Duke wished he would take them lest Government should think that they, the Rebels, would not lay a hand on him, but desired the s-d Lyons or his Party should not alarm the Ladies, and this Informt. saith that upon delivering s-d message the said Cooney disappeared and as this Informt. believes returned to the House of his s-d Master''.

This deposition was sworn before a William James and 'the Informant' bound in £500 to prosecute the information before the Lord Lieutenant and Privy Council of Ireland. The Duke himself sent a more sober account to the Viceroy. On 23 July he had been at Carton. When, on hearing that "Maynooth was in arms", he had, we are told by the Duchess, immediately dispatched his Secretary to Dublin to inform the military and waited up all that night to resist the insurgents. The letter penned in the small hours from Carton reads:

"My Lord — "It is with infinite concern that I am to inform your Excellency of a very extraordinary event that took place last night at Maynooth. The town had been alarmed in the course of the day by a report that the town was to be attacked by a set of people, and that they intended to stop the mail coach last night. As the report was so universal, and so much talked of that I thought it would not be intended, knowing that various reports were spread. Had they only mentioned the mail coach I should have informed the Post Office, but the report mentioned there was also to be a Rising in Dublin, but I did not think the reports came to me from good authority.

"However, before ten o'clock, just at dark, a number of people sallied out of the different public-houses, better dressed, as I am informed, than the commonality of labourers, marched about the town, arm in arm. After some time they stopped a carriage, fired a pistol, and gave a huzza, and then all was quiet and no noise heard. They soon after parted, and the great part of them went off towards Salins. About thirty, they say, stayed to attack the mail coach, which, I understand, escaped by the coachman driving; that one of the guards is wounded. There certainly was not much firing, as I had people up all night watching. Indeed, I did not go to bed till daylight.

"There being no troops at Maynooth, I since understand they carried off two inhabitants with them, and several horses; that they went towards

101

Kill on the great Munster road, where they expect to be joined by the people from the mountains. I should hope that your Excellency will be so good as to order a part of the Army to Maynooth, as I understand there are but very few at Kilcock.''

Lady Emily records in her diary that the following day troops arrived at Carton and after having some refreshment under the colonnades marched to Maynooth. The Duke and the young Lord Kildare occupied a bay window in the inn after going round the town to warn people against joining the insurrection and next day persuaded the people to surrender their arms — they were pooled in the hall at Carton before being sent to Dublin.

Epistles were buzzing about the place. The *State of the Country Papers, 1803* in Dublin Castle contain immense material about the Maynooth area. The attacks on the Mail Coach are described more than once and a letter from as far away as Co. Waterford on one of those days says: ''I have this instant seen a gentleman who left Maynooth at three o'clock. He states everything was as bad as possible at that hour''. The rebels around there were numerous whatever about the rest of Co. Kildare. Thomas Keraghan was a farmer from Crew Hill, about a mile from Maynooth, Thomas Frayne and Owen Lyons were also farmers nearby. There were many others — Edward Kavanagh a labourer, Edward Kenny a mason, Peter Hacket a carman and Daniel Fogarty who is described as a vagabond. The Castle has long lists of all who were in any way concerned including even the innocent Cooney ''servant to the Duke''. They came from Rathcoffey, Celbridge,

Lucan and Straffan as well as from Maynooth itself. Many from Maynooth may well have been men who were working on the College buildings, for they comprised bricklayers, carpenters and painters, together with tailors and general labourers. Conolly and Collison were witnesses for the Crown. Informing was rampant in the area, informers informing on informers without realising it. And, as in the case of the '98 rebellion, when both the local rebel leader and the army commandant in the area were called Aylmer, so now similar personages on each side had the name of Fox. The depositions continued to be taken. On 23 July the Lord Lieutenant held a Council in Dublin Castle, attended by Colonel Aylmer from Donedea, Co. Kildare, who brought him up to date on the situation there. On the 28th Thomas Connell of Tullybane explained to the Privy Council how various people of the town of Maynooth were involved, while on 6 August Daniel Collison sought to improve on his evidence. It was still going on by 5 December when Timothy Daly of Griffinrath told all he knew about Carter, Conolly and Keraghan.

The students of the College were mostly away during the course of the ill-fated rebellion. It was almost the same as had happened in '98. On 27 July one who had remained behind was writing to a fellow student who had left because of bad health that the examinations had concluded satisfactorily and the year ended well despite "the distressing accidents that disturbed the public mind and rendered it unfit for laborious exertions" That day the Trustees had come for their usual meeting (although as in '98 only four attended) and had assisted at the distribution of prizes in the Lay College. Next evening the Duke of Leinster dined at the College with them and invited them to dinner at Carton. The scene was decidedly *déja vu*. But the people around the place were not so easy. That August the Duke was in receipt of a letter from the inhabitants of Kilcock asking him to allow Colonel Aylmer and his troops to remain. The signatories included the Parish Priest, Fr. Arthur Murphy. Likewise we learn that a report to Edward Lees at the Castle came in from Maynooth the same month pointing out that a quantity of arms had been lodged at the house of Quigley of Rathcoffey for safekeeping but there is a danger that the depot may be discovered and raided as some of Quigley's family had been with the rebels. "Be assured the minds of the people here are by no means tranquil, and if Government are not prompt in their measures, much mischief will ensue". Rumours were rife. It would appear to be about this time that the Viceroy wrote to his brother: "It is suspected by some persons whose letters I have seen that Buonaparte has assured the Roman Catholics that if they will undertake to aid him to conquer Ireland, he shall establish a Roman Government . . . . The students of Maynooth are, I fear, among the disaffected. That seminary will excite much indignation, and I think it will bear a question whether the priests would not be more civilized by a foreign education. But this is, of course, private". Late in August he goes so far as to describe the recent events in the country as "the rising at Maynooth". It had indeed been very much that as the uprising in Dublin had entirely misfired.

Now the misadventure was over. Towards mid-August, 1803, what was left of the insurgents about the Maynooth district marched in arms into Celbridge and surrendered. Some of their names were to crop up during Emmett's trial, notably that of Quigley, "a bricklayer or mason" at Maynooth, who with other on the day of the rebellion is said to have had uniforms like that of Emmett but with only one "epault".

These were the products of the College tailors, one of whom, Terence Colgan from Lucan, gave evidence of their being made. The tailors had gone to town and taken some drink, after which they had set to making green jackets and white pantaloons the Sunday previous to the insurrection. It is all to be found in the *Trials of the Insurrection of 23rd July, 1808* in the library of the Royal Irish Academy, Dublin. The tailors, or at least one of them — hopefully Colgan — had made themselves scarce, for one discovers that on 14 September at the Custom House: "Sir Richard Musgrave presents his compts. to Mr. Flint, and informs him, that the taylor (sic.) who worked with fourteen others in the county of Kildare, in making uniforms for the rebels, is gone to Ennis in the county of Clare". Collison, true to form, was only too eager to uncover the whereabouts of all such felons. In October he informed the Castle that he had just "this moment received a letter from Maynooth acquainting me with the retreat of John and James Mitchell, both of Maynooth. They are to sleep this night at the house of Thomas Frayne near Dunboyne". Quigly found the pursuit too hot and, together with six others (including Thomas Frayne) submitted to the mercy of the Government, offering to render it "services". They were all at it now. An account of Secret Service money applied in uncovering treasonable conspiracies for November shows N. D. Harvey, gauger, of Maynooth in receipt of £5-13-9 for services rendered. It was a sad end in the one place in Ireland that had stood by 'the darlin of Erin'.

THE GAELIC TRADITION

All was not ended with Emmett. From the day of its foundation there persisted in Maynooth College a genuine spirit of nationalism. It was something that did not escape notice by its enemies when times were such as to dispose one to be anxious about parading it. At the end of the first quarter of the 19th Century, enemies, the Reverends Wm. Phelan and Mortimer O'Sullivan — parsons — were to animadvert that between the foundation and 1800 no less than ninety students had been expelled from the College for excessive indulgence in Irish, or anti-Anglican feeling. This was surely a travesty but it served to make their point. The nationalism of the students manifested itself particularly in an adhesion to the Irish language. In many ways this should have been the language of the College but that would have been too much to expect. It was the native language of one of the early President, Dr. Crotty of Cloyne, also of another much later, Dr. Renehan of Cashel, probably that of Dean Montague to whom reference has already been made, as well as of many of the junior Irish Professors. And as already mentioned too, it is indeed a tribute to the original trustee body, none of the lay members of which are likely to have known Irish, that they set up a Chair of Irish as one of the first ten Chairs. That it was not occupied immediately was not their fault and in 1802 the young Paul O'Brien, who had matriculated in 1801, was appointed lecturer in — teacher rather of — Irish by the President. He became Professor in 1804 at £40 per annum, "with the usual allowance for groceries". This seems more likely to have been the chain of events than what is commonly thought by those writers on College history who date his appointment to the Chair from 1802.

O'Brien had been born in 1773 in Co. Meath and had studied on the Continent. On the advent of the Revolution he had escaped to Ireland and completed his studies at Maynooth. The salary which he received when appointed to his Chair was from the general funds of the College, derived from a legacy for the teaching of Irish made in August by John Kinin or Keenan — of £1,000 — to give £60 per annum. In actual fact, this legacy was not paid to the Trustees until June, 1820, after a lawsuit which began in 1815. The incumbent was quite adept. A grand-nephew of Carolan, the poet and musician, he was steeped in the Irish tradition. Among his works were to be poetical efforts in Gaelic, translations of parts of Hesiod, Homer, Horace and Virgil and an Irish Grammar and elements for a Dictionary. Described by O'Reilly in his *Descriptive Catalogue* as "a living magazine of the poetry and language of his country", he was offered the Presidency of the Royal Irish Academy. It is a pity that Healy should have dismissed him in a few short lines.

Fr. Paul steps from the founts of Gaelic culture into the portals of Maynooth. One of his earliest poems in the language is about a lovely young girl who was 'after him', in another version of which her place is taken by a hag. About this the collector of Irish manuscripts Peadar O'Galligan writes:

"Rev. Paul O'Brien in his youth established himself as a superior of an Academy or literary establishment in a place called Culaville, Co. Armagh, and in his schoolrooms he had an assortment of beautiful birds of every description in cages. Amongst this collection was found the Owl, which he had in his bedchamber as a nightly companion, in which he was delighted. The young gentlemen of the vicinity came on a visit to see Mr. O'Brien's schoolrooms, and were highly delighted with his collection of curious birds, and also of his Academy. One of these young men asked if he was married, to which he replied that he was. They being anxious to see his conjugal partner inquired of him where was she, and he brought them into his sleeping chamber where they saw no person, but only the owl. Being astonished at this, Paul told them that she and no other was his mistress".

One of them is supposed to have written the verses but Galligan is persuaded that they are O'Brien's. This is certainly so in the case of the

Agallaimh idir an tAthair Pol agus Maire. This is from the time before his ordination when he lived for a while in the neighbourhood of Bawn-Breakey and had a housemaid whose name was Mary Farrelly, who killed (not accidentally it would seem) a gander of his and who, though he saw her do it, tried to make him believe that it was some of his neighbours did so. There was also the *Agallaimh idir an tAthair Pol O'Brien agus an Fuischid:* he apparently liked a little drop.

O'Brien was a great friend of Donncha O Floinn of Cork, namesake of another Corkman of the 20th century, a successor of O'Brien's in the Chair of Irish. As early as 1804 a correspondence is starting between them, designed to give mutual support to the Gaelic. O'Brien in a reply to O'Floinn avers that the Irish language will always be welcome at Maynooth while he is there.

The O'Curry Letters contain the exchange. Nearly all are prefaced with versification, a trait of Gaelic scholars. O'Floinn is soon writing again, saying that the printer of Vallency's dictionary has referred him to material "in the College" and he does not know "whether there was question of Maynooth College or Trinity College"! He asks whether there are any old books at Maynooth? The letter ends curiously with an oblique reference to Lord Nelson, whose whereabouts or that of his fleet O'Floinn does not know. One wonders was it a coded message and, if so, for what purpose? *"Ni feas ca hait de'n mhuir bhraonaidh ina bhfuil mac Eibhlin* (Nell's son) *na a choltach".* It may be that at Maynooth the French adversaries of the occurrences in their homeland had found an ally however unlikely!

HUGH FITZPATRICK'S BOOK-LABEL
(Stoyte House and a harp, with crown, on the left, are balanced by the figure of St. Patrick, with ruined abbey and round tower on the right).

In 1806 O'Brien made a contribution to the *Transactions of the Gaelic Society of Dublin,* in such exalted company as Theophilus O'Flanagan, and in 1809 published his *Practical Grammar of the Irish Language,* issued by Fitzpatrick's of Dublin, now publishers to the College. Its appearance had been held up for three years by pressure of other publications, for which Fitzpatrick apologises. He is sorry that he has not been able sooner to "gratify the undergraduates of Maynooth, for whose particular use it was originally intended". He pens his introduction as publisher 'To the Lovers of Irish Literature'. He regards the grammar as "a work in the publishing of which I considered my ambition somewhat flattered, even as an humble instrument, for facilitating the acquirement of the long-neglected, yet venerable language of my forefathers, a language which has the singular advantage of surviving centuries of discouragement, and being now acknowledged by philologists as the purest branch of the Celtic now in existence, and the matricular tongue of the Greek, Latin and other European dialects". O'Brien's own introduction was less pretentious. His purpose, he said, was "to exhibit our native language in its present form . . . still exhibiting proofs of its ancient grandeur". He shall never "blush at my attachment to the language of my forefathers, whose memory and whose virtues I shall ever revere, in the only memorial that remains to us of them".

Alas, shortly after its appearance, a copy of the grammar was to come to grief when a poet hedge-schoolmaster of Kerry, Tomas Ruadh O'Sullivan, lost his books when his boat was wrecked crossing Derrynane harbour. His poem, in Irish, *Amhran na Leabhar,* commemorates the loss. In translation a stanza runs:

> "There was Paul O'Brien, the grammarian,
> Who put Irish into shape for us,
> And gave us the rules of song and story
> So that all could read them".

We find this in the *Humphrey O'Sullivan Mss.* in the Library of Maynooth today. A whole host of other Irish manuscripts there conserve remembrance of O'Brien and his prolific output. There are pious poems and sarcastic ones, poems of all kinds. There are poems dedicated to O'Brien by his friends. One, entitled *Oide Gaoidheilge a n-ardchoil Mhaodhaud,* commemorates the Professor of Irish in the College:

> "Guide of the youth in the wisdom of the ancients;
> The upright godly professor,
> He guides along in the path of the Lord in flawless wisdom,
> He also directs the interpretation of the commandments of
> the law".

Another, by Michael Og O Longain, written in Cork in August, 1815, is equally complimentary. In September O'Brien himself contributed some lines to *The Dublin Chronicle* "occasioned by Daniel O'Connell Esquire and Mr. Peele . . . . having an affair of honour to decide . . . ." O'Brien welcomes back O'Connell after his winning the duel. At the same time he is versifying a blessing on Conchubhar O Corcartha on his leaving Cork to study divinity at Maynooth. The message is not to forget his Irish language when he gets there. Forget about his luggage but not his language — Irish is the real to key to learning.

Paul O'Brien died on 13 April, 1820, and was buried in the College Cemetery. A later President Dr. Renehan, erected a monument over his grave with an epitaph, part of which runs:

"Hic in spe dormit
Donec absorbpta est mors, in victoria
Rev. D. Paulus O'Brien
Linguae Hibernicae olim Professor
Quem luci Media, clero Armachana
Disciplinis Academicis, altaribus sacris
Literarum famae, coelisque moerens
Manutia dedit".

During O'Brien's lifetime there must have been two million people who spoke the Irish tongue and his grammar must have been one of the first to be published in Ireland, where the Continental editions were not easily available. There is little doubt but that his efforts helped not only fatherland but faith, for in another O'Brien's — Eris O'Brien's — *The Dawn of Catholicism in Australia* one can find a poignant letter by an early Irish missionary to that land, a Fr. Connolly, to Dr. Poynter, Vicar-Apostolic of the London district, requesting priests for Van Diemen's Land who were proficient in Irish: "The knowledge I have of these Colonies points out to me the sort of Clergymen that are fit for them. Among the Curates in Ireland in country parishes is the most likely chance to find them . . . . A very respectable priest in Dublin lately suggested to Government such addition to the annual grant to Maynooth College as would provide a few places for the education of Priests for these Colonies . . . The necessity for a Priest to know Irish here is very great indeed". Without doubt Van Diemen's land was coming to be populated after the '98 and Emmet's rebellions. And it was not the fault of Paul O'Brien if the poor fellows there had not more priests to minister to them through the medium of the Irish language.

Chapter VI

Regency Bucks

What today is known as the process of socialization — marked by conflict as well as co-operation — was, as in all nascent institutions, a feature of Maynooth in its early years. Bishops and Government, students and staff, students *inter se,* and especially Frenchmen and Irishmen, all had their tugs of war. Some of these were serious, some half-joking and some just funny. It could naturally be assumed that Fr. Paul O'Brien would be in the middle of this and so he was. *The Life of the Most Rev. Doctor Crolly,* Professor in the College from 1810, by his nephew, another Dr,. Crolly, also a Professor later, contains an amusing passage:

"When Dr. Crolly was appointed to a chair in Maynooth, a great many of the professors were Frenchmen, who had been expatriated at the time of the Revolution, and even the Irishmen who held offices in the college, were for the most part, educated in foreign countries. The result was, that French was almost the only language spoken at table.
"Father Paul O'Brien, whose memory is still green in the college, was then Professor of Irish. With him the late Primate, the present Bishop of Achonry, and, indeed, the whole of the junior lecturers and professors, entered into a league, offensive and defensive, by which it was stipulated that those who knew Irish should immediately commence to learn it under Father Paul's auspices, who opened a private school for this purpose, and that in the meantime they could be at liberty to talk any kind of gibberish they pleased, provided they could interlard it with as many Irish words as would make it pass off for genuine Gaelic at the head of the table. No story or anecdote was told in French without a return of twice its length being made from the foot of the table in Irish; and whilst the former was listened to with solemn gravity, the latter was sure to be

received with unbounded applause. Sometimes a genuine story was told, which very few understood; but more frequently, one of the juniors, under the pretence of telling something very amusing, merely treated the company to a piece of oratory in an unknown tongue, which rather increased than diminished the fun. This proceeding soon had the desired effect; for the Gallican party were glad to compromise matters, by making English the ordinary medium of communication at table . . . .''

DOMESTIC FACTIONS

Innumerable stories are told about the French professors and their bouts with their colleagues and pupils. The *Irish Ecclesiastical Record* for 1884 carried some of these. They are quaint and worth retelling. ''To those of my readers who studied at Maynooth everything in it must be interesting, the grounds and walks, the trees, the buildings. But, for those who saw it at the earlier period, many changes have been made, and noted objects effaced. On the terrace near the Senior Infirmary there was a hawthorn called the third year's Divines Bush, because the budding of its leaves in Spring gave notice to that class, then the highest, to prepare for flitting . . . . In the garden there was a Harp formed of boxwood, planted so as to represent beautifully the frame and strings; and it was always kept neatly trimmed into form. It was said by some to be the work of Paul O'Brien, the Professor of Irish; by others, of the French Professors, who were believed to have a great taste for such things; for the tradition varied on the subject. The latter account is rendered more probable by the following anecdote which was formerly current. On some Visitation day, when the Judges were visitors, Lord Manners, the Chancellor, was looking at that part of the garden where the Harp was, amongst the flower beds, accompanied by some of the Professors, who acted as cicerones; when Lord Norbury, who was in the garden at the same time, came towards them, and exclaimed: 'Oh, my Lord, I regret it will be my duty to report you to Government, as I have caught you with the Maynooth Professors in a French plot.' . . .

''As for college *facetiae,* they are numberless. If they could be collected from the different generations since the beginning, the electric flashes crackling around the Poles, in every varying colours, would but faintly represent the wit and fancy displayed in them. But they should be used with caution by a writer, not knowing where, like shells, they might explode; perhaps in his own hands, *'Horresco referens'.* Soubriquets applied to individuals were also numerous, but as they might offend, it would not be well to quote any of them. They were applied also to classes. Those in the Physic Class who were not successful in their studies were called 'Doctors'. Some students who seemed of such manners or

110

disposition as would deserve to be only subordinates, and to have the rough part of the work put on them, were called 'Sappers'. These may be taken as samples.

"Of the old college stories I will mention a few. Some of the Professors played a practical joke on Dr. Delahogue. A large turnip was scooped out, the rind alone remaining, and eyes, nose and mouth cut on it, to represent a man's face; and it was placed, with a lighted candle inside it, in Dr. Delahogue's room, on the table. When he opened the door to enter his room, and saw the spectre, as he thought, he ran off in terror to Paul O'Brien, crying out, 'O Father Paul, *vidi deamomen in cubiculo;* he is persecuting me for that treatise I wrote *de Ecclesia'.*

"In the examinations of the Church History Class, Dr. R. asked a student to give some account of the 'Tria Capitula' controversy. The answer not seeming sufficient, the Professor asked the same question a second and third time, with the same result, when the student said: "I believe, sir, in the three answers I have given I have replied indirectly that I don't know anything of the matter".

"But if the professors could press the students hard at examinations, sometimes the students would occasionally reply in good humour. An aged Professor examining a student in logic, asked him to explain a 'morally universal' proposition; and gave as an instance, *"Juvenes sunt inconstantes'.* While explaining it, the student, fearing the inconstancy was intended for himself, gave, instead of the professor's example, *'Senes sunt queruli';* at which a great laugh was raised in the Hall, by all present; in which the professor heartily joined. This, it should be observed, was all in good humour.

"Whether any of the Freshmen, coming for the first time to the College, were treated as Mr. Pucker was at Oxford, when Verdant Green became an undergraduate, I cannot say. I knew no instance of it; but there was a tradition certainly of some having been hoaxed in that way by students pretending to be Examiners. Some accordingly would approach the entrance gate with great fear; and the Sphinxes on the gate-piers seemed to remind them of the fate that awaited them".

But the plots and the pressing and the pranks took on a different aspect when factions began to appear. It was probably inevitable that after the rebellions in the country had passed, both staff and students had time for domestic wrangling. A new era seemed to have arrived. On 9 January, 1806, Lord Nelson was buried in London; on the 23rd of the same month Pitt died and on the 29th word was received of the death of Cornwallis, then Governor of India, at Ghazepoor, the previous October. On 13 September died Charles James Fox. It did seem therefore warranted to assume that a new era had begun.

On 27th June, 1807, a new President, the Reverend Patrick Byrne, was appointed, Dr. Dunn to remain on as Acting President until his successor had arrived. Dr. Byrne was a Doctor of the Sorbonne and late President of the Irish Seminary at Nantes. On 18 July his appointment to Maynooth was confirmed by the Lord Lieutenant, then the Duke of Richmond, and he took the prescribed oath the following November.

That there was trouble in the College even before he arrived is clear from enquiries made by the Trustees into the state of the College on the day before his appointment. The reasons for this had been outlined in a letter to Cashel by the Bishop of Ossory the previous Autumn. For one thing, said the latter, Dr. Dunn had not been gifted by nature nor qualified by his attainments to be President. Then too, "for sometime back there was no professor of Rhetorick, nor of Scripture in the College. Heretical and devilical works were read by some of the young students in Theology. Permission was readily granted to young men to go to Dublin and to remain there days and nights without a companion. Lastly, an ecclesiastical spirit and spirit of piety pervade not the house. If piety was cultivated and flourished there, would it not supersede the necessity of constantly adding to the multitudinous regulations established for the College".

Dr. Byrne inherited a problem. On the very day of his appointment the Trustees ordered that a low wall outside the iron railing at the entrance of the College be raised to a "competent height", while, at the other end of the scale, they had just fended off an appeal to the Judges in their quality as Visitors made by a student who had been expelled during the previous year. In January — Lord Fingall signing — they had solemnly confirmed his expulsion by Dr. Dunn. Now, in an effort to sidestep the matter before the Visitors could act, the Trustees had accepted his "submission" and were prepared to reinstate him. It would appear, however, that his case did go before the Visitors who ordered the reinstatement. According to a much later issue of Cox (January, 1813): "The Chief Judge of the King's Bench, the Chief Baron, the Chief Justice of the Common Pleas, and the other members of the board, held many meetings in the College . . . . I am not warranted in saying what were the feelings of the court at the time, but I have heard him (the student) say, that on several subsequent interviews with Lord Norbury, his Lordship complimented him with the appellation of a *second Luther*". The court, says Cox, ordered him to be restored but the law did not require that orders be conferred on him. What an interesting judgment in view of the future!

His name was James Kennedy, of the Diocese of Ossory. The occurrence was most likely the reason for Dr. Dunn's resignation and was ill-calculated to help the new President. The Trustees themselves were also to reap the whirlwind.

As for the new President, *Cox's Irish Magazine* for March, 1808, was virulent in its criticism of his treatment of the reinstated Kennedy. Claiming information from the most authentic source, it came out with the assertion that the reason for the troubles in the College of late was the undue influence on its government wielded by:

"A certain lay Lord (it was Lord Fingall) who holds a very predominating place in the cabinet of the Bishops . . . . He has carried his high crushing principles so far, that in the course of last year, he persecuted with the most unabating animosity, a young man, a student of the College, for no other known reason, than because the young man resented an unjust and wanton expulsion pronounced against him by the President, who happened to be a favourite with the lay Lord. The student appealed to the Trustees for redress against his Lordship's minion. His Lordship presided at the board, and the unassisted student (whose bishop was induced to withdraw his protection from him) was treated with the most sovereign contempt. The student, however, determined if possible to clear his character from the stigma of expulsion and boldly brought his cause before Lord Manners and the other visitors at the triennial visitation in June last. The lay Lord, who himself had retained counsel against the student, had the impudence to sit on the same bench with the Judges, but in despite of all his endeavours, the student was triumphantly reinstated in the College.

His Lordship's minion unable to bear the shame of remaining in a situation he had filled so badly, resigned in disgrace, and the consequence was a considerable change for the better, both in the discipline and studies of the house. The student, however, in the end, fell a victim to the increased resentment of his Lordship, for his bishop was prevailed on to refuse him ordination, declaring at the same time his conviction of the pure and upright character of the student, and the 'necessity he was under of yielding to an opposition against him, respectable from rank, and formidable from numbers' ".

Here we have the usual mixture of truth and tergiversation for which Cox's magazine was noted. We do not know what was the case against Kennedy, but it is interesting to find the Trustees as early as then in a case before the Judges. Had such Judges remained on as Visitors, recourse to the Supreme Court would not have been necessary in the 20th century. The Trustees survived as always. Dr. Dunn survived too and cannot have been too alienated from the College, for he later returned from being Parish Priest in Dublin and died there as Librarian in

1823. Speaking of the Library in 1807, Cox maintained that it was scarcely ever open to students, that it was necessary to be of four years standing in the house before being admitted to it and even then only with the leave of a professor, of which power the professors had made bad use, not giving tickets except to a few of their own favourites. It would be ironical if Dr. Dunn were later to put things right here if that was necessary. As for Kennedy, the last of him had not been heard either. In June, 1808, a memorial from him seeking damages was read to the Trustees and ordered to be referred to the law agents of the College. The episode concluded in September, 1808 when, according to the *Journal of the Trustees,* the Secretary was directed to inform him "that the Trustees have been instructed by Council (sic.) that they are not bound to agree to his claim of pecuniary compensation and that on the remainder of his memorial, after due consideration, they think it inexpedient to take any steps".

It was of little consolation to Dr. Byrne that in June 1807 his salary as President was augmented to the sum of £300 per annum. He was now on a par in this respect with Alexander Knox, Parliamentary Agent for the College, who later admitted that his office had no duties. Dr. Byrne's certainly had. In some ways it is amusing, looking back on it all now, that one of his first difficulties was with a student called Theobald Mathew involving a problem about drink. Let Mathew's biographer, John Francis Maguire, tell us about it:

"Having gone through the usual course of studies necessary as a preparation for Maynooth, Theobald Mathew was sent to that College under the auspices of the Most Reverend Dr. Bray, and matriculated in the Humanity Class, on the 10th of September, 1807 . . . .
"Theobald Mathew was not destined to finish his scholastic career in the halls of Maynooth. The rules of that institution were then, as now, strict in their character, and rigid in their enforcement. Thus, for instance, it is not allowed that one student shall visit another in his room; as, were it lawful to do so, irregularities and abuses would be likely to follow in consequence; one of which would be the interruption to the studies, which, at a certain period of the year, the student prosecutes in private. But if two or more students assemble in the room of one of them for the purpose of eating, which is defined in the technical phraseology of the college by the term *'commessatio',* they do so at the risk of expulsion. It may have been that young Mathew did not regard this rule in its serious aspect, or that the temptation of feast-giving was too strong for his powers of resistance; but it is the fact that he violated the rule in a marked manner, by giving a party to a few of his special friends among the students; and the meeting being of a convival character, the attention of the authorities was attracted to a circumstance extraordinary and unlooked-for in such a place. The master of the feast was at once put under censure; but anticipating expulsion as the result of the formal in-

vestigation which was to be held in due course, he quitted the College of his own will, and thus probably avoided what would have been regarded by many, who would never have too closely scrutinised the real cause of offence as a stigma upon his moral character . . . . He left the college in 1808 . . . .

"One might be disposed to think that this unexpected severance of his connection with Maynooth was specially intended by Providence: for, had he gone through the usual course in the classes of that college, he might have become a rural parish priest, even have worn the mitre; and though he was certain of being beloved by his flock, whether of a parish or a diocese, the world at large would, in all human probability, never have heard of the name of Father Mathew."

It is in no way unexpected to find the Trustees, at their meeting on 30 June of that year, resolving "that any wine which may be necessary in the Infirmary be ordered by the President during the actual illness of any Student, provided that such wine be ordered by the Physician and the Apothecary". As it so happened, during the Winter of 1808-09, an "epidemic sickness" prevailed in the College.

Now is perhaps the time to take a big leap forward, to the occasion when the 'converted' Fr. Mathew came to Maynooth to administer the pledge. It was many years afterwards. He was then a Capuchin. The visit is covered again by J. F. Maguire:

"I had the good fortune to be present in the great hall of the college when the professors and students knelt down with edifying humility under the inspiring eloquence of a humble priest. The scene was majestically grand; it threw back the mind upon itself; it drew forth in full light all that is high and amiable in the Irish heart; and to a day-dreamer, like myself, recalled in tender recollection the memory of other times and looked for a while like their revival. On an elevated bench, which extends along one side of the quadrangular room, stood the Apostle of Temperance, 'reasoning of justice and temperance and the judgement to come'. The able and amiable Dr. Hughes, Bishop of York, was present on every occasion, and showed by his feelings how deeply he loves the land of his birth. Mr. Mathew was supported on either side by the masters and professors of the college. The room was piled to the utmost extremity by the students, and several distinguished strangers were occasionally present. A small vacant space under the bench was the hallowed spot consecrated to the virtue of temperance. The words of wisdom which he uttered were followed by deep emotion, they won the heart and subdued the judgement. No pen can describe and none but an eye-witness can conceive, the stirring effect produced on a thoughtful spectator by the appeals of Theobald Mathew, the conflicting emotions of joy and astonishment in

115

his audience, and the thunders of involuntary applause that greeted each new accession of converts as they moved deliberately forward in successive files, and with eager emulation to the arena of virtue and heroic self-denial.

"The discipline of the college wisely separates the senior and junior parts of the community. The good man, after his first successful essay in the senior College, requested to be led to the junior house. He briefly stated the object of his mission. They listened in silent wonder, their humility alarmed by the exalted virtue they were invited to imitate. No postulant appeared, and the holy man retired with perfect composure, but not without hope. Their reflections created a speedy revolution of sentiment, and they requested him to return. He hurried with eager zeal to see them again, and the little Benjamins, as he endearingly called them, repaid his paternal solicitude by fully emulating, at each successive visit he paid them, the generous enthusiasm of their seniors."

That was a long way ahead. At Maynooth in 1809 'little Davids' were preparing slings for the powers that were. Signs of this had already appeared in June, 1808, with the publication of a letter in the newspapers by 'Academicus', a student of the College, complaining about the distribution of prizes for that year. They were reinforced in October, 1809, by another letter, to the *Evening Herald,* this time signed 'Hibernicus', also believed to be a student of Maynooth, which contained much criticism of unnamed politicians both English and Irish. A certain Mr. Sheehan was suspected. It gave some substance to Lord Portland's wishes, expressed shortly before, to the effect that steps should be taken "to render Maynooth less suspect and increase the respectability of the clergy on the establishment". The President had worries of a more immediate 'political' nature, for insubordination had broken out amongst the students. In June the Trustees had resolved that, in view of "disorders, particularly insubordination and general relaxation of Discipline prevailing in the College, caused principally by the want of cordial co-operation between the Presidt., Dean, Professors and Masters, a Committee is hereby appointed. . . . to inquire in to the state of it and report the result of their investigation and their opinion on the remedies to be applied for the better Government of the College and the restoration of Discipline". The Professors would seem to have been quite remiss because the same meeting resolved "that in the opinion of the Board the Professors should attend the Publick service of the Church!" How history is destined to repeat itself! The disorders among the students have not hitherto been recounted in published writing about the College. It has been thought that they must remain in obscurity. In fact they are fully covered by two documents in the *Clogher Archives.* These are unsigned and we do not know who wrote them, but they are to be found among Dr. McNally's papers. He entered the Logic class at Maynooth in the year 1808. One is headed 'Connaught lie down', a clear reference to the factions that then divided the College. Much too long for complete transcription (anyhow it is illegible in places), it bears with being summarised and sometimes quoted.

The writer is disabused by both students and staff in the College. The spirit of discontent which prevails therein is contrary to that of religion! He lays before his reader (who this was we know not — possibly the then Bishop of Clogher) the facts about it as he has experienced them. Dr. Byrne's administration during the present year has been marked by grave disorders. One gentleman, notorious for irregularities, had to be lifted one night "at full length" to his room. Towards the middle of the year, eighteen students who had been convicted of drinking were, despite the President's promise not to promote them to orders, thereto promoted. That this was connected with the Mathew affair seems clear, for the account continues:

> "that on the night of the above detection, the Dean on entering the room of one gentleman said he smelt of spirituous liquors, upon which the President was sent for, but so far from assisting in the detection of such violation of the statutes, he (said) that it was all false, that he had as good olfactory organs as any other and that a search should not be made. The bottle was found the next morning under the very room, as it appears thrown out not long before . . . . It is also notorious that a Mr. Matthews who was publicly detected in a violation of the statutes prohibiting revelling of any description offered to convict the forementioned 18 but his deposition was rejected".

There is much more to be reported. There was "scurrilous lampoonery", which defamed the Archbishop of Cashel and others, this "libellous system" having become almost general "between the two provinces of Ulster and Munster". Two students had been detected by the Dean "in the act of card playing", yet it was allowed to pass by the President, who, we are told, was very concerned with his popularity. The more "virtuous part" of the student body had appealed to him by letter to check the abuses, but to no avail; instead he had read their letter to a full meeting of the theology class. Partisans of one of the factions frequented the sacristy until twelve, one or two in the morning, but the President only fulminated against those who decried this, calling them non-conformists and Jansenists. He induced the culprits to subscribe to another letter commending him. "This party" — of Munster it would appear — had become almost intolerable to their fellow students and to the Dean.

Obviously, in circumstances such as this, violence could not be too far off. The account proceeds to tell of how the President indicated that the tactics of the Dean were "like unto a cat watching a mouse" and unnecessary. "Thus was piety and its votaries treated with contempt. A gentleman of unblemished morals and upright character was consequently so sorely persecuted that his patience must at length be necessarily worn out. Hissed by this man, laughed at by that and even

117

kicked (perhaps) by a third, till at length on being tripped by a certain bully he turned about no doubt in a passion and kicked the person who had been so near tumbling him on the open area and perhaps breaking his neck". Some, says the account, had dubbed the President 'Turkey Cock'. He had on every occasion shown the most palpable partiality to his own party and had declared that he would crush "the Connaught faction" . . . . "and their Metropolitan". Hence it was that the Dean — himself a Connaught man — found himself very much at the mercy of his opponents. He was distracted by the organizing of sessions for that very purpose as well as "by flinging stones, buckets, whistling, shouting, etc. at the time he gave the Benedicamus . . . . by ringing the bell at an advanced hour of the night . . . . trumpeting, blowing flutes and such instruments, yelling, if possible to be surpassed by those of damned alone, emptying buckets against and into rooms of orderly students and many such irregularities". The bell was to be rung again at advanced hours in the latter half of the 20th century. On one such occasion the culprit was caught by a fleetfooted President.

But to return to 1809:

> "Finding that measures were adopted for the prevention of further abuses of this kind by the seniors, these gentlemen had recourse to a far more intolerable plan, namely crowding together in close array and appropriating to themselves a certain portion of the prayer hall, and their extinguishing lights in order by those means to be better able to insult and abuse the Dean by not answering to their names when called or answering for one another, or if they ever chanced to answer him by doing so in the most insulting tone of voice and in case of a reprimand to insult him still further by scraping the floor, hissing etc., in so much that he was frequently obliged to desist from calling the roll. The well disposed being scandalised at such conduct in the awful hour of prayer and in the very presence of God went in to this part of the hall in order thus, if possible, to check the further progress of such unpardonable conduct. But they, alarmed and terrified at the idea of detection, insulted, struck, abused them and even had the unparalled effrontry to strike a student in Dr. Byrne's arms, in his immediate protection. Who can without horror hear of their profane (fictions) . . . . (of) how the sacred minister turned his garter to a stole. Good God! More than Turkish impiety!"

In the end violence did break out with a vengeance commencing in the prayer hall it would seem. Mr. McGrath was struck and Mr. Burke also assaulted in the refectory, in consequence of a signal made by Mr. Sheehan. A number of others had been assailed in like manner, whereupon:

> "Mr Magennis, at all times remarkable for irregularity, took up an empty bottle and swore by the living Christ that he would beat out the brains

of the first person he met that was not of the party (which of the parties is not clear) and Mr. Power (could it have been the Vice-President?) ran hastily to his room and thence brought a large bludgeon obviously for the purpose of riot . . . . Mr. Browne on the night of the tumult in the prayer hall threw off his jacket lest it should afterwards encumber him . . . . his intention is manifest from his (having) instantly struck Mr. McGrath . . . . Cummins and Sheehan publickly hallooed 'Connaught lie down' ''.

Enough. Patently things were in a bad way. The document referred to sometimes addresses itself to "My Lords", as if it were a complaint to the Trustees or Visitors, which it may well have been or a draft of same. It may even have been prepared by the Dean himself, Mr. Coen. Things had got to such an impasse that by November a meeting of Trustees was called for 1 December to inquire into the causes of the disturbances. Not too surprisingly, given the situation, only five of the Board arrived. Plunkett of Meath went away because of this but was summoned back by the Primate to get on with the work. He returned on the 7th and remained until the 11th when — understandably too — they adjourned to Dublin. The deliberations of the Board did not terminate until the 13th.

A lengthy series of resolutions ensued. It was resolved:

"That any member of the College convicted of writing anonymous letters on any subject whatever whether printed or not, or circulating them in the College or elsewhere, shall be expelled;
"That any Member of the College convicted of exciting riot, or of making disorderly noise in the prayer hall, shall be called and placed according to seniority on benches or forms to be numbered for that purpose, and not allowed on any account to choose places;
"That any Member of the College convicted of making disorderly noise in the Corridors, Halls or Refrectory shall be expelled;
"That Inspectors, or Monitors, be appointed in each Corridor to observe the conduct of the students and to report any irregularity to th Presidt. and Dean;
"That the Introduction of newspapers and other periodical publications amongst the students has alienated them from the necessary attention to their studies and other duties, and that the Presidt. be hereby required to prevent it;
"That any Student convicted of writing or signing or circulating defamatory letters, addresses or remonstrances again the President, or any of the Superiors, Professors or his fellow students, or soliciting signatories thereto shall be expelled;
"That any Student opposing the entry of President, Vice-President or Dean into his room shall be expelled;

119

"That no student be henceforth appointed to the Procurator's department, and that he be appointed in the manner prescribed by the Statutes;
"That, after the most strict and diligent inquiry with respect to the author or writer of a letter in the *Evening Herald* of the fourth Oct. 1809, signed 'Hibernicus', and which, in our opinion, contained a libel on the Government and Legislature of the country, we have been only able to ascertain that Kennedy told Mr. Montague, the Procurator, that Mr. Sheehan was the author of said letter and that the above named Mr. Kennedy (possibly the one mentioned earlier) stated to the Board that a student whose name he would not mention, asked him whether he had seen the said letter. On his (Kennedy) replying in the negative, and adding that he believed it was not yet published, the student above alluded to said 'No matter for that, come in here and I will show it to you', that he (Kennedy) went into said student's room, where said student took a written paper and read a part of it to him. Resolved: that our law agent be applied to for advice how we are to proceed in this case''.

That the College was split down the middle is undeniable. Even such a jaundiced source as Cox (December, 1813) can on the whole be believed when he says: "Dr Byrne's administration . . . . was distinguished by an alarming division among the students. What was denominated the Munster Party solicited through the medium of the public prints for the removal of Mr. Coen from the office of Dean. The Connaughtmen, identifying their own honour with that of their countryman, united in his defence". There is probably nothing very extraordinary about this line up for we know that on the Continent not so long before there was a similar division: Munstermen almost solely went to Bordeaux while at Salamanca there was discrimination against Connaughtmen. At Maynooth, as is evident, the President was not of the latter nor did he and the Dean hit it off together. His difficulties were compounded by the fact that he was also *persona non grata* with the French Professors because of his removal of a Mr. Crowley (although from Cork and of whom also more later) from office in the College. Cox, going back on the thing in 1814, says that Dr. Byrne:

"had to bear against the storms which the jealousy and resentment of Crowley's friends had raised against him. The Frenchmen, enraged at the loss of their cherished panegyrist, gave no limits to their indignation, and the Dean, the Kitchen-officer, and a mercenary hoard of Connaughtmen, were equally determined to oppose the progress of the new administration. Many other causes concurred to throw the college into a violent tumult (Cox says that tumults are of the essence of Maynooth) . . . . Dr. Byrne . . . . was unwilling to be a spectator of French intrigue and Connaught ferocity, and accordingly resigned his place in Maynooth". That would have on 27 June, 1810.

120

GALLICAN INTRIGUE

But first **what** about that French intrigue? We have come across plenty of the ferocity of the Connaughtmen and of the Munstermen too for that matter. Cox for January, 1810, carries a 'Letter from Maynooth to the Earl of Fingal' on the present state of that house, in which it avers it has always shown an interest:

"When it was founded, there were a number of French emigrant priests burdensome to the tables of every rich Roman Catholic here; that nation has the gift of impudence, and pretends to everything, and frequently the claim is allowed. The first blunder of Maynooth was to take in upon its foundation a swarm of these jabbering pretenders, who no sooner got inside the door than they effected to usurp dominion . . . . Abbe Darre is there yet . . . . Monsieur Delahogue (another Gascoine)is there too — the gentleman who fired the boys into meeting, by calling them a parcel of plebians; for which mutiny Collins, one of the first clergymen of his years in Ireland, was expelled, and that by the pointed interference of your Lordship. It was your Lordship, chiefly who Frenchified the college . . . . There are at present two Frenchmen, two barbarous Connaughtmen and a vulgar Northern in office there, which five ought to be removed . . . . The insolence of the French is insupportable".

Cox had never liked the Frenchmen. In April, 1808, he had described "La Hogue" as one who "retains all the imperious and disgusting self-sufficiency, all the narrow and despotic bigotry. . . . of the Sorbonne". One feels that there was a good deal of truth in this.

In the College, after the resolutions of December, 1809, things were still far from settled. Two letters, signed provocatively 'Monitor', sent to Cox and published next February, bewailed the fact that the recent actions by the Trustees were all on the side of the authorities and had neglected the students. "How can we put those laws into execution? Will the students be willing to undertake the disagreeable task? No generous or independent student will do it. Shall we request the professors to leave their darling chambers and keep the nocturnal watch on the corridors? It would be a dangerous insult. To whom than shall we resort? Why, doubtless to the Dublin Watchmen, who probably preferring an academical to the civil state, may be ambitious enough to shake their rattles in our corridors, or bring to the tribunal the daring delinquent, if any such can be found". This, it is added, will save expense, "for such is the mild temper of the Dean, that when any opposition is ever made, a broken door will immediately be the consequence". These were answered by another letter from the same source, signed 'Inspector', also in February, 1810. While this did not see in the earlier correspondence anything other than "the unbiased language of spirit and independence", it did agree that the Investigation of 1809 — in which the writer claimed to have participated — should have caused a change in the administration. This, it says, was manifestly the desire of every member of the community. Yet of the same time the *Weekly Orthodox Journal of Useful Knowledge* was to say that "disappointed students, who would be no honour to any Seminary, have assailed everything and everyone belonging to the college with low and vulgar calumny. This was well calculated to please the vilest faction that ever cursed a country."

The French professors can hardly have been pleased when, on 17 February, 1810, Bonaparte formally annexed Rome and the Papal territories to the dominions of France. It must surely have been a time when they were at one with their 'hosts'. one wonders whether Crolly's story about Delahogue dates from around that time?

> "Dr. Delahogue used to tell, very often, a story, or rather fable, about a contest between a mule and an ass, as to their relative claims to gentility. The mule made a long oration on the good qualities of his mother, in which, along with other things, he declared that the best blood of France flowed in her veins, and that she was nearly related to the first families in the Kingdom. The ass waited patiently until his antagonist had finished, and then drily asked — "And your father, what was he?". This conclusion was always received with a burst of laughter, in which the learned and good old Doctor heartily joined, imagining that it was the effect of his story, whereas it was, in reality, produced by the absurd way in which he asked the question".

In June, 1810, things came to a head with the Triennial Visitation which was held on Wednesday, 20th inst. Everybody was commanded to attend "on pain of amotion from the College", unless he had a sufficient cause. It was followed by a Trustees' Meeting on 27 June, at which the President, Dr. Byrne, "signified his resignation" and "Mr. Coen promised the same in September". Cox tells us that the Trustees, conscious of the 'Munster-Connaught' division and "wishing to avoid the imputation of favouritism to either party, thought prudent to institute a public investigation to depose on oath whether he was 'fit' or 'unfit' for his situation?" This is much more likely to have been decreed by the Visitors. But to continue with Cox's narrative: one J. S - n (assuredly Sheehan in any book) is said to have been foremost in accusing Dean Coen but felt that the decision would go against him. Fearing that "decimation" would follow in order to quell the dissentions, on the second day of the investigation he became an ardent defender of the Dean. As things turned out, after a few months Dr. Coen left the College. He was soon afterwards to become Bishop of Clonfert.

The precise circumstances surrounding his resignation have not heretofore been clear. Healy gives as reason his treatment of the aforementioned Mr. Kennedy of Killaloe but it should by now be established that there was much more to it than this. Where Healy may well be correct is in saying that neither his nor Dr. Byrne's resignation was completely spontaneous, although nowhere is it stated that they were asked to resign. Still, the usual thanks for their time in the College is not recorded in the *Journal of the Trustees.* Cox, as usual self-confident, said that the Dean was "removed as unfit" while Dr. Byrne resigned the Presidency "at the expostulation of his friends". We are never likely to know the full truth. But the Vice-President at least was glad. He wrote to Bray of Cashel on 16 July, 1810: "I am much obliged to Your Grace for the pleasing accounts from the last board at Maynooth. I hope that health, order, discipline and piety will take the place of confusion and faction, with their train of evils, in our national college". Alas, as Cox was to note, the troubles were not yet at an end. Speaking of the Dean it says: "He had not, I am confident, arrived at home, when S - n returned again to the head of his party".

On 29 June, 1810, it was decided that the Reverend Patrick Everard be requested to accept the Presidency of the College. He had been mentioned on an earlier occasion for the post. He was Headmaster of a school at Ulverstone in England. He arrived at Maynooth on 23 July to the gratification of the Trustees. Most Reverend Dr. Murray, the new Coadjutor Bishop of Dublin, wrote to Bray of Cashel from Maynooth three days later:

"My dear and most honord Lord — I have singular pleasure in being able to announce to your Grace the arrival of Dr. Everard here, and his acceptance of the important task you have reposed in him. Nothing more providential than this event could possibly occur for the salvation of the Establishment. He is here but three days, and he has already gained the hearts of all the good members of the Community, and the manly and energetic manner with which he Commenced his government has completely overawed the disorderly into submission. No one who knows the miserable state of disorder, in which he found the College, could believe it possible to effect so much in so short a time; but, my dear Lord, he must be supported, firmly supported, or all will be lost . . . . The incessant occupations which engage every moment of his time do not allow him, at present, to have the pleasure of writing to Your Grace: he begs, therefore, that thro me you will accept the assurance of his high consideration and respect — I remain, my dear Lord, with all possible esteem, Your Grace's most faithful and devoted servant, Dan.l Murray".

Those were the days of courtesy whatever else may be said of them.

It is hard to say whether courtesy was extended by the students to the new President. Dr. Murray's hopes were certainly premature. Some years later *Cox's Irish Magazine* devoted a lot of space to 'An Unbiased Account of Maynooth College, since the Commencement of Rev. Mr. Everard's Administration'. How unbiased it was is open to speculation. Cox's articles were usually of the type that newspapers of a later period reserved for their week-end columns. But it would appear that Mr. Everard did not exactly impress his students on his *debut*. He appeared, Cox, tells us, to inspect the buildings, accompanied by some Bishops, equipped with a cane and a spy-glass and wearing a moustache. The reaction of the students can be imagined "as Colleges are usually the nurseries of ridicule". Yet neither was the "frivilous" attitude of the students lost on Dr. Everard who straight away divested himself of the "imported foppery of the sister country". Cox goes on: "He retired to an apartment in the house — stripped himself of the incumbence of a white bang-up small cloths, and a no ordinary pair of moustaches. Thus equipped, he appeared again — called the entire community to an interview in the assembly hall "and announced himself the president of the future. He promised to overlook the past, to treat every man according to his future deserts, expressed his intention to bring about regularity and to "banish the demon of discord". He offered unconditional forgiveness to both factions in the College. "Entire condonation was promised to all who would . . . . publicly confess that he was guilty of high treason against his culinary Majesty Mr. Montague, of calumny and slander against Connaught Coen and of blasphemy against the Gallican professors".

The honeymoon did not last for long, although a couple visited the College that August — "W. W. Pole . . . . together with W. Scott and a lady, 'both yellow and tall' ". The 'willowy blonde', in today's parlance, who accompanied Scott, was something unusual to the College. The President and students received then in the Assembly Hall and afterwards the President paraded by with the lady "hanging from his arm", such a sight being of "infrequent appearance" in the place. As a result, Cox tells us, he was invited by Mr. Pole to Dublin, to be introduced to the Lord Lieutenant, the invitation being read to the students from the pulpit. He spoke of Pole and Scott and others for three days. It seemed the inauguration of a liberal régime, even though the students might have had some reservations. Cox again:

> "Faint, however, ... as this promised ray of liberty might have been, it scared those night owls, the Gallican professors, almost out of the right use of reason . . . . The president had no sooner retired to his apartment than they flocked about him . . . . represented . . . . the unrelenting aversion of some students to them; adding that propriety would never attend the house as long as their reputed enemies had existence in it. He gave an open ear to (them)".

It was the start of the feud again. Students told their side of it through Cox, just as the side of the anti-establishment has usually continued to get publicity long since: "He assembled us the next day — proclaimed hostility to every man anywise obnoxious to our Gallican domineers. That day commenced the persecution that raged ever since unabated, that grinds whatever talent and genius there is amongst us''. In furtherance of his determination to restore discipline, the President one night ''alarmed the community at the very unseasonable hour of four o'clock in the morning, declaring that he saw from his chamber many young men, at that time, beyond the precincts of the College. In a few minutes we were assembled, our names called — and, to his great confusion, everyone was present''. He, however, believed that they had scaled the walls between the time of alarm and of assembly, and. according to the same source, wept over the vice and irregularity of the students and offered a reward of £50 to any informer who would tell him what exactly had taken place. This was then the extremity of insult in Ireland after the perfidy experienced during the rebellions. On hearing it the students ''burst forth into open manifestation. From one direction he was saluted with 'A fitter you would buy with it a breeches for your daddy'. From another — 'We scorn the corruptor and his bribe'. This last had scarcely reached his ears, when they were again assailed with an universal shout of 'Put the bribe where Davy put the beans'. Upon this seized with a holy zeal, he leaped out of the pulpit to detect the offenders or die in the attempt, but all was in vain''. Still, ''when . . .

time had been given to point out the suspected enemies of the Gallican intolerants, eighteen students, most of them were greatly advanced in their academical course, were expelled from the College . . . . These young men . . . . were introduced into the public hall — stripped of their cap and gown and delivered over to the care of some of the Frenchmen's partizans, who, with the guarded circumspection of so many practised Macmanuses, held them by the collar, until conveyed beyond the bounds of the College''. One of them complained to his Bishop, who asked the President to state the reason for his expulsion.

The President was in no mood for nonsense and nobody could blame him. If his methods were not immediately successful or shrewd, he could be pardoned. Cox is hard on him, saying that he set up ''the Connaught party'' to spy on the other students, authorised them to open rooms, search chests, desks and the like. That Cox is wrong in this is clear from his statement: ''Thus originated that diabolical system of *monitors* which to this day grinds the students, malignantly rejoices in the repression of genius, and feasts with furious voracity on the learning and happiness of the College''. The monitor system had been established before Everard. But Cox is too fascinating to let down. The monitors, it says, shortly after their ''incorporation'' met and declared a particular place for each student in chapel, with punishment for absence; the use of Holy Water on entering and leaving same to obviate suspicion of ''Protestant innovation''; the obligation to ''uncover'' in the presence of a monitor to avoid suspicion of insubordination; and the need to obtain permission from a monitor ''to go to the temple of Cloacina'' during hours of study.

The students were put into ''divisions'' between monitors. These sought to be excellent. Many of them ''walked about in silent meditation, even during the hours of recreation. They . . . . avoided the usual amusements . . . . The ball-allies

. . . . were by them condemned as only fit for bullies who wished to exercise their athletic powers . . . . From the want of social concourse, so necessary an ingredient in the oeconomy (sic.) of the human constitution, fifty of the godly battallion were in a few weeks bedridden in the infirmary. Thus did God at length interpose his chastizing arm''.

It was in 1810 that a Mr. Phelan, already mentioned but of no great fame, visited the College and called to the room of a student, to which, after "rapping" for some time, he was admitted, being told that the reason for the delay was caused by the student endeavouring to conceal Johnson's *Rasselas,* which he was reading and which would have caused his expulsion if he were caught. Phelan was quick to publish this but another student in a pamphlet, entitled *Calumny Refuted,* insisted that "no such prohibition ever existed in M......''. That there was violation of rule there cannot be denied. The *Liber Poenarum* of the College has an entry for 3 May, 1810: "I Thos. O'Neill, Student of the College of Maynooth, do accuse Francis Mangin also a student of said College of having stolen out of my Trunk in my Room one Silver Table Spoon, about three months ago, as well as a Shirt, which I detected on his Body, to all which he acknowledged and to the truth of these accusations I am ready to swear to''. The entry continues, signed by Dr. Byrne, that "Mangan" was expelled the same day. To Cox's mind the President was impetuous: he is said to have got a search warrant from the Castle to inspect the students' rooms:

"We were most insultingly commanded, on the authority of civil law, to surrender our keys, and throw open our rooms to be ransacked . . . . The moment we had obeyed . . . . we were driven out of the college, and all the great doors were locked to prevent our entrance. In this state of exclusion from our rooms we passed a considerable portion of the day in the adjoining fields, actually afraid to speak a single word to one another. When the authorised prowlers had finished their rounds, the exultation of their countenance proclaimed the day well spent. In the minuteness of the search, they found among the papers of a young man, a copy of a letter which he had sometime before written to a priest in a distant part of the country. The letter merely contained a simple statement of the proceedings of his Reverence . . . . yet for this alone his removal from the house was determined on''. 'His Reverence' was likely to have been Dr. Everard. The expulsion was apparently there and then proclaimed, in the presence of the searchers, who were "covered with dirt''.

The Trustees were entirely satisfied. Discipline was being restored. In August Dr. Moylan of Cork wrote to Dr. Bray of Cashel welcoming Dr. Everard's work in Maynooth — "May God be praised and glorified" — and wishing "that worthy Ecclesiastic good health and length of days to compleat the good work''. The good Doctor gave the annual retreat in September, at the commencement of the academic year, lengthening the year thereby by a week. The students were not amused. Those who were in the habit of informing Cox assured it that he gave no sermons but only stories, for two days proving that Queen Elizabeth had been no virgin and devoting the third to his travels through Yorkshire. "Captain Whiskers"! During the retreat, S - n, of fame in Dean Coen's time, "declared in the public prayer hall that he had accused Mr. Coen falsely" and was prepared to accept punishment. Evidently Dr. Everard's retreat was not without some fruit. He replied: "Well done, thou second Austin. I shall esteem thee more than if thou had never sinned". This was received with peals of laughter by the audience. How could the amour of Captain Whiskers convert anybody? The retreat does not seem to have been a great success. The retreat master was guilty of indiscretion when he attacked the character of Irishmen under the name of 'Teigue'. Paul O'Brien was visibly incensed for we learn that "our Milesian professor of the Irish language openly reprobated it in class. He let his pupils know that Teigue was a name sacred in the annals of Ireland, and that to laugh at it was to deny our country".

On 19 September Everard wrote to his Bishop Dr. Bray of Cashel. His own words about his position are eloquent:

"In obedience to your Grace's desire I have entered on the very arduous duties of President of this national establishment. I should have had the honour of communicating this information on an earlier day, were I not distressed by the many extraordinary difficulties which I had to encounter here, and which were of a nature totally different from what I anticipated. Indeed these were, my dear Lord, from a source when I expected only consolation and co-operation!!! But I am distressed in being under the necessity of *confidentially* acquainting your Grace that some of the Prelates themselves ——. But I long for an opportunity of opening my whole soul to your Grace on the numberless causes of anxiety that harass my mind. Oh, my good Lord, what a task you imposed on my weak powers! It is true that the prospect before me is now less dark; but it still is far from being bright. The evils of this house are of an inveterate and of an extremely complicated nature. This is a very unpleasant subject, for which I entreat your Grace's indulgence; but my heart being oppressed I find some alleviation in pouring out its sentiments before you, my good Lord, whose prayers will be addressed to the Father of Mercies to remedy the deplorable state of this College, and to direct the heads and hearts of all its inhabitants . . . . We are now in retreat".

The going was obviously hard, not for the first time or last time either, as was also the President's lack of support from some of the Bishops.

Why this last we know not now. It may have had to do with the apportionment of places in the young Dunboyne foundation of which more later. Or it could have had to do with the expulsions. Whatever it was, in October the Trustees resolved "that any interference in the concerns of the College save only by the Visitors or Trustees at their Boards, or any correspondence between the Prelates or their Clergy and the Students touching the Regulations and discipline of the College must be subversive of that subordination so essentially requisite in such an Establishment, and we therefore earnestly entreat that such things may not take place thereafter". The Archbishop of Cashel had not let down his Tipperary man.

Gradually Everard made his way. After the retreat and in spite of Cox's doubts, Mr. Sheehan became a model student. Cox had to admit it. "Mr. S - n became very pious . . . . stripped his cheeks of an exuberant pair of whiskers . . . . (and) modelled his fashionable surtout (got on the very week of his recantation) after the grave simplicity of a Quaker . . . . smiled — grimaced — at Everard" and was appointed as head monitor. "The Munstermen regarded him as a base deserter; the Connaughtmen as a hypocrite". He was given the nickname 'Porteus', the 'Arch Spy'. A contribution to Cox signed 'A Whig' tells us that the monitors as a whole were not too happy at his advancement. "Though they were the very dregs of the community, they thought their character would suffer from the undeniable infamy of their intended master". A council was called at which they agreed unanimously to resign if S - n's appointment was not cancelled. The resolution was handed to the President, with proofs of Sheehan's guilt. For a week they refused to submit to his authority. He however was not to be put off easily and resolutely "reviewed the students' bedchambers for the least disorder". He outlawed *Twiss* as unpatriotic, which had anyhow been "projected from the window" at him. One can gather from Constantia Maxwell's *Dublin Under the Georges* that the reference here must be to the wealthy English eccentric, Dr. Richard Twiss, who travelled through Ireland in 1775 and whose observations on the country were regarded as impertinent by the people, in consequence of which a Dublin manufacturer of earthenware had the idea of having the offender's portrait printed on the bottom of his chamber-pots, a countenance, we are told in Maurice Craig's *Dublin, 1660-1860,* with his mouth and eyes open ready to receive the libation". These wares were very popular. Lady Clare, wife of the Lord Chancellor, even thought it fit to compose some lines on the subject:

> "Here you may behold a liar,
> Well deserving of hell-fire:
> Every one who likes may p—
> Upon the learned Doctor T—".

Which, says Constantia Maxwell, illustrates the "aristocratic humour of the time". In truth Georgian days were different from Victorian, although it is said that in Victorian Ireland the same utensil was also produced in some quantity with Victoria's head on the bottom. These are now rare objects, even if deriving from a period after the dateline for antique antiques. They are to be found if at all, in California, as containers for mixes at cocktail parties. We are not told really whether it was Twiss's guide to Ireland, his earthen monument, or its contents, that was delivered on the hapless Mr. S - n. We can exclude at least the book. For Philip Luckombe in his *Tour of Ireland* of 1776 tells us that a *Twiss* was the name commonly used to designate the vessel in question. Now we have some idea of what was meant when we read of *Twiss* "being projected" on Mr. Sheehan. And although some friends may be disposed to think otherwise, it was unfortunate that he may have been a Limerickman!

In one way or another discipline was restored. On 15 October, 1810, the Trustees passed the resolution: "That we witness with the greatest satisfaction the improvement in Subordination and Piety so manifest since the appointment of Dr. Everard to the direction thereof, that we highly approve the measures he has found it expedient to adopt and that we will support him to the utmost of our power in these unremitted and zealous exertions which so strongly mark his conduct". It was also resolved "that the President, after taking the advice of his Council, is empowered to remove from the College any scholar, who shall appear to him unfit for the clerical state, or if in holy orders, who shall appear disqualified to remain in the College, consistently with the good order thereof". Lord Fingall was in the Chair. We learn years later from Cox that the expelled students set themselves up in Dublin as a group. It speaks of a "board of Deists, lately formed in Dublin by an unshod assembly of fellows who were driven out of Maynooth College, for exercising their wisdom, and smuggling whiskey into the College". These were undoubtedly Cox's informants about happenings in the College. They would appear to have lost the faith . . . . At the College their old enemies the French professors found themselves isolated, most likely because of their interferences, however well-intentioned. In November, 1813, Delahogue wrote to Troy, now a very old man, pointing out how sad it was that for three years the Board (of Trustees we can assume) was divorced from the Masters of the College: *"Il est bien triste que depuis trois ans le bureau se fait entierement isolé des Maitres du College, sans avoir avec eux aucune communication.* He felt that the Trustees needed to be enlightened about affairs in the College: *"me parait-il necessaire que Mess. Les Trustees soyent instruits de tout".* The Trustees, one imagines, were tired of it all. It was only a matter of time before Darre departed for France, on 24 June, 1813. His post in Natural Philosophy was given by the Trustees to two of his students Messrs. Denvir and Boylan, at 20 guineas per annum each. Denvir was later to become Bishop of Down and Conor. Boylan too had a distinguished career. They were much criticized by Cox when given the job: others would have been much better "some of whom are now a living monument of Maynoothean vengeance and persecution" — an old refrain to be heard again and again later. Darre wrote to the two from London on his way back to his native land. He thanked them for their friendship and help and wished to be remembered to the students, especially those of his class. "I shall forever be rememberful (sic.) of the interest they showed to me and on account of my health and at my Departure. My heart is always in the middle of them and I cannot be happy until I see them again''. *Toujours la politesse.*

SCANDAL AMONGST THE STAFF

In 1811 the College was shaken by the defection of one of the staff. The Reverend Mathias Crowley perverted to Protestantism. Crowley's time at Maynooth had been long and varied and always controversial. His first appointment was in 1802 to a Junior Lecturship in Divinity. He had been admitted as student in 1797 but expelled for non-attendance at prayer one day and for absenting himself from College to go to Kilcock without leave, although at the time he was an extern, lodging out of College. The main reason seems to have been that he returned late for prayers and in a state of intoxication. His expulsion was by solemn sentence, publicly announced in the hall. He went home to Cork for a year, then to Carlow College for two years. But he was back in Maynooth in 1802 as assistant to Delahogue who, whatever might have been his principles about Junior Lecturers, seems to have been happy with his aid. Crowley, we are told, repeated Delahogue's lectures as there was no formal treatise on theology in use in the College at that time. His salary between 70 l. and 80 l. a year and he dined at the Professors' table. He was certainly a go-getter for shortly afterwards we find him engaged in music teaching as well. An 1808 publication, *Papers Presented to the House of Commons relating to the Royal College of St. Patrick, Maynooth,* contains a list of staff members for that year. It notes that Mr. Crowley was Lecturer in Dogmatic Theology at £75 and Teacher of Church Music at £10.

Cox devoted a lot of space to him as might well be expected. In 1814 in 'Memoirs of the Rev. Mathias Crowley' it gave details about his time as lecturer, insisting that it was in a position to know the facts. The writer claims to have the best interests of the College in mind but shows himself to be very critical of it. He may have been one of the ex-students. Of Crowley his writing is not flattering:

"On many occasions the President, Vice-President, and Dean would be summoned to his lecture hall, in order to quell the tumult which Crowley's unfortunate disposition had excited in his class. An occurrence which happened in the very commencement of his career, I shall . . . . mention in this place . . . : In the class of Divinity it is the system of the College that both the professor and the students should deliver their sentiments exclusively in the Latin tongue. Mr. Crowley was, unfortunately, almost a stranger to this language and accordingly expressed himself in a most uncouth and barbarous manner. At one time it happened that his intellect, disordered by the irregularity of his ideas and the want of expression, rendered him for many minutes incapable of uttering a syllable, to the great confusion of the master and the scorn and contempt of his pupils. During this time a dead silence reigned through the hall; at length availing himself of the opportunity (he) interrupts the silence by a reiterated exclamation of 'Bees Wax' — 'Bees Wax', cries out the professor, leaping from his chair in a most dreadful rage; now (he adds) let me see the Vagabond that dare say 'Bees Wax'. This curious piece of mummery threw the whole class into a most violent tumult; some were laughing at the idea of the wax; many enjoyed themselves in beholding the disfigured attitudes of the discomfited professor, and it was with difficulty that peace and order could be restored''.

Crowley remained, nonetheless, the protegé of the Professor — Delahogue. He is said by Cox to have been appointed in the first place through "French intrigue". Because he "used to have recourse to La Hogue for the elucidation of theological difficulties, he was usually denominated the 'French wag-tail' ''. He received a set back when Dr. Dunn left and Dr. Byrne assumed the Presidency. That was in June, 1807. For Dr. Byrne decided to remove Crowley. At the time the Bishop of Cork, Dr. Moylan, was in need of priests so a suitable excuse for getting rid of him was found. His lectureship was discontinued but — and in view of history this is not hard to believe — Mr. Crowley remained on in the College, earning thereby, if for no other reason, a place in Fitzpatrick's *Wits and Worthies*. On Dr. Byrne's departure and Dr. Everard's arrival, the Frenchmen and Crowley's friends made solicitation for his reinstatement, this time as Professor of Scripture, which was done in October, 1810. At the beginning of his new office he was mild. Then, after a while, "he would frequently fly in a rage with any student whom he should find studying a comment or the dictates of his predecessor, in preference to his own". The predecessor was the Reverend Francis Eloi who stay in the College had been short. Mr. Crowley's aversion to his 'dictates' did not disturb the French professors. Perhaps it was because Eloi was believed to be of German extraction. He may have left because he did not get on with them. But the students regarded him as "a man of great talents and of universal reading and . . . . had respect for his memory".

At the end of 1810 Dr. Everard went to England for six months, leaving "the house to the guidance of a snarling Dean and a merciless junto of monitors". The Dean was now the Reverend William Fitzpatrick of the Diocese of Dublin, who had been appointed 'provisionally' the previous July and 'absolutely' in October. Whether snarling or not, the Dean seems to have been quite happy at the President's absence. He wrote to his Bishop in Dublin to tell him that all was well in the College but that the Bishop should not mention this to the President, as it might retard his return. "This I did in my letter to him, not considering that I was forging bolts for myself". As it so turned out, he was. In March, 1811, the President was still in England and the Vice-President did not know when to expect him back. He reports that "everything is going on here with the most edifying

131

regularity". Eventually the President did return sometime in the Spring. The monitors briefed him on the scene. A pass-book had been found on one of the public walks, which accused the Vice-President of remissness and also the Professor of Irish — hardly surprising although it is surprising that the incident should have occurred at all — of giving a wrong reply to a *casus* in morality proposed at one of the evening classes, even though he had afterwards called on the students to testify that his answer had been different. One would love to know what the *casus* was. But to get back to Mr. Crowley. His already varied career now took on more colour by his being appointed as Dean on the resignation of Mr. Fitzpatrick. The *College Records* have it so for 2 May, 1811, even though Healy does not list him among the Deans. Mr. Crowley was appointed Dean at least temporarily. According to Cox, he himself did not welcome the appointment, following Mr. Fitzpatrick's being "obliged to withdraw on account of his unfitness". But Dr. Everard had his way. The students were summoned to the Common hall and told that "the Dean's department was now in a state of Widowhood". He would set over it a "man of God".

At their next meeting the Board of Trustees did not sanction Crowley's appointment and Fr. Andrew Hart was appointed in his place at the following meeting. This was the occasion if not the cause of Crowley's apostasy. Fitzpatrick — the writer not the ex-Dean — tells us that the moment Crowley learned of this "he in a fit of anger went directly to Pastor Ashe, the Rector of Maynooth, and read his recantation". Cox has more to say about it. According to it, just before the Summer vacation, Crowley tried to have a number of students expelled, a move which did not receive the approval of higher authority — whether of the President or the Bishops we are not told. Whereupon he attacked everybody and "was therefore commanded to lay down his office and depart". Where to? That was the question. For one who had been Lecturer in Dogmatic Theology, Professor of Scripture (at least pro tem.), Music Master, Dean and, according to another source, also at one time had "a quasi-Lectureship" of Logic and of Physics "which he was then learning for the first time, a return even to Cork would not have been attractive. There, one gathers, his most intimate relations were turned against him: there was the disgrace of a second removal from the College. Hence his turning his coat. He was received as Minister in the Church of Ireland by the Archbishop of Dublin and appointed Chaplain to the Blue Coat Hospital, where he was captivated by Miss Fanny Crofts, the then housekeeper. "Discipline and peace" were "found established" in the College on the occasion of the June, 1811, meeting of the Trustees.

In view of his rejection of Romanism, some of Mr. Crowley's poses now seemed nothing short of ludicrous. A writer calling himself 'Aldhelmus Hibernicus' brought out a *Series of Letters to Wm. O'Donnell Esq. . . . . on Interesting Subjects — the causes of Matthew Crowley's apostasy and the Squalid Pages signed James Crowley*. It was published in Strabane. Referring to Matthew Crowley as the "musical professor of his own musical theology", it went on in student vein (indeed the author had obviously been a student) to say of his lectures:

"Nothing could we get but what was before us in the written lectures of the Professor. True, indeed, we amused ourselves with many interrogations, and so did he us, and with many prettily and literally delivered historical tracts, from Eusebius and the Councils, etc. These hereticks who broke off from the Church. These went down very well with the Minors of the Class". Aldhelmus Hibernicus continues: "This unfortunate man was raised to the office of Temporary Dean, and of course, removable at pleasure. He frequently made application to get a permanent situation, but this was not granted him, certainly from a conviction that he was inadequate. By the frequent recurrence of disappointed ambition, the inferior man weakly gave up . . . . Darkness came upon him; and with his then associates, against the President, he exclaimed in the language of revolt, 'We will not have this rules over us'. He immediately rushed forth — he read his recantation . . . . At the time of . . . . (his) secession it was much rumoured by our family that some of the Professors of Maynooth, and many of the Students would follow the example . . . . Here I confess I felt much indignation . . . . No Sir, the Students of Maynooth were Gentlemen of strict regularity, who knew how to command their passions, allowing still for individual exceptions which will be ever found in communities, so long as society exists. Yes, I shall say, nor shall I dread the petty frowns of low-bred envy, or the nasty sneer of those who know not Maynooth. The Students of Maynooth were of a quick and discerning mind, and of strong natural abilities. They were in the aggregate, allowing, as I have said, for exceptions, a portion of young men, at least equal to any of equal numbers all over Europe. Here again, I say, I do not fear the frown. What did a venerable foreigner, a man of profound learning and unaffected manners say? 'I have spent my years in study', said he, 'I have filled a Professor's chair in the University of the Sorbonne — I have taught in Maynooth — I have been these forty years a Professor, and never have I witnessed such examinations. There are here who would do honour to the academy of Paris' ".

In the March of 1811 this reputation was to stand by Maynooth. On Tuesday, 2 April, the *Freeman's Journal* reported a debate in the House of Commons on the Maynooth estimates. The grant at the time had to be renewed yearly. On this occasion it was moved by Mr. Hutchinson, who advanced the view that it was but a pittance in comparison with that voted for stationary for the Customs House. Learning in Europe owes much to the Irish, whether on the Continent or in England. Bede is quoted and reference made to Erigena. Yet the Professors of Maynooth are badly paid. "Could there be a greater indecency than such a paltry allowance to those professors, who ought to be among the most learned men of Europe?" Surely the grant could not be refused? It was not: Mr. Hutchinson's motion was carried. Mr. Crowley, however, benefitted little from it. He was on his way out of the place. Cox, naturally, made the most of it, pointing out that the Blue Coat Hospital had been founded for the education of the sons of poor tradesmen, as the Foundling Hospital had been for the illegitimate offspring of popish parents. Of Crowley it says: "If Mr. C. kept up his countenance and remained on terms with Everard, he would most undoubtedly enjoy a share in the Dunboyne bequest. The French doctor is the only man on whom the appointment depends, and as Crowley had always gratified him by committing to memory a few pages of his compilation, I should hazard the assertion that he would have been continued the corner stone of the new institution". The references here are to Delahogue and the new Dunboyne Establishment. In August, 1811, Cox had printed that "the conversion of Mr. Crowley has become a public theme of thanksgiving among the elect of the Board of Grace" — whatever that was, hardly the Board of Trustees, even though they may be fairly thought to have been glad to be rid of him. His "enlargement from the rules of celibacy procured him many offers in a matrimonial way . . . . We hear he had made his selection" and that the day of the wedding is appointed. At present he is on a visit "with the Scotch Bishop of Kildare, at his Lordship's Seat near his turnpike at Glasnevin". He had been pressed by offers from the different Boards of Grace in the city, inviting him to be lecturer in Whitefriar Street, etc. He has chosen York Street. Cox was taking a chance. The previous May, as a short note in the *Evening Herald* (for Monday 27th) informs us, Mr. Walter Cox had received sentence for a libel of which he had been found guilty: "To be find 300 l., to be imprisoned for 12 months to be computed from the expiration of his former sentence and not to be discharged until he enters into security for his future conduct, himself in 1,000 l. and two other persons in 500 l. each". A very heavy sentence and richly deserved.

Cox was insuppressable. By September he was expatiating on a sermon preached by Crowley in Glasnevin Church. The hearers consisted "like all our country Churches in Ireland, with the exception of the Bishop and his family, and the sergeant of the guard (for the soldiery are everywhere), the Sexton, his wife, the school mistress, her lap dog and spectacles". Crowley, or rather "Crawley", as Cox puts it, had arrived at the Bishop's place in Wood Street in a coach to be received by the "Board of Grace". October saw the appearance of a pamphlet from the Roman side on the affair. Signed A Clergyman' — a copy carries a pencilled note "evidently by one of the old French professors — it bore the grandiloquent title *A Letter on the reasons which led the Rev. Matthew Crowley to change from the Roman Catholic to the Protestant Religion*. It was all hot and bothered and defensive: Mr. Crowley had not been Professor of Scripture at the time of his leaving Maynooth. He had been allowed to fill the Chair for some time but was removed to the place of Dean, which was the last situation he held in the College, "and he would have been dismissed from this, on account of his late conduct, had he even continued a Catholic''. He knew not Hebrew and is not a master of Greek. He "merely literally and drily selected passages from Commentators, which he gave in the shape of a dictate", his merit being "neither more nor less than a totally good memory". (A point was made there). He was challenged by the pamphlet to prove that the Established Church was the true Church.

Crowley had not been the only dissident who left Maynooth and Rome at that time. The Reverend Daniel Sinnott, lecturer in Moral Theology, who also gave lectures in the Lay College, was one of them. He joined no Church. There was also a Mr. Cousins, and a Mr. Molony who wrote pamphlets after leaving: in other words he took up journalism as a career. Not for the last time was such a thing to be heard of. Another was a Mr. Nowlan. He, however, repented and in April, 1811, address a 'Letter to the Roman Catholic Archbishop's (sic.), Clergy and Laity of the Diocese of Dublin'. He, Mic. Nowlan put on paper:

"I by leave to address myself to my respected friends and contempories of the College of Maynooth, who are to be the future support and ornament of the Irish Catholic Church, and to implore their forgiveness and commiseration for a deluded child of that establishment, who, for many years, had heard the doctrines of religion, of virtue, and of morality, taught and inculcated there. And now I reckon on their acquittal on the score of my present regret and retraction. I humbly request that my misfortunes may proclaim to them a happy lesson of religious circumspection and punctuality in every duty belonging to their state, and thereby preserve them from ever experiencing sorrow like mine''.

This was followed up by the publication of *A Letter to the Rev. Mathias Crowley . . . . on his Apostasy, containing the Rev. Mr. Nowlan's letter with some observations respecting him.* It went into three editions within the year. Crowley's case was contrasted with Nowlan's. "The contrast between you and Mr. Nowlan is this : You are a man of *mere memory*, without genius or talents; Heaven has denied both the one and the other, therefore eternal silence is your duty; you have drawn your little store of information, not from a comparison of facts, but from books, which you have literally got by heart; you have not abilities enough to be the founder of a heresy . . . .''.

The Matthew Crowley controversy, if it may be called that, was clouded by the publications at the same time of a Mr. James Crowley, also a presumed former student of Maynooth. In 1811 were published two pamphlets under his name. One was entitled *Reasons for Embracing Popery and Afterwards Recanting* (put out by Thomas Johnston, 20 Crow Street, Dublin), which made reference to "the religious dissentions which recently agitated Maynooth College, and the departure of some educated individuals from the Romanish communion". The other, entitled *Thoughts on the Emancipation of Roman Catholics,* had as its theme the enormities of Catholic belief. The writer underlines that as a student in Maynooth

135

he had studied the works of some of the most eminent Protestant divines, and had been convinced by them. "Indeed one of our professors (Could it have been M. Crowley?), a very sensible and well-informed man, said, in my hearing, a few months ago, that the religion of the Church of Rome could, by no means, bear examination; and, that, for his part, he often secretly laughed at the stupid credulity of the Roman Catholic laity". One Patt. Rogers, described as a lover of science and religion, made a reply to this, entitled *Observations on Thoughts of Catholic Emancipation — A Libel on the Roman Catholic Church by James Crowley,* which took Crowley's assertions to pieces *seriatim* but like all such efforts was not as forceful as the other. Aldhelmus Hibernicus, to whose pamphlet reference has been made already, called James Crowley to task more tellingly. He chose to denigrate rather than enter into argument. Was not James Crowley's publication sent round in the penny post and "left at the corners of Thomas Stret, Dublin, that the poor might pick it up and imbibe its principles?" It had even been translated into Irish through the efforts of Protestant ministers in Derry. "This production of this non-existing Crowley" is intended to deceive Catholics and to confuse the M. Crowley incident. One is compelled to wonder whether there ever was a James Crowley? It would not be the last time such subterfuge was to be adopted. True, another Crowley — a near relative of Matthew and also a Maynooth student — perverted as well but his Christian name was not James. It is hard to be sure. James Crowley may well have been the James Crowly (sic.) of Cork who matriculated in 1800. In Ald. Hib's view "the falling off, from time to time, of such droning theologians as Crowly (sic.) or Cousins, never will injure Maynooth".

Cork came to the rescue of its son Mathias as it always does for its sons. In March, 1812, was published there (by Joseph and Robert McMullen) a *Vindication of the Conduct of the Rev. Mr. Crowley . . . . now a Clergyman of the Established Church.* It was a theological treatise which frequently referred the reader to "Mr. Buck's Theological Dictionary". The year passed away. In September the *Freeman's Journal* had reference to a comet and in October quoted the *Gazette of France* as having reported the discovery of coal gas and its uses. Meanwhile Cox was retailing that Counsellor Clinch, one of the learned editors of the *Evening Express,* was preparing a collection of his essays for printing and that the Reverend Mr. Eustace (undoubtedly the former Maynooth professor) had dined with Lord Louth. Eustace always cultivated the gentry. Cox continues to complain: most of the prizes in the College go to the monitors, also the stewardships, for example that of the kitchen which brings £30 per annum. Somebody had his ear again. . . . And Kennedy is heard of too. In 1813, in a 'Letter from Kilkenny' and one on 'Maynooth Kennedy', Cox returns to his favourite topic — Maynooth. But it is hard to know who precisely he is speaking of, the James Kennedy, infamous some years before, or a Thomas Kennedy who had arrived in the College in 1802 and was removed sometime afterwards. In May, 1814, he records the death of a James Kennedy, calling him 'Monkey Kennedy' in an awful obituary. If it were indeed the former student of Maynooth, broken possibly by trials though some may have been of his own making, may he rest in peace. Whoever he was, may God keep him. As for Crowley, Cox informs us he is now teaching in the Foundling Hospital, living a "miserable existence . . . . The unfortunate wretch is suffering for his pride and apostasy": Crowley was at home with his wife . The ecumenical spirit of that time in some ways surpassed that of later times. Whether because of this or old friendship — more probably the latter — right up to 1835 some of his former colleagues used to visit him, hoping perhaps, says Fitzpatrick's *Wits and Worthies,* to induce him to return to the Church. "Mr. Crowley sang beautifully, and after he had treated his visitors on one occasion, to a vocal effort of great melody and volume, touching allusion was made to auld lang syne when he had sang the High Mass.

A big tear rolled down the Parson's cheek; Mrs. Crowley saw that he stood upon dangerous ground, and the gentlemen were bowed out with a degree of frigidity which prevented them from ever after repeating their visit". No comment. The good Vicar was to end his days in Newbridge, where he is buried. For a while it was said that no grass grew on his grave. One asks thereafter whether weeds have not grown on it?

MEASURES OF VARIOUS KINDS

The President's health had not been good for quite a while. He spent long periods out of the College, usually in England. He does seem to have been an Anglophile, despite his Tipperary origins. We are told by Peel's biography that, as Archbishop of Cashel in 1818, he made a private approach to the Government proposing that £1,000 should be granted annually by the State to subsidise a special house for ten young priests from Maynooth who would preach obedience to the law to the lower classes of Ireland — a petition which Peel rejected, on the grounds we are also told, that the character of the Maynooth educated clergy hardly afforded much hope for the success of such a venture. Everard could not last long in Maynooth. One source has it that in the Spring of 1811 Dr. Lingard, the learned Lancashire priest, had been urged by Bishop Moylan to accept the Presidency. If so it may have reflected these absences as well as the situation in the College. But it may equally have been merely a matter of patronage, coupled with a possible qualm on the part of the Bishop of Cork after the Lanigan affair. One does gather that in general the Irish Bishops had a high opinion of Lingard, and were ready to offer him almost any post at Maynooth if he were willing to accept it. There is no disputing the fact that the *Journal of the Trustees* contains an entry for October, 1811, resolving that he be requested to accept "the place of Professor of Sacred Scripture and Eloquence in the College with a salary of two hundred pounds per annum". A surprising offer in a way in view of Lingard's specialty, ecclesiastical history. But then the other was probably a greater priority. Father William Murphy, the noted preacher, is supposed to have been offered the chair of Rhetoric and also declined. Lingard declined too, it would seem.

137

But a more grevious matter was that of the Presidency, for Dr. Everard resigned in June, 1812. The pressing nature of the problem facing the Trustees can be gathered from the fact that on the same day they appointed the Coadjutor Bishop of Dublin, Most Reverend Daniel Murray, as President. The account in the *Records* reads that Dr. Murray "was requested and prevailed upon to superintend the direction and management of the College provisionally". The minute of the Trustees goes: "That M. Rev. Dr. Murray be requested to accept the office of President — This request is made in the perfect conviction of the high advantages which must result to Religion and to the College from his acceptance". It was the Archbishop of Dublin, Dr. Troy, who prevailed upon him. For his part, Dr. Everard, although still in ill-health, was to go on later to be Archbishop of Cashel. When question of this came round in the July immediately following, one of his stoutest supporters was his successor in Maynooth, Dr. Murray. In fact he wrote to Rome stressing Everard's suitability for Cashel owing to his success as President of Maynooth, where he had demonstrated his zeal, prudence, forcefulness, piety and learning. On 1 July Rutland, the Lord Lieutenant, furnished the required approval of Dr. Murray's election as President and, as before, on 7 July an official attestation was made out — signed by Thomas Bouchier, Deputy Clerk, Crown and Hanaper in the Court of Chancery — that the new President had taken the required oath. One of the ironies of the situation was that in Murray the Crown had come closest perhaps at Maynooth to one who had contact with the United Irishmen of former days when he had ministered as a young priest in the Wicklow mountains. In '98, in fact, he had to flee to Dublin from Arklow following threats from the soldiery.

Murray himself seems to have been under the impression that Everard might be able to return as President. Less than a week after his writing to Rome recommending the latter for Cashel, he was writing to Bray, still Archbishop of Cashel but in declining years, saying that, while Dr. Everard's health was very poor to the extent that he had been in danger of death during most of the Winter and not able even to write a letter, a year's rest would do him good. He, Murray, tells of his own acceptance of the government of the College *for one year* (underlined), in the hope that Everard might be able to be President of Maynooth again. It would be a great misfortune if he were not able to resume. Presumably, in recommending him simultaneously to Rome for Cashel, Dr. Murray was thinking ahead.

It is hard to know what to believe about these strange times. The official *Life of Dr. Murray* maintains that he (and Fr. Peter Kenny, the Jesuit and later founder of Clongowes Wood College, who had been appointed Vice-President of Maynooth in November, 1812) "found the discipline in the college, from one cause or another sadly relaxed; and a spirit anything but ecclesiastical too widely diffused among its inmates — insubordination and moroseness, and foppish estimates of independence". Fr. Kenny as Vice-President composed a series of meditations for the use of the students, "one of which was preached each evening for almost the entire period of his stay in the College". Dr. Murray, who in-

138

troduced the Vincentians into Dublin, gave them the "privilege of presenting their most distinguished pupils — applicants for the priesthood — to certain free places in the College", something that was to be pregnant of future events. During his one and a half years as President, Dr. Murray also visited the city regularly each week, preached to parishioners at St. Andrew's church every Sunday morning, assisted the Vicar General at the Archbishop's Council on Monday and returned the same day to Maynooth.

In those days the rapidity with which people attributed to themselves or had attributed to them imediate success was remarkable. Fr. Kenny wrote to Plunkett of Meath (apparently as acting Vice-President) in October 1812: "I have for the present acceded to Dr. Murray's earnest desire to fill the office of vice-president in this house, and have every reason to be satisfied with the present good order and earnest application to duty which prevails amongst the students"!! But even already he is interested in finding a house for a Jesuit 'seminary': Clongowes was in fact taken by the Jesuits in 1814, Fr. Kenny going there from Maynooth to be head. Evidently he had kept his eyes open while at Maynooth.

Trouble with the 'Masters' had to be dealt with as much as that with the students. A loose leaf in the *Liber Poenarum* may refer to this period. It obviously deals with staff grievances of which there are quite a number:

"1. We find upon inquiry that serious inconveniences arises from the want of a cellar, in which the wine, spirits and other groceries may be deposited. For the present, we are of the opinion that partial benefit may be obtained by using the dark room as a repository for the wine and spirits; and Mr Anglade's cellar, with his permission, for the tea and sugar. We find upon examination that some negligence occurred in superintending the storage of the wine and spirits. We ascribe this neglect in a great measure to the circumstance of no persons being specially delegated to take this charge and we therefore recommend that the Purchasing Committee for the time being should be charged with the superintendence of said storage.

"2. We find that the duties of the Acting Committee have not been equally discharged; and that from this inequality much inconvenience did occasionally arise. In compliance with the suggestion which we received from several of the Gentlemen concerned, we beg leave to recommend that the office of Steward be filled by one Gentleman only for the period of one month — reserving to the individual acting as Steward the right and liberty of entering into any arrangement with any other member of our society who may be disposed to share with him the trouble and responsibility of the office.

"3. To prevent every colour or pretext of complaint, we beg to recommend that in no case whatsoever, under no circumstances however peculiar, should groceries of any description be removed from the Parlour to any private apartment.

"4. We beg leave to suggest, that it be the duty of the acting Steward to see the sugar broken and tea made.

"5. Owing to the manner in which the stock of groceries on hands is arranged and the accounts not having been kept with a view to any report being made thereupon, it is found impracticable to lay before you the exact amount of the annual expenditure. But as far as the partial data supplied enable us to form an estimate of these expenses, we would venture to say that they do not exceed 17 or 18 pounds per annum.

"In this expenditure we have no hesitation in saying that a strict attention on the part of the acting stewards to the several duties of their office would effect a considerable saving — Our attention has been specially called to the waste of wine and spirit occasioned by negligence with respect to the bottles. It has frequently occurred that wine was mixed with the spirits; and wine and spirits put into bottles which were not clean — The member of the Acting Committee may be requested to attend in giving out tea to the number of the Gentlemen likely to be present morning and evening.

"6. We take leave to submit to you the expediency of considering whether, when a *clergyman* is entertained and wine served after dinner only, two bottles of wine should *not* be deemed a sufficient contribution on the part of the Gentleman inviting him — Should more than one Clergyman be invited, an additional bottle for each he invites. The original rule to be observed when wine is served during dinner or any Lay Person is invited.''

Also recommended "to be considered" was "the propriety of subjecting the gentleman who entertains only after dinner, to the obligations of giving only two bottles of wine for one guest, and one for every other", and "to be submitted to the body whether two loaves of sugar be a sufficient contribution on the part of the President to the common stock". Despite their shortcomings, these were truly interesting days and spacious ones in matters of wine. Georgian Ireland at Maynooth was living up to its reputation for capacity in this respect. They were the days when the Irish exiles in Bordeaux — the Catholic McCarthys from the South, the Protestant Bartons and Johnstons from the North — thrived on their lucrative businesses. Scotland bought more than twice as much wine as did England at the end of the 18th century and Ireland up to four times as much! We are told by those in the know that the figures are somewhat unreliable in that in the case of Ireland they might easily be capable of revision upwards by reason of smuggling — into little coves in places like O'Connell's Kerry. That the Irish might be tempted to do this — apart from the fact that they were! — could be attributed as much to their thirst as to the fact that they paid three-quarters as much less than the English for a cask. The 'punt' was good in the E.M.S. of the time. Actually the 'Irish connection' with the French wine trade is of absorbing interest. Thomas Barton, or 'French Tom' as he came to be called, had settled eventually in Bordeaux and owned his own business by the age of thirty in 1715. By the middle of the century he owned concerns in such *bouquet* places as St. Estaphe in the Médoc as well as an estate in County Tipperary! His grandson, Hugh, who had married into the Johnston family, was known as 'Citizen Hugues Barton' after the Revolution, although he did at length have to leave the country.

It mattered little to the Maynooth Masters, to adapt the title of Nicholas Faith's book *The Winemasters,* whether their wine was of revolutionary vintage. That they should have it and in sufficient quantity was what counted. And so we find a resolution of the College Trustees, dated 11 November, 1812: "Resolved, that the allowance made to the Masters for wine and groceries be increased". It could have been a coincidence that the very next day the Trustees ordered that Baily's work on morality should be printed for the College! On the same day a further resolution laid down that no student be allowed to go home during vacation who did not have the permission of his Bishop and of the President. Student discipline at least had been restored whatever about the Masters. Measures then as always were varied.

Chapter VII

Life, Learning and Lucre
c. 1810-20

After the foregoing chapters it may be thought that there is not much left to say about life in general at Maynooth during the early part of the nineteenth century. It would be a mistake to think so: there is. By the middle of the second decade the College had somewhat settled down to a more normal kind of existence yet there was much that was colourful in its texture.

One of the more interesting facets of life at that time was travel, and travelling to Maynooth has had its narrators. Some naturally relate to students, who came there, first on horseback or by carriage, later by canal boat or railway train. It was a long shot from the motor bus or private car of later years and one awaits the helicopter or aeroplane. They came from all over the country, some from more formal junior schools, others — the majority in all probability — from the 'hedge schools' that then dotted Ireland. While it is true that these latter were frequented more by the ordinary folk, in many places they were the only sources of the kind of education that was a prerequisite to entering Maynooth. A *Statistical Survey of Kildare* made in 1807 says: "All over the county are numbers of schools, where the lower orders have their children instructed in writing, arithmetic and reading'', while in 1808 Lord Palmerston of Sligo declared: "The thirst for education is so great that there are now three or four schools upon the estate. The people join in engaging an itinerant master; they run him up a miserable mud hut on the roadside, and the boys pay him half-a-crown, or some five shillings a quarter. They are taught reading, writing and arithmetic and what, from the appearance of the establishment, no one would imagine, Latin and even Greek''. Such schools were particularly numerous in Munster, from where many 'Poor Scholars' came as well as the better off.

GOING UP TO MAYNOOTH

The kind of journey they made is illustrated by Sir Richard Colt Hoare in his *Journal of a Tour of Ireland in 1806.* Hoare travelled from Dublin, through Maynooth and on to Trim. He describes Maynooth as 'a modern town, with a spacious inn. Adjoining the town is a school for the instruction of Roman Catholic Youths, upon a large establishment, and called St. Patrick's College''. Rather more generous really than the *Irish Times* guide for July, 1979, which, however, mentions Maynooth College, at the end of the town, as worth a visit "if only to calm the nerves''. Those in the know would no doubt want to ask "whose nerves?'' But to return to Hoare. Maynooth was taken in by him in his Northern Tour, but it could just as easily have fitted into a Western or a Southern one. He took the lower road, between the Liffey and the Phoenix Park, to Chapelizod, there crossed the Liffey and then on to Leixlip where the Liffey was crossed again. He mentions that 'post horses' were kept at Kilcock. Another of the many tours through Ireland for which the 19th century was famous — that of J. Gough — informs us that the old bridge at Lucan was swept away by floods in the year 1806.

Water brings to mind the canal era. The Royal Canal was *par excellence* the Maynooth waterway. It had been extended there by an act of George III in 1790 to enable the Royal Canal Company to complete the enterprize. At the time it was said to have been brought through Maynooth in order to please the Duke of Leinster who wanted it to pass near Carton or, as the Rev. Caesar Otway writing in 1839 was to say, to pass by "his town of Maynooth''. What? A canal as well as a College? In 1845 *Hall's Ireland* carries a full description of the journey and the boats used. But we are well before that time as yet. In 1796 there was a gala opening of the Grand Canal. The *Diary of Lord Clonmell* recounts the day's events: "Saturday, 23rd April, 1796, St. George's day — Lord Camden, with a vast concourse of people, nobility, gentry, and rabble attended at Ring's end, with music and cannon; and a public breakfast, given by the governors of the Grand Canal at the opening of the new docks, and sailing into them of a vast number of ships and small boats. The Judges and Bar left the courts to attend so new and splendid a sight''. December 2nd of the same year saw the opening of the extension of the Royal Canal to Maynooth and beyond. *Walker's Hibernian Magazine* for that month contains a graphic account:

"Yesterday, the passage boats commenced plying on the royal canal, between Dublin and Kilcock. Two very handsome boats (named 'The Camden' and 'The Pelham') started, one from each place, at nine o'clock, and arrived at their destinations, making allowance for a little delay occasioned by the ice from the intense frost of the preceding night, within five hours and a half — they passed within a quarter of a mile of Lucan and Leixlip, and through Maynooth, amid the acclamations of multitudes (the day being remarkably fine) who hailed this auspicious beginning of the trade, so likely to contribute to their cheap and comfortable accommodation, and the establishment of a permanent income to the company, to whose enterprising spirit and undaunted perseverance, through difficulties hitherto not encounted in canals, they seemed disposed to show every mark of respect and admiration. The boats met at Lucan harbour, at near twelve (about half-way) where they stopped for a few minutes. The construction of the boats is such as to remove every apprehension of their over-sitting (a discovery highly favourable to this infant undertaking) and the management of them through the locks, eleven in number, and the promptitude, zeal, and attention of the several persons employed by the company were very conspicuous. As friends to inland navigation, we beheld with infinite satisfaction, by the extension of this canal, the prospect of an aquatic communication with Cloncurry, Kinnegad, Mullingar and Athlone, and, with them the great western trade of Ireland — a period, in our opinion, not very far distant, if the same zeal and anxiety for their country's improvement animate the company''.

Actually, the passenger boat services on the Royal Canal, between Dublin, Maynooth, Mullingar and Longford were neither as grandiose nor as profitable as those of the Grand Canal, largely owing to the lack of adequate hotel accommodation along the route. Early in 1800 an advertisement appeared in the *Dublin Evening Post:* "The Public are requested to take notice, that in order to accommodate the passengers from Meath, Westmeath, Longford and Connaught, or any other distant part, the Packet Boat shall not leave Newcase, West of the Nineteenthmile House, on the Mullingar road, until 11 o'clock, from the 6th day of February next, and from and after the 1st day of March, at 12 o'clock. The Boats from Dublin to start from the 6th day of February at 7 o'clock, and from and after the 1st day of March at 6 o'clock''. Travellers to Maynooth had to rise early.

A graphic description of travel to Maynooth by canal boat was penned in 1837 by Charlotte Elizabeth, a traveller from England. Even though her journey took place after our period, it undoubtedly provides an authentic account of what the scenario must have been between 1810 and 1820. She got on the boat at nine a.m.:

"Many things concurred to render the moment of embarkment very

depressing. You may judge whether my spirits received a cheering impulse when I discovered that, with the exception of the corner which I occupied, and the one over against me, the long narrow cabin was entirely
filled with priests, bound, as it appeared, for Maynooth. Some especial
work had called them to Dublin. I suppose; and this goodly freight of
eleven was returning to College; all were evidently men of some standing
in their vocation; and, prejudice of every kind apart, I regretted that
habit of studying countenances which has from childhood made me a
physiognamist, in spite of myself. Whether some untoward occurrence
had called the darker passions into exercise, or whether an instinctive
dislike of their company occasioned it, I know not; but looks more
ominous of ill I never encountered, than from under the slouched hats
and bent brows of my fellow voyagers, during the three hours that I was
part of their society. W. (a young boy who was travelling with her),
preferring the pleasant look-out from the open boat, soon left me to enjoy alone my singular privilege — singular in several respects, for I had in
the portmanteau at my feet a great folio of Foxe's Acts and Monuments,
in my pocket Dr. Newland's cutting exposé of the antiscriptural Education Board, and in my lap the plank that I had brought from the top of
Vinegar Hill''.

No doubt Charlotte was self-conscious in the open possession of this relic of a
United Irishman's defeat. She was clearly self conscious too in the presence of her
fellow-passengers, many of whom were most probably students. It is amusing to
read how she was attracted to them yet put her attraction away like a bad
thought, concentrating on the erroneous nature of their ways. For their part they
threw her the odd look and equally curtailed it.

"Fancying myself in the Holy Inquisition, I could not but think how it
would fare with me had all these silent witnesses (i.e. her 'guilty' possessions) been produced, and their testimony received; nor did it require any
great strength of the imagination to suppose such a juncture. Had I been
a man, openly observing them and their country, asking information or
taking notes, I can readily imagine how bland, how courteous, how
frank and agreeable the gentlemen around me would have become (yes
— she would have liked to talk with them), but a female plainly attired,
accompanied by a school-boy, and giving no token of reverential homage
to 'the clergy', was not calculated to induce any disguise on their part.
Glances of stern displeasure, quite unprovoked, frequently crossed my
view, as I took a peep towards the opposite windows. The conversation
was low, and much of it in Irish, as W., who knows a little of the
language, informed me. I cannot say that, with the exception of one
elderly man, who looked mild and thoughtful, and said very little, there

was a face that I could have wished to see again. Yet some of them very handsome men, and all had a most gentlemanly manner and demeanour. Each was habited in black — good broadcloth it appeared, with a fresh gloss on it; each had the distinguishing badge of a Romish priest, a broad-hemmed collar of white lawn turned down, about two inches in depth, over the upper edge of his black stock; two had clerical slouched hats, and one of these wore the habit of some monastic order, a coat rather loose, with exceedingly wide sleeves, the cuffs of which folded over one another as he sat with closed hands. I felt as if under the influence of an uneasy dream: I strove to pray and did pray for these destroyers of their own souls and the souls of the poor. I thought of our blessed Reformers, every one of whom had been as they, before the Holy Spirit enlightened their darkness; I thought of Nolan and others, actually brought up among those very individuals yet now preaching the faith which once they destroyed. These recollections encouraged the secret prayer, but no effort would dispel the gloom that overhung me as I realised the presence of the very priests of Rome; contrasting as I could not help doing, their expensive attire, and the look alike of high feeling and high-mindedness, with the penury, the privations, the deep depression, to which their wicked machinations had reduced the dear servants of Christ, the faithful, devoted ministers of the Irish Church. Had they assumed an aspect less dark and haughty, I might not have felt these impressions with equal force; but the reality of the case could not have been affected by any externals; and miserably uncomfortable as it made me, I rejoiced that it was not my lot to be imposed on by the lamb's face, so easily assumed at the dragon's will . . . .

"When the boat approached Maynooth, a general preparation for paying the fares was made. Each drew forth his money, to be in readiness for the expected demand. The silver counted out, and gathered together on a narrow table, was far from diverting my thoughts into a pleasanter channel . . . . and yet again I prayed that I might never be permitted to fall into the snare of seeming to consent to, or to connive at, or to tolerate, any scheme whatever that would in its operation leave a single soul for a single day under the power of that mystery of iniquity whereof the men around me were the worn, the active agents. A smart jar, as we touched the pier, gave the welcome signal of release. I sat next the entrance, and as they severally brushed past me, and stooped to avail themselves of the low, narrow doorway, I did indeed breathe over each a prayer from my inmost heart, that God would convert him from the deadly error of his way. I felt a pang too of remorse for not having attempted to win them to converse on a subject that might have laid the foundations of an answer to that prayer . . . . From all false charity and expediency-loving unfaithfulness, good Lord deliver me. Disbursed of our priestly freight, the boat sped lightly on. I just sent a parting glance after them, as they wound, a long black line, upon the innocent green sod towards the great curse of Ireland, the foul blot of England's unrighteous legislation — Maynooth; then, without being tempted even to look upon its outline, I turned to the opposite bank, and breathed freely''. And yet Charlotte was not able to forget those Maynooth men hurriedly. As she passed through the flat country after Maynooth, through the bogs of the Midlands, while she mused whether they might be drained and used for agriculture, she again breaks out: "Certes, whatever else my plan of improvement might leave the bog, Maynooth should be fairly out of it''.

Dear Charlotte. How unthoughtful of those Maynooth inmates to have travelled on that canal boat.

The majority, of course, still came by road. One such was John McHale from Tuam, who matriculated in 1807. A vivid account of his journey up to College is given in his biography by O'Reilly, publshed in New York in 1890:

"Early in September, John bade farewell to brothers and sisters, and to the kinfolk and neighbours who had come to bid the boy God-speed. One of his brothers, Thomas, accompanied him on his long and pleasant journey, both being mounted on two of their father's best nags, with a well-filled purse to enable them to travel comfortably.

"In truth, it was a most pleasant and most instructive journey to the two young men. Every district through which they passed, every town on their road, every country inn at which they put up at night, had monuments or memories . . . .

"In Dublin, the two youthful travellers found a capital discrowned, dispirited, and despoiled of the wealth and industries created and fostered by the brief and brilliant period of national self-government. The stately edifices erected before the Union — the Parliament House, the Four Courts, the Post Office, and Custom House still displayed to the eye of the citizens or visitors their classic fronts, pediments, and colonnades; but they were all, the Hall of Justice excepted, as lonely and silent as the grave. The busy commercial thoroughfares, Westmoreland Street, Grafton Street, Dame Street, etc., were no longer thronged with customers; and many of their shops were closed. The houses of the nobility and gentry were untenanted, many of them "for sale" or "to be let''. The proprietors had migrated to London with the Irish Parliament .

"And so, in mid-September, 1807, the two brothers took their way from Dublin to Maynooth. The rich level country along which they rode was then thickly populated. The frequent villages through which they passed; and the well-cultivated fields stretching out on every side, gave evidence of the care of the landlords and the husbandry of farmers and laborers . .

"But here they are at Maynooth. The townsfolk, as the two horsemen pass up the main street, look with friendly eye at the manly youths, noble specimens of the budding manhood of Tirawley; and many a 'welcome', and 'God bless them', are uttered by women old and young, and by men, too, ere the travellers reach the massive, ivy-mantled keep of the Geraldines, which towers aloft near the gate of the College. By and by John Mac Hale will have leisure to learn the history of the Geraldines' ruined castle. Now his heart beats more quickly, as he alights at the porter's lodge . . . ."

A good deal less fulsome yet respectful passage about Maynooth students in 1813 appeared in 1815 in A. Atkinson's *The Irish Tourist*. It too is worth giving at length not only because of its coverage of the students but because what it relates took place during their journey home on vacation from Maynooth:

"Before the accomplishment of my business in this city, as usual, I fell sick — sick in body and sick in mind, through the fatigue and disappointments necessarily connected with the duties of this wandering life, which in point of embarrassment, yields only to the still more anxious cares of a large family. I was, however, in some degree compensated for those embarrassments, by the conversation and patronage of several persons of distinction; and by the pleasure I derived from a new kind of society, which, during the summer vacation of 1813, I found at my hotel in Dublin. This new addition to the ordinary company of the house, consisted of several students from the College of Maynooth, who had taken advantage of summer vacation to visit the city, in their progress to the north of Ireland. I requested one of those gentlemen, (who with the zeal of an apostle had just before laid down his knife and fork at table to dispute with me about Eucharist,) to accept of my book which treats on principles, and studiously avoiding the investigation of mysteries, recommended to the attention of these young men, as I had opportunity, that philanthropy of the gospel which forms a most glorious feature in the character of a christian minister, and the necessity of education in this country, in order to prepare the public mind for the attainment of so inestimable a gift. Without any solicitude on my part to express my opinions, I was, during our joint residence at this inn, several times drawn into those conversations, which cost me dear by the treatment which I afterwards received at that house; . . . .

"With regard to those students, into whose company I was thus accidentally thrown, nothing could be more correct than their whole behaviour; and save that one of them endeavoured to defend the cruelties of those sanctimonious murderers, who on the ground of political necessity, had burned or otherwise destroyed heretics in popish countries, appeared disposed to cultivate the sentiments of philanthropy.

"The discipline of Maynooth College, as stated to me by one of these young men, I thought highly exemplary. The appointment of each student, in his turn, to read to the remainder (who are bound to abstain from all conversation) during meals, is a regulation of that college, so evidently calculated to improve time, to seal instruction upon the minds of youth, and to establish them in habits of reflection and self-government, as, in our judgment to recommend itself to the esteem of mankind; and in the same spirit of justice with which we censure the abuses of the romish religion, we hold up this law of the College of Maynooth to public view, as a deserving object of imitation to all Protestant seminaries".

EVERYDAY PROBLEMS

It had taken Maynooth quite some time after the '98 and Emmett rebellions to achieve the kind of life described by Atkinson. The area around was very upset for years. In 1801, between the rebellions, at a court in Leixlip in May two men swore that as they were going to the fair at Maynooth they had been held up by two highwaymen, armed with a blunderbuss and a pistol, and robbed. Such disorder was bound to make itself felt in the College and we have seen how disturbed the place was. In 1801 Eugene Conwell, still a student then, complains that a person who owed him seven guineas only gave him half a guinea. At least his silver spoon does not appear to have been stolen as happened to another student. Among *Major Sirr's Papers* in Trinity College is to be found a typically Georgian account of this theft which took place in November, 1801. Sirr was the much unloved Chief of Police that had been responsible during the years immediately preceding for great harassment of the people by the security forces. The incident referred to here is all the more fascinating because of involvement in it on the part of Matthew West, the outstanding silversmith of Georgian Dublin. The paper reads:

"The Information of Matthew West of the City of Dublin, Jeweller, who having duly sworn and examined saith that on Saturday the seventeenth inst. about the hour of Eleven or Twelve o'clock a man who calls himself Hugh Lynn came to Inft's shop in Shannon Bow and offered for Sale one silver Table Spoon, which was broken. Inft. saith that he asked said Lynn if he had the other part of the spoon which was broken off, who answered he had not. Inft. suspecting Lynn searched him and found in his coat pocket one Table Spoon and the upper part of the handle of the spoon he gave for sale and Inft. has reason to believe that said Hugh Lynn feloniously stole said spoons from the College of Manooth (sic.) or knew of their being stolen as by the Motto on said spoons they appear to be the property of said College and Inft. is further induced to believe that the said Lynn either stole the said spoons or recd. them knowing them to be stolen from his prevarication and denying he had the other part broken in his possession — Sworn before me this 17 Nov. 1801, Henry Sirr, Matt. West''.

West brought trouble on himself, as he was bound to prosecute under penalty of £50. In the early 1970's two halves of an old silver spoon were discovered thrown away in some College cupboard. Their date could no doubt have been established from the hall marks although that was not then done. But it could scarcely have been within the bounds of credibility that these constituted the stolen broken spoon! It is curious that a report on the sale of the Major's books some years later lists 'A History of Maynooth College' amongst them. What this was one cannot now even surmise. In spite of hazards, silver objects were common at the time on the part of the well-to-do. On ''December ye 28th'', 1810, the Reverend James Duffy at Maynooth received word from one Alex McDonnell that he was sending him on ''a silver box inlaid with gold'', which he had bought for Duffy's uncle on his way home through Portugal. One wonders did it come through safely so treacherous were the times.

Health problems plagued the College as well. in June, 1802, Conwell complains of toothache, proceeding from Rheumatism, according to Drs. Purcell and Burke who attend the College and who have recommended him ''the use of Salt water early in Summer''. Not that a dental service was likely to have been lacking, for around this same time a printed leaflet was circulated in the College headed: 'To the Gentlemen of Maynooth College' and proclaiming:

''It is some years since I was introduced to the Gentlemen of this College by the Right Rev, Bishop Cruise. Should there be any of these Gentlemen remaining, they may remember that I was of great use to those who employed me, by the prevention and Cure of all Diseases arising from the Teeth and Gums. I have since made many valuable Discoveries, which I wish to be permitted the honor of delivering in a Lecture, and which will be found to be of the highest importance. During this visit I will cleanse and settle Teeth and Gums, on very moderate terms — I remain, Gentlemen, Your very humble Servant, Edward Brehan, etc., etc.''.

Still, general facilities were not great. We learn that during William Crolly's student days, a bath was something ''ordered by the doctor'' as far as the students were concerned. And the doctor's orders were not always respected by the authorities. When the physician arraigned the President (Dr. Dunn) before the Trustees on the charge of causing two students to die without medical assistance, he is supposed to have said ''I hold my place from the Lord Lieutenant and you cannot bring me to account''. Cox had it that the reason for the tragedy was because ''an apothecary's boy'' had been recommended to Dr. Dunn by Surgeon

150

Rooney and given the title of "Doctor". The veracity of this, strange though that may be, is borne out by a letter of J. Murray M.D. of Dublin to the Bishop of Meath in May, 1810, in which the doctor says that he has just spent a few days in the College with his friend the Vice-President "Dr. Power" (he actually calls him 'President'). The ills of the students kept him busy. He hopes for the resignation of Dr. Egan, to be replaced — one accepts naturally — by himself. Egan, he remarks, only visited once a month, the sick being in the charge of a "young apothecary". Apparently Cox's information was not always off the mark. Crolly recalls that there was no place to see visitors except on the public walks or in ones bedroom, and that, as regards refreshments, "the College generously provides . . . . cold water and nothing else".

This was the College into which young McHale entered in 1807. Yet his later nineteenth century biography was able to enthuse about it after the fashion of its time. The superiors in the College, it says, knew only too well "that the longer and more serious the strain on the mental faculties required by the daily and weekly toil of the students, the more these needed occasional relaxation".

Hence they allowed them on pleasant walks around Maynooth, a sentence beside which a student of later days wrote 'Hum' on the margin of the copy in the College library. At Summer vacation time, the biography continues, the young McHale, even though longing for the mountains of Tirawly, was often more attracted by the said library than holidays at home, on which the student comments 'Great Scott' while another adds three exclamation marks. The spirit of McHale was shown during his very early years in the College when he confounded the loyal French Professors, who had set up in a flower plot an ornamental post commemorating the King, by erecting a similar one nearby dedicated to St. Patrick.

On 26 November, 1809, the much respected professor, Edward Ferris, Vincentian priest, died. He had once been First Assistant to the Superior General of the Lazarists in France as well as Superior of the Seminary at Toul and Vicar General of the Diocese of Amiens. What a time! He was beloved of the students. Even *Cox's Magazine* honoured him by carrying as frontispiece for its edition of the previous May a fine engraved likeness: a few numbers of Cox were entitled *The Irish Catholic Magazine and Monthly asylum of neglected biography,* though nobody could ever be terribly proud of it. It reminds one of certain late 20th century periodicals. To return to Fr. Ferris, his friendship with the Limerick students was to be underscored a century and a quarter later when Archdeacon John Begley, historian of the Diocese of Limerick, was to come across in Dromcollogher, where he had been Parish Priest, a letter from Fr. Ferris at Maynooth to a Limerick priest. As a document from Maynooth it provides a welcome change from so many that have been referred to up to now, for it is intensely spiritual in content. He hopes his friend is "faithful to God and to his duty, edifying all in his conduct, employing his time in study, prayer and all kinds of good works, instructing the ignorant, visiting the sick comforting the afflicted, assisting the poor for whom he will receive contributions according as his charity for them will impress this virtue in the hearts of others. The only comfort of a priest is in the internal peace of a pure and irreproachable conscience and the practical feeling of a diffusive goodness''. Archdeacon Begley sent on a copy of the letter to Father Boyle the Vicentian President of the Irish College, Paris, with the comment: ''How strange: I sending you a copy from the place where the original arrived about 114 years afterwards and where it is still preserved''. Maynooth, despite its tribulations, was sending out many good priests and also had pious men on its staff.

Learning too proceeded apace. Publications began to flow from the College. In 1809 three Dublin printers — Hugh Fitzpatrick, Peter Blenkisop and Richard Coyne were each appointed ''Printer, Bookseller and Publisher to the Royal College of St. Patrick, Maynooth''. They had their offices at No. 4 Capel Street, Irish Catholic printing having by now come out from the narrow lanes around Cook Street where it had been hidden away for so long. Fitzpatrick printed a Latin text by Delahogue, as well as Baily's Moral Theology and Menochius on the Scriptures, also Paul O'Brien's Irish Grammar and, in 1813, Darre's *The Elements of Geometry with both Plane and Spherical Trigonometry, designed for the use of Students of the R.C. College, Maynooth.* Mark Usher composed an English Grammar and Spelling Book. James Bernard Clinch was active in the field of political pamphleteering, publishing in 1810 a *Speech at the General Meeting of Catholics of Ireland,* whatever that was. The writers had at all times to be careful, for 'Big Brother', in the shape of Government, was always watching. In 1813 returns were demanded by the House of Commons of the treatises in use in the College. Dr. Murray, the then President, replied about this to Wm. Gregory Esq. In Dogmatic Theology they consisted of Delahogue's tracts, *De Sacramentis,* etc., which had been named in the House earlier. In the sphere of Moral Theology, Antoine was followed as explained by Dr. Anglade ''and accommodated to the laws of these countries by occasional references to the Commentaries of Judge Blackstone. The Professor is not bound to support in every instance the opinions of the author''. Thus goes the 'Letter from the President of Maynooth College' in the *Parliamentary Publications* for 1812-13. One definitely gets the impression that in those days the Irish Bishops were adept after the manner of their 20th century counterparts in Communist-dominated Poland. With a view to satisfying the desire of the House to be acquainted fully with the Maynooth course of studies, Murray transmits another theological work published by Dr. Delahogue for the use of the College 'On the Trinity and the Incarnation', which had not been named in the House before. He could have been fairly sure that neither of these topics had any direct political implications. He did announce, however, that certain works for use in the College were in the press. These were the aforementioned *De Poenitentia* by Delahogue, Menochius's *Commentary on the Scriptures* and Baily's *Moral Theology.* The theology of Peter Dens must surely have been followed too, if not in a prescribed sense, for in 1808 a new edition of this — to the number of three thousand copies in eight volumes

— was published with the approbation of Dr. Murray.

The Government was also curious about the College Library. In 1810 the Commissioners of Public Records of Ireland were pursuing investigations on several fronts. From their report, published later, we learn that the Oath of Loyalty by the President of Maynooth was usually taken in the presence of an "Officer sworn into office by the Clerk of the Crown", together with the Lord High Treasurer, the Chief Baron and Puisne Barons of the Exchequer and the Clerk of the Crown and Hanaper in Chancery — with the possibility of others too, all high-sounding dignitaries. The Mikado wasn't in it. To the Commissioners' queries concerning the library, Dr. Dunn — then Secretary to the Trustees — replied on 6 November, 1810 in a letter to the Secretary:

"Sir — In answer to the Queries directed by the Right honourable the Commissioners on the Public Records of Ireland, I can state authentically, as Secretary to the Trustees, and Librarian of the Roman Catholic College, that there are not in the Library of the College, or in any other repository belonging thereto, any original Records, Rolls, Instruments, or Manuscript Books and Papers, containing any Acts or Proceedings by Royal, Parliamentary, Judicial, or other Public Authority; nor are there in the custody of the Trustees, or any Officer of the College, any authentic Manuscript Copies of any such original Manuscript Records, Rolls, etc.". Not that the library itself was ill-stocked. Far from it. Originally set up in 1800, it had benefitted from private purchases, donations and official acquisitions as well as enjoying virtual amalgamation with the collection of its first Librarian — Dr. Dunn — which collection was purchased in 1815. That it was expanding rapidly can be assumed from the resolution of the Trustees on 3 February 1813, "that the Librarian do with convenient speed compile a Catalogue of the Books in the Library". When, in the same year the Reverend James Hall (one asks whether he had any connection with the later Mr. and Mrs. C.S.?) brought out his *Tour through Ireland* — "particularly the Interior and Least Known Parts, containing an accurate view of the Parties, Politics and Improvements in the different provinces; with Reflections and Observations of the Union of Britain and Ireland; the practicability and advantages of a Telegraphic Communication between the two countries and Other Matters of Importance" (2 vols., London, 1813) — he was flattering in his reference to the College library: "From Balbriggan I went to see the Roman College at Maynooth, so liberally provided for by Government. The young men here have many advantages; such as learned professors, a good library, excellent food, and extensive gardens and ground wherein to amuse themselves".

He continues however:

"The great fault is, they seem too much excluded from the company of

153

Protestants. The Professors give as an excuse for this, that, at some colleges, the students have too much liberty. So they have, if what Robinson, of Cambridge, the reputable well-known author of The History of Baptism, etc., etc., in one of his tracts says, be true: that ladies of a certain description, dressed in a gown and band, like clergymen are sometimes seen arm in arm, at churches and elsewhere, with the young men of the university. Whether the nine or ten thousand pounds, which flow yearly into the college of Maynooth, through a Protestant channel, will tend to corrupt the purity of the Catholic doctrine, I shall not pretend to say. Poison the fountain, and the streams will soon become impure. It is this idea which has put the Roman Catholic bishops and clergy in Ireland on their guard, and, unfortunately, makes them adhere more closely to the most absurd dogmas of the Roman Catholics. Were the young men allowed freely to mingle with Protestants, by degrees they might see their peculiarities, and become Protestants. But the Professors, dreading the consequences of the young men mingling with Protestants, will scarcely allow them to see one at a distance''.

Not altogether on the library, to be sure, but worth reproducing. About the same time, another Englishman — John Gough — visited the country and subsequently published his *Tour in Ireland.* He, of Maynooth, says only that it is ''a great building, and well-regulated'' but that was something. Gough had come through the Phoenix Park and the Strawberry beds, afterwards so-called but then literally covered with strawberries for three miles on the right hand side, by the charming plantations of Edmundsbury and Hermitage, through Lucan and Leixlip. Hall and Gough were among the first of very many foreign visitors to 19th century Ireland who included Maynooth in their itineraries.

In the College life was quiet. The College clock had been erected in 1810 and was to survive for a long time — unfortunately not long enough; it surely could and should have been kept going even still somewhere in the College. To the period of reconstruction in the 1950's that prided itself in its College *cognoscenti,* the failure to do so cannot be pardoned. But back to the early 1800's. The years 1812 and '13 were notable mainly for the controversy surrounding the writings of 'Columbanus' — i.e., the Reverend Charles O'Conor, in a series entitled *Columbanus ad Hibernos.* The Irish Bishops were not enamoured of any of his ideas; in fact he was not personally welcome in Dublin. In July, 1812, the Archbishop of Cashel conveys to the Bishop of Limerick that Dr. O'Connor is there consulting manuscripts in Trinity College and saying Mass without having applied for faculties. In mid-November there appeared a printed Address by the Bishops to the clergy and laity warning them of the errors in the O'Connor tracts. These, said the Hierarchy, were ''fraught with misrepresentation and calumny''. Amongst other things, he had been highly critical of Maynooth. His sixth tract contained the following gem:

154

"One of the tales of the Roman breviary, which I have read in the office of this day, the 6th of November, informs me that S. Nicholas was a pious faster, even from his birth; for on Wednesdays and Fridays he abstained from his mother's milk. With a spirit of holiness, worthy the imitation of all the Students of Maynooth, he turned his little pious lips from the profane spring of maternal nourishment; and surely, how can any pious *Maynoothian* complain, if he fares on Wednesdays and Fridays, not more sumptuously than S. Nicholas?"

He criticises too how "they teach at Maynooth, that they can depose any priest, however acceptable to his flock, unless he will subscribe to any new Test Act they may think proper to impose, and, even in unqualified terms, receive the political discipline of the Council of Trent, as they receive the doctrine of the Seven Sacraments". He was indeed sailing close to the wind, questioning not only some dogmatic aspects of Trent but also some disciplinary aspects, in particular the power of the Pope. The riposte of the Bishops infuriated him. To what he called the 'Barrister Theologues' he hurled: "Go — in virtue of the drowsy title of your Maynooth Diplomas, and take your seats, soporiferously dull, amongst the clean or the unclean beasts of the Ark of Noah!" The Trustees, as usual, were not flurried. A triennial visitation was held in June, 1813, and nothing remiss discovered. The Judges were there, together with Drs. O'Reilly and Troy. The minute in the *Records* says that the Chancellor "expressed in flattering terms his satisfaction at the prosperous and orderly state which this silence so loudly proclaimed". As was to happen again long afterwards, a period of great unrest in the College was to be followed by a period of calm.

In November, 1813, Dr. Murray resigned the Presidency, to be followed by Dr. Bartholemew Crotty of Cloyne, formerly of the Irish Seminary at Lisbon. In view of this it is intriguing to find a letter from Dr. Bray of Cashel to Dr. Crotty in Lisbon in 1802, regretfully replying to the latter's request for funds for the Lisbon College because of the fact that the Government has decided to grant large sums to Maynooth and would not favour the idea of subscriptions being sent to "a foreign establishment". Now Crotty was President of Maynooth. Whitford, the then Lord Lieutenant, approved and the President took the oath. The following Saturday, at the beginning of March, 1814, he was formally installed. Back again too was an old figure, the Reverend Wm. Fitzpatrick, Curate at St. Michan's, Dublin and former Dean, this time to succeed Fr. Peter Kenny who had departed to take over Clongowes which had just been acquired by the Jesuits. We are told that when this was done, Peel, then Secretary for Ireland, sent for Kenny and threatened that the property could be confiscated by the Government, to which Kenny is said to have replied that it could but should not, and instead invited him to send his son to Clongowes for a sound education. Great stuff this. At Maynooth the erection of new buildings was approved. The R.C. Church in Ireland was certainly on the march. The years 1814 and '15 saw little of particular importance. Eighteen fourteen began with heavy snow in Dublin and the surrounding districts. There were letters to the papers on how to remove it, reminiscent of those in Chicago papers in early 1979.

Cox continued to flourish! During 1814 it carried quite an absorbing article 'Observations made on a Tour from Dublin to Lucan', which gives a glimpse of what at least part of the journey from the capital to the College was like then. It began with the "profaneness and debauchery of Barrack-street", at 10 o'clock in the morning, amid a multitude of "strumpets" and young recruits, drunk and using profane language. The traveller was struck at by one of the soldiers, who stumbled and was run down by the mail coach. Having got to the Park Gate he crossed himself and returned thanks to God and his guardian angel. They then passed the "great artillery barrack at Islandbridge" with its roll of the drum, piercing fife and grating trumpet, together with the passing and repassing of soldiers. On to Chapelizod, which has falled on evil days as its former trade is now a thing of the past: "at present its inhabitants are a few naked peasants" and clerks attached to the military and the "Pike Office"— for manufacturing, buying and discovering pikes. Keeping the Liffey on the left, our travellers then "passed the ruins of several printing yards and woollen factories, which had very recently flourished" but had fallen victim to the English monopoly. Descending Knockmaroon hill, he entered the road to Lucan "which for beauty and rural scenery is not surpassed by anything of the kind in the world" — with neat cottages and the like. Then on by the Spa, much used in Summer, with a fine hotel attached to it. Eventually to Lucan, where the new bridge had just been completed.

He did not continue on to Maynooth. But during the same year the *Magazine* carried another article which sought a classical education for all in the College. Addressed 'To the Trustees of Maynooth' and signed 'M — ' (probably a staff member, student or ex-student as almost always):

"I must beg leave to disavow every idea of lessening the credit of Maynooth, I speak not to vilify but to exalt, not to enforce but to improve; I am fully confident that no house encloses more genuine and sterling talent than St. Patrick's walls, making such restrictions as must necessarily occur in giving the general character of a large community, and in proof hereof I challenge any place of education to produce students more ably versed in logic, theology and metaphysics, or more persevering in the drudgery of dry, and, sometimes, useless study. This declaration, if proceeding from myself, I might suspect to be the offspring of prejudice or partiality; but it falls far short of the flattering compliment publicly paid by a French professor in that house, who though marked for his jealous antipathy to the Irish character, and enthusiastic attachment to the Gallic honour, confessed that none of his compatriots could compare with them in point of exertion and perseverance, and none exceed them in point of talents . . . . I shall not at present interfere with the contrast commonly drawn between Maynoothians and Continent priests, highly flattering, I must confess, to the latter gentlemen; from the plumes of the Continental Doctors, I would not willingly pluck a feather . . . . I would surely be silent, on reflecting that to a Continental education we are indebted for the transcendent merit which renders your Lordships enviable in the eyes, even, of our most inveterate foes".

It was at this time that John McHale, now a sub-deacon, was appointed Junior Lecturer to Dr. Delahogue in the Chair of Dogmatic Theology for one year. He was proposed by Delahogue who intended him as his successor. McHale's biographer, O'Reilly, paints the picture. By the way, the *Journal of the Trustees* speaks of a "Rev. M. McCale". In 1816 he had come to be referred to as "Rev. John McKeal". It was some time before "The Lion of the West". But to O'Reilly:

"Dr. De la Hogue had made it a custom, long before 1814, when age and ill health had begun to tell seriously upon him, to call around him some twice a week the principal professors in the establishment, and to discuss with them — especially on the most controverted points — the most powerful arguments brought forward in establishing or defending the revealed doctrines, as well as the most formidable objections put forth against them by the enemies of religion. This method of thorough discussion, even on the subjects most successfully assailed at that day by secular science, was admirably adapted to form young professors, as it was to give to the oldest doctors greater precision, skill, and power in exposition and refutation.

"Although Doctor MacHale was only appointed lecturer on theology, and not professor, while Dr. de la Hogue still had that office and title, — the latter, knowing the young man's uncommon abilities, and wishing to form him thoroughly, made him at once a member of their Theological Club or Circle.

"Every one of the members made it his duty to read and master the opinions and arguments of some of the great lights of theological science on the dogmas which were soon to be taught in the Class of Theology; of these, the names of St. Thomas Aquinas, Duns Scotus, SS. Bonaventure and Anselm, Suarez, Vasquez, Benedict XIV., Cardinals de Lugo and Bellarmine — to omit some other great men — are familar to scholars. While among these, and among the Fathers of the Church, such as St. Augustine and St. Irenaeus, — there is perfect unanimity on all matters of revealed or defined doctrine, there is a great diversity with regard to the method of scientific exposition or defence. Men like those who, about 1814, read up the works of theologians and Fathers, and reduced to the briefest and most lucid form their arguments on each subject, rendered each other, and the young men they were training, a service beyond all price.

"Such intellectual discipline as this gave Dr. Mac Hale's mind not only uncommon precision and vigor, but that confidence in one's own knowledge which can alone be derived from the scientific analysis of sacred truths, and the clear perception of what is divinely revealed, what defined by the Church, and what is still left open to free discussion . . . ."

To Dr. McHale is attributed the following advice concerning students:

"The relative superiority of speaking or writing is a subject of grave and serious controversy, which has a long time divided the learned world, and which I feel as unwilling as I am incompetent to decide. To avoid, therefore, any undue partiality for either excellence, I endeavour, in my estimate of merit, to blend both these qualities, unwilling to depress the talents of oratory or composition, but manifesting a preference when the readiness and profusion of the one would be seconded by the precision and accuracy of the other.

"I feel all the difficulties of adjusting the nice shades of discrimination between such a vast number of persons, a task in which no one can plead exemption from error . . . . I register my judgement before the name is disclosed, a judgement which afterwards remains undisturbed through favor or affection. Nor shall I, I trust, ever imitate those whose first unbiased judgment of an unknown writer would be found with the fluency of mercury to rise or fall in obedience to the warmth or the coldness of their feelings . . . .

"Were I, abstracting from my duty as professor, to give my opinion of the gentlemen of the class in any other relation, I have no hesitation in saying that there are some in the class whose virtues and literary acquirements will confer as much lustre on religion, and perhaps more, than those who are most highly distinguished.

"The Church is not confined to one species of excellence; and, as the Apostle well remarks, there are but few who excel in a variety of attainments. Hence a diversity of natural and divine graces, springing from one common origin, which imparts to one the word of wisdom, to another the word of knowledge, to a third the grace of healing, to another the discerning of spirits, to another divers kinds of tongues . . . . Of all which gifts it is as doubtful which is the most excellent, as of the organs of the human frame which is the most perfect.

"Let those, then, who may be disappointed console themselves with the approbation of Him whose vigilance never slumbers, and whose judgment never strays, inviting us to a competition into which the spirit of jealousy never enters; holding out a reward for which all may strive, and which all may acquire." . . . .

"I could talk to you a great deal and dispense a variety of formal admonitions on the dangers which you are to meet, and on the prudence with which you are to avoid them. But, with a saint who was asked by another to give him some lessons on the great affair of salvation, I answer, 'Be in earnest'.

" . . . . It is thus with you; be in earnest about the magnificent designs of benefiting your country and your Church by your labours, and you will infallibly succeed.

"If, then, there be any one that requires incessant vigilance to guard him against wrong, let him not enter into the Church, since even the eyes of Argos could not follow him everywhere.

"Nay, if there be any whose dispositions are not mischievous, but of that passive kind, requiring to be roused by incessant admonitions, let him not enter. No outward action could sustain his languid career against the *vis inertiae* of his own indolence.

"You must not only possess that singleness of eye, which will direct you in the right way, but also the strong and ardent spirit of zeal; that *vivida vis animi* ('that intense energy of soul'), which moves the living body, which no obstacle can hold back, and no exertion can tire . . . . borne along by the force of its own velocity, and kindling, as it moves, by the vehemence of its own action."

What wonderful sentiments! That the students did not quite come up to them may be discerned from the fact that in 1815 the Trustees found it necessary to order that all meetings "for literary or any other purposes . . . . should be discontinued". The following year the students defied this and the President was directed to take action against the offenders. But in 1815 other matters also claimed the attention of the hard-pressed Trustees. At their January meeting they "ordered" as against "resolved",

> "that the President be allowed to keep two horses at the expense of the College according to the following allowance: to each horse fifteen pounds of Hay per diem and one barrell (sic.) of oats per month, with the necessary quantity of straw, the same treatment for one horse is allowed to the Procurator and for the two horses employed in the general work of the College, twenty pounds of Hay per day and one barrell and a half per month is allowed to each. No grass is allowed to any of the above".

It does not say what the horses thought of the package deal. Most likely they consulted their union. That same year the Lower Corridor in the front of the College, later to be called Long Corridor, was ordered to be repaired and arches erected under it and a goodly sum also expended on the purchase of "a Physical apparatus", not a bad idea in the year before Nicholas Callan came up to College. Meanwhile the College basked in the reflected glory of one of its former professors, John Chetwode Eustace, who had left it long before and whose *A Tour through Italy, exhibiting a View of its Scenery, its Antiquities, and its Monuments, particularly as they are objects of Classical Interest and Elucidation* had been published in 1813, in its first volume. *The Quarterly Review* had raved about it: "It is gratifying to us to meet with a traveller, who has directed his attention to subject more important than dirty inns, sandy roads and surly postillions". On the Friday of 17 February, 1815, the evening *Freeman,* in its section on 'Literature, Arts, Sciences', announced that "Mr. Eustace is in Italy collecting materials for a third volume of his Tour". Alas, before the year was out, he was dead, carried away by fever in Naples. Sickness was not the only danger which travellers in those days had to brave. In 1816, a future rather than past Maynooth professor, the Reverend Nicholas Slevin, wrote from Brindisi to Michael McCormick at Naples, relating that he had been assaulted on his journey thither by robbers who "threatened me hard, but finding I had really nothing, let me pass without stripping me of anything else than a few carlins, 2 shirts and some handkerchiefs".

Life in the College at the time is well covered by Crolly's life of Crolly. It concerns, however, that of the staff more than that of the students and its highly personal approach can be seen for itself:

> "It is quite a mistake to imagine, that a college life either is or that it ought to be dull, insipid, and sombre. It is a retired, a studious, and

160

laborious life — a life in which our books are our most constant and cherished companions.

"But for this very reason, those who lead such a life should be gay and cheerful when they meet together. It is related that one of the saints replied to a person who found fault with him for joining in childlike amusements, that he relaxed his mind by those innocent sports, in order that he might be able afterwards to give it entirely, and without distraction, to God. It is for the same reason that the professor gives up his mind to innocent mirth in his moments of relaxation — that, being refreshed and invigorated, he may resume with more success the studies which he had for a brief space interrupted. Many persons would as soon think of spending their life in gaol, as of immuring themselves within the walls of a college; and yet, I question whether, unless in some similar place, so many youthful hearts could be found under gray heads. I, of course, speak of Catholic colleges; for the man who has a family in the next street, does not lead a college life at all.

"With this brief introduction, by way of apology, I shall relate a few anecdotes which have reference to the period which Dr. Crolly spent in Maynooth, and which all regard either himself or his most intimate friends, although I am sensible that they lose their chief charm when deprived of his inimitable way of telling them.

"(As well as Dr. Delahogue) The Abbe Darre, Professor of Mathematics and Natural Philosophy, was also a Frenchman. They were both accomplished gentlemen, and, I believe, members of noble French families; Abbe Darre was very much addicted to boasting about his feats of horsemanship when he was a young man, and he insinuated that he could still perform prodigies when mounted on that noble animal. He gloried, perhaps, more openly in this accomplishment because his two inseparable companions, Drs. Delahogue and Anglade, were notoriously very shy horsemen. As an instance of the latter gentleman's ideas of equestrianism, I may mention, that Dr. Denvir, the present Bishop of Down, having selected a horse for him at Dycer's in Dublin, he went to that establishment to see the animal, before the purchase should be finally concluded. The groom took the horse out of the stable, mounted him, and, by way of recommending him to the purchaser, galloped to a five-feet bar, which he cleared in gallant style. 'Be certain', said Dr. Anglade, 'but that does disqualify him for me'. In vain he was assured that the horse was very quiet and gentle, and that he would not leap unless he was urged by his rider. To every fresh remonstrance the old gentleman returned the same answer 'Be certain that he is disqualified for me'. Abbe Darré was, of course, quite safe in boasting of his equestrian feats before those gentlemen, who were sure never to put it to the test; and nothing could induce him to go out with the other professors, who would, he knew, by some means or other, contrive to bring him into a scrape. But at last he was caught. A new horse had been purchased for him at, I think, Ballinasloe fair; and he urged his two companions in vain to accompany him for a short distance across the country, to witness the performance of his new steed. Some of the juniors, however, persuaded Dr. Delahogue to go out with him to the Duke of Leinster's demesne, and, when there, to ask him to cross a tolerably large ditch, just that he might observe the action of the horse. No one dared to follow them, lest he might be discovered, and thus spoil the whole sport; but their return was watched with great anxiety. To the astonishment of every one, they did not appear even at the hour for dinner; but just as the cloth was about to be removed, Dr. Delahogue entered the parlour. Every one asked where was Abbe Darre, and what had detained them. He stood a moment, looked round the table, and then pronounced these words with the utmost gravity: 'There was separation'. The truth is, the poor Abbe was thrown into the ditch, and was obliged to get himself scraped, before he could venture home through the town. From that day to this, if any gentleman connected with the College of Maynooth, happens to part company with his horse in a sudden and unpleasant manner, it is never said that he fell, or was thrown, but simply that there was separation . . .

"One of Dr. Crolly's earliest and most attached friends, was the late President of Maynooth College, the Very Rev. Dr. Montague, who held the office of bursar whilst the late Primate was a student and professor in that establishment. Like Dr. Crolly, he was a good horseman, and fond of riding, but could never be induced to venture into the fields. Once, however, he had occasion to visit a farm which was eight or ten miles from college; and Dr. Crolly, whom he had requested to accompany him, induced him to proceed by a near way across the fields, assuring

him, as he firmly believed at the time, that there was no impediment in the way. When they had proceeded about three miles, they came to a small stream, with pretty high banks, which it was absolutely necessary for them to cross. Dr. Crolly immediately leaped over; but Dr. Montague, instead of following him, declared that he would go back. The former then returned, and asked the latter to dismount, and he would lead his horse over.

This being agreed upon, he took Dr. Montague's horse by the bridle, and, taking a long sweep, came to the stream at full gallop. But the led horse being totally untrained, planted his forefeet firmly on the bank; and when Dr. Crolly got over, he found that he had taken nothing with him but the bridle. The horse, finding himself at liberty, galloped back to the college; and Dr. Montague, after easing his mind a little, by declaring that no one ever would have luck who kept Dr. Crolly's company, was obliged to return on foot, and to submit ever afterwards to the accusation of having got separation.

"Shortly before Dr. Crolly left Maynooth, a gentleman connected with the establishment became deranged in his mind. The chief delusion under which he laboured was that he was dead. One morning, before any person was aware of the matter, he went into Dr. Crolly's rooms, and complained bitterly that he had neither gone to his funeral, nor employed any person to bury him. 'Why', said Dr. Crolly, 'the fact is I would have gone to your funeral, but Father Paul would not come with me; and I think you have far greater reason to complain of him than of me'.

"He immediately went to Father Paul's apartments, and asked that gentleman, whom he found in bed, what objection he had to attend his funeral. Father Paul declared he had no objection whatever; and that he had not heard of his death, or he would certainly have been present at his interment.

" 'Oh! you need not tell me such a story,' said his visitor; 'for I know that you not only staid away yourself, but prevented Mr. Crolly from coming'. 'Anyhow', he continued, 'I will be buried here, and nowhere else; and you must write an epitaph, and put it over me'.

163

"He then lay down under the hearth-rug. Father Paul had by this time hastily dressed himself, and began to think in what manner he could get rid of his unwelcome visitor. Being commanded to prepare the epitaph, he took a sheet of paper, and wrote upon it the following distich:—

> 'Your scraggedy snout shall snuff the moon;
> Why, d—————— your eyes, did you die so soon?'

'I'll not lie under that epitaph', cried the dead man.

'You must,' answered Father Paul.

'I'll not,' said he, starting up, and rushing out of the room.

"Whilst Dr. Crolly was a professor in Maynooth, a student from his native diocese, whose name was Dan M'Mullan, entered Maynooth. As frequently happened in these times, he was ordained before he came to college. It is not often that persons succeed, especially in literary pursuits, who have not been trained to them from their youth. Mr. M'Mullan was, in one department, an exception to this rule. Whilst still a student, he had become so famous a preacher in Dublin and its vicinity — a kind of fame, by the way, which does not always require great learning — as to excite the jealousy of Father Barnaby Murphy, who, having published a book of sermons, thought that it was intolerable assurance for a student to preach at all in the city which was honoured by his eloquence. Dr. Crolly, who was, on the contrary, a steady patron of Mr. M'Mullan's, took care to procure for him abundant opportunities for the development of his oratorical powers. He also introduced Mr. M'Mullan to his friends; and as he was a delightful singer, his society was greatly sought after.

"The late Primate sometimes took him to dine with some of his Dublin acquaintances, and on one of these occasions they met Father Barnaby, whom they knew by character to be sometimes very unceremonious in his manners, but they were entirely ignorant of his particular antipathy to Mr. M'Mullan. Very soon after dinner, he flatly contradicted something which the latter gentleman had asserted. Mr. M'Mullan ventured to sustain his opinion, probably without what Father Barnaby considered becoming deference to so great a man; whereupon he became wrathful, and told Mr. M'Mullan, amongst other things, that he should not be allowed to preach without knowing his theology. The latter attempted to propitiate him, by saying that he had studied a little theology, and that he might get a good printed sermon by heart without any risk of heresy. All this had no effect; for Father Barnaby replied, in Johnsonian style, 'No sir, you may not, for you might mistake the substance of the sermon.' 'Indeed,' replied Mr. M'Mullan, 'you are quite right; and lest I might make any mistake of the kind you mention, I shall confine myself, for the future, to the sermons published by the Rev. Barnaby Murphy; and as there is no substance in any of them, I cannot possibly mistake it.' "Dr Crolly himself was not always secure against Mr. M'Mullan's sly witticisms. I have mention that the latter was a most enchanting singer — a gift which nature did not bestow on the late Primate. They frequently dined at Castle Baggot, where Mr. M'Mullan delighted the company with his sweet songs. He made it a point invariably to call upon Dr. Crolly as soon as he had finished himself, assuring the company at the same time that he was a delightful singer. The latter was so much pressed, in consequence of these repeated calls, that he resolved to give one specimen, to prove, he said, the truth of his own assertion that he could not sing; still he seemed determined to do his best, for he put himself under Mr. M'Mullan's tuition, from whom he learned the famous old ditty, 'Cruiskeen Laun.' They agreed that when they next went to Castle Baggot, Mr. M'Mullan should sing first, and Dr. Crolly afterwards. After dinner, Mr. M'Mullan was, as usual, called upon for a song, but he positively 'declared that he would not sing unless Dr. Crolly promised to sing after him. The latter readily gave the required pledge, and the former immediately sung, in his rich and melodious voice, 'Cruiskeen Laun'. When he had finished he called upon Dr. Crolly to redeem his promise, and told the company that they would now, at length, get a specimen of his powers. Of course he could not attempt to spoil a song which had just been sung so delightfully, nor had he any means of getting out of the difficulty except by candidly telling the whole story. 'Cruiskeen Laun,' however, continued to be his only song during his entire life, and he sung it, on some rare occasions, amongst his clergy after he became bishop, and even after he became Primate. The last time was, I think, in the College of Maynooth, about four years ago, in the course of a very happy evening which he spent with the professors. I have mentioned these anecdotes not merely as bearing on the personal history of Dr. Crolly, but also as a specimen of those little pleasantries which diversify the monotony of a college life . . . ."

The aforesaid Mr. M'Mullan was an able dealer. Although how it got there is a mystery (possibly the recipient wanted his identity established or acceded to his request) there is a letter of 1811 in the *Dublin Diocesan Archives* from him to a Mrs. Talbot, at Baily's College Green. He explains that, although he is ordained, he has to make up some studies and is staying at the Lay College, Maynooth, as priest students are not allowed to stay in the ecclesiastical side of the College. He has that there is a vacancy at the College and the residence rule would not apply to this. He asks her to approach the Archbishop of Dublin on his behalf.

So College life was not all that bad compared to life outside! Yet death too showed itself. In May, 1817, a new College cemetery was opened and on 5 June received the mortal remains of the Reverend Francis Power, first Vice-President and first occupant of the burial ground — *"huius Coemeterii Hospes Primus"*. The year 1817 also saw the death of the 'Lay College'.

THE 'LAY COLLEGE'

Whether one should speak of the death or the murder of the Lay College is impossible to say. The *Report of the Commissioners of Irish Education Enquiry,* 1826, said that it had become "apparent that the different system of education which is deemed necessary for those who are to undertake the duties and obligations of the priesthood, and the additional restraints to which they are subjected, rendered the lay college an inconvenient appendage. It was discontinued in the year 1817, and the buildings and land, which had been appropriated to it, were applied to the use of the clerical students". 'Discontinued' is a vague term. What is certain is that a meeting of the Board of Trustees that year "finished the purchase of the Lay College".

The same had had a good innings, from the time of its reconstitution in 1801 under new Trustees and a new President, Rev. Mr. Long. In 1804 its Trustees were Lords Jenico and Gormanstown, Most Rev. Drs. Troy, O'Reilly, Bray, Dillon and Plunkett, John O'Shea Esq. and David Henchey Esq. In 1805 a notice stated that its "plan of education comprises the Latin, Greek, French and English Languages; History, both Sacred and Profane; Geography, Arithmetic, Book-keeping and Mathematics". The Prospectus for that year was comprehensive:

> "Young Gentlemen are admitted from the age of ten to fifteen years; each to provide two pairs of sheets, two pillow cases, six towels, a knife, fork, and silver spoon, which he is at liberty to take away on his departure from the College. The holy day dress is uniform and consists of a coat of superfine blue cloth, with yellow buttons; waistcoat, buff. Terms — Ten Guineas on admission of which Five will be returned on departure, and Thirty Guineas per annum; to be paid half yearly in advance: Three Guineas washing and repairing. Students who are sufficiently advanced, and who wish to profit of the Royal College course, and continue their education through the higher classes of literature and the sciences, pay Two Guineas to the Professor whose class they attend. Music, Drawing, Dancing and Fencing are extra charges . . . . The President and Masters dine at the same table with the students. During the hours of recreation a master will constantly attend, to prevent irregularities, and enforce an exact observance of order and gentlemanly deportment".

The *repertoire* of the Lay College was such that in 1806 the Reverend Mr. Robertson, teacher therein, was also employed "for the next academical year" to instruct the scholars of the Royal College in Sacred Oratory. And, although the Lay College and the Royal College were distinct, premiums were distributed in both on the same day each year. In fact in 1806 there was a competition for prizes in *Litterae Humaniores* between the lay and clerical colleges, on which occasion Mr. Patrick Cruise (probably a relative of people in high places) stole the prize for translation from Greek from the ecclesiastical students.

The lay students were an extraordinary bunch, in the Ireland of that time. Their *provenance* was good as was their subsequent performance in general. They included such notables as the future Lords Fingall and Killeen, Sir Joseph Laffan the well-known physician and Sir Dominic Corrigan equally famous, Dr. Christopher Fleming and Christopher Boylan, Professor of Elocution in the College after Usher Judge Corballis and Stephen Woulfe, the first Catholic Chief Baron, Robert fFrench Whitehead the future Vice-President of St. Patrick's College, Richard Lalor Shiel the orator and dramatist, John Sweetman, James Blake, Arthur Plunkett, Valentine Dillon and many others of note. In view of this, what a pity the Lay College ever ceased: Maynooth must endeavour to overcome the wound. The staff of the Lay College is less known. Apart from the President, Reverend Mr. Long, it consisted in 1810 of Rev. Messrs. Lovelock and MacNicholas and Mr. Simon Lonergan (Profs. of Belles Lettres), Rev. Mr. Milet, a Frenchman (Prof. of the French Language), Mr. Cornelius McDermott (Prof. of Mathematics), Mr. John Morris (Prof. of Arithmetic — how he distinguished himself from McDermott those who are aware of the vagaries of the exponents of these estoric sciences in learned establishments will know), and Mr. Mark Usher, also of St. Patrick's College (Prof. of the English Language). In 1816, some of the students of the Lay College subscribed to the publication of his *Synonymous Terms in the English Language Explained.* In that year ten of them proceeded to Trinity after their course at Maynooth had ended. *O tempora; O mores.*

During his visit to Maynooth in June, 1807, the famous English ecclesiastic Dr. Milner was intrigued by the Lay College. On 27 June, as agent of the Catholic Bishops, he met the Trustees and on Monday,, 29th, spent the day writing letters from the College. Of the Lay College he observes that this is "for Catholic young gentlemen intended for the world". He goes on: "The Lay College has no other communication with the former except that its members frequent the same Church, and attend the same lectures in Philosophy with the ecclesiastical students". He adds how much better it is for Catholic parents to send their sons for education there where there were frequent religious exercises and a rigid discipline than to a "mixed University"!! He notes that it has been asked both outside and inside Parliament: Why a separate College? Why not send them to the universities? But he has already given the answer: 'You' want the latter to keep them liberal; 'We' want the other to keep them separate. He is led to animadvert on the former glory of Irish learning which illuminated Britain. And he also mentions that Maynooth College mourns "the loss of their landlord and friend, the late good Duke of Leinster". His remarks are contained in *An Inquiry into certain vulgar opinions concerning the Catholic Inhabitants and the Antiquities of Ireland,* published in London in 1808. His final letter from Maynooth on 30 June, 1807, relates to both the lay and clerical courses of studies:

> "I will endeavour to give you a general idea of this course. An indefinite time, perhaps two or three years, is employed in the study of English, Irish, Latin and French Grammar. After this, a distinct year is appointed for the study of poetry, and another year for that of rhetoric. At the end of each year public examinations are held, at which the literati of the neighbourhood, of whatever communion they may be, are invited to assist, and also bear a part in them. This forms what is called the course of Humanity Studies; after which begin those of a higher order. One whole year is always devoted to logic and metaphysics, upon Lock's (sic.) system; and another to mathematics, physics and astronomy, in which Newton is the chief guide. The whole of this philosophical course the student must publicly defend, not by answering a few questions well-known beforehand, but by solving the objections of each individual present amongst the company indiscriminately invited to the defensions (sic.). To the study of philosophy succeeds that of divinity, which takes up four whole years, under three distinct professors, (at least there is this number of them at Maynooth) a professor of speculative theology, a second of morality, and a third of the holy scriptures. The divines, no less than the philosophers, are required publicly to defend their several treatises".

As far as the clerical students went, Milner was really off-beam. Their normal course consisted of two years humanities and philosophy and three years divinity.

In 1807 the Lay College was completely separated from the esslesiastical. Not without reason, one fears, on reading the *Evening Herald* of 9 November of that year. Therein we are told of how a number of students from the Lay College visited the Celbridge Academy for the purpose of presenting an address to their late President, Fr. D'Arcy, who had changed over to Celbridge. The evening was rainy and they were wet when they came back so they retired to the tavern at Maynooth for punch and supper. The rest can be imagined. A Master from the Lay College came and ordered them in — before they had finished, although it had been paid for, which was not to be taken lightly; Nor did they. They returned to College but "elate, volatile and giddy" and threw down and broke various items — the President was away in Dublin. The same President, Dr. Long, seems to have been essential to the well-being of the Lay College. When, following Napoleon's first defeat, he was sent in 1814 by the Irish Hierarchy as their representative to the French Government and was made administrator of the Irish College, Paris, by Louis XVIII the following year, the Lay College at Maynooth could not but have been the poorer. In actual fact, Dr. Long was recalled by his Bishop in 1818, thereby causing grave misgivings on the part of Dr. Coppinger,

Bishop of Cloyne. He expressed "the unanimous entreaty" of the Munster Bishops that Dr. Anglade "should undertake the Presidency of the Irish College in the French metropolis assisted by some qualified subject of Maynooth". He had communicated this to the President of Maynooth Dr. Crotty — his own 'subject' — who, however, "has not condescended to favour one with a line in answer, upon this important subject". Crotty was to succeed him as Bishop of Cloyne. Returning to the Lay College, it ended, as said, in 1817 — end such as it was . . . . The Trustees of the Royal College bought its property for the sum of £1,000, through their agent Randal McDonnell. The main building, known as Riverstown Lodge, became the seat of the College Bursars. It has sometimes been called 'Tara', understandably insofar as this refers to High Kings.

QUESTIONS OF FINANCE

Financial matters were to loom large around 1807. That year the Whig Government proposed to increase the grant to Maynooth but the adversaries of the College bitterly opposed it. In a curiously entitled pamphlet *Maynooth and the Jew Bill* we are told of how Mr. Perceval prepared to speak against the measure. And so indeed he did. When, on 4 March, following the report of the Committee of Supply, it was moved that the grant be raised from £8,000 to £13,000, Mr. Perceval advocated the eight, on the grounds that Maynooth was not in the interests of Catholics at Trinity College. In reply, Sir John Newport maintained that this was irrelevant in that it was unthinkable that those intended for the Roman Catholic priesthood should be educated by Protestant professors. Grattan chimed in with the old refrain that it was better that these be educated at home than in foreign countries: "The Roman Catholic laity in Ireland amounted to three millions. Could £8,000 a year for the education of two or three hundred priests be thought too much when, for between six and seven hundred thousand Protestants, twelve hundred clergymen were allowed? Was it desirable to starve religion and learning, in order to save £5,000 a year? Had not the committee just voted to the Protestant Charter Schools £21,000? to other Protestant establishments £20,000, to the education of Protestant foundlings £20,000, to Presbyterian schools £9,000?" Lord Howick likewise supported the grant on the principle of connecting the Irish Catholic with the State. It was particularly necessary to promote the domestic education of the Catholic clergy now that an extensive institution had been founded in Paris. The £13,000 was voted without a division. The Trustees were naturally elated. Hotfoot on the announcement Troy wrote to the Prefect of Propaganda telling him that the Parliament has added £5,000 *scudi* to the annual grant of 8,000 *scudi* for Maynooth. Money is also to be expended on providing more accommodation for students and domestic staff.

But it proved difficult to keep the higher grant. With foresight, in November an extraordinary meeting of the Trustees was held for the purpose of signing a petition to the Imperial Parliament to provide £13,000 next year. They were beginning to be up against it. That year Lord Redesdale, then the Lord Chancellor of Ireland, had sent a dispatch to the Duke of Portland's Cabinet in which he made several complaints about Maynooth: The visitors have no power; no student dare complain; "No college of Jesuits was half so dangerous to any Catholic kingdom". He went on: "What may be the consequences of this institution to the peace of Ireland, it is difficult to foretell in their full extent. It is easy to perceive that it must ever be the greatest obstacle to the extension of the Protestant religion, and to the quiet settlement of the country". Cox was not at all helpful. An issue of March, 1808, gave out that the College was in receipt of funds for which it did not give a proper account — again something that was to be heard again, however wrongly. The argument at that time was that at his matriculation each student paid eight guineas but "to whom or for what purpose this money is given or expended we have not been able to ascertain". Then there were the profits from the produce of the College land, which "are not publicly accounted for". Cox also spoke about a bequest to the College from an Irish gentleman who died on the Continent. It was only to be expected, therefore, that when, on 29 April of that year, after a long debate by the Committee of Supply about the grant in the House of Commons, on a division the numbers for the larger sum were 58, those against it 93. When the House carried the matter further, the College's old friend Sir John Newport was supported by Colonel Montague Mathew who "had been within the last ten days at Maynooth, and he could assure the house, that unless the whole of last year's grant should be voted, the buildings upon which former grants had been expended would fall. There was no lead on the roofs, and the rain penetrated through them". The Duke of Wellington made a brief intervention in favour, but to no avail. The grant was curtailed. It is not only possible but likely that damage had also been done to the College by an informer. Among the *Peel Papers* in the British Museum can be found a letter of 1825 from a man called Lyon to Peel. This man was one William Lyon, a Protestant, who had served on the staff of Maynooth College as a music instructor from 1805 to 1816. Through him the Government had a good idea of the attitudes of everybody in the College. He posed as a Catholic and, having gained access to the inner sanctum as it were, reported that he had found both students and professors holding forth private feelings hostile to the Government. They regarded emancipation, so he said, as an objective secondary to separation from England. In his letter to Peel, Lyon also asserted that he had once given information to Lord Castlereagh which led to a cut in the Maynooth grant from £13,000 to £9,000. Surely this is proof enough.

The Trustees were quick to react. The Primate writing from Maynooth to an Armagh priest in late June, 1808, remarked: "Our meeting this time will be a full one. We shall have important business to do at it". They had and did. Seemingly they had recourse to powerful friends especially in the House of Lords, for on 11 July the Duke of Bedford is writing from Woburn Abbey to the Secretary of the

Trustees informing him of a Protest which has been made to that House about the reduction in the Maynooth Grant. A copy of this is enclosed. The undersigned dissented with the recent Bill:

"First, Because by the Introduction of a provision in this Bill, granting to the Rom. Cath. Seminary at Maynooth the sum of £9,250, being a reduction of £3,750 from the grant made in the last Session of Parliament, this House is thereby fettered in its judgment and precluded from the exercise of its discretion in deciding upon the propriety of such a reduction on its own exclusive merits. Secondly, because in our opinion, the policy which suggested the Establishment of the Royal College of Maynooth ought equally to operate in affording a liberal support to an Institution of such manifest advantage to the Rom. Cath. population of Ireland. Thirdly, Because we have reason to believe that the restricted sum of £9,250 is insufficient to the object of educating the number of students adequate to the exigencies of the Rom. Cath. Ministry in Ireland, the necessary and immediate consequence of which must be a recourse to foreign seminaries to supply the deficiency, and the evils likely to result from such a necessity, when almost the whole of the continent of Europe is either directly or indirectly under the control and dominion of the Enemy, cannot be too strongly guarded against. Fourthly, Because it is peculiarly incumbent upon us when the two Houses of Parliament have so recently thought fit to refuse to take into their consideration the restrictions and disabilities under which the Rom. Catholicks of Ireland unfortunately labour, to endeavour with all the means within our power to improve the condition of this numerous and loyal class of His Majesty's subjects, to excite among their lower orders an attachment to the constitution and a just regard for the Laws of the Country, to strengthen the bonds of affection and charity by which we ought all to be united, and to afford the best and most extensive means of enlightening by moral and religious instructions our Christian Brethren of the Roman Catholick Communion; all which objects may be materially obstructed by the reduction of the grant to this useful and laudible Establishment — a measure in our opinion impolitic and unwise, if it arises from a narrow spirit of economy; and which cannot be too loudly censured and condemned, if it proceeds from an intolerant feeling of bigotry. (Signed) Bedford, Vassal Holland, Rosslyn, Lauderdale, Ponsonby''.

On receipt of this, the President, at that time Dr. Dunn, replied on 19 July, apologizing for his delay in writing — he has been residing for some time at Lucan Spa, near Leixlip, on account of his health — as "a state of debility produced by the confinement attendant on the duties of the President of the College has obliged me to resign the situation". But he is not short in expressing thanks on behalf of the College: "Indeed, My Lord, the Bedford Government in this country will be long remembered with gratitude by a people not devoid of sensibility, who have not always had the happiness of possessing Governors disposed to investigate their wants, or willing, or perhaps able to administer to those wants. But the hope of final success in any cause must be exalted into confidence, when it is known that in the Judgement of the wise, the good and the truly great, that cause is supported by every feeling of just regard to the genuine welfare of the nation and of the Empire". Well, it would be hard to better that. After their October meeting, the Trustees themselves sent an address of thanks to Bedford, through Dr. Dunn and the Right Hon. William Elliott: "Sir — did the publick importance of those whose names are prefixed to the enclosed address equal the sincerity with which it is offered, it would not be unworthy of your best acceptance. As a testimony of your genuine patriotism which, superior to personal or local views, looks only in publick measures to publick good, it will not, I trust, be unacceptable". On 12 October Bedford replied from Wells expressing his appreciation of the resolution: "The truly respectable names prefixed to the resolution stamp an additional value on a record so highly flattering". The Trustees did not let up. On 11 November, the Earl of Kenmare in the Chair, they again petitioned Parliament for the sum of £13,000, to make possible a larger number of students and an improved system of education. Peel made notes to the effect that Vesey Fitzgerald the Chancellor of the Exchequer — and an Irishman — favoured the request but that the Lord Lieutenant Richmond was hostile. Peel, then a young Secretary, had consulted verious members of the Cabinet. Liverpool was in favour, Vansittart evasive, Sidmouth against, Castlereagh favourable. Peel was showing an early interest in Maynooth affairs. Finally, in March, 1813, Richmond gave his Secretary freedom to decide for himself.

The original annual grant had been something under £8,000 (Irish). It had been raised to over £12,000 during the Greenville administration, then reduced to £9,673. There were separate grants for buildings. Now what was being looked for annually was in fact £700 more than the previous high point. This increase was sought to effect improvements costing £1,200. The Trustees could provide £500 from endowments but £700 was asked for from Government. Peel opted for this, advising the Lord Lieutenant that it was more politic to do so as a means of preventing trouble. "It is hardly worth while perhaps to give up office on the Maynooth grant". He was to do exactly that towards the middle of the century. The Government, however, hoped to maximize its profits from such generosity. In 1813 Grattan presented to the House of Commons a proposal for a Catholic Relief Bill allied to a Veto by the Crown over episcopal appointments. This matter had been dead duck since 1801, when Troy of Dublin had sent on to Cashel a document from the then Lord Lieutenant to the effect that insurmountable obstacles to the bringing forward of measures of concession to the Catholics had emerged and anyhow that the Ministers in favour of these had retired from His Majesty's Service. This is why the 'Veto question', to use Bishop Young's phrase, had "vanished like vapour". Now the whole thing was back again. The position of the Bishops respecting it had hardened. In 1808 a General Meeting of the Bishops respecting it had hardened. In 1808 a General Meeting of the Hierarchy had rejected the idea, including most of the original Maynooth Trustees who had once been prepared to concede it. The matter had been revised in the Commons in May of that year in the context of a debate on the restoration of their political rights to Catholics. In fact not until then had it been publicly disclosed that in 1799 the Trustees of Maynooth had intimated to Castlereagh that they would accept the measure. O'Connell was opposed to any such thing both in 1808 and 1813. At a meeting of the Catholic Board on 29 May, 1813, he vigorously rejected the arguments of Councillor Bellew that a Veto might be entertained. His speech was able but typically full of acerbity and biting invective and Maynooth got a lash of his tail. Of Bellew, he said:

"he tells us that he is council to the College of Maynooth, and, in that capacity, he seems to arrogate to himself much theological and legal knowledge. I concede the law, but I deny the divinity; neither can I admit the accuracy of the eulogism which he has pronounced on that institution, with its mongrel board of control — half papist and half Protestant. I was, indeed, at a loss to account for the strange want of talent within the college. I now see it easily explained. The incubus of jealous and rival tolerance sits upon its walls, and genius, and taste, and talent fly from the sad dormitory, where sleeps the spirit of dullness. I have heard, indeed, of their Crawleys and their converts, but where, or when, will that college produce a Magee or a Sandes, a McDonnell or a Griffin? When will the warm heart of Irish genius exhibit in Maynooth such bright examples of worth and talent as those men disclose? It is true, that the bigot may rule in Trinity College; the highest station in it may be the reward of writing an extremely bigoted and more foolish pamphlet; but still there is no conflicting principle of hostile jealousy in its rulers; and, therefore, Irish genius does not slumber there, not is it smothered as at Maynooth".

Even though Archbishop Troy wrote to O'Connell to say that he agreed with him on the Veto question against the views of Councillor Bellew, as far as Maynooth is concerned there never seems to have been any warm relationship with 'the Liberator'. On occasion he did speak in favour of the Maynooth Grant during the many debates which took place about this in the House. They are all to be found in James Lord's *Maynooth College, or the Law affecting the Grant to Maynooth, with the Nature of the Instruction there Given and the Parliamentary Debates thereon,* published in 1841 and covering the period up until then. On a few occasions he defended the College incisively, lauding the priests whom it produced as having the entire confidence of the people and assiduous in their care of the poor and the dying (5 August, 1831), contending too that it was not true that Maynooth had not produced as able men as any that had been educated abroad or that its student body was made up only of the sons of persons in humble life (31 August, 1831). But it may have suited him to have done so on those occasions. In general his support of the grant was for broad reasons relating to Catholic rights which did not involve him in specific defence of the College as such. For one who is praised so much for what he did for Catholic Ireland it is somewhat significant that he left such little impression on Maynooth College. In point of fact, towards the middle of the century when he and his son paid a formal visit there, the reception they got was quite cool. But to conclude about the Veto, on 25 May, 1814, a Synod of the Irish Bishops began at Maynooth. It lasted for three days and ended with a clear rejection of any Veto. The College staff member, layman James Bernard Clinch, who had written an enlightened pamphlet on the matter in 1808, was present, presumably on a consultative basis. He is described as "not merely . . . . learned enough to be a priest — he was sufficiently learned to be a bishop"! This is surely saying something! Always loyal, he defended the ten Bishops who had assented to the Veto at Maynooth in 1799. They had been, he said, "terrified men" and he hoped that they would shortly undo the charge that they acted for gold. At all events, now in 1814, the College had successfully maintained its grant without the Hierarchy being tempted to allow a Veto.

To be very factual, the grants to Maynooth, between the year 1810 and 1820, were anything but excessive when compared to others. The following list should prove the point:— Protestant Charter Schools, £372,106.13.0; Foundling Hospital, £318,967.7.8; Marine Nursery, £26,803.7.8; Temple Orphan House, £24,834.4.7; Association for Discounting Vice, £40,976.3.1; Kildare Place Society, £38,504.0.0; Maynooth College, £92,350.0.0.

MAINTAINING STANDARDS

One of the points which the College had to contend with in debates on the grant during these years was the accusation that its academic and disciplinary standards were neither high nor politically reliable. Sir John Cox Hippsley was a more ardent defender of the College than O'Connell. And he kept in contact with it for that purpose. Amongst the Clogher papers pertaining to Delahogue we find a communication from him to the latter in April, 1813, relating how he had countered a motion by a Mr. Ryder which had demanded that there be laid before the House a full account of the course of instruction in divinity followed at Maynooth.

"I think now it will be sufficient for your President to sign his name under the title page *of each of your three publications* and then, in a paper accompanying them, to state that those publications of the Pro-

174

fessor of Dogmatical Theology contain, in fact, the tracts, both of doctrine and discipline, taught in the College — that References may also be made to the works of Hooke, Baily, etc., etc., etc., as Ecclesiastical writers of high principles and such as will not be found to contain any principles derogating from the soundest duties of allegiance to His Majesty . . . . I shall be very much obliged to you, if, *for my own information,* you would send me the pages of your Tract *De Ecclesia,* which contain the most pointed passages to illustrate *the independence* of your Church in respect to the authority of foreign jurisdiction of a questionable nature . . . . Mr. Percival quoted the last page of your Tract *De Ecclesia* to prove that the *whole* discipline of the Council of Trent was considered *obligatory at Maynooth.* I afterwards referred him to another passage . . . . I observed also that the *discipline* of the Council of Trent had not been submitted to by the Gallican Church and that your Treatise did not comprehend the *objectionable parts of the Discipline of that Council* — much less that of the Lateran. I shall be happy to receive from you a short statement upon this subject before the next debate''.

Delahogue replied promptly. He was careful. He teaches, he says, the doctrine of the Sorbonne, which can be found more explicitly in Tournely and Collet, whom he follows. His silence on mixed matters proves nothing as regards what he teaches at Maynooth. But the matter continued to drag on. Again, in 1817, John Leslie Foster, Esq., in a Speech in the House of Commons that May, referred to the Transalpine Doctrine, which accepted the authority of the Pope in temporal matters, as one which ''has been so vigorously repelled, that as this hour there are but two spots in Europe on which it can rest its foot; and one of these spots is the Vatican and the other at Maynooth''. The witch hunt was on again. On 23 June Hippsley sent the first of three letters to Delahogue. He would much appreciate having a line from him by return letting him know whether any new class books have been adopted at Maynooth since the returns of 1813, also confirmation of the fact that Delahogue's teaching continues to be that of the Sorbonne. Referring to what Foster had said, he hoped that Delahogue has ''expelled the opinions of Bellarmine respecting the indirect power'' of the Church on the temporalities of princes. In a second letter he says that his friend Lord Fingall has ''gone over'' to a meeting at Maynooth and may be able to assist Delahogue ''in deciphering this hieroglyphick''. A third letter followed seeking clarification on a number of points as the debate is coming up soon. They are the same as had already been brought up. Delahogue replied on the 27th. The teaching is the same as in 1813 and as regards Bellarmine he refutes him not only relative to any direct but even indirect temporal power of the Pope. He is annoyed. *''Il est etonnant qu'on est avance qu'il n'y avait qu'au Vatican et a Maynooth qu'on soutient la doctrine transalpine''.* His treatise *De Ecclesia* was printed in France last year after having obtained the consent of the Government and no word has been changed either on the temporal power of rulers or on the infallibility of the Pope. Hippsley was well armed for the debate of 7 July and made good use of his equipment.

In 1817 the teaching of Scripture at Maynooth was attacked by a Fellow of Trinity College, Dublin, the Reverend Willliam Phelan, in a tract entitled *The Bible, not the Bible Society,* which was quite critical of Catholic scripture teaching in general. A Maynooth student took up the cudgels on behalf of his College — "an humble student of Maynooth . . . . an undistinguished, I must add, an inexperienced member of a community, whose obscurity has been classed with the causes that accelerate the fall of the Roman Catholic Religion in Ireland". Phelan's tract must have occasioned the kind of thing long afterwards satirized by a great poet, Patrick Kavanagh, in his 'House Party to celebrate the Destruction of the Roman Catholic Church in Ireland', written in all likelihood after the publication of another infamous tract shortly after World War II:

> "Her book was out, and did she devastate
> The Roman Catholic Church on every page!
> And in Seamus's house they met to celebrate
> With giggles high the dying monster's rage".

The student's reply, entitled *Calumny Refuted,* did its best, such as it could. Phelan must have been dismayed when a fellow Protestant, the Reverend R. J. McGhee brought out a counter tract criticizing him highly. McGhee found Phelan's views on Scripture, whether knowingly or not, as Popish as could be and quite acceptable to the Professors of Divinity of the Popish College of Maynooth, including the Reverend James Browne, Prof. of Scripture. Browne was later to become the inveterate adversary of McGhee in public controversy about scriptural matters. On this occasion it was Phelan who replied to McGhee in another round of the context — Maynooth being in the middle. The affair blew over.

The Library too came under fire. Warburton, the historian of the City of Dublin, writing in 1818, reported that the books were principally on theology and the professor of philosophy was obliged "from paucity of books" to dictate his material to his pupils. This is highly unlikely in view of the fact that Anglade's *Institutiones Philosophicae* had been published in Dublin in 1817. Warburton does agree, however, that the courses of study are extensive — those in Humanity covering Sallust, Virgil, Horace, Lucian and Xenophon; those in Belles Lettres covering the Acts of the Apostles, Cicero and Pliny; those in Philosophy, Locke, in Theology, Bailly, Collet and Tournely. Perhaps more importantly, "prayers are offered on Sundays and holidays for the King in prescribed form". As far as the library went, it was, whether Warburton was aware of it or not, in the process of becoming a rich repository, including quite a number of *incunabula.* There was Sir Joshua Reynolds's gift to Richard Burke, which had been presented by his father, also a large Atlas rescued from the Great Fire of Moscow — how that got there is a mystery — a Sarum Missal with the word 'Pope' and the feast of St. Thomas of Canterbury deleted from the calendar, an edition of St. Augustine which was the first book from the press of Anton Sorg of Augsburg in 1475, one of Appian from Venice in 1477, an Index to the works of St. Thomas Aquinas (1497) with one of the earliest woodcuts of the great Doctor lecturing to seventeen rather elderly students — and "the great typographical achievement of the 16th century", i.e., the *Polyglot Bible* printed at Antwerp between 1568 and 1573. Whether all these were in the College Library in Warburton's time one cannot be sure but some certainly were. They were not, of course, student textbooks. But these were not likely to have been in short supply. There are continued references to the cost of them: that of Menochius in 1819 was thirty shillings! The College had published a large quantity of it with a nice engraving of the house on the fly-leaf. Perhaps it was because of this that the Trustees passed a resolution on 3 March of that year compelling students to buy the classbooks printed by the College. The College could not afford to lose on them. A resolution of 4 March says that "as the principal article of expenditure is the subsistence of the Masters and Scholars, the Bursar is advised to use all possible economy in the Parlour and Refectory". In fact a couple of years later the Trustees were so desperate financially as to order that "henceforth no person indebted to the College be admitted to a place on the Establishment, and that the President be requested to inform those students who are indebted that until other debts to the College are discharged they are not to be promoted to Holy Orders". At the same time they ordered "that a Book containing the names of Donors, for what purpose donations made and in whose names such donations stand in the publick funds, as also of Burses, by whom made and how funded, be kept by the Secretary and laid before the Board at each of its meetings".

The year 1819 came and went, though it was not uneventful. It saw the consecration of the Coadjutor Bishop of Elphin, Dr.Burke, in the College Chapel and ejectment suits brought against the Trustees by the Duke of Leinster for recovery of some land. A compromise was arrived at in 1820 on the Trustees agreeing to surrender two small plots, including the old castle grounds and the piece in front of the entrance to the College. One cannot but regret parting with the old castle. It would have added to the College more were it in its possession and probably have been kept better too. In 1819 there was also a triennial Visitation, by Lord Chancellor Manners and the Chief Judges. Although these visitations were usually quite short, this time they had to deal with an appeal by a student named Shannon against his expulsion from the College. The *Records* have it:

> "The Lord Chancellor declared that this College was practically an Ecclesiastical establishment and that a student not qualified for the Eccl. State was not a fit subject . . . . (but added) if a student was removed in the beginning of his course before there was any question of his pro-

177

ceeding to orders, the President in that case might be supposed to act from prejudice, making the qualification for orders a pretext for expulsion. Lord Norbury on the same occasion said he knew well of the intention of the Government in establishing this College, that he had frequent conversations with Mr. Pelham, now Lord Chichester, about it, and that it was intended to supply the place of foreign Eccl. Colleges, from which the Catholics of Ireland were, on account of the war, then excluded''.

It was around 1819 also, it would appear, that a student called Molony became a 'seceding Presbyterian'. He had been a divinity student in the College, who had preached against the establishment of schools in Ireland. Afterwards, during the brief meditation before supper, the Dean cautioned him against such use of intemperate language, lest enemies should hear of it: ''the institution at Belfast'' had been deprived of a yearly endowment of 1,500 l. in consequence of a similar happening. He was told to ''return home till Midsummer'' — the only example of rustication that can be found at the time — and come back afterwards. He did but later perverted. In many ways this period was a watershed in the History of Maynooth, particularly in that it marked the culmination of an effort to secure for it University status. But that is another story.

Chapter VIII

The Thwarting of a University

From its very beginning Maynooth College — irrespective of the slanders that were regularly made on it — acquired a reputation for profound scholarship. Irrespective too of the many disruputable occurrences which have been chronicled here and which sullied its good name in its earlier days, this learning was coupled with a reputation for decorum. Even Cox in 1808 of all times, was disposed to remark that, the first Dean, Dr. Ferris, raised the College to such a pitch of discipline "that for sanctity of manners, Maynooth in 1800 and 1801, might be styled the Bangor of modern times". At this stage one may well speculate as to how much of what Cox said is to be believed! Walter — or Watty — Cox was the son of a Westmeath blacksmith, described as a hanger-on of the revolutionary party of 1798, who, according to Webb's *Compendium of National Biography,* "proved faithless both to his own side and to the Government". He established *The Irish Monthly Magazine,* "a medley of truth and falsehood . . . . (and) carried it on from 1808 to 1815, being subjected to numerous fines and imprisonment for opinions expressed therein". His dates were 1770 and 1836. *Duffy's Irish Catholic Magazine* is more reliable and it has a lot to say about the reputation of the College even in its days of infancy. The recollections are those of a native of the town of Maynooth, whose childhood mind was duly impressed by both the staff and the students of the College. His name was Wm. McCabe.

'THE BANGOR OF MODERN TIMES'

"My first recollections as a child were, that the Catholic Church was a great, a paramount, nay, the pre-eminent power in Ireland; for it was my good fortune to have been removed from Dublin to Maynooth when about six years of age, and to have remained in Maynooth until I must have been at least ten years old. As a child, I remember the impressions produced upon my mind, by comparing the ruined castle of the

179

Geraldines which flanks one side of the College, and the finnikin-looking, sneaking-seeming, tiny Protestant church which hangs upon the opposite side of the College. Bigness is one of the elements of grandeur, in the mind of a child, and the size of Maynooth College — its long front — its multitudinous windows — the newness, the freshness, the whiteness of the building — its flower — plants — the sun-dial — to me a most marvellous thing, all these tended to demonstrate that the Catholic church was greater than the Geraldines, for they, it was plain, were not able to save their own house from being 'blown about their ears', whilst as to the Protestant establishment it seemed to be reduced to so low and so contemptible an ebb, that it could not afford to keep its solitary large window free from dirt, and dust and cobwebs.

"Then there was next the students in Maynooth College. Priam did not look with half the wonder and admiration, from the walls of Troy, upon the assembled leaders of the Greeks, as I did upon them. They were — although the bloom of youth was on their cheeks, to my childish apprehensions — great old men — such old men — the youngest of them could not, I thought, be less than twenty; and to the child of six, or seven, or eight, that seems to be 'so very old!' and then their dark robes and their graceful caps (I never could endure the Dublin Trinity College caps, because of my love for that of Maynooth), and then their decorum and their gravity, and what amazed me most of all, the fear, the reverence, and the respect evinced by these old grown men, for other men so much older than themselves — for professors, for president, and for vice-president — and their awe of the Dean! Why, I used, as a child, to tremble even to hear that the Dean was in sight, even though I can remember his once presenting me with a most delicious rosy-cheeked apple. What was George III, on his throne of gold, in my apprehension, as compared with the Dean of Maynooth College? And then, there was the High Mass on Sundays, the lights, the vestments, the music, the censer, the pealing voices of thousands, as I thought, answering from the choirs. I remember kneeling from its commencement to the close, awe-struck with wonder and delight.

"I have since then seen many grand sights, and among the rest the coronation of the Emperor of Austria in Milan, when forty mitred prelates conducted his imperial majesty to receive, from the hands of the Cardinal and Milanese Archbishop, the iron crown of Italy; but never have I beheld anything which filled me with a thousandth part of the awe, or inspired me with anything like the mingled feeling of rapture and wonder which used to fill my mind, when kneeling Sunday after Sunday at the corner of the rails fronting the high altar in the chapel of Maynooth College, during the celebration of High Mass."

Cox can never be ignored. While castigating Dr. Flood's failure to fill the Chair of Irish in 1800, due to some unknown difference with Mr. Theophilus O'Flanagan which prevented the latter from employing his talents for the good of his country by lecturing on a language he was so eminently qualified to teach, as well as the President's failure to fill the position in Hebrew, it also issues a eulogy on Maynooth that would be hard to beat: "Trinity College in its best days never possessed a greater number of learned men, than were at this period at the head of the classes in Maynooth". There was Dr. Aherne, whose fame "was spread thro' all the Catholic colleges of the Continent". Then there was Dr. Delort, "a great and universal genius. He was a polished as well as an erudite scholar; adding the most refined taste to the most profound and well-selected knowledge. He was in great repute amongst the literati of Paris, an intimate acquaintance of Langlois, the mathematician, and Lavoisier, the famous chymist (sic.). His mathematical acquirements were in such esteem that tho' a roman catholic priest, he was solicited by the fellows of Trinity College to become a professor on their establishment". As for Clinch, "unless Dr. Johnson, perhaps a greater prodigy of learning has not appeared in modern times".

And Usher, the descendent of the famous Archbishop; Enough said even if the Archbishop was Protestant and an eccentric to boot. Hussey too was to be admired: "His aim was to inspire the scholars with a dignity of mind and an elevation of sentiment equal to the character which he wished them to fill afterwards in the world. He planted in Maynooth the germ of literary and moral excellence".

Of studies in the College in 1802 Cox writes:

"So great was the progress made in the languages by the scholars under Mr. Clinch, that Greek appeared to be almost their vernacular tongue. As an instance of this proficiency, we will relate an anecdote of one of them, which does equal honour to the abilities of the master and the disciple. A Hungarian, who translated some of Ovid's Elegies into Greek verse, travelled through these countries in the year 1802. He had been to both the English Universities, in Edinburgh, and at the college of Dublin, at each of which places he had conversed with the cleverest men, in the Greek and Roman tongues. After being some time in the college of Dublin, curiosity led him to Maynooth. It was during the Summer recess, and most of the Professors and students were from home. He met a lad about 20 years of age, with whom he entered into conversation. He asked several questions concerning the internal economy of the college; and amongst the rest, if there was a professor of Greek on the establishment. The young lad, indignant at the affront offered to his *Alma Mater,* spoke to him in that language with the most astonishing fluency. The Hungarian was struck with wonder and afterwards declared, that the best Greek scholar he had conversed with since he left his own country, was a student of Maynooth College. This young man's name is Patrick Connery, he is now a clergyman and is a native of Ballyragget, in the County of Kilkenny".

Cox's hostility to the Dean — Coen — is illustrated by his making out that the latter tried five times to have Mr. Connery expelled, such was his aversion to learning! A little bit far-fetched, one feels.

There is no doubt but that already the name and fame of the College as a centre of scholarship was building up. So were its facilities, the staff, the halls, the library. In 1802 we find Janico Preston of the Gormanstown family writing to Archbishop Troy from Liege to inform him and the Board of Trustees of a big sale of theological, canonical, historical and other books in that city. The property of a former seminary Professor, they would go cheap because of present circumstances and, if commissioned, he would buy them for Maynooth. It looks as if this was done because in a further letter of March, 1803, to Dr. Troy, Preston supplies the titles of a number of books asking Troy to mark those which he would like to have purchased for Maynooth. Presumably they were contained in a present of volumes made to Maynooth by the Archbishop during the years 1806-7-8, a list of which is preserved in the *Dublin Diocesan Archives.* It covers ten pages. So, between one thing and another, one is not taken aback to find Maynooth, no less than Trinity, being lampooned for what were regarded by some as pretensions. W. M. Letts, in his *Songs from Leinster,* which came out around 1802, let them both have it:

> "It is a pity I have,
> And that is a truth,
> For the Trinity men
> And the men of Maynooth
> The men of Maynooth are the like o' the rooks,
> With their solemn black coats an' their serious looks.
> An' the Trinity men are no better at all,
> For when they're not studyin' deep in their books
> Their only diversion is batting a ball,
> An' that is a truth".

Truth or no truth this, Maynooth was set on the way to academic greatness. From the start, of course, it had been what was later called a third level institution. And while it was not formally a university, this being then reserved to Trinity College, Dublin, it was the next best thing. Given the opportunity to develop within it a centre of higher learning (of post-graduate studies in effect), the time would be ripe for pitching its cap at university status.

MILORD DUNBOYNE'S FOUNDATION

The story of John Butler, Roman Catholic Bishop of Cork and Baron of Dunboyne, who had perverted to Protestantism but reverted to Catholicism on his death bed, is well told in Con Constello's book *In Quest of an Heir* (Cork, 1978).

CUM DEO.

AUSPICE

REGE NOSTRO AUGUSTISSIMO ATQUE MUNIFICENTISSIMO,

GEORGIO III.

FAVENTE

NOBILISSIMO CAROLO MARCHIONE DE CORNWALLIS,

DOMINO LOCUMTENENTE GENERALI ET GENERALI GUBERNATORE HIBERNIÆ.

PRÆSIDE

PETRO FLOOD,

SACRÆ FACULTATIS PARISIENSIS DOCTORE THEOLOGO.

COLLEGIUM REGIO-CATHOLICUM, S. PATRITII DE MAYNOOTH, POST ACTAS FERIAS ACADEMICAS, LECTIONES SUAS
HOC ORDINE RESUMET, DD LUNÆ MENSIS SEPTEMBRIS XVII.
ANNO DOMINI M.DCC.LXXXX.VIII.

MAURITIUS AHERNE,

Sacræ Facultatis Parisiensis Licentiatus Theologus, ac Theologiæ Dogmaticæ Profeffor, dicet de Sacramentis et Incarnatione Verbi Divini, horis Xᵃ matutinâ ac Vᵃ pomeridianâ.

—— DE LA HOGUE,

Sacræ Facultatis Parisiensis Doctor Theologus, Scripturæ Sacræ ac Juris Canonici Profeffor, dicet, pro tempore, de Contractibus, de Obligationibus ac practicis Pœnitentiæ Quæstionibus, horâ XIᵃ matutinâ; de Canone vero Scripturarum Sacrarum horâ Vᵃ pomeridianâ.

PETRUS JUSTINUS DELORT, J. U. D.

Naturalis et Experimentalis Philofophiæ Profeffor, dicet, pro tempore, de Mathesi, horâ Xᵃ matutinâ; de Physica vero Experimentali horâ Vᵃ pomeridianâ.

ANDREAS DARRE, A. M.

Philofophiæ Profeffor, dicet de Logicâ ac Metaphysicâ, horâ Xᵃ matutinâ de Ethicâ verô horâ Vᵃ pomeridianâ.

JACOBUS BERNARDUS CLINCH, A. M.

Rhetorices Literarumque Græcarum Profeffor, Artis Oratoriæ Elementa tradet e Latinis et Anglicanis Scriptoribus, horâ Xᵃ matutinâ, eadem repetet e fontibus Græcis, horâ Vᵃ pomeridianâ.

CAROLUS LOVELOCK, A. M.

Literarum Humaniorum Profeffor, Authores Clafficos explanabit, Regulafque Orationis Latinæ, tàm strictæ, quàm folutæ, tradet, horâ Xᵃ matutinâ; Selecta e Græcis Scriptoribus exponet horâ Vᵃ pomeridianâ.

MARCUS USHER. A. M. Profefforâ Vice, dicet, pro tempore, de Orthoepeiâ Linguæ Anglicanæ, horâ post meridiem IIᵃ

FRANCISCUS POWER, Pro-Præses, A. M. ftatutis horis aget de Gallico Sermone.

PETRUS FLOOD, Præses, ftatutis horis dicet de Legibus ac de Concordiâ Sacerdotii et Imperii.

Ineunte Menfe Julio proximo, publicæ habebuntur in Aula Collegii Concertationes, in quibus finguli Alumni facturi funt industriæ fuæ periculum. His peractis, qui in unoquoque ordine præ cæteris, ex fententia Judicum excelluerint, præmiis, ex curatorum generalium placito, folemniter donabuntur.

DUBLINI, FACUDERUNT M FITZ'ATRICK, & PATRITII COL TYP. ET BIBLIOP.

It is a story which resembles that of King Henry VIII insofar at least as the apostasy was caused by the nobleman's anxiety to continue the family line. The Bishop had resigned his See in 1786, on the death of his nephew, upon which he succeeded to the title and estates of the family. He then appealed to Pope Pius VI for permission to marry, which appeal had been predictably turned down. Hence the walk out from Rome. It is with Lord Dunboyne's return to the fold that we are concerned here, linked as it was to his making a substantial bequest to the Trustees of Maynooth College. The will was made on 1 May 1800. On the following day Dunboyne wrote to the Pope expressing his repentance and also to Dr. Troy, who immediately had the Augustinian friar, Father William Gahan, call on him. He died on 7 May, 1800. Naturally, news of his reversion to Catholicism travelled swiftly and gave satisfaction to Catholics. Luke Concannon wrote from Rome to Troy on 12 July saying that he had received Troy's letter with the details and that the Cardinal (Prefect of Propaganda we may take it) was delighted and will inform the Pope. He wished, however, that Dunboyne had been more moderate and discreet in his bequest to Maynooth.

It is doubtful whether the Trustees had any such reservations but his relatives, the O'Brien Butlers, definitely had. A lawsuit was quickly filed by his sister on 31 October of the year he died. The particulars are all contained in a booklet, published by Fitzpatrick in 1802, with the kind of long title so common in those times: *Some particulars of the Case wherein the Lessee of Catherine O'Brien Butler was plaintiff, and the Rev. A. Dunn, Sec. of the Roman Catholic College of Maynooth, Defendant.* The Trustees prepared to defend their end of the stick. On 19 November they met and ordered that Lord Fingall, Dr. Troy, Richd. Stronge Esq. and the Secretary be a Committee for carrying on the lawsuit about Lord Dunboyne's legacy. The trial began in the Court of Chancery in 1801 and was put back to the Trim Assizes for 24 August, 1802. . It had many elements of the bizarre in it, not least the fact that the Judge — Lord Kilwarden — was one of the Visitors to Maynooth College and had to doff one of his hats for the occasion. Sergeant Moore and Standish O'Grady appeared for the Plaintiffs and Mr. Ponsonby and John Philpot Curran for the Defendants. The matter turned on Father Gahan's refusal to say what transpired between him and Lord Dunboyne when he visited him before he died. The version that has come down to us is that the reason for Father Gahan's refusal was a fear on his part that, should he say that Dunboyne had declared himself to be a Catholic, he might be exposing himself to the risk of penalties, under the existing law, on the score of having assisted a person to pervert from the Protestant to the Catholic religion. There may have been more to it, for if it were established that Dunboyne did indeed revert, would he have been legally entitled, under the same law, to make the bequest? Fr. Gahan was in a dilemma. His refusal to testify fully to the satisfaction of the Court brought him a sentence of a week's gaol in Trim, to the boos of the crowd in the court at the Chief Justice. He had scarcely been escorted away by the Sheriff when, following further evidence and submissions which Lord Kilwarden deemed to be of such a nature as to render Fr. Gahan's testimony unnecessary, the Chief Justice ordered his immediate discharge, which was welcomed by the crowd. It was an interesting insight into the intricacies of the legal mind. Kilwarden undoubtedly meant well. He was in a quandary, one might say, between justice and equity, and he tried his best to be fair, although people held his first sentence on Fr. Gahan against him. He sought now to divest himself of the entire matter, declaring that it was so complex that it should be tried again next term at the Court of the King's Bench, but advising the parties to try to reach an amicable settlement. Here, one feels, he has again donned his second hat, that of a Visitor of Maynooth. This they did, but before they could end the matter an Act of Parliament had to be passed enabling the College to effect the dispositions necessary in respect of land.

This was the Maynooth Act of 1808, officially entitled *An Act to amend two Acts passed in Ireland, for the better Education of Persons professing the Roman Catholic Religion, and for the better Government of the Seminary established at Maynooth for the Education of such Persons, so far as relates to the Purchase of Lands, and compounding Suits.* It was 48 Geo. III. By it the Trustees were given full power to receive donations and to purchase or acquire lands and to compromise any suit relative to any property claimed by the College on such terms as they saw fit. As a result, in May, 1809 a compromise was reached between the Trustees and P. O'Brien Butler.

On the 7th of that month Dr. Plunkett hastened to Dublin "for the purpose of giving effect to the compromise entered into by the College of Maynooth and Mr. O'Brien Butler". The College benefitted very substantially from the bequest, receiving £500 per annum. It was on the basis of this that the Trustees sought a further £700 from Government in 1813 to enable 'improvements' to be effected. These 'improvements' consisted in the provision of an establishment for higher education, to which purpose the Trustees decided to devote the Dunboyne money. They wasted no time, nor were the Bishops remiss in preparing to send students to the new institution. So much so that in July, 1810, Dr. Murray of Dublin had to write to Dr. Bray of Cashel telling him that the President, Dr. Everard, "entreats Your Grace to suspend the appointment to any subject on the Dunboyne property, untill the next meeting of the Trustees", and asking him to communicate this to his Suffragans. One of them, Young of Limerick, was, already in August, pointing out to Bray that there would be six additional places allotted to the Province of Munster in Maynooth "in consequence of Lord Dunboyne's bequest". He wonders whether his one is perpetual or in rotation. His concern was wide. In November of 1810 he wrote again to Bray:

"In order that the Resolution of the Board, which concerns Lord Dunboyne's foundation, should prove of general utility, the number of Professors at Maynooth ought to be increased, for the further improvement of such as may be found qualified to be put on this establishment. There should be a professor to instruct them in the canon law, another for speculative Divinity, and controversy, for the time must come when some of the Maynoothians must be put into the highest offices of the Church, and of course that college ought to be in a condition to enable them to become well versed in those branches of ecclesiastical science necessary to render themselves and their functions respectable. I was always and am still an enemy to the scanty course there of three years Theology''.

Young, as has emerged earlier, was a Louvain man. Good though they were, his suggestions for the young 'Dunboyne Establishment', as it was quickly called, were not followed up — unfortunately, for one feels that, even though great were its attainments during the following century and a half, it would be better placed ultimately by the implementation of Young's ideas. Instead, it got one special Professor — the Prefect of the Dunboyne — in general charge of its students, who were selected by the President after their ordinary course in Divinity for a further three years study 'on the Dunboyne'. There were eleven of them by 1826 although the Dunboyne fund could support up to twenty. The building which houses them — known afterwards as 'the Dunboyne' — was begun about 1814 and completed about 1817. It was added to in 1822 and finished entirely in 1823. Simultaneously, a plan of studies for the Dunboyne students was adopted provisionally. Their attire too was attended to. They wore a distinctive dress, particularly the cap, which was described as being similar to the Jesuit cap worn at Clongowes! All was ready for take off — an application to be erected into a university.

IN SEARCH OF A CHARTER

In spite of the fact that some documents referred to before now make it clear that Maynooth early on had no university ambitions and sought simply to provide education for priests for Ireland (no degrees), the question of its being raised to university level goes far back in its history. There were strange interludes, such as that of 1804 when the four Archbishops wrote to Cardinal Doria, the Cardinal Protector of Ireland, seeking that Propaganda should make available places for Irish students because the Bishops feared that they could not rely on the annual grants from Parliament to Maynooth, for which they have to ask each year. It was hardly the pose of people with an interest in securing university status for the College. But to be fair, the question had not arisen as early as then. It was not, however, to be long delayed. In that same year — 1804 — the first English Catholics entered Cambridge in the person of a Mr. George Petre, nephew of Lord Petre. Until then both Oxford and Cambridge had been closed to them. Maynooth could be pardoned if it felt that it had students — apart altogether from its staff — who were worthy of university recognition. In fact it was John

186

Chetwoode Eustace, formerly Professor in Maynooth College, chaplain to Sir Wm. Jeringham at Costessy in 1799, and three years later to make his famous tour of Italy with three Irish gentlemen, who, on his return became tutor to George Petre and accompanied him to Cambridge. Eustace fancied himself as a verse composer. In late 1796, he had transmitted some through Burke to Earl Fitzwilliam, who duly acknowledged receipt of them. In April, 1808 he penned "an Elegy by Rev. Mr. E ———— e", inscribed "to the Duchess of Leinster on the death of an infant son, left on a little urn in a little temple erected to his memory":

"Oh: then a sickly, dying babe, no more,
But decked angelic, with each heavenly grace,
And fairer far, and loverlier than before,
Then shall he rush, to meet thy fond embrace".

But blood is thicker than water, as they say, and during the Rebellion of 1798, Eustace's blood was boiling so much at the treatment of his native land that he recanted his ode to Camden on the Foundation Day of the College. Naturallly, Cox is our source (April, 1808). On this occasion Eustace delivered himself of a very long composition. The final stanzas run as follows:

"What! Whilst beneath the savage Camden's reign,
My injured country bleeds in every vein,
Whilst boys, whose bosoms yet with virtue glow,
Must die for crimes, the perjured only know . . . .

Shall I, a dastard parasite, profane
The poet's laurel's, and the muse's strain!
And brand with C—— n's odious name, the lays,
That truth makes sacred . . . ."

In general Eustace's writing betrayed advanced liberal opinions which evoked the wrath of Milner — surely sufficient proof of his being university material, if one were to follow some later ideas on that subject, including some at Maynooth! The fact that it was not a university may, extraordinary though it be, have put off some prospective students during its early period. One of these may well have been the Rev. William Phelan whom we have come across already. Phelan was born in Clonmel and, though of Protestant schooling, was a Catholic, whose father's wish it was that he should enter Maynooth and study "for the Papal Church". At an examination held in Waterford for entry to Maynooth, he was chosen but declined to accept. Instead he entered T.C.D. in 1806, giving his name as a Protestant. He became a Minister of the Church of Ireland and eventually a Fellow of Trinity College.

In the Autumn of 1806 printed copies of a decree by Napoleon were sent to Ireland from Milan via Hamburg! By it were united the English, Irish and Scotch ecclesiastical institutions in the French dominions, under Dr. Walsh, Superior of the Irish College in Paris, who at once invited the students of the Irish College, Lisbon, to repair to Paris for their studies, expenses defrayed: No problem. In January, 1807, however, the Trustees of Maynooth met in Dublin and disapproved of this, in a letter to Dr. Crotty, then Rector of Lisbon, afterwards to be President of Maynooth. A copy was sent to Lord Howick and Mr. Secretary Elliott — always make sure to be on the safe side. It read: "Bound as we are by every tie of gratitude to the present Government, for its very liberal support of an ecclesiastical establishment at Maynooth, and which, under the auspices of the present administration, we hope will very shortly be considerably enlarged, we . . . . feel it our duty to declare, in the most unequivocal terms, our reprobation of such attempts to seduce the youth of your house".

At about the same time it seems that some kind of offer was made to the students at Lisbon by the Catholic Institute at Paris. Nothing seems to have happened until 1814, when the Irish Bishops appear to have endeavoured to get control over the burses of the Paris College that have been set up by officers of the former regiments of the French Army for the education of their descendants and relatives in France. When Louis XVIII was restored that year an Irish prelate arrived in Paris for the purpose of securing these burses. Fr. Ferris, who had been nominated to the Irish College by the King on 21 June, 1814, reacted strongly against this move. The pamphlet which he issued is to be found, in incomplete form, in the *Archives of the Irish College, Paris:*

> *"L'erection de Seminaire Collegé de Meynooth (sic.) paroît devoir mettre fin a l'emigration des étudiants en théologie pour le continent. L'intention des prélats et clergé d'Irlande ne peut être d'appliquer au seminaire college de Meynooth les revenus annuels de ces fondations, parcequ'alors le but que se sont proposé les fondations, ne serait pas rempli, puisque ils admiettent, pour occuper ces bourses, des étudiants en médicine et en chirurgie concurrement avec les éleves en theologie, et que ces connaissances ne peuvent pas être acquises au seminaire College de Meynooth".*

The burses simply could not be redirected into the Maynooth coffers, said Ferris, because *"Ces fondations ont été faites pour des étudiants en théologie, médicine et chirurgie indistinctement"*. He was not the only one to be annoyed at the proposition. On 24 December, 1814 in Paris, not a bad night for camaraderie and good cheer, fifty-five officers of the old régime, incensed at the proposal to endow Maynooth, "a stranger to us", drew up a memorial addressed to the Minister of the Interior condemning the proposal. Amongst those who signed was Count Charles Hegarty, Lieutenant Colonel in the French Army.

In July of 1814 the Irish Bishops had reiterated their petition to the Holy See to provide some places for Irish students in Propaganda on the grounds that Maynooth was proving inadequate to supply all the priests which Ireland needs.

188

This is reflected in a resolution of the Trustees of 26 June, 1817 by which "it is earnestly requested to the Prelates of the Kingdom to allow the Scholars of their respective jurisdictions, unless in cases of pressing necessity to remain in the College until they shall have completed four years in the study of Divinity". Obviously many Bishops were in short supply of priests. Hence they had also sought the restoration of the Irish College, Rome, to the Irish after the Napoleonic period. Their comment is calculated to irk many: if it were then sold and the revenue given to Propaganda, the latter would be in a position to take as many Irish students as the income warranted. Then suddenly came the burgeoning of the Dunboyne Establishment. In June, 1817, a Committee of the Trustees was appointed to draw up a plan for it. Hot on the tail of this went a letter from Dr. Troy to a Signor Felice Argenti, an agent of the Irish Bishops, in Rome. Troy's message was that some Irish Bishops and its administrators desire that Maynooth — "the Royal College of St. Patrick" or "Regio Collegio Manutiano S. Patrici vulgo Maynooth" — "be given the privilege of a university". The reason put forward was that the students, after their ordinary course had been completed, should, after a further three consecutive years of study and the public defense of a thesis, secure the degrees of Baccalaureate, Licentiate and Doctorate in theology. It was a scheme clearly designed for the infrastructure capped by the Dunboyne. Long forgotten now was Troy's note of 1793 to the effect that the "colleges" which the Bishops were then seeking were not to be on a par with universities but rather "private" schools for the clergy. Rome replied, through Cardinal Litta, to the June, 1817 letter during the following August, acknowledging its receipt. Rome has always been interested in the setting up of Catholic universities.

The matter had now been formally raised and the business was on. The same August Argenti wrote to Troy concerning the matter of the request for "Maynooth University", enclosing letters for the four Archbishops requesting their opinion. On the same day Cardinal Litta wrote again to Troy, making some queries about Maynooth College preparatory to granting it the faculty of conferring degrees in Theology and Canon Law. In passing he remarks how dilapidated the Irish College, Rome, now is. All this correspondence, when not contained in the *Dublin Diocesan Archives,* is to be found (and that is by far the greater portion) in the manuscripts of the *Archives of Propaganda.* Came 1818 and in June a letter of Troy to Litta again concerning the Maynooth petition. Its administrators seek no other privilege of a university except to confer the Doctorate in Theology and Canon Law. There are Professors of both of these disciplines at Maynooth and also professors of Logic, Physics, Mathematics, etc., all of sound doctrine. (Why it should have been necessary to include reference to secular subjects is any man's guess). There is also a copious library. It is true that the doctrinal orthodoxy of some members of staff has been questioned. "To reassure you on this point I will take the first opportunity to send you the books which are being used". The consent of the Government to confer these degrees is not necessary but simply convenient in the opinion of some. Troy was only doing what the Trustees wanted. According to the *Journal of the Trustees* for 24 June, "Dr. Troy at the request of the Trustees promised to apply to the Holy See for powers to enable the Prelates members of the Board to confer degrees on such as may merit them: the degree of Bachelor in Theology will be conferred at the close of the first year's examination on such as shall be judged duly qualified".

Whether he realised it or not — surely he did — Troy had already touched on the two main obstacles to recognition of Maynooth as a Pontifical University — its doctrinal orthodoxy and the attitude of Government. Rome replied on 4 July, 1818 but the real action was yet to come. The Maynooth Trustees sought to be ahead of events. At their meeting of 24 June they laid down that at the end of each academic year a concursus should take place between the Dunboyne students for the purpose of ascertaining their respective merits. The President, Professors of Divinity and Scripture and the Lecturer in Theology should each put two questions. This should be supplemented by a thesis written by any three of the students whom the President should appoint, and defended in the presence of the "Board of the Community". One half of the students should defend it, the other half object. The students who defended on the first day should object on the second. On the basis of this course of studies for the Dunboyne the Trustees found it quite in order to expect the Baccaulaureate to be conferred at the end of the first year, the Licentiate at the end of the second and the Doctorate at the end of the third.

From Rome Argenti sent words of encouragement. He had shown, he says, Dr. Troy's letter of 26 July to the Cardinal Prefect and is glad to be able to say that His Holiness, at audience on 9th August, granted the request of the "University of Maynooth" to confer the Laureate in the same way that Propaganda does for its students. A brief will follow. This is merely advance news. It was August, 1818. That Argenti was being over sanguine is clear when we find, on the following 12 September, Propaganda writing to Troy asking for details regarding the studies at Maynooth. The decision of the Congregation had been to await the report of a Consultor concerning them. Truly, the College was in a difficult position, even if not for the first time. At home it had to defend its teaching before Government in matters such as the power of the Pope in temporalities, at Rome before Propaganda it had to do likewise — not by any means an easy task if reconciliation of interests was necessary. The indefatigable Argenti was not to be put off: He would be helpful in all circumstances. And so, during 1819, we find him in touch with Dr. Troy about sending on the books concerning "Maynooth University", keeping the pot boiling in Rome, and finally, in August, informing Troy that he has sent on the books used in Maynooth to the Counsellor appointed by Propaganda to examine and report on them. He promises to forward the Consultor's comments when he learns of them. Propaganda took due notes about the whole thing, headed "the supplication by the university of Mainooth" to be given the right to confer degrees. What a strange way of putting it! The name of the

Consultor was Dr. Pietro Ostini who, on 29 August, the day after he had got the books, wrote to the Secretary of Propaganda agreeing to undertake the task of scrutinizing them but asking for time proportionate to the number of volumes which he has received and the profound nature of the matter that they contain. He covers himself in respect of one of them — the first volume of the moral course — which is missing; just in case it may have been sent to Propaganda he wishes them to know that he has not got it.

It was at that time that the interference started, from quarters least expected. Irish friars based in Rome and an Irish Bishop at home became very active against the interests of Maynooth. The first to engage in this Quisling let-down, although in charity it was most likely intended in the Church's best interests, was Fr. Giovanni Browne, Secretary to the Franciscan Provincial in Rome. In a letter of 17 Deptember to Fr. Olivieri, an Italian, to be given by him to Cardinal Fontana, Prefect of Propaganda on 12 October, Browne argues that it is a big scandal in Ireland that many priests are attracted to Gallican principles. The reason for this, in confidence, is that the first Maynooth professors were Frenchmen. They have been taken up and refuted by Fr. Peter Magennis, in the matter of the supreme authority of the Pope, infallibility, the doctrine of grace, indulgences and other questions. At home an Irish Bishop was also sharpening his knife. This was Dr. Robert Walsh, Bishop of Waterford. The same year of 1819 finds him sending a long letter directly to Propaganda, marked 'Secret and Confidential' about Maynooth. It deals with whether the College should be elevated to the status of a university. The writer proclaims himself motivated by a sense of religion, which impels him to offer certain observations and information to the Cardinal Prefect. The situation is firstly that Maynooth is dependent totally on the Protestant Government that founded it. The Visitors include the Protestant Judges. There is a right of appeal to the Protestant Chancellor of the Realm from anybody's decisions, even those of Bishops — some expelled students had been restored as a result. Secondly, its elevation, without the formal consent of the Government, could excite the anger of Parliament and of the Protestant university in Dublin and it could be deprived of resources and disappear in a moment (*in ictu oculis*).

Would it not be better to await the emancipation of the Catholics of Ireland, when these difficulties would no longer hold? Thirdly, should not the Bishops of Ireland as a whole, who have students there, be also previously consulted? Fourthly, could it not endanger relations between the Holy See and the British Government? And the real rub: Should it be done without the maximum of caution regarding the teaching of its professors and the books used? The students are taught against the infallibility of the Pope. For the past eight years in many parts of the country, priests have been abjuring the Catholic faith and marrying and writing books against the Catholic faith and the Holy See — all of them having been educated at Maynooth. There is Signor Crowley, a dean of the College and Prof. of Sacred Scripture, Signor Tinnot (Sinnot), who had been a "quasi-professor" or moral theology and had abjured his faith in the College, Signor

191

Cozens (of Ferns) who became a Protestant minister, Signor Nowlan (of Cashel), Signor Crowley (of Cork), brother of the other, who did also abjure and left the country, and from Waterford itself, Signor Brown, who preached from the altar against the use of holy water, Signor Kernan, who spoke against the Supreme Pontiff, Signor Morrissey, who maintained publicly that it is not necessary to wear a stole or use a candle when administering the sacraments, and Signor Tailor, who spoke even in Rome against miracles. *"Isti omnes qui fuere educati in aliis seminariis per totam Hiberniam sunt sanae fidei, iis solum exceptis alumnis de Maynooth, quare haec differentia? Judicet sacra Congregatio"*. It was a powerful indictment of Maynooth. The Bishop followed it up in a further letter of 9 December to Cardinal Litta, expounding the state of his Diocese of Waterford. As far as the Seminary there goes, it is now, by reason of the size of the College, the number of its professors, the regularity of its studies and renovation of its discipline, the rival of Maynooth. The clergy have been reformed and those guilty of improprieties (all educated at Maynooth) have been dismissed. Rome must have been quite confused about the state of affairs at Maynooth, especially when another Irish Bishop, the famous J. K. L., wrote to his brother in religion Fr. Rice at the same time — the letter is to found in the documents of the *Congressi (Irlanda)* of Propaganda — pointing out that Maynooth was *"non un seminario vescovile, ma un collegio nazionale"*, which could equally have been counter-productive.

It was, therefore, unnecessary for Giovanni Hogan, in May of the following year, to write to the Bishop of Waterford — through the Superior of St. Isidore's and, believe it or not, Signor Argenti — complaining about Crowley, Cozens, Synot (sic.) and others, who had become heretics at Maynooth, saying that the Pope should know of the scandal. He already did, or his civil service did. The whole thing somewhat resembles the attacks made on Maynooth, on the doctrinal level, by Hamish Frazer and the followers of *Catholic Approaches* around 1970. And unlike the latter occasion, at least to any great degree, some of the mud stuck. It is a great pity that, unlike later times, the Irish Bishops as a whole do not seem at that period to have had any effective representative in Rome. The lack of an Irish College was showing its consequences. There was nobody there like Kirby or Cullen of the period that had not yet begun. Fancy depending on Argenti, a two-faced timer as far as can be found. In 1820 he is writing to Troy to tell him that Propaganda does not approve of the Gallican propositions being taught at Maynooth nor of de la Hogue's treatise "all the more because these Frenchman know well how dangerous and harmful such maxims are". The books used at Maynooth, which Dr. Troy had sent on, are being examined. Understandably, Troy prepared a draft submission to Propaganda, pointing out that the Trustees and Archbishops had asked him to reply to the accusations that had been made to the Holy See about the College. It is utterly untrue that unsound doctrines are being propagated there. So goes the draft, preserved in the *Dublin Diocesan Archives.* In April, 1820, he did write to Propaganda, reviewing his petition that the "College of Maynooth be given the privilege — which universities have — of conferring the doctorate, *servatis servandis,* on its students". He recalled that the Archbishop of Dublin, Giovanni Lech in the time of Clement V, year 1312, had applied for the faculty of having a 'Universita Scolarium' in Dublin, which was not issued to him as he had died. HIs successor, Alexander Bicknor, had reapplied for it from Pope John XXII in 1320. We find Troy's letter among the *Acta* of Propaganda for 1820. It was a truly great letter, demonstrating the interest in and powerful advocacy of Maynooth which was then and has since again manifested itself on the part of the Archbishop of Dublin, who, perhaps, more than any other member of the Irish Hierarchy, has been in a position to exercise influence on Government, whatever about Rome. Troy's references to his predecessors related to a Bull of Clement V obtained by John de Lech, actually granted in Dublin and to the petition of Alexander de Bicknor in 1320, which had resurrected de Lech's initiative. But by then this had languished and disappeared.

Whatever of Troy's influence at home, it does not appear to have counted for much in Rome as far as the Maynooth question is concerned: that of episcopal appointments is a different matter. A note in the Propaganda archives for 19 June, 1820, gives the impression that the suggestion about a university at Maynooth came up in the full Congregation for the first time on that day. Shortly afterwards the Congregation was to be in receipt of a communication on the subject from the Primate in Armagh, Dr. Curtis. Writing on 28 July he confesses himself saddened at hearing that Maynooth was thought of badly in Rome. The charge, ". . . . *praefatum nempe Collegium male audiri Romae, ibique haberi pro coetu pseudo philosophorum, vel turba hominum Religioni Catholicae, et Sanctae Sedi praecipue adversantium, etc."* is rejected as *"plane absurdum".* Curtis insists that the Trustees do exercise vigilance, for example, when some students about twenty years ago had conspired secretly concerning new things, they were expelled. One is forced to wonder whether this point, however well-intentioned, carried the cause far. Rome would have been shocked at the very idea of 'secret conspiracies'. It is all very reminiscent of the early years of the 1970's when, just while a student strike was occurring in the College, some Bishops were taking the view that not only should this sort of thing not occur there but that it could not occur. That attitude changed afterwards but at the time it was not at all helpful to the President. One Archbishop reminded him of a sentence from Don Boyne's *I Remember Maynooth* (1937): "In order that Maynooth College should force its way into the headlines and become universally talked about . . . . something in the nature of a general strike among the students would be necessary".

To return though to Archbishop Curtis in 1820. He refers Rome to the College textbooks which have been forwarded by Archbishop Troy. It is true that De la Hogue's treatise in theology follows the Paris school on Infallibility but in this respect it has never been widely followed in Ireland *and does not prevail in the College.* Indeed he would prefer to write an encomium on *"transmarine nostra Seminaria"* but refrains from doing so. Propaganda replied to him courteously on 9 September. It acknowledges that it is not proved that Gallican views are followed there. Indeed it opines that the French themselves are beginning to reject them, as witness the recent work by De la Menais, in other words, de Lammenais as he came to be 'spelt' later! But Rome inculcates the need for vigilance. The books relating to the College have been received and are being given attention — a diplomatic letter if ever there was one. On 12 February, 1821 came the moment of truth. The Congregation met *"sul Privilegio del Collegio di Maynot"*. The agenda for the meeting was printed. The discussion took place under the Chairmanship of Cardinal Somaglia and proceeded impersonally to deal with some problems raised by the Archbishop of Dublin in his letter of 24 April, 1820, already referred to here. The basic question was that about raising Maynooth College to the status of a University. Lech and Biknor were duly recalled. That was fine as regards the past, but as regards the present for two years the Congregation has been receiving "not good" reports on the doctrine of the College. The meeting recalled how the Congregation had written to Dr. Troy in September, 1818, asking for details about the studies there. The Archbishop had forwarded the books being used, which were given to Ostini for examination but who had not yet finished his task. Curtis's letters and the replies of the Congregation were also produced. The decision, once again, was to await the Report of the Consultor. The matter was still hanging fire in 1821. During that year J.K.L. sent off to Rome what was clearly intended as a root in favour of his own seminary at Carlow which, since 1792, has "sent forth well instructed workers of good morals", not only into his Diocese but over all Ireland. The dice was loaded against Maynooth.

In April, 1821, Cardinal Fontana wrote about abuses in Ireland that were undoubtedly being attributed to Maynooth: Priests were said to hear confessions of women without screens, marriage bans were not being published and in some dioceses parishes are being provided with concursus, causing favouritism and quarrels. He adds: the examination of the Maynooth texts has not yet been completed and no decision has yet been reached. But the portents were not good.

THE SPECTRE OF TRINITY COLLEGE

An element in all this that was of as much significance as that of doctrine was the role of Trinity College, the University of Dublin. Signs of this have already appeared, notably in Bishop Walsh's letter to Propaganda. Its relevance — and the influence of Walsh's letter with it — became painfully evident in 1821 when a referral of 24 April from Cardinal Fontana to Troy was received. The Cardinal comes quite clean. Propaganda has got the Archbishop's communication asking for advice on the petition that Maynooth be raised to university status after the books used there have been examined. Propaganda needs some clarification. It has been reported that some students had lapsed from the faith, others expelled for sedition who received heavy sentences from the civil powers, several behaving arrogantly, obeying neither their superiors nor the Holy See. Is this true? Can Troy assure Propaganda that it has ended? Also it was reported that the Board included a Chancellor and four Protestant Judges to whom the students could and did appeal against their own superiors and that expelled youths had been reinstated by order of these Board Members. If the Pope granted university status, the Government and Dublin University might be displeased and cause the grant to the College to be stopped and then it would collapse. He asks Dr. Troy to give full information on all three points so that he — the Cardinal — can deal with the business. It was almost a paraphrase of Bishop Walsh's letter. Before anything of consequence could happen, Pietro Ostini delivered his report — on

24 June, 1821. It spanned twenty-three pages. In thoroughgoing fashion it examined and reported in succession on the Philosophy of Anglade, the Theology of Delahogue and the Theology of Bailly who, although not a Professor at Maynooth, was followed there. The Philosophy of Anglade was contained in three volumes, one in Logic, one in Metaphysics and one in Ethics. There is nothing objectionable in the first two but in the ethics yes. The author teaches not just a 'probabilism' but something approaching a 'tutiorism' of a kind condemned by the Church. Even though Jansenism was not mentioned by name the rigorism of Jansenism was what was in mind. The Theology of Delahogue, in five volumes, was subjected to careful analysis. The *De Religione,* while over critical in its approach to Scripture, might be overlooked but the *De Ecclesia* was Gallican in its content, not only in regard to Papal infallibility (on one page it explicitly poses the case of the fallibility of the Pontiff) and his superiority to Councils, but actually injures his authority as Pope and the dignity of the Holy See, also his primacy of jurisdiction and finally even the authority of the General Councils of the Church. The Theology of Baily, in four volumes, is in like vein.

With this the game was really up, even though on 30 July Primate Curtis is writing again to Propaganda urging Maynooth's case: Despite what may have been said of it, it is worthy. The whole world had been caught up in troubles some time ago (so how could Maynooth be expected to have escaped). And there is no need to worry about the University of Dublin once it is understood that the degrees which Maynooth will be conferring have nothing in common with those of the former. Then — in a most interesting foreshadowing of Faculty rather than University structure — Curtis says that it is not necessary that Maynooth be constituted into a university. It would be sufficient if it were given the power to confer Baccalaureates, Licentiates and Doctorates in Theology. That Maynooth had a real claim is evident. There was a sufficient staff and sufficient students at the time, not merely for a Faculty but for a University. It had too a blossoming institute of higher theological and canonical education. It was humiliating that some of its best students, despite competent training in Maynooth, had to attend Trinity College for degrees in certain subjects. For instance, around 1820 the Reverend Christopher Boylan, Professor of Hebrew at Maynooth since 1816, found it incumbent on him to stay in Dublin for nine months, supported out of College funds, for the purpose of studying the Oriental Languages under a Fellow of Trinity, the famous Vice-Provost Jackie Barrett, with a view to teaching them again in Maynooth. Or so we are told years after by Eugene O'Beirne, no friend at all of Maynooth and whose reliability as a reporter on the affairs of same, while undoubtful in its opportunities for accuracy (he had previously been a student there), is open to question for the slant which he gives.

Sometime during 1821 Archbishop Troy replied to Cardinal Fontana's request of the previous April, for on 8 September we find the Cardinal returning the compliment, professing himself consoled by Troy's report on the present state of the College and promising to do what in him lay to enable it to grant the degrees envisaged. But — and here again is the rub — lest the Civil Power or Dublin University should be offended, the Lord Lieutenant's consent is necessary, not just orally (as would seem to have been assured by Troy) but in writing. As if Charles Chetwynd — Lord Talbot — Lord Lieutenant from October 1817 to December 1821 — could be envisaged writing to Propaganda, if that is what was meant! Probably not, but even a letter from Talbot to Troy or anybody else after the manner required by Rome, was equally had to envisage. Besides, one could not be sure if it would do the trick, because Fontana still harked back to the reports about abuses stemming from Maynooth — hoping that they had been eradicated by the Bishops in their Dioceses but silent in his implications. Curtis of Armagh got a similar letter simultaneously. The Roman machine was, as always, well oiled. Curtis contacted Troy at once — 8 November, 1821. He seems to think that Fontana is more disposed to favour Maynooth than he had been. He had asked Lord Fingall to favour the petition by mentioning it at the Castle: approval from that quarter would count with Rome. But Fingall is apprehensive. It can be discussed at the next Bishops' meeting. Curtis was carrying coals to Newcastle in telling Troy what would curry favour with Rome.

In Rome itself the stage is again limelighted by another friar, this time Fr. Philip Crane, O.S.A., the Augustinian Provincial for Ireland, who approached Propaganda about *"dr della Houge* (sic.) *primarius hucusque in nationali collegio Minuthensi* (sic.) *professor"*. Crane's 'information' — to use an old '98 term — was that in a new book Delahogue says that outside the Church those in invincible ignorance can be saved, whereas the opposite opinion (we are glad that he spoke just of 'opinion' so certain were men in those days) has always been held in Ireland. The *"doctrina minuthensis"* is Latitudinarianism or tantamount to it. How complex a jungle we are in — with Maynooth being slated on the side of its moral teaching for a narrow Jansenism and on that of its dogmatic teaching for an over-broad tolerance! We cannot but think of the erratic Fr. Leonard Feeney, excommunicated by the Archbishop of Boston in the middle of the 20th century for teaching that the dictum — contained in the most orthodox treatises since Trent — 'Outside the Church there is no salvation' — should be taken literally. Footnotes in all the dogmatic treatises has indicated otherwise, yet not until the *Decree on Non-Christian Religions* of Vatican II was notice really taken of the footnotes, except by Cardinal Cushing of Boston — a great man if ever there was one. Fr. Crane, O.S.A. is of more immediate historical concern. He informs Propaganda that his brother in religion, J.K.L., another Augustinian whose portrait has been hung in the great refectory of Maynooth, promises to keep "Maynoothians" silent in his diocese and that his former disciple, Fr. Rice, will explain this further if necessary.

The Bishop of Achonry, Patk. McNicholas, could write to Cardinal Somaglia, Pro-Prefect of Propaganda in 1822 (how the personalities change even within the brief of our work) to assure him that his students at Maynooth were well instructed, but things were at an end. In Roman style, little happened for some years and then, on 6 October, 1824, we suddenly find in the *Archives of Propaganda* a letter from the Archbishop of Dublin to Cardinal Somaglia. Its immediate concern is the Irish College, Rome, which the Archbishop wants restored. A Monsignor Caprano of the Congregation had opposed this proposal and for a strange reason. In his view, Maynooth College in Ireland, although supposed to have good reports as regards the ability of its Professors, is highly suspect as regards the theological and canonical principles that are taught there. This is confirmed by the books used there. And so, naturally, these would be the principles which almost all the students of a restored Irish College would bring with them. The admission of such could be interpreted as an approval by the Holy See of these same principles. To say that Maynooth was hemmed in from every side would be the understatement of the century. Even more: From Callan, Co. Kilkenny, came a letter from the Augustinian Prior then there, Fr. John Furlong, to Somaglia, also complaining of Delahogue's teaching on the possibility of salvation for unbelievers in invincible ignorance. He was speaking of Delahogue as "Professor Manutinensis". By now we are so accustomed to diverse spellings for 'Maynooth' as not to be taken by surprise. Bray of Cashel tried to 'inform' Rome, in the best sense of that term. Writing in 1825 (and his letter too is in the *Archives of Propaganda*) he put it that the opinions of Delahogue, now taught by many clergy in Ireland, about the possibility of salvation outside the Church, could be held through one's "being virtually a Catholic" and therefore in some sense within the Church. It was all very predictable and orthodox but profited little in Rome.

Sometime in 1825 — it was more likely June — the Primate, Curtis, wrote to Dr. Blake in Rome that he has just returned from a meeting of the Board of Trustees at Maynooth. The prelates were concerned about the "alarming attacks" that have been made in Rome about the "doctrine, morals and discipline . . . . in the College of M". At their request he has made since some years back more than one statement on the subject to Propaganda and has received answers from Cardinals Fontana and Somaglia stating their perfect satisfaction. The Primate continues, however, to say that even more attacks have been made since and appear to have been entertained by the learned Mgr. Capiro (sic.) Secretary. He had latterly been persuaded to address Curtis, which he did, and conveyed the exact results of the triennial Visitation of Maynooth by the Lord Chancellor and the Chief Judges, together with the investigations carried out every six months by the Board of Trustees. If there is impropriety, it is to these it should be attributed, rather than to the subordinate members of the College.

> "To these Trustees then, rather than to the subordinate members of the College, should be attributed any improper doctrine, morals, discipline or other abuses, supposed to be taught, tolerated or even practised there. They have consequently felt inexpressible pain, and wish indignantly to repel so fowl and unjust a stigma, which they would have long since

refuted, in full and solemn manner, had it been intimated to them, as they justly expected, by the Holy See, and not merely by the contemptible medium of popular rumour''.

Curtis asks Blake to find out from Caprano what exactly is deemed to be wrong at Maynooth, as he (Curtis) is approaching his 80th year and consequently his ''final dissolution'', and he would like to remedy matters before this if they need to be remedied. Truly a just man. HIs remonstrance found its way to Propaganda. Whether it made its way there then or later is an open question but, to all appearances, it did go there then. The outcome was bleak for Maynooth. No decree issued from Propaganda granting it the facility to confer any degree. And there is no denying that the spectre of Trinity College hangs over the unanswered question as to what would have happened if Maynooth had been granted this. It played a major part in the thwarting of Maynooth's university prospects at that time. But then time goes on . . . .

Chapter IX

Investigation by Order of the Crown

The 1820's marked a special period in the history of Maynooth. It was in 1821 that John J. McGregor's book appeared — *A New Picture of Dublin . . . containing a Complete Guide to everything Curious and Interesting in the Irish Metropolis.* It was published by Johnston and Dees of Bachelor's Walk. Naturally, it gave some place to Maynooth:

"Though this establishment is not situated in Dublin, yet, from its vicinity to the capital, it may justly be classed among its literary institutions . . . The building consists of a centre and two wings, the whole extending 400 feet in length, and containing a neat chapel, refectory, extensive dormitories, and a library of about 5,000 volumes, chiefly on theological subjects. In front of the building, is a fine lawn of two acres, laid out in gravel walks, and separated from the street by a handsome semicircular iron railing . . . The number of students in the college is about 300. Each student pays eight guineas entrance money, and his personal expenses throughout the year are estimated at twenty pounds. The course of study comprehends humanity, logic. mathematics, divinity and modern languages. There are two public examinations held in each year, and premiums are given according to the merit of the answerers; the period of study is usually five years. The strictest discipline and decorum are enforced by the internal regulations of the college. During meals the Scriptures and other useful books are read, and the students are allowed to read no books but those recommended by the President and Professors. The officers of the establishment consist of a President, Vice-President, Dean, Bursar, Sub-Dean, eleven Professors, three Lecturers, a Treasurer, Physician, and Agent. The salaries amount to above 1800 l. annually. This respectable and useful establishment is supported by Parliamentary grants, and aided by private donations and legacies".

THE LETTERS OF 'HIEROPHILOS'

The previous year had seen the publication of *A few friendly Hints to the Rev. Harcourt Lees, Baronet, with an Epistle to the Protestant Prelates of Ireland,* by the Rev. Charles B. Stennett. The *Anti-Jacobin Review* for September of that year in reviewing this had said that it was "an authentic work, issuing from the Romish college of Maynooth . . . in which the author has been domesticated for some time". He is referred to as "priest Stennett". The *Review* assures him that "he is as dangerous to the Protestant Church in Ireland, in his hood and cowl at Maynooth, as he possibly could be at the head of his grenadiers in the North York Militia". Who he was escapes us. In the same 1820 his opponent, Sir Harcourt Lees, brought out another pamphlet entitled, in the short way that the time espoused, *The Mystery: being a short but decisive counter-reply to the few friendly hints of the Rev. Charles B. Stennett at present an officiating popish priest in the Religious Colleges of Maynooth and late a lieutenant of grenadiers in the North York Regiment of Militia.* It was addressed to "The Rev. Lieutenant Stennett", who has exchanged his "helmet for a Maynooth cowl" and gone "into the services of the Pedagogues of Maynooth College", otherwise known as "the Friars of Maynooth." Sir Harcourt Lees went further by all accounts, bringing out also another pamphlet, equally short in title — *Strictures on the Rev. Lieutenant Stennett's Hints to Sir Harcourt Lees, by the Anti-Jacobin British Review for September, to which is prefixed a Short Introduction containing a most important letter from a Gentleman, educated and intended for the Popish Priesthood.* This one is addressed to the "Most Rev. Grenadier" and says that the reply 'Mystery' nearly occasioned Stennett's death, or at least so the writer is informed. And so he goes to town: "Let some of your pillars and brightest luminaries try to confute one single argument I ever advanced, and you will then see where I will place him within twenty-four hours after his work appears, whoever he may be — I challenge the entire body of your Heads, Professors and Principals, from Dr. Milner or the Jesuit Gandolphy to the Titular Archbishop of Tuam, Dr. Kelly — from Rome to Maynooth." Fancy that — not from Maynooth to Rome!

The identity of Stennett remains obscure but not of John McHale. It is true that he had been listed in the College *Records* as John McCaule and even in 1820 the *Journal of the Trustees* has it that, on the resignation of the Rev. M. de la Hogue from his Chair, in compliance with a resolution of 25 June, 1818, whereby he will get an annuity with lodging and commons, he is to be succeeded by the Rev. Mr. McKeal as Professor. McCaule, McKeal or McHale, whichever one calls him, was going to leave his mark. He became Professor of Dogmatic Theology on 22 August, 1820. Finance-wise he came to his chair at an unpropitious time. At the June meeting of the Trustees that year the salaries of the staff were reduced. The Vice-President, Procurator, Profs. of Divinity, and Sacred Scripture and Hebrew were to have £100 p.a., allowances included, Professors of Philosophy were to have £90, those of the First Class of Humanity £80 and of English Elocution and Irish £80. Those of the Second Class of Humanity were to be in receipt of £70 as well as those of all other classes and the Junior Dean £70. On that day also the Reverend Loftus was appointed in the place of the deceased Paul O'Brien. On that day too, as the *Journal of the Trustees* puts it, "the particular attention of the Presidt. is requested to the cleanliness of the College both in and out of doors and to the dress of the scholars conformably to the regulations". The 'Professors' were not doing badly at all, even though neither then nor since could it be expected that this would be acknowledged, thank you. The spiritual life was a different domain, one hopes, but with experienced incredibility, unaffected by things material. In July, 1820 Dr. Doyle — J.K.L. — had a great retreat at Carlow for some "one thousand priests and nearly every prelate in Ireland". It was regarded as quite a 'happening', because retreats had fallen into disuse although "a few attempts had been made at Maynooth, from 1795, to restore that great piece of ecclesiastical discipline". The Limerick Novena of the 1970's was far off.

Back to McHale: The first series of his letters to the daily papers, signed 'Hierophilos' and against antagonists in Dublin, the English in general and Canning in particular, appeared in 1820. McHale himself was a cultivated and tolerant man but he did not stand for nonsense — or ceremony for that matter, even though he was a frequent visitor to the Duke of Leinster at Carton, as were also, we know, the French professors. The year 1820 has also seen the formation of the Iberno-Celtic Society, with the President of the College and the soon to be deceased Paul O'Brien as members. When the *Letters of Hierophilus* appeared, the College public was prepared for them. Technically, they were but a reply to a pamphlet by 'Declan', a Fellow of Trinity College. They were patriotic to the highest degree and castigated the Government of the time. They made no great impact in the College but it is no great wonder that they drew a response from the defenders of the status quo. In 1821 was produced *Irish Priests, or the great obstacles to every measure intended to promote the Tranquillity, Civilization and unanimity of Ireland.* It reported: Students for the priesthood are first instructed in a Catholic Academy "at about from 18 to 30 years of age". After a year or two "the predestined imposter is translated to the College of Maynooth" of which "the very name is a burlesque upon learning, and, to anyone acquainted with its nature, concentrates in the mind a term expressive of everything contemptible and vile . . ." It has "swarms of unfledged pedants . . . with demure and crafty looks . . . a scholastic and awkward air . . . vigorous limbs, disguised in the unaccustomed trammels of glossy black broadcloth, plump and shining cheeks, puffed up with the recent luxury of station . . . with averted eyes, crouching brow, and settled smile, endeavouring to conceal the rancorous bigotry of their hearts". Charlotte Elizabeth could not have been bettered. A 'tit for tat' reply came as always: *A Reply to a Malignant and slanderous pamphlet entitled 'Irish Priests'; containing a general glance at the Orange System and a brief vindication of the Roman Catholics of Ireland.* What an interesting combination! It was published by Richard Coyne in 1821 at 4 Chapel Street, Dublin.

'THE BUST OF HIS LATE MAJESTY'

On Monday, 6 November, 1820, the Queen's trial entered its 49th day in the House of Lords. Poor Caroline of Brunswick — she may have been somewhat uncouth but she was ill done by the nobility of England in general although not by the common people. On 15 November the *Freeman* of Dublin carried an elated account of her legal victory. On the following Saturday, 18 November, it tells us of illuminations (a custom of the time) at Oxford on the previous Monday night, even though a placard had been put up, signed both by the Vice-Chancellor of the University and the Mayor of the City, asking for no such thing lest 'Queenites' should break the peace. Yet "a great part of the City is illuminated and those parts that are not, it is thought will require glazing tomorrow"! Still, on Monday, 20 November, the *Freeman* expressed doubt about the wisdom of such illuminations. What of Maynooth College? Were there any illuminations there? On Tuesday, 28 November, the *Freeman* carried the following: "We have unquestionable authority for stating that the account given in the *Weekly Register* of Saturday, of illuminations said to have taken place in the R.C. College of Maynooth, is totally destitute of truth, and is supposed to have originated in a feeling hostile to the peace and prosperity of the Establishment". It is of some interest too to recount that in the same November the *Freeman* reported that "Mr. Godwin has just published a work on Population, in which it is his object to show that the doctrines advanced by Mr. Malthus on the subject are altogether unfounded". This was the William Godwin who predicted that the day would come when the whole world would be able to grow its food supply from a single flower-pot. It is a hypothesis worth considering . . .!!! In Ireland of 1821 it was even more preposterous. On Friday, 1 May, the *Freeman* reported: "Not for twenty years has the Spring been remembered as so backward in this quarter of the century, nor the weather so severe. The crops make little progress, and the poor condition of the cattle marks the insufficiency of the pasturage and the inclemency of the weather".

At Maynooth the College was concerned with litigation — not for the only time; it survived. The *Journal of the Trustees* has an entry for 3 February, 1820: "The Case respecting two ejectments on the title being served by the Duke of Leinster, one for the purpose of impeaching the grant of the 9th Sept. 1795 from the late Duke of Leinster to the Trustees and the other for 16 perches of ground on which has been erected the Porter's lodge and Mr. Bellew's opinion thereon, being laid before the Board that it was proper that a compromise should be entered into between the Trustees and His Grace. Resolved, that it be referred to Mr. Bellew, the counsel to the Solicitor of the College to take the necessary measures to effect such compromise in the manner most advantageous to the College". As we know before, on 20 February, 1821, a new lease on the part of the College from the Duke of Leinster was signed. It was all part of the time. The *Catholic Directory* for 1821 directs attention to other matters: "In Navan is kept the Roman Catholic Diocesan School . . . in which vast numbers of young gentlemen from every part of Ireland have been educated, some of whom have excelled in the various learned professions. The plan of education embraces the diverse branches of Literature which are calculated to fit the young Gentlemen for the College of Maynooth, Dublin, etc., . . . Army, Navy, etc." In the College of Maynooth the Trustees, at their meeting of 26 June, that year, had more mundane matters in mind. They resolved that "the Sub-Committee appointed yesterday having reported and recommended the following works, repairs, etc., viz. a Bake house, benches for the aisles of the Chapel, a Store room to be floored, Necessaries to be built" and so forth, this should be done. At the same meeting it was also resolved that a special Committee should "point out a proper situation where the Bust of the late King be placed". George III, of — memory was gone. The said 'Bust' had many repositories. During the early 1970's it was found by the then President, in little more than a rubbish heap in the carpenter's store, whither it had been dispatched years before in an excess of patriotic enthusiasm. It was then placed in the President's office. If no more, it is a fine portrait by the Italian sculptor Turnerelli. Afterwards following some further viscissitudes, it was removed to the rooms of the President. History repeating itself again.

On 26 June, 1821, with the alacrity common at that time (sub-committee or no sub-committee) the Trustees decided on "the placing of the Bust of his late Majesty in the Hall". This was undoubtedly done and 'his late Majesty' probably reposed there until the revolution of 1916-'21. As far as the College went, February, 1822 saw the Trustees deciding that "a sum not exceeding two thousand pounds be expended in building a continuation of the South wing of the College". And College people will remember, with either mirth or nostalgia, the resolution of 1822: "That the Bursar subscribe to the farmer's Journal". That same Trustees' meeting decreed that the College Buildings Committee should look into the ventilating of the four great halls of the College, "with cold and warm air", and also the refectory and prayer hall "with cold air"! Their remit was monetarily up to 200 guineas. What a time. What a currency. Finally, on 21 June, 1822, it was 'ordered' by the Trustees "that the Bust of the late Majesty be placed in a niche to be formed in the South Window of the front Parlour before 25th August". As it so happened in the following January it was put in the President's room "until otherwise ordered". It would seem that there was some reluctance on the part of the College to place 'his late Majesty' in a prominent position. We have related 'his' subsequent history to date.

THE 'MAYNOOTH MANIFESTO'

The dilemma in which the College was caught — of loyalty to both the Crown and to Rome — continued to show itself regularly and a lot depended on one's point of view as to which side should go more emphasis. That the teaching was coloured by Gallicanism cannot be doubted. In 1823 the student Francis Patrick Kenrick wrote from Rome to his uncle the Reverend Richard Kenrick, P.P. of Francis Street, Dublin: "I fear my theological treatise on Papal prerogatives might not have entirely met with your appreciation, but I hope the abundance of your charity will make allowance for our speculative dissension. You were educated at Maynooth and if I mistake not under French preceptors; I at Rome whence we might not be expected perfectly to agree in opinions at issue between France and Italy . . .". On the other hand, in his *Views of Ireland,* published in London in 1823, John O'Driscoll, Esq. wrote: "There was more of the spirit of Rome at Maynooth than at Rome itself . . . and we are sure the Pope has less of popery in his mind and character than some of the young students of that College".

Naturally, it was in the Dunboyne studies, of a higher nature as they were, that these 'opinions' were canvassed most. We know, for example, that in 1823 Nicholas Callan, then a Dunboyne student, advanced a thesis entitled *De Sacrificio Abrahae.* It was at a public disputation in the presence of the assembled Trustees. By all accounts it was a famous occasion which went down in College folklore for many a year. The later Archbishop of Tuam, Dr. McHale, then Professor of Dogmatic Theology, played a big part in it. We are not told a lot as to what it was all about but it seems likely that it is the same occasion that is referred to in Fitzpatrick's *Life of Doyle.* Dr. Doyle — J.K.L. that is — gave the retreat at Maynooth that year and the disputation may have taken place just before or after it while he was in the College. At any rate he did attend at a disputation at which Dr. McHale expressed an opinion different from that advanced by Dr. Slevin, the then 'rector' of the Dunboyne class. Dr. Doyle stood up and said: "The opinion of Dr. Slevin is more in accordance with our natural feelings than that of Dr. McHale. The opinion of Dr. McHale, however, is more in accordance with the words of Almighty God". The argument apparently was whether human sacrifices were acceptable to God. It is well that any of the Gallican 'opinions' were not being discussed or there would have been sparks flying with a vengeance. Dr. Doyle was particularly interested in opinions of a political nature. In May, 1824, he contributed a Public Letter to Mr. Robertson on 'The Concilation of Ireland' to *The Morning Chronicle* of London:

'The Minister of England cannot look to the exertions of the Catholic Priesthood; they have been ill-treated and they may yield for a moment to the influence of nature, thought it be opposed to grace. This clergy, with few exceptions, are from the ranks of the people, they inherit their feelings, they are not, as formerly, brought up under despotic governments, they have imbibed the doctrinces of Locke and Paley more deeply than those of Bellarmin or even Bossuet on the divine Right of Kings;

They know much more of the principles of the Constitution than they do of passive obedience''.

It was true that at that time some of the younger clergy were campaigning actively for emancipation, which was not far off. In May, 1824, a priest of the Archdiocese of Tuam sent on to his Archbiship some letters he had received from some of them who were participating in the agitation, ''to show Your Grace what a contrast between the sentiments of the young and the old''. The Maynooth staff, or at least the more conservative of its members, were worried lest some of this would rub off on the College to the detriment of its interests. Hence they determined to counter it by an open statement of their loyalty. It was suggested afterwards that their action was the result of an appeal by the Lord Lieutenant, Lord Wellesley, who wished to neutralize Dr. Doyle's letter, which was looked upon as seditious. The 'Maynooth Manifesto', as it came to be called, was got up by the French professors. Fitzpatrick describes it as an ''effort of antiquated French divinity'' to suppress Dr. Doyle. Its authors — the Sorbonnistes — were certainly men of the old r'egime. The story of how they produced it after dinner one evening and got the whole staff to sign it (even chasing into town after the young Dr. Browne of Kilmore and pretty well forcing him to sign) is told fully by Fitzpatrick:

> ''On the 4th of June 1824 appeared the manifesto from Maynooth, of whose advent Dr. Doyle had already been advised. ''In consequence,'' it said, ''of recent public allusions to the domestic education of the College Clergy, we, the undersigned Professors of the Royal College of Maynooth, deem it a duty which we own to religion and to the country solemnly and publicly to state, that in our respective situations we have uniformly inculcated allegiance to our gracious sovereign, respect for the constituted authorities, and obedience to the laws''.
> ''Dr. Doyle promptly addressed a letter to the editor of the *Post,* assuring him that the 'publication signed by some gentlemen at Maynooth had his full and entire approbation'. He observed that a recent letter of his had been designated as 'seditious' by a noble Lord in the House of Peers. 'In Ireland,' he added, 'no such mistake as that of the nobleman alluded to could occur, because here my efforts to support the laws and check disaffection are too well known, and the principles of allegiance as inculcated by me are recorded in my writings.'
> ''The Right Hon. R. L. Sheil writes:— 'Dr. Doyle's announcement of what is now obviously the truth created a sort of consternation. Lord Wellesley, it is said, in order to neutralise the effects of this fierce episcopal warning, appealed to Maynooth; and from Maynooth there is issued a document, in which it is well understood that the students, and even the President, Dr. Crotty, did not agree, but to which the names of

five of the Professors were attached. The reputation of Dr. Doyle was more widely extended by this effort of antiquated French divinity to suppress him..'

"Three of the Professors who signed the Maynooth declaration of 1824 became members of the Irish Episcopal bench. One of this venerable trio informed us of the precise circumstances under which the document was drawn up. The late Rev. Paul O'Brien, a priest of great tact and talent, was then attached to Maynooth College. 'He would sometimes,' observed our informant, the late Dr. Brown, Bishop of Kilmore, 'read aloud a random passage from a book, and by means of using a peculiar tone and emphasis, would turn his hearers completely against it. Again, by shifting the tone and reversing his manner, that passage which previously disgusted rarely failed, the next minute, to fascinate. It was Mr. O'Brien's aim, in the present instance, to charge Dr. Doyle's paragraph with the unfavourable tone; and one fine evening in June, while the Professors were at dessert, O'Brien took up the letter and read it aloud. The Irish Professors present listened in silence; but the French theologians, Delahogue and Anglade, who had belonged in their own country to the ancient r'egime, at once pricked up their ears, and assumed a mingled expression of disgust and alarm. *'Mon Dieu!'* exclaimed Delahogue, *'est ce possible qu'il preche la Revolution?' 'La Revolution!'* echoed Anglade, *'c'est horrible!'* It was decided then and there, that, lest the Royal College of St. Patrick or its Professors should be in any way compromised by Dr. Doyle's letter, they should forthwith, and in the most public manner, repudiate all connection with it. 'I signed the document with great reluctance,' continued our informant. 'I long shared the friendship of Dr. Doyle, and rather than be called upon to sign it, I proceeded to Dublin when the matter was started. But it was not long ere my retreat was discovered by Dr. Anglade and Delahogue, and, yielding to their expostulation, I at length very reluctantly gave my signature. Although the document was pointedly aimed at Dr. Doyle, his friendship for me suffered no diminution, and on my elevation to the episcopacy, a year later, he wrote me a beautiful and most affectionate letter of advice, and prayerful aspiration for the success of my untried abilities. I preserved this truly eloquent letter until recently, when I destroyed it with many others, which I now greatly regret!''

Copies did survive however, The Manifesto, also known as 'the Sorbonne Manifesto', is printed in Healy and it is also contained in a pamphlet issued in 1824, entitled *Correspondence with Members of Parliament on an Union of the Churches to which are appended a letter from the Right Rev. Dr. Doyle and a Declaration from the Professors of the Roman Catholic College of Maynooth.* Actually the manifesto was headed 'Royal Catholic College of St. Patrick, Maynooth' and was a fawning protestation of loyalty.

The full text is as follows:

"In consequence of recent public allusions ot the domestic education of the Catholic Clergy, we, the undersigned Professors of the Roman Catholic College of Maynooth, deem it a duty which we owe to Religion, and to the country, solemnly and publicly to state, that in our respective situations, we have uniformly inculcated allegiance to our gracious Sovereign, respect for the constituted authorities and obedience to the Laws.

"In discharging this solemn duty, we have been guided by the unchangeable principles of the Catholic Religion, plainly and forcibly contained in the following precepts of Saint Peter and Saint Paul:-

"Be ye subject therefore to every human creature for God's sake; whether it be to the King, as excelling, or to governors sent by him, for the punishment of evil doers, and for the praise of the good; for so is the will of God, that by doing well you may put to silence the ignorance of foolish men: as free and not as making liberty a cloak for malice, but as the servants of God. Honour all men, Love the brotherhood. Fear God. Honour the King . . . For this is thanks worthy, if for conscience towards God a man endures sorrows, suffering wrongfully, for what glory it is, if committing sin, and being suffering for it you endure? But if doing well you suffer patiently, this is thanks worthy before God." *1st Ep of St. Peter, c.2.*

"Let every soul be subject to higher powers: for there is no power but from God; and those that are, are ordained of God. Therefore he that resisteth the power, resisteth the ordinance of God. And they that resist, purchase to themselves damnation. For Princes are not a terror to the good work, but to the evil. Wilt thou then, not be afraid of the Power? Do that which is good, and thou shalt have praise for the same . . . Wherefore be subject of necessity, not only for wrath but also for conscience sake." *Ep. to the Rom. c.13.*

"Our commentaries on these texts cannot be better conveyed than in the language of Tertullian. "Christians are aware who has conferred their power on the Emperors: they know it is God, after whom they are first in rank, and second to no other. From the same source, which imparts life, they also derive their power. We Christians invoke on all the Emperors the blessings of long life, a prosperous reign, domestic security, a brave army, a devoted senate, and a moral people." *Apology,* chap 30.

"Into the sincerity of these professions we challenge the most rigid inquiry; and we appeal with confidence to the peaceable and loyal conduct of the Clergy educated in this Establishment, and to their exertions to preserve the public order, as evidence of soundness of the principles inculcated in this College. These principles are the same which have been ever taught by the Catholic Church: and if any change has been wrought in the minds of the Clergy of Ireland, it is, that religious obligation is here strengthened by motives of gratitude, and confirmed by sworn allegiance from which no power on earth can absolve.

L. E. DE LAHOGUE, Fellow of Sorbonne, and Emeritus.
    Professor in Sorbonne and Maynooth.
JOHN M'HALE, Professor of Dogmatic Theology.
FRANCIS ANGLADE, Professor of Moral Theology.
JAMES BROWN, Professor of Sacred Scripture.
CHARLES M'NALLY, Professor of Logic and
    Moral Philosophy.
June 2nd, 1824''.

It is doubtful whether this manifesto produced the effect which its authors wished. It may have only served to draw even more attention on the College, and its political sentiments, the very thing that they did not want. Dr. Brown in his own way also drew attention to the College. In November, 1824, we find him taking part in a public argumentation at Carrick-on-Shannon between three Roman Catholic Priests and three Clergymen of the Established Church. The function was organised by the Leitrim Bible Society. One of the priests was Dr. McKeon, Vicar General of the Diocese of Ardagh and the Pope's Legate in Ireland. Fifty tickets were issued by the Protestant Curate of the Parish and fifty by Dr. McKeon. The subject was the propriety of circulating the Scriptures and whether good men of every persuasion may be saved, as against "the doctrine of exclusive salvation. Between one thing and another suspicion began to hang over Maynooth as regards its loyalty and the exact nature of what was being taught there. The government had begun to take fright. It mattered little that the Maynooth Professors took the oath of loyalty on their appointment and that the appointment of the Prefect of the Dunboyne Establishment had the approbation of Dublin Castle, if the views of the Professors about the meaning of the oath were questionable, which is thought to be the case. Did they regard it as "an empty formula", to employ a phrase heard much later? There was only one way to satisfy one's queries about such matters — through investigation by order of the Crown. Delahogue was resigned to it all. He had made his will in October, 1823, leaving most of his effects to his brother and sister and the residue to Anglade whom he appointed executor. He continued to live in the College as Professor Emeritus until his death in 1827, unlike Fr. Braughall, a former student now retired also who, about the same time was offered rooms in the College by the Bursar, but who, we are told, "preferred to end his days with the Benedictines at Monte Cassino, an order which had already given forty-four Popes to the Church". Monte Cassino was certainly quieter than Maynooth in the 1820's.

In March, 1825, a prelude to what was to come was enacted in the Select Committee of the House of Lords on Ireland. The theme was the profound changes worked on the Irish Catholic priesthood by the substitution of Maynooth for the old seminaries of the Continent. It was good for O'Connell to be up against it, given his previous record on the subject: he was now being heard again specifically on it. Lord Binning was in the Chair. It was 4 March of that year. Asked 'what class of persons are the Catholic priests educated at Maynooth?' O'Connell replied: "The are mostly the children of peasants or small farmers but lately several gentry are becoming priests; there are a good many of them now at Maynooth". He was catching up, long after he should have done. Asked: "Is there not a very great want of books at Maynooth College?", he replied: "They complain of wanting books; the funds there are totally inadequate for the College" — again *a Tadhg an da thaobh*. He considered this lack of books acute as the students "are kept almost isolated from the world, not allowed so much as a newspaper . . . living under a rigid discipline in point of hours, living very temperately in point of provisions and secluded from the politics and pursuits of the world". As regards the course of education pursued there, all he would — or maybe could — say was that it was available from Coyne's of Capel Street for a few pence or a few shillings. No, O'Connell was not going to be enticed into speaking about Cabassutius or Menochius or Virgil or Euclid — he was too canny for that. He did say that he had a nephew at Maynooth — this may explain the 'recent' entry there of gentry — who "when he comes to my house at Dublin it is a great treat to him to be allowed to go over the newspapers, four or five or six weeks old". Asked: Are the students "allowed to mix with the gentlemen and others residing in the neighbourhood?" — reply: "Not at all". It was crisp and entirely incomplete. Question: "Then are the Committee right in supposing the Maynooth College has very much the appearance of a very strict monastery?" Answer: "It has a good deal of monastic discipline. What surprises me most, with respect to the young men educated at Maynooth, is not that they acquire a classical and scientific knowledge, but that they really acquire a style in the English language that is of a very superior order; they write admirably well". How surprising. But then: "The Priests, who were educated in France, had a natural abhorrence of the French Revolution, which bore so much on the Catholic Clergy. They were very strong Anti-Jacobin, if I may use the expression. By that means there was among them a great deal of what is called ultra-royalism; but, with the Priests educated at Maynooth, the Anti-Jacobin feeling is gone by, and they are more identified with the people, and therefore in the phrase that is usually called loyalty, they do not come so much within the description of it as the Priests educated in France". He himself, of course, as a schoolboy had been with the Josephites in Louvain. There were further submissions to the Select Committee — including one by our old friend The Reverend William Phelan — but we need not delay over them. It suffices to say that they were not on the side of Maynooth. Neither was that of the Protestant Archbishop of Dublin, who claimed that De la Hogue taught the "doctrines of exclusive salvation". In his eyes, like those of O'Connell, with all its disadvantages a foreign education is preferable to an education at Maynooth. To be sure, there are circumstances which account for this presently at Maynooth, due to the unfortunate state of the country.

> As a result "it would seem that whatever withdraws for some time from the scene of the fermentation and party a considerable portion of the Roman Catholic youth, and especially those of that description who are to have a leading influence upon the principles and feelings of the mass of their population, must in its own nature be highly advantageous. In Maynooth the student still breathes, if I may say so, the atmosphere of inflammation. . . . (also the education there is illiberal) . . . There is too much reason to apprehend that in Maynooth a feeling hostile to cordiality is fostered . . . It is generally amongst the young priests who have been educated at Maynooth, as far as I have been informed, that the forwardness . . . to intermix spiritual with political concerns, principally prevails. Therefore with respect to the Maynooth institution, I am obliged, upon the whole, to give it as my opinion, that, as it is at present constituted and conducted, it is not favourable to tranquillity, nor, I fear, to the principles of a sound civil allegiance".

He gives no proofs to support his opinions. It is heresay only. But there it was. O'Connell had been of no help. The die was cast.

MR. DANIEL O'CONNELL, M.P. LIBERATOR

UNDER SCRUTINY

It was not for the first or the last time that the College was investigated. We recall 1812 when it was ordered that the books used there be submitted to the examination of the Government. On that occasion — to be precise it was in a speech to the House of Commons on 24 April, 1812 — John Leslie Foster had said:

"The College of Maynooth has now subsisted for seventeen years and I have never met with any person who could inform me of the course of studies actually pursued. Is this a matter of no consequence? Did there ever exist a Catholic Government who thought this a matter not necessary to superintend? A Return indeed, was made a few years ago, to an Order of this House, of the books which form the basis of these studies: among which, I will candidly acknowledge, I was a little surprised to see the name of Locke. The Return, however, goes on to State that after all, these books are not what is there read, but that the lectures are delivered from Manuscript Courses, and a reason is assigned in 'the paucity of books' . . . By some I have heard the studies represented, if not as very enlightened, at least as very harmless: but others I have heard with equal confidence assert that the course consists not of the Logic of Mr. Locke but of the Logic which his writings overturned, curiously compounded with the Theology of the Jesuits, and both administered under the discipline of Sparta".

Now in 1825 — on 20 January — Foster took up his cause again, Writing to Peel:

"My late tour of inspection gave me full opportunities of comparing the Maynooth priests as a class with the foreign educated clergy, and O'Connell would have found in the latter but a rope of sand if he had been obliged to deal with such for his materials. But it is plainly Maynooth that has enabled him to construct his organisation. The students who enter it are literally peasants. They leave it with as great an ignorance of the world as they brought into it, but they acquire in it an *Esprit de Corps* which it is impossible to describe, of which a taste for religious controversy and a keen anti-British feeling are the leading features. These are just the men to influence the people and to be led themselves by a bold demagogue".

If the *Journal of the Trustees* for 11 February, 1825, is any indication, festive times, such as Christmas and St. Patrick's Day, were occasions for the manifestation of student views because it records a resolution to the effect that on those days an allowance of wine was to be continued but for one hour only after dinner, during which conversation is permitted. It reads in full:

212

"Resolved: that as soon as may be convenient after dinner the students shall as heretofore have their allowance of wine for taking which one hour is deemed sufficient. During this hour conversation is permitted. But the Board hopes that the good sense of the student will show them the impropriety of anything bordering on uproar or discord, more especially on those solemn festivals on which they are supposed to have complied with the most sacred duties of religion and to be more than ordinarily impressed with the feelings which the discharge of their duties is calculated to produce. After leaving the refectory the students may amuse themselves in their respective halls until 7 o'clock, and may sing songs; but it is hoped that here too they will conduct themselves in a manner becoming of Gentlemen and Christians".

Strong language itself indeed.

Whether they were aware of it or not — and they possibly were not — both staff and students at Maynooth were in for a rude awakening. It was all very fine for somebody to say that the famous Manifesto "was laughed at by the Irish priesthood" but what was about to overtake the College was no laughing matter at all. In October, 1826, the Commissioners of Irish Education Inquiry, having completed their other work, announced their intention of investigating Maynooth. The extent of their inquiry, published in 1827, can be judged from the fact that it runs to 456 closely printed foolscap-size folio pages. It was conducted in Dublin Castle, whither came on command the President, Vice-Pesident, Dean, Bursar, Professors, Prefect of the Dunboyne and a selected number of students past and present. The examination tends to be repetitive. Strangely enough, we cannot cull a great deal from it about the everyday life of the student. The Commissioners were interested more in the political views of everybody there, in their beliefs concerning the infallibility of and temporal power of the Pope, their attitude towards the oath of loyalty and similar 'mixed' items. Some of those examined were from those who had conformed to the Established Church, including the Reverend Matthias Crowley, then "a curate in Great Connell, in the diocese of Kildare and vicar of Jerpoint in the diocese of Ossory". He had gone places. The Commissioners were naturally quite interested in what he and his likes had to say. They also availed themselves of the opportunity afforded them to find out something about the background of the students. Those whom they chose to examine must have left them somewhat puzzled. Mr. Furlong from Wexford declared that his parents "hold land in the barony of Forth"; Mr. Reynolds stated that his father "keeps a general shop in Kilcock, he also holds a considerable tract of land, something beyond two hundred acres"; Mr. Leahy from Tipperary informed them that his father "is engaged in the surveying and engineering department"; Mr. McGauley of Dublin that his people "possess some houses in Kilmainham", his father being also some sort of maintenance man; Mr. Aylward of Kilkenny that his father "is a farmer"; Mr. Chapman of

Ferns that his mother "holds between 250 and 300 acres under the Marquis of Ely, in the Barony of Shelbourne; Mr. Roger from Cork that his father "is a woollen draper and an army contractor for men's necessaries and accoutrement on a large scale". And that was it, apart from Mssrs. Delany from Cork and Marmion who were not asked the question and Mr. Cassidy from Fermanagh (planter's territory) who said simply that his parents belonged to "the middling order" of society, meaning "persons who can live independently, and who, perhaps, could provide for their children a situation that would be more lucrative than the priesthood". The Commissioners had got more than they bargained for in their sociological survey into backgrounds.

On the issues of infallibility and the temporal power of the Pope they were in all likelihood more satisfied with the answers. Whether Rome would have been is an entirely different thing, for it does emerge very clearly that Maynooth was a hot-bed of Gallicanism as might be expected due to the French influence. Even French cultural influence can be deduced from the fact that in those early days all students were obliged to attend classes in the French language. On the infallibility of the Pope, Dr. Crotty is unequivocal that it is only if something is decreed by the Pope in communion with the majority of the Bishops that it is regarded as infallible — not precisely because it is a decree of the Pope. Similarly, the former Vice-President, Fr. Peter Kenny, S.J., agreed that an assertion contained in the oath of allegiance that it is not an article of Catholic faith to believe that the Pope is infallible "is a doctrine which Jesuits as well as all other Catholics maintain; but the proposition which asserts that the Pope is infallible, when, *loquens ex cathedra,* he declares, that such or such a doctrine is an article of Catholic faith, is an opinion which each man is free to hold whose conscience and judgement lead him to that conclusion". Likewise, Anglade was definite about this. Speaking of the fourth article of the 'Gallican liberties', which is generally understood to deny the infallibility of the Pope, speaking for himself, and independently of a general council", he assured his inquisitors that this article was held generally at Maynooth, although "one may be for one side and another for the other, for it is not an article of faith". The wily old boy. But he was unswerving in his answer to the question: "If the Pope and a Council properly constituted, were to declare tomorrow that the Pope was infallible, would it not then become an article of faith?" Answer: "It would". Dr. Higgins took a like view. On being asked: "The question whether the Pope has nor the gift of infallibility is a mooted question in the Roman Catholic Church?" he replied: "Yes, it is question left perfectly free for professors and students to discuss as they may think proper".

These Gallican liberties occupied a great deal of the Inquiry, that relating to the temporal power of the Pope even more than than about his infallibility. Anglade gave a comprehensive explanation of them. And he still held them. More particularly: "I do hold that the Pope has only spiritual jurisdiction, but not as an article of faith". "Do you not reject the doctrine that the Pope has any civil or temporal power?" "I do reject that doctrine." Mind you, at a time when the

Papal States had been restored . . . Small wonder that Mr. Anglade kept away from Rome. Crotty was equally certain that he did not regard the Pope as having any temporal power: "I mentioned his interference in temporal matters and disclaimed his right to interfere . . . Temporal matters I conceive to include all the rights and prerogatives either of the King, or of whatever civil government may be established in any country, and I hold that the Pope has nothing to do in the management of such matters". Is it possible that Crotty was making a subtle distinction between the Pope and his government managers? Dr. Higgins was un-prevaricating in avowing his adhesion to the Gallican principles: "I do most willingly subscribe to those principles", while Dr. Montague declared that the Gallican principles were "substantially adopted", inasmuch as "the principal propositions on which the Gallican liberties are founded, are defended by the Professors and Students of Maynooth", and Dr. Dowley asserted that "the Trans-Alpine doctrine has never been taught, inculcated, or encouraged in the College".

So far so good; on this the Commissions were probably satisfied. But what about the understanding of the oath which these Maynooth men took? Dr. Boylan, Prof. of Rhetoric, when asked: "Have you ever met with any student who thought it would be lawful for him to break that oath, because it was taken to a Protestant sovereign?" told how he "had paused for a moment, from a feeling of indignation at the general charge that is brought against us, and against our religion, of indifference to oaths" — it was an intolerable question he thought. Needless to say, he has come across no evidence of any student "who would not fully participate in these sentiments". Was it a parry, having taken some time to recollect himself? This is unlikely, for we know that some years before the Inquiry Dr. Milner had met the four Irish Archbishops at Maynooth and had agreed with them a formula concerning the oath. But the Commissioners must have been prevented by Boylan's hesitancy. Worse was to follow. The Reverend Thomas William Dixon, a former Maynooth student now a clergyman of the Established Church, did not put a tooth in it. When he was a student, he said nobody took any great notice of the oath: "We thought that these oaths were required of us, in order to save appearances". The Reverend E. Moloney, another pervert, corroborated on the grounds that the Pope could dispense with any oath as he saw fit. There must have been some commotion at this. It took the appearance of Dr. Crolly, Professor of Moral Theology, to endeavour to put things right. The fact was, he outlined, that while parts of the oath of allegiance were perfectly acceptable to Catholics, certain parts were not, but Mr. Arthur O'Leary had explained how these might be regarded by one talking the oath, an explanation that was at the disposal of the Maynooth students: "There were some parts requiring us to swear with regard to the power of the Pope and things of that kind, which young men at the age when they generally enter college did not well understand; of course it was necessary to have some explanation given on these points, and O'Leary's explanation was perfectly satisfactory to me, and I believe to the others". Father Peter Kenny, in true Jesuitical fashion, tied them up in knots. While agreeing that an oath had to be taken very seriously, he agreed also with the Professor of Moral Theology but expanded on what the latter had said by pointing out that there were two kinds of oaths, that of which the subject matter is lawful and that of which it is not. An example of the second would be where one under obedience took an oath contrary to the good of his community — which oath his Superior could certainly invalidate as already subject to his jurisdiction ("controul"). The Commissioners must have been dazed. One feels that they were glad to fall back on the clearcut, no-words-lost reply of J. R. Corballis, Esq., formerly of the Lay College, a Barrister, who when asked: "Has the sentiment . . . with respect to the sacredness of an oath, been a sentiment which you have heard universally inculcated?", answered "Universally".

Perhaps it was better to turn to the nitty-gritty and in every case the Commissioners addressed themselves to a greater or lesser degree to trying to establish the political behaviour and outlook of the students and their part in any rebellion, all of which was taken as connected with discipline, including the books and periodicals at their disposal. The President gave an excellent account of himself, he had no qualms about the general political purity of the students even though there might have been the odd problem now and then of general indiscipline, which was quickly dealt with, and even though, while many of the students possess Mr. Locke's *Essay on the Human Understanding,* "the Professor is not bound to adopt in every instance, the opinions of Mr. Locke. There are some things in him that we consider erroneous, and we consequently hold the contrary doctrine. Whenever the Professor finds in necessary to touch upon those parts, he remarks that Mr. Locke's doctrine is not considered quite sound". He fended adroitly. Dixon and Delaney, as on all other subjects, were calculated to put the fat in the fire. Delaney gave evidence to the effect that he had often heard it "brought forward as a subject for regret", at Maynooth, "that the union of England and Ireland had taken place, and that it has destroyed this kingdom", and that as regards the Established Church he had heard it said there "that it has been a very tyrannical and intolerant church; unjust in depriving the Roman Catholics, as a body of monasteries, and of their properties and so on". The Commissioners must have been a little uneasy all the same. But Dixon put the tin hat on it. To the question as to whether "the connection of the British Islands with each other" (what a very British way of putting it) and whether the connection could be "dissolved" was regarded as desirable at Maynooth and spoken about? — he agreed: "Certainly, when we all went out to walk together, we have talked about that; and it was natural that such conversation should arise, in consequence of several of the students having been actually engaged in the late rebellion, and expelled from Maynooth in consequence of it, so that it was not a novel thing for feelings of this nature to exist, and to gain considerable strength among the students at Maynooth". To the further question: "do you mean that those persons who spoke to you in this manner had themselves been engaged in

rebellion?'' His reply was: "I do not mean that they really had; but I really at the time felt that it was a noble cause to engage in rebellion, and to rid my country of the chains of a foreign government unjustly imposed''. Tut, tut. There really must have been some coughing then, perhaps even snuff-boxes produced. Even some monocles may have fallen off and perukes become in need of steadying. Another question quickly came: "Did it not occur to them to apprehend that the greater power of England would afterwards necessarily recover the country through scenes of great carnage and desolation?''. Reply: "Yes; but it has been sometimes thought that there was a possibility that there could be some auxiliary force obtained that might have a depot on the other side of the island, where the bays and the harbours are very fine, and that would enable them in the course of time to resist an invasion from England''. Sure, as always: 'The Year of the French' and all that: "Oh the French are on the Sea, says the Shan Van Vocht'', the same refrain as earlier in ''My Dark Rosaleen': "There's wine from the Royal Pope upon the ocean green'', the same refrain in truth that lifted through the Irish Volunteers in 1916 hopeful of help from Germany: "Tis better to die neath an Irish sky than at Sulva or Sud-el-Bar''. Coming from Dixon, it sure must have caused a flurry. And when asked whether there were many students who were for maintaining the connection, his answer again must have disappointed: "There were very few among the students that used to take that side''. Once again it took Corballis tersely to correct impressions. "From your general knowledge of Maynooth, would you believe that the students there were in the habit of expressing a wish for the separation of Ireland from England, and for the overthrow of the Protestant establishment, and the destruction of Protestants in this country?'' Reply: "Certainly not''. After all, the inquirers may have over-worded their question and left themselves open to the good barrister's powers of distinguishing.

But it was the Prefect of the Dunboyne, Nicholas Slevin, that really gave them their money's worth. His examination, which ran for eight days and fills nearly a hundred pages of the *Report*, is a book in itself. Slevin was noted for learning and was also a bit of a crank. Both qualities helped him now. His display of erudition was only immense. He too was Gallican, in matters pertaining to infallibility and temporal power, even though he had risked Papal Italy. He was quizzed on a wider front — concerning the Catholic position on mixed marriages and any claims on its part to have a right to punish heretics. He fielded beautifully on every topic. The 5 December, 1826 was remembered as the day when he really put them down. The discussion was ranging over obscure and thorny ground, Slevin having let himself go all the morning about whether loyalty to the Pope was in conflict with loyalty to the Government. The Turkish occupation of Antibaris in Albania came up. Could the Turks ever acquire a title to this contrary to the wishes of the Pope? No. All right. Then, is it therefore "a maxim of Canon Law that no mere length of possession can give a title by prescription or other wish against the church?" A trap had been laid and Slevin reacted: "It is not; if it were, Benedict the 14th, one of the most enlightened men of the last century, would have been worse than an idiot to have composed such a rescript". It may well have been at this point, that, as one account tell us, a member of the Inquiry kicked a colleague under the table, for he was delighted that the questioner, who was evidently endeavouring to display his prowess, had been unceremoniously put back in his place. It is good to know that the Commissioners had the kind of humanity that shows itself so often still at similar gatherings. That Slevin was taken seriously can be gauged from the fact that he was the only one of the Maynooth staff to be asked to revise and correct the report of his voluminous evidence to the Inquiry. He did add copious notes but he did not change the last-quoted sentence, even though it was possibly hoped that he would do so. Unfortunately, in the discharge of this task he caught a cold (it was Winter, 1826-'27) which terminated in a fatal decline. In February, 1828, he was granted leave of absence by the Trustees because of the poor state of his health. He never returned but died in November of that year in Bourdeaux (sic.) — a Gallican to the last. Notice of his death appeared in *The Dublin Weekly Register* for 15 November 1828.

The *Report of the Commissioners,* when it came out during 1827 (how quickly they printed in those days), was regarded as a triumph for the College. A quarter of a century afterwards *Duffy's Magazine* carried an exhaustive article on it:

"In that year 1806, the property of increasing the annual grant from £8000 to £13000 was brought before the British parliament by Sir J. Newport; on that occasion Lord Howick adverted to the efforts made by the French government, through the agency of the Rev. Dr. Walsh, ex-president of the Irish College at Paris, to induce the Irish, English, and Scotch ecclesiastical students, then on the continent, to re-unite in one grand seminary in that metropolis, and under the patronage of Napoleon, Hugh Murat, &c. This Dr. Walsh went so far as to invite the students of St. Patrick's College, at Lisbon, to repair at once to Paris, holding out to them various inducements to do so, and this invitation was considered of so much importance, or so much danger, as to draw

218

forth an indignant protest against Dr. Walsh's proceeding, addressed to Dr. Crotty, at that time president of the Irish College at Lisbon, by the Most Rev. and Right Rev. Dr. Troy, Dr. Bray, Dr. Dillon, Dr. Moylan, Dr. Plunkett and other prelates. 'Bound as we are,' they say, 'by every tie of gratitude, to the present government, for its very liberal support of an ecclesiastical establishment at Maynooth, and which, under the auspices of the present administration, we hope will very shortly be considerably enlarged, we not only feel it our duty to declare, in the most unequivocal terms, our reprobation of such attempts to seduce the youth of your house, but are determined to use the authority vested in us in order to prevent even the possibility of excuse on the part of any of our students, who might be tempted to accept of that insidious offer," and they conclude by declaring "that any person being in holy orders so accepting incurs suspension, ipso facto, and that all others acting similarly will never receive ecclesiastical faculties in their several dioceses.'

"Doubtless, the allusion to this attempt of the old Gallic enemy to get into his hands the education of our clerics, had a salutary effect on the decision of the House of Commons; at any rate, the sum of £13000 was voted to the college of Maynooth. But this was only a transitory ebullition of British generosity, or, rather an exercise of British prudence. A short two years had scarcely elapsed, ere, the Whigs being displaced, the hereditary foes of the Catholic body proposed to reduce the grant to £9250; it was in vain that Sir John Newport remonstrated; General Mathew, the staunch and consistent friend of the Catholics, upon that occasion said that "he could testify, from personal inspection, that the original buildings of the college would soon tumble about the ears of the inmates, unless the whole of last year's grant was voted;" He added a very explicit and apparently an authentic statement, regarding Napoleon Bonaparte's offer to restore all the Irish bourses, provided the Irish student would come to Paris for their education; he very plainly charged the ministry with being swayed in their determination to reduce the grant to the College by the sinister interference of a member of the royal family - which drew forth a rather equivocal denial from the chancellor of the exchequer. The grant, after all, was reduced to £9250; and at that figure it continued, for many years, to furnish a pretext, from year to year, for many a dreary exhibition of impotent yet rancorous bigotry. A few months since, it was increased to about £26000.

"As might be expected, the doctrines taught in the college and the discipline therein prescribed, have been always the principal points of attack for its enemies — furnishing convenient matter for misrepresentation, or pointing many a sorry and stupid sarcasm. There was a double object attained by even a partial success on the first subject; it raised an outcry against the college and the vote by which it was supported, whilst through its sides the blow might reach the Church itself, inasmuch as identity of doctrine amongst all the members of that church is at once its greatest boast, as well as its most glorious characteristic. Both the doctrines and the discipline of the college were subjected to a searching enquiry in the year 1826; a year that will be memorable in the history of Maynooth College, for then, indeed, was it put upon its public trial.

"Five gentlemen had been appointed by his majesty to report on the general state of education in Ireland, and their enquiries led them, in due course, to the redoubted gates of Maynooth College, armed with sovereign authority to lay bare all its mysteries, and to turn it, as it were, inside out, for the pity or edification of all his majesty's lieges. Their names were T. Frankland Lewis, J. Leslie Foster, W. Grant, J. Glassford, and, last, not least, A. R. Blake, the only Catholic on the commission.

"The examination of witnesses commenced on the 19th of October, 1826, with the president of the college — at that time the venerable B. Crotty, the late bishop of Cloyne and Ross — and closed on the 7th of November following, with that of A. Knox, Esqr., law-agent for the college. The witnesses examined were in number thirty-three, comprising superiors, professors, students, with a due admixture of some unhappy men who had been formerly alumni of Maynooth, but subsequently conformed to the established church. As we speak just now of those persons, we may passingly observe, that, with one very gross and discreditable exception, they alleged very little against the doctrines and discipline of the college — with so many motives of interest or revenge to do so, were it at all in their power. But what shall we say of the great body of the evidence? It must indeed have astonished if it did not convert or convince such as Leslie Foster — plain, sound sense, a thorough knowledge of what may be called their own professional business, perspicuity of statement, and a transparent candour that, much more effectually than sleight of cunning, foiled some unfriendly attempts to embarrass and confound them; all these were the salient characteristics of this evidence.

"It might appear invidious to particularize individual excellence, during this trying investigation, were it not that one remarkable course of evidence stands out clearly and unmistakeably transcendent, we mean that of the Rev. Dr. Slevin, professor of the Dunboyne establishment. For nine successive days, did this profound scholar explain those doctrines of his church that had reference to the *questiones vexatae* of the temporal power of the Pope, his dispensing power, his infallibility, &c., elucidating, as he proceeded, those rescripts and bulls that might seem to be susceptible of an adverse interpretation; the interrogations put to him were evidently furnished by a professional hand of no small cunning, and Dr. Slevin's replies evince a quantity of information, and a power of

220

memory to recall that information, merely equalled, and perhaps never surpassed; briefs, canons and decretals, church property, mixed marriages, all come in for inquiry, whilst the Corpus Juris Canonici, the Hibernia Dominicana, the councils of Lateran and Trent, and the works of Benedict XIV are severally ransacked for the obnoxious opinions so often imputed to Catholics: but nothing comes amiss to the invincible Doctor, who appears ready-armed at all points, so that it might really be supposed that the one or two 'great facts' fished up each day out of the depths of ecclesiastical history for his special bewilderment, had formed the most recent subject of his study and investigation. .

"A most interesting examination, likewise, is that of Dr. McHale, the present distinguished Archbishop of Tuam. During his resident at Maynooth, as professor of Theology, he had written and published those remarkable letters which bore the signature of Hierophilos, and which attracted universal admiration for the graces of their style, whilst their bitter but polished invectives against the monstrous abuses of the established church in Ireland, provoked the numerous partisans and dependents of that establishment beyond all bounds. The statutes of the college stringently prohibit the publication of political pamphlets by any member of the college; and, besides, they require, before the publication of a work of any description, that the sanction of the President should be asked and obtained. Stoutly and pertinaciously did the Commissioners contend that Dr. McHale had violated both these statutes, and with firmness and ingenuity did he maintain that such penal enactments are to be interpreted with indulgence, and that they had not infringed the spirit or counteracted the end of those laws, framed as they were to prevent the dissemination of those works which might be injurious to religion, public order, or the interest of the college itself. Thus far baffled, they next, with all due and stern solemnity, produced some of the most caustic passages of the letters, in which are depicted, in no mincing phrase, the evils inflicted on this unhappy land by English dominion and the minions and agents of England. And right boldly did the unbending prelate adhere to these convictions and published opinions of his college life, and the garbled and isolated passages cited by his interrogators he explained by counter-passage, or by showing their true signification from the entire context.

"In this eight report of the Commissioners, which serves as a kind of useful preface to the body of evidence, under the name of an appendix, nearly filling the goodly folio, we find the Commissioners stating, that 'they did not conceive it fell within their province to examine into the tenets of the Roman Catholic religion, except where they appear to be connected with the civil duties and relations of Roman Catholics either to their fellow-subjects or to the State'. Tis hard to reconcile this assertion of theirs with their perserving and almost impertinent inquiries about some pious sodalities established in the college; and whose mysterious bonds of union, and supposed cabalistic pass-words, seemed to have put some of them on the keenest scent to discover something of ulterior design. Upon the examination of the late Rev. Dr. Dowley, at that time Dean of the College and now the president of Castleknock Seminary, they were very curious to ascertain what were the peculiar advantages or inducements to belong to these sodalities. 'As members of this pious confraternity', replied that gentleman, 'they have no inducements or advantages but such as are entirely and exclusively spiritual and religious. Here, with sentiments of great respect for this Board, I beg leave to submit whether subjects purely and strictly religious, practices merely of Catholic discipline adopted in the college, are legitimate matters of investigation. The authority of the visitors of the college is restricted by an act of parliament, and does not extend to points which belong exclusively to the doctrines or discipline of the Roman Catholic religion. Whether the powers of this commission are more extensive, it is not for me to determine.' Dr. Dowley was asked no more questions on this topic.

"Nor were the students of the college unrepresented before the Board of Inquiry on this occasion. They were directed to choose by ballot a certain number from amongst themselves, to afford whatever information was in their power to the commissioners; and amongst those thus selected by their fellow-students, we find the names of the present newly-elected Bishop of Cork, Dr. Delaney, Professors M'Gawley and Furlong, whose after-career fully justified the confidence then reposed in their ability and discretion.

"Having previously observed, that the various harsh things said and written about the college have reference in general to its doctrines as there taught, and its internal discipline, we have deemed it right thus to call attention to this government inquiry, because on that occasion there was a strict investigation into both the one and the other, and the result as published, has been a most triumphant one for the college. Upon the subject of the doctrines taught in Maynooth, as we have observed before, it was not merely a fencing between laymen and practised ecclesiastical taciticians; for to any one looking even cursorily through the evidence, it will be apparent how admirably supplied the commissioners were on all the knotty points and damaging facts, and dangerous precedents that might affect Catholicity. What, for instance, could these gentlemen be supposed to know of the *Decretum Gratiani?* or the bull *Singulari nobis?* or what could the father of the cashiered commissioner of Poor-Laws — Mr. Lewis — know about Benedict the Fourteenth's elaborate decrees concerning church property, or the Turks in Antibaris, or the fifth book of Gregory the Ninth's Decretals? Yet on all these points the commissioners were diffuse, nay, argumentative".

How argumentative they were when all was over is debatable. One hears no more from John Leslie Foster who was one of them and it is notable that they made no attempt to assess the evidence that had been put before them but confined themselves to publishing it. It is hard to see how they could have done better. As we have seen, there were some amusing moments. Even if not to the Commissioners it must have been amusing to the Maynooth team to find so much interest being shown in the 'Sodality of the Sacret Heart'. True, it had been a Jesuit introduction and therefore naturally suspect, possibly even of being a seditious cell. The Commissioners were also anxious to know whether Fr. Peter Kenny had used his position while Vice-President of Maynooth to further the Jesuits in Ireland by helping to acquire Clongowes and whether many of the students there came afterwards to Maynooth? Whether they suspected that Clongowes was a sort of recreated Lay College for Maynooth or Maynooth a feeding place for young Jesuits from Clongowes one cannot be sure. One can only smile when one comes across Dr. Crotty assuring them, on their asking "whether it would constitute a ground of objection", in the election of a person to hold the post of Professor, "that he was a Jesuit?": "I believe that, considering the present state of public opinion (I mean that of the Protestant portion of the Empire), the Board of Trustees would not wish to appoint a person, professedly a Jesuit, to any situation in the College; but I beg leave to state, that I think they would not reject him on any other ground". He had said earlier of the superiors at Clongowes that, while they are generally reputed to be Jesuits, he did not know. "I have it only from public fame. I never asked one of them whether he was a Jesuit . . . They wore a dress which would indicate that they were ecclesiastics, but it was not the dress of the Jesuits with which I had opportunities of being acquainted . . . I believe they were educated in Sicily . . . I think it was at Palermo".
Why the Commissioners should have fastened on to the Jesuits about the alleged Jansenism of Maynooth is any man's guess, but they did. Fr. Kenny was the one. He was of the Jesuits who had been at Palermo and they asked him about the conformist Cousins. Kenny had given one of the first retreats in the College. The outcome of the exchange should disabuse anybody who may be disposed to lend credence to the charge of Jansenism in the *Report*. To quote Cousins in reply to the question: "You stated that you believed the Roman Catholic bishops in Ireland wished to patronize the Jesuits, will you state your reasons for that opinion?" Cousins, by the way, had just said that Dr. Ferris seemed to him to have "had a leaning to Jansenism". Now in reply about the Jesuits — and Jansensim — he said:

"The Jesuits and Jansenists are two opposite parties; the Jesuits opposed the Jansenists in France, and crushed them there. Maynooth was probably suspected for a leaning to Jansenism in my time, and upon that ground I would conclude that the Roman Catholic Bishops might have patronized the Jesuits, and got up the establishment at Clongowes for the purpose of checking that disposition. I was going to mention a circumstance with respect to Mr. Ferris; a question was put to him in class on merits of saints, and his observation was the merits of saints, compared with the merits of Christ, was no more than a drop of water compared with the ocean; he could not have gone further, consistent with the Roman Catholic doctrine, in crying down the merits of saints; and I understand that this is one of the doctrines of the Jansenists. There was also a feeling of regret in the college that the schools of Port Royal, in France, had been put down, and the Jansenist institutions destroyed; the students were also partial to a clergyman charged with Jansenism, Doctor Lanigan. These circumstances have often led me to conclude that the Roman Catholic bishops of Ireland at that time suspected that there was at Maynooth a leaning to Jansenism, and probably wished to counteract it . . . I have heard a Roman Catholic bishop say that the French church went to the very verge of heresy; he had been educated at Salamanca; and I have heard a Maynooth priest charged with Jansenism by a Franciscan friar''.

Still, when he was a student at Maynooth, the works of Jansenius ''were condemned''. However, ''On that subject I beg to explain; there were five propositions said to be extracted from the book of Jansenius, and these were condemned; but they who were called Jansenists, while they condemned those five propositions, said they were not contained in the book, and therefore read the book though they condemned the propositions''. He adds that he did not think that Dr. Delahogue ever leaned to Jansenism. It is a story of fact and fancy but to those who are conversant with the history of Jansenism it should produce sufficient evidence that there was some adherence to Jansensim at Maynooth at least during its early period.

Towards the end of the 19th century the whole question of the orthodoxy of Maynooth was controverted at length — anonymously — in the pages of the *Dublin Review*. The issues are not now easy to get at although the matter is of importance. Extended quotation would seem to be in order.

''I do not for a moment think of asserting that in the earliest days of the College the full circle of doctrines defined in the Council of the Vatican was explicitly taught in Maynooth, as a theological creed in regard to which no difference of opinions could be allowed: in regard to some of these points, as for instance the infallibility of the Pope, the question was for many years — but by no means for so long a period as the learned author of the Article seems to suppose — treated, not merely as open to discussion with the limits of orthodox faith, but as one on which it might safely be left to the discretion of theological students, having before them a fair statement of the arguments on both sides of the questions, to adopt the side which commended itself to their reason and judgment. And here, perhaps — although, of course, it is by no means necessary for the purpose for which I have undertaken to write — it may not be out of place to mention that a different, and more fully satisfactory method of dealing with the question was adopted in Maynooth at a much earlier period than the writer of the Article is at all aware.

"A venerable dignitary of the Irish Church, who was a student of the College just fifty years ago, has authorised me to mention a fact regarding himself which, even if no other evidence were in existence, would be absolutely decisive on this point. 'At the close of my College course,' he says, 'I was appointed to a place on the Dunboyne Establishment, but I went in preference to Rome where I was anxious to study for a few years in the Schools of Theology. Dr. Cullen, who was then Rector of the Irish College, suggested to me, before coming home, that I give our Archbishop a proof that I had not mis-spent my time in Rome, I should make a public defence of the usual kind, to obtain the degree of Doctor in Theology. I was then directed to prepare a list of forty propositions, and, among them, as a matter of course, I put down the infallibility of the Pope, a doctrine of which I had not, and could not have had, a moment's doubt or uncertainty from the time I had read that portion of the Treatise, 'De Eclesia,' under my professor, Dr. O'Hanlon, in Maynooth. The defence was made in the College Romano — Father Perrone and others being the objectors. It so happened that the proposition selected for discussion was this very doctrine of the Pope's infallibility. I defended it there in the Roman College, simply and solely from what I had learned in Maynooth; for, as it happened, from my being engaged in the study of other portions of the theological course, I had never received a word of instruction about it, or heard a reference to it, during the two years that I was in Rome." . . . .

"Let us consider for a moment the incident of the rebuke administered by one of the Professors of Theology, as mentioned by the writer of the Article in the case of a student who had quoted some opinions of Saint — or as he then was, the Blessed — Alphonsus. The name of the Professor is not mentioned in the Article; but as the incident is one with which we are all familiar, as handed down by tradition among the College notabilia of former days, I fortunately have no difficuty in supplying the omission, and in stating that the Professor in question — Dr. Magennis — was one, the mere mention of whose name is sufficient, in the minds of all who knew him, to overturn at once the entire structure so carefully built up in the Article, as to the connection of the rigid principles of our school of Moral Theology with the alleged predominating influence of

"Gallicanism" in the College. Noted among the Professors of his day, as Dr. Magennis was, for the decided, not to say extreme, character of his views on every subject of which he undertook to treat, and for the emphasis of the language in which he usually gave expression to them, he was, I am assured, not more decided in his views or more emphatic in his language on any other topic than in his outspoken maintenace of unmistakably "Ultramontane" opinions in Theology. It is, indeed, a somewhat curious coincidence that of the many interesting and valuable communications I have recieved from Irish priests, old students of Alma Mater, bearing to me the expression of kindly wishes, and directing my attention to sources of evidence and to facts that might prove useful in her defence, the last is one that has reached me only to-day, the writer of which says — 'When I was reading my first year's Theology, under Professor Magennis — now over forty years ago — he one day denounced Gallicanism in the most earnest manner and in the strongest language. Having given us a thorough history and explanation of the matter, he concluded by saying — 'This, gentlemen, is what is called Gallican liberty, but what I call Gallican slavery'. Applicable then to 'Gallicanism' as such epithets as 'intolerant' and 'unreasoning' may be, their application will have to be justified on some other grounds than the rigorism — however we may deplore it — of so decided an anti-Gallican as Dr. Magennis of Maynooth."

"Maynooth . . . got her first professors from France, and with them an importation of genuine French theology. French theology was exclusively studied by her alumni, and French theological authorities alone consulted by them for generations. Indeed it takes not many years to count back to the period at which French principles still continued to tincture her teaching, and through it the views of the Irish clergy at large. We must be understood as speaking of the French theology of the past, for the French theology of our times has, almost universally, wisely assimilated itself to the receiving standards of the theological teaching throughout the Church. But a bitter set of exclusivists were those early French professors. The Most Rev. Dr. Denvir, late Bishop of Down and Connor, when Professor of Physics in Maynooth, one day on his return from Dublin, announced in the presence of Dr. Anglade, Professor of Moral Theology, that he had purchased a copy of Lacroix. 'Lacroix!' exclaimed the doctor, 'but did you bring him home? Believe me, I would not sleep in the same room with him.' This abhorrence of the less rigorous theology was not merely sentimental, as the students were made to know and feel. If one of them was found in the public library reading the same Lacroix, or any of the probabilist theologians, he would at once become suspect. If the Casuist Diana was found in a student's hand, in all human probability he would never be promoted to orders; certainly never without thorough purgation of the contempt thus shown to the principles of rigid morality in which he was being trained. An *'Index pro-hibitorius'* was regularly established, which included the greatest and most authoritative writers *'in re morali'*. Liguori himself, even after his beatification, was not safe from censure. A student on one occasion venturing to quote an opinion of his, was abruptly checked by the professor, who gave his estimate of our great guide in moral theology thus — *'homo equidem eximiae pietatis, sed perdite laxus.'* And this professor was only the pupil of the Frenchmen. What an unreasoning intolerant was the Gallicanism' . . . .

"Louis Aegidius Delahogue, Doctor of the sacred faculty of Paris, Fellow of the Sorbonne, and Professor Emeritus of theology in the Sorbonne schools, *'coelum non animum mutans',*was chosen professor of dogmatic theology in the Seminary of Maynooth, and lectured to and composed treatises for successive generations of the students thereof. These treatises for moral theology of Bailly, they were obliged to purchase. They were their class-books, There was no alternative from the Sorbonne theology for them, except what lay silent in the tomes of the college library, sources of knowledge which, as we have already seen, they were not at all encouraged to approach. Hence, as an inevitable consequence, the Irish clergy became Gallican to the core. The classic theologians of the Church, Suarez and Lugo, and Molina and Petto, were to them names unknown or proscribed; they were a little familiar with Bellarmine, *'de Sacramentis',* and *'de Eucharistia',* but Bossuet was the great central theological luminary, not of the French Church only, but of the Church universal. An alien theology, possessing for us neither national nor other interests, thus balefully affected the youth and the manhood of the Irish Church, narrowing their views, misdirecting their professional studies, and, if not entirely estranging their feelings of allegiance, at least sensibly weakening them towards the true object of Catholic loyalty.

"Dr. Louis Delahogue wrote a treatise on the Church, and lectured the students of Maynooth in dogmatic theology in the early decades of the present century. Dr. Patrick Murray wrote a treatise on the Church, and with his associate professors lectured in dogmatic theology, of another stamp, in the fifth, sixth and seventh decades. The anomaly of a 'Council above the Pope,' as a tenable proposition, exists for them no longer. The theological puzzle of a centre of unity, to which all Catholics are bound to conform, and which, though itself errable, could not lead them into error, exercises their ingenuity no more. The straining of judgement and of inventiveness to reconcile the privilege which Christ asked, and doubtless obtained, for Peter that he should 'confirm his brethren,' and the commission which He gave him 'to feed his sheep,' and 'to feed his

lambs,' with the fallibility of Peter's successors, is at length at an end.
"Romanus Pontifex jurisdictione superior est omnibus Episcopis con-junctim, sive dispersis sive in Concillio generali congregatis." "Romanus Pontifex universam Ecclesiam obligatorie docens, infallibilis est." Murray *de Ecclesia,* Disp. xx., What a transition is here recorded! and in so short a period of time! And without any theological revolution to account for it! There was no local discountenancing of the old teaching; there was no importation of professors trained up in other schools; but, by the sheer honest following out of principles inculcated on them by Gallican masters, the Irish-born theologians of the College of Maynooth forced their way through the lines of Gallicanism, and formed a successful junction with the grand theological army of the Catholic Church.

Good old Maynooth. It was hard for it to win, certainly in the 1820's. Just while its staff were boldly contending with His Majesty's minions in Dublin Castle, Dr. Blake of Dromore was writing to the Archbishop of Dublin that Monsignor Caprano of Propaganda dislikes the Maynooth establishment, especially the works used there, and more especially Bailly "whom he considers worse than De La Hogue . . . as unsound throughout being everywhere infected with Gallican principles. He frequently visits the Pope". Ominous words indeed. That was in February, 1825. In March, 1826, Blake wrote again to say that he had been interrogated by Propaganda concerning the doctrine taught at Maynooth. He has assured them, in a letter sent on 19th inst. to Caprano. On 27 April he writes to say that he has reason to believe that his letter was found satisfactory at a meeting of the Congregation. Things moved fast in those days despite the less sophisticated means of communication. Maynooth deserved some respite. One can only gasp at that which it got from its old adversary the Reverend Charles O'Connor who, on his death-bed that same year is understood to have said that "an esoteric doctrine of the high transalpine school was taught in that seminary." It was certainly esoteric whatever about being transalpine. O'Connor's statement may have done something to palliate the effect of James Glassford's *Notes of Tours in Ireland in 1824 and 1826,* which described the Maynooth students as living "in a hot political atmosphere".

THE SPLEEN VENTERS

The great scrutiny (the first one) was over, and Maynooth had come out of it. But it had learned some lessons. One was that a poor view was taken by the powers that were if Bibles were not freely available to all students. It's an ill wind . . . In June the Trustees, in anticipation of this, had accepted their publishers offer to supply the College with 500 copies of the Holy Bible at 14/6 each. In June, 1825, McHale, soon to be 'in the dock' and all the more difficult for his elevation (He refused to answer one question put by the Inquiry on the ground that it as none of his business) was conscretated Bishop of Maronia (Coadjutor to Tuam)

228

at Maynooth — his old friends Delahogue and Anglade among the congregation, together with Mrs. (sic.) Catherine Mac Auley, foundress of the Sisters of Mercy. The Theology classes presented him with a silver chalice. The consecrating Prelate was Dr. Murray who had ordained him priest. Things were not going too badly. That same June the accounts for the College for the previous year were presented to the Office of Public Accounts signed and elaborately sealed three times, giving details of the amounts received, paid and owed, the latter, £400, to Messrs Henry and Mullins for part of an enclosure wall. The lease of ground on the Canal Bank which had been taken from the Royal Canal Company for the creation of a walk was ordered to be prepared. Wellesley's confirmation of the appointment of Drs. Curtis and Murray "in the room" of Dr. O'Reilly and Dr. Troy was registered. On 12 July Walter Scott, then at the height of his fame, with his son in law Lockhart and daughter in law Anne, left Glasgow by steamer to pay a month's visit to Ireland, Scott Junior being then a Captain in the army and stationed in Dublin. The group was warned not to travel too much even in the vicinity of Dublin after 7 p.m. because of highway robbers. There were some notable ones around Lucan. The visitors did an extensive tour of the country, but there is no record of a visit to Maynooth. A young man who was to become illustrious came up to College that August to sit for matriculation. He was Charles Wm. Russell of the family of the Barons of Killough. He waited on for the result. He was then aged fifteen. He wrote home: "When we get up in the morning . . . we have to dress ourselves, make our beds, clean our shoes, sweep our rooms, and wash ourselves in twenty minutes". Then, having given the horarium: "I paid part of my pension on Saturday, £20-3-10; ten pounds more must be paid in March. I engaged a washerwoman at Mr. Kenna's recommendation. I am to pay her 7/6 a quarter . . . I bought . . .a bed and furniture for £5-5 . . . The Lay College is quite separate from the ecclesiastic, and it is one of the rules not to hold any intercourse with those in the other College". He must have been talking of what was later known as the Junior House. Obviously, the recently founded Convent of Presentation Sisters in the town had not yet started a laundry. The Superior, Mrs. McKeever, wrote that May to the Bishop of Dromore to say that the community "reside in a temporary house in Maynooth . . . The Professors are exceeding kind, the youngest is their chaplain, Mr. Anglade is Confessor". The first postulant, a Miss Fleming from Waterford, entered the convent in 1826 but unhappily died the following year. She was interred in the College Cemetery, there being no cemetery at the convent at that time. With or without a laundry, things were looking up in the Fall of 1825. In September the President was instructed to take "immediate measures" to provide "a shower bath and a warm bath" in the Infirmary, and in January, 1826, under the signature "ffrench", it was ordered that the exterior of the College be annually painted.

All that was before the great investigation. It would seem, however, that this left the place comparatively unruffled. Maybe that is what annoyed its enemies but they did vent their spleen on the place for some time afterwards. Peel wrote to

Leslie Foster in September, 1829 wondering what to do about the Maynooth grant. The letter is marked 'most private'. Foster did not wish to get involved again, for he replied that "after every consideration that I have given to this institution, I really do believe that, bad as the results of Maynooth have been and are, anything we could do with it would more probably make it worse rather than better. Their system is to take young Irish peasants from their native mountains, and keep them close prisoners for seven years, in order to convert them into machines fitted for their purposes. Any regulations which would prevent their doing so they would of course indignantly reject, and any that would leave this part of the system in its vigour would appear to be at least useless". He had given up. Peel did so too. Later, for his own reasons, he became an ardent defender of the grant. Others were far from giving up. One such was Lord Bexley, who made a biting attack on the College. The R.C. Bishop of Kildare was furious. Writing from Carlow to Dr. Donovan of Maynooth on 4 December, 1826, he, J. K. L. pointed out "the duty of defending yourselves" which lay on the Maynooth people. Who is to do it? "Anglade is old and a foreigner, unable to express his sentiments fully". The "duty devolves naturally on the President . . . I beg you will see Dr. Crotty and get something done . . . I can safely assure you that the charges against the College are working more mischief than any occurrance of this present time and God knows that is saying quite enough". Fitzpatrick relates that Maynooth still kept silence, one leading professor saying: "Woman are never admitted or even named at Maynooth; Lord Bexley is an old woman, and we will not notice him". But in the end they had to formally reject Bexley's charge that the Pope exercised dispensing power as regards the oath of allegiance. It was too serious to let pass, especially after the ambiguities of the Inquiry. And so it fell to the lot of Dr. Crotty, in March 1829, to bring out *A Letter to the Right Hon. Lord Bexley, in reply to charges against the College of Maynooth*. He was thorough in his refutation. Newspapers, pamphlets and reviews have, he said, teemed with the contributions of every venal scribe criticizing the College, forgetting that it is the subject to a triennial visitation. He harked back too to the answers of the professors at the Inquiry, especialy in matters related to politics. In particular he rebutted the charge by Bexley that Maynooth was under the influence of Clongowes Jesuits. He, Crotty, has not visited Clongowes more than once a year for fifteen years. He has never consulted any member of that establi hment on anything connected with the goverment or discipline of Maynooth, although if necessary he would because he respects the Jesuits. Fr. Kenny, S.J., had been Vice-President of Maynooth for only eight to ten months. To quote Crotty:

> "Some matters of minor importance remain yet to be noticed, upon which I do not mean to detail your Lordship. You say that Doctor M'Hale, whilst professor of theology, published, without my approbation, a pamphlet under the signature of Hierophilus. grossly reflecting on the established church; that he presented it to me in person, and that I

did not enforce the rule of the college which subjected him to expulsion. This omission you further adduce as a strong illustration of the discipline of Maynooth College . We thank you, my Lord, for your friendly solicitude for the discipline of the College of Maynooth; and in return, I will take leave to remind you of one of the canons of dialectics, which forbids to draw a general inference from particular premises. It is as unjust as it is illogical to infer from a solitary infringement of rule, a general relaxation of discipline in any such establishment. But you complain that the violation of statue in this instance was not visited with heavy chastisement. During your collegiate course did you never witness more than one infraction of rule, and observe the severity of law tempered by the mildness of authority, particularly if the case presented features which justified the exercise of clemency? The publication of the letters of Hierophilus without the consent of the President was a violation of rule: but I confess that I was disposed to view it also as a violation of form towards myself; and such offences I have always felt more inclined to pardon than to punish. The circumstances of extenuation were, that Dr. M'Hale took up his pen to vindicate the Catholic Church of Ireland against the virulent and unprovoked abuse, which, for years, was unceasingly poured out against her doctrines and her clergy. If, in doing so, he transgressed the limits of legitimate defence, he was certainly guilty of no injustice against his agressors. Your Lordship will also please to recollect that Dr. M'Hale was then preparing to leave college; and that his removal, therefore, would have been deemed a work of vexatious supererogation.

"But was it within the limits of my authority to have removed him, for the alleged violation of rule? I am not quite clear that it was. Your lordship, it is true, states that Dr. M'Hale presented his pamphlet to the president; but you omit to state that he did so without acknowledging himself to its author. I felt that I could not trace the production juridically, to its authors, otherwise than through his own acknowledgement or through the testimony of the printer. Through his own acknowledgement I did not attempt to trace it, because, as I stated before the commissioners, "I should think it not quite fair, in such a case, to oblige a man to become his own accuser." Through the testimony of the printer I felt equal reluctance to trace it, inasmuch as it would have compromised his interests by involving what might be considered a violation of the confidence reposed in him by the author. Accordingly Doctor M'Hale himself says, in his sworn evidence: It would be difficult to prove that I am the author: there are many things which are matters of notoriety, and yet could not be legally proved . . . The President had no official knowledge of the publication of Hierophilus: I never told him that I was the author; supposing that the President had wished to institute an inquiry, it would have been very easy for me to say, which I could say to any one except to such as I had avowed it to be, 'if any thing comes under my name, I am liable to be brought to an account for it; this is not published under my name; you cannot prove that I am the author' ''. Doctor M'Hale adds: "If I presented it to the President, I very cautiously abstained from ever noticing the author, by putting 'the author's compliments' or any thing that would lead him to know I was the author."

"But, my lord, your quiver is not yet entirely exhausted. The society of the Jesuits is next to be linked with Maynooth College, and the odium which attaches to their name in the minds of the Brunswickers of Kent, is to be shared by us. In Maynooth, as in every other Catholic college, its inmates commence and close the academical year with a spiritual retreat. It has sometimes been deemed expedient to vary the course of religious instruction, by requesting a clergyman, not a member of our community, to conduct these spiritual exercises. On two or three occasions it happened that the person requested to discharge that duty was a member of the neighbouring college of Clongowes. From this circumstance, and from that of Rev. Mr. Kenny's having, in compliance with the request of Most Rev. Doctor Murray, acted as Vice-President of Maynooth for eight or ten months, your lordship wisely infers that 'a jesuitical influence of a very suspicious kind, has been allowed to establish itself there at different times.' I have held my present situation for more than fifteen years, and I can declare, for your lordship's gratification, that I did not visit Clongowes during that period oftener, on an average, than once a year, although the distance does not exceed four or five miles; and I will add, that it has been visited, at least as often, by several of the neighbouring Protestant gentry and nobility. I can also state that never, in any one instance, did I consult any member of that establishment, on any thing connected with the government or discipline of the College of Maynooth, and I need not observe that they are too discreet and judicious to obtrude their advice. For each and every individual member of Clongowes college I feel the sincerest respect and regard; and had I occasion to ask advice on any thing that concerned myself personally, I would apply to them as willingly and with as much confidence as to any other class of persons with whom I am acquainted. But as President of Maynooth College, my advisers are the Protestant and Catholic visitors, the trustees, and the officers of the establishment, whom the statutes command me, when necessary, to consult. Your lordship will hence infer that my opinion of Jesuits does not accord with yours; but I trust you will also perceive that this my opinion has had no influence whatever on the discipline or government of Maynooth College. But in truth, my lord, I cannot persuade myself that you are so much alarmed by the phantom which you thus conjure up. You know the Brunswickers of

Kent, and the contrivance, although possessing little merit in their way of invention, was well calculated to fright their imaginations and enlist their prejudices . . ."

It took the President all his time to dispel the spleen that was being spewn out both in public and private against Maynooth. The *Sirr Papers* contain information, dated 24 to 27 December, 1830, which describe a Popish Plot, in which Bishop Blake and a number of Catholic laity are supposed to be implicated, together with "twenty-three officers, i.e., young priests from Carlow and Maynooth", who are alleged to have been sent by different coaches to various parts of Ireland, all charged with "secret missions of a most formidable character". The Presbyterian Minister of Killorglin and the Rector of Dunmanway added their voices. Talk about the Skibberreen eagle keeping an eye on Russia! There were big placards displayed with large lettering 'Murderous Maynooth'. Strolling lecturers were employed in English towns to instruct the public about it. Even the high-class *Edinburgh Review* was enlisted in the cause, with Lord Mountcashel, Keynon and Newcastle. But the College defended itself nimbly now. "One student was found to be a paid spy in the College; and *in poculis* wandered into the town of Maynooth and attempted to assault Dr. Whitehead. He was a man of length, breadth and magnitude. With his servant, he disarmed, belaboured, and expelled the reveller, Mr. O'R., who soon became a parson near Newry. The cause of each expelled and censured man was questioned in Parliament". Petitions from Armagh, Aberdeen and other places were made against the grant to Maynooth, led by Lord Mandeville. It was then that O'Connell defended Maynooth, also in face of another petition from Dundalk, presented by Mr. Gordon, M.P. O'Connell maintained that "he knew the students well, and could assert that few bodies of young men in any place of education possessed more extensive information that they did". Yet there were similiar petitions from Fermanagh, Drumkeeran, Innismacsaint, Hamsterley, West Alvington, Penzance, Colsterworth, Eusham and many other 'prominent' places like them'. Nor was the Maynooth image improved by the publication around then by Carleton of *Denis O'Shaughnessy Going to Maynooth*. Contained ultimately in *Traits and Stories of the Irish Peasantry,* it appeared originally in *The Christian Examiner* for September and December, 1831. It has been described as "an example of the evils of Popery admirably suited for Evangelical purposes", which turned into something different and was suddenly terminated in December, having no moral but being just a good tale. We get a picture of Denis as comical yet sympathetic, his anti-heretical bias and his efforts to get called to Maynooth by the Bishop. On the eve of his departure, health and success are drunk to him by the locals: "May he soon be on the Retreat in the vivacious walls of the learned and sprightly seminary, Maynooth".

Carleton himself visited Maynooth on one occasion although it is hard to establish the precise date from his autobiography. In this he tells us of his decision to visit the place: "I was more anxious to see that College than I had been to see Lough Derg itself". What an interesting comparison. He did visit the College, after visiting Clongowes Wood, where he was refused "a post" and sent off with a meal and 15 shillings. Thus furbished he came to Maynooth Village. He did not immediately seek 'audience'. To give him his due he animadverted: "What communication could a nameless wanderer like me expect with such an establishment?". He does seem to have been on good terms with Dr. Patrick Murray, the well-known Maynooth Professor of the mid-century. But then Murray had not yet attained to position, or so at least it would seem. Carleton therefore bedded down in a boarding house in the village, where, he spent the night. Next day he was conducted through the College by none other than Fr. Paul O'Brien. His entire account of his sojourn at Maynooth — to be found in the said autobiography - is not exactly marked by distinction. Indeed his writing this, as in *Denis O'Shaughnessy,* did little else than damage to the College.

Far greater damage was done during the 1830's by an expelled student called Eugene O'Beirne. He had got the door in 1830 and immediately petitioned the Duke of Northumberland, the then Lord Lieutenant, to issue a writ for an extraordinary visitaton. He got a reply saying that this could not be done as he had not mentioned the cause of his expulsion in his memorial. He then waited on the Attorney General, who suggested that he should repair to Maynooth and, in the presence of a witness, inquire of the President the reason for his expulsion. He returned, therefore, to the College with a friend for this purpose but was denied what he sought. On the contrary, he says, he was "offered personal violence" by the President. Again he 'memorialed' the Lord Lieutenant but to no use, whereupon he retired to the country, determined to await the ordinary triennial visitation to be held in June, 1831. This was duly held in the May of that year but O'Beirne had thought it was to be in June. He came back for the June meeting but found it was too late. His next move was to petition an investigation of his conduct by the Board of Trustees. He did so through Lord Forbes to Dr. Murray, who replied that this would be done on 22 June. And yet, he maintains, when the appointed day came, he was refused, on the grounds that he had previously applied to a lay tribunal. So he resolved to await the next triennial visitation. He revealed all this in a statement to the *Dublin Evening Post* for 19 May, 1831. The public prints are always convenient vehicles for such material and often utilized as either a first or last refuge by people like O'Beirne. He was later, in 1834, to publish his version of the whole thing in the book *Maynooth in 1834*, which had quite a success and went into a second edition in 1835. Things had gone wrong for him during the visitation of 1834. On 8 May he had come to the College — on this occasion definitely on time — and had waited on one of the visitors. He found that the visitation was going to take place on the following Saturday. When the day came, to his consternation, the Chief Justice told him that he could not investigate his case as the President who had expelled him had since been appointed Bishop of Cloyne, and also because he had not served notice of pro-

234

ceedings with his complaint at that visitation. Evidently the visitors knew their man. At which he gave in, except for having resort to the newspapers and writing his memoirs. It did not carry him far, no farther than the Regency politicans who, as Sir Shane Leslie puts it in his *George the Fourth* (London, 1926), "often committed actual suicide, instead of using more cumbrous method of writing their Memoirs". The *College Records* for 10 May, 1834, dismisses him in one short paragraph: "Mr Eugene F. O'Beirne, who had been removed from the College in 1830 for nonpayment of his pension etc. etc., attempted to lodge a complaint with the Visitors on the subject of his alleged expulsion, but they refused to entertain the complaint because Dr. Crotty who was alleged to have expelled him was not then a member of the College, because neither Dr. Crotty nor Dr. Montague nor the other parties complained of had been served with notice of O'Beirne's charges and his intention to advance them at this Visitation — and because he had not brought forward this charge at the visitation held in 1831, when the facts of his case were fresh in the memories of all the parties and of the witnesses when Dr. Crotty was in the College. He but waited till Dr. Crotty and many perhaps of the witnesses had left the College and then attempted to accuse them in their absence and without giving them any notice of a charge which they could not well expect at the time". The sub-title of his volume was *An Impartial View of the Internal Economy and Discipline of Maynooth College.* How impartial it was may be judged by the addendum: "containing an account of the system of tyranny — mental, moral and physical - pursued therein". And he followed that up: There is only one real Doctor of Divinity on the staff (Callan — the title is given to others only out of courtesy). The Vice-President (Renehan) used to snuff a lot. As a lecturer, "now he thunders forth a citation from some Jewish Rabbi on the Canonicity of the Maccabees — now he clutches at the objection of an Arian Adversary — now he nibbles at the 'Prolegomena' of Genesis — now he quotes Josephus's attestation of the Christian miracles". O'Hanlon was of "a clownish appearance" and had a repulsive manner. He is complimentary, however, towards Magennis, Furling and Russell. Such are the tit-bits to which we are treated in his impartial *expose,* sold by three bookshops in Dublin, one in Belfast, one in Cork, one in London and one in Edinburgh. It was then as always — the sensational had a market.

Dr. Crotty had gone, Dr. Montague became President on 24 June 1834. The spleen venters did not give up. The Saturday before he was appointed a 'Great Meeting was held at Exeter Hall, London, to give Protestants an opportunity of holding forth on the errors of Catholic teaching. Exeter Hall was to figure again, very prominently, in 1845, when an enormous campaign was launched against the Maynooth grant. That was in the high Victorian period about which not now, but it is amazing to find all the chief actors of the 1845 scene present earlier at the 1835 meeting — the Earl of Roden, the Reverend E. Tottenham, P. Dixon Hand, the Revvs. Ed Nagle, R. J. McGhee and M. O'Sullivan. The proceedings were published in a booklet, to be followed later by a more thorough account by

O'Sullivan and McGhee. Another meeting was held, appropriately in the Amphitheatre, at Liverpool in October. There was a great deal of discussion on both of these occasions as to whether Dens's theology, which was violently opposed, was taught in Maynooth. In April, Dr. Montague, had listed the texts in use there, which did not include Dens. Nevertheless, Coyne's Catalogue for 1832 had shown that a limited edition had been printed following a resolution of the Bishops in 1808: McGhee claimed it numbered 3,000. It was argued that if Coyne were not able to keep Delahogue and Bailly in stock (they were evidently less hated than Dens who had shaken off Gallicanism), he should no longer be retained as bookseller to Maynooth. It was all very well for Mr. Woods in the *Hereford Times* to have quoted a letter of the Maynooth Board in February, 1809, saying that it had unanimously rejected Dens after it had been prepared. The truth was rather, it was suggested, that even though Dens had been approved and brought out and intended for Maynooth, it had been thought better by the Board not to adopt it formally as a textbook. The insinuation may have been correct. After that, said a speaker at the Liverpool meeting, Dens "went to sleep" for eighteen years but was now again to the forefront. Nowlan, the ex-priest. is cited as saying that it was read at Maynooth, though not as a textbook. It was also a reference book to be found in the Library. McGhee went so far as to say that it was the standard although unofficial work in Maynooth in 1814. Further meetings in Glasgow on 27 September, 1836 and at Bristol on 12 June, 1837 carried on the war, at the last named one day Rev. M. Paterson lamenting the fate of students who "tumbled into Maynooth, to wallow like so many serpents amidst the impurities of Dens". Exeter Hall too saw a crowded meeting on 11 July on the same subject, reported later by Dixon Hardy, and there was another in Hereford in September. There was also, to use its published title, some *Correspondence of the Rev. R. J. McGhee with the Rev. Dr. Murray on the Subject of Dens Theology (London, 1835)*. During these months *The London and Dublin Weekly Orthodox Journal* interested itself in the proceedings but threw no great light on the matter while the Reverend T. Maguire of Kilmore, who for some time had been making a name for himself as a Maynooth product with debating skill, challenged the "Exeter Hall'ites" to a disputation in Manchester.

The Siege of Maynooth (or 'Romance in Ireland') published in London some time before had nothing to do with our subject. *The Case of Maynooth College* (Dublin, 1836) had and it was not friendly. Another tract, published the same year, was: *Letter to Sir George Sinclair on his notice of motion touching Maynooth and its Moralities*. The former was based mainly on the 1826 *Report*. It was not quite sure what it was about, for even though it attacked Maynooth for its textbooks, it urged a much better salary for the President. "To secure the services of such an individual, instead of £300 a year, twice or three times that sum ought to have been allowed". It also recommended big increases for the Professors of Theology: "I do not mean that the *present* professors are not paid as much as they deserve. But how could better be expected for the salary?" Both

236

Presidents and Professors of a later period will surely take note . . . The *Dublin Review* for December, 1836 had an article on *The Case of Maynooth,* O'Beirne's book and the 1827 *Report of the Commissioners on Education in Ireland.* Another publication which saw the light (in one sense only) in 1836 was *Roman Catholic Morality as inculcated in the Theological Class-Books used in Maynooth College.* It too was published in Dublin, as so often with tracts of this kind by Milliken. It was at a loss about what to do. Who would blame it? It had made its own inquiries and had found that Protestants "are dealing with Roman Catholic tradesmen and confiding in Roman Catholic servants". It is important to ascertain whether they are honest or lax according to the principles taught to them. Was that of occult compensation then taught one asks . . .? John Barrow, in his *Tour around Ireland* (London, 1836), held that money for the College of Maynooth "is spent on the education of men who on all occasions exhibit . . . a rancorous hostility against every attempt to enlighten the lower orders" and in 1837 there appeared *The Roman Catholic Confessional Exposed in Three Letters to a Late Cabinet Minister* (Dublin, Dixon). An attack on Dens, Bailly and Delahogue, it was also therefore an attack on Maynooth. It is only fitting, therefore too, that we should leave 1837 with the 'poem' on the College, called *Maynooth the Offspring of Degenerate Times* (London and Dublin, 1837 by 'Protestans Hibernicus'. It is not often mentioned by name but known simply as 'The Monster'. The lament could apply to the loyalists of 1979:

> "Britains distinctive glory, they,
> With sorrow, see has passed away!
> No more, among the nations, she
> Rules separate from Popery;
> No longer is the Government
> Pre-eminently Protestant;
> The jealous guardians once of the Truth;
> But now — the FOUNDERS OF MAYNOOTH".

Thus ends a poem and a chapter in the history of "Ireland's greatest curse, and the foulest spot on Britain's glory, the Royal College of Maynooth" (Protestans Hibernicus, 1827).

Chapter X

Awaiting Victoria

During all the hub-bub of these times life went on as usual in the College itself. There were many new appointments between 1827 and 1838 the year of Victoria's accession to the throne. Despite the usual complaints from within (to say nothing of those from without), positions there were envied and well paid. In 1827 the President commanded £316 p.a., the Senior Dean and Professors of Theology £112, the Junior Dean and Professors of other subjects £102. The President is allowed two horses, groceries, washing, postage and letters, the "fifteen Masters have no allowance but Commons". The Physician got £52-10-0 p.a. and the Apothecary ½ guinea for each student. The Scholars on the establishment had £26 each and the Dunboyne Scholars ('Senior Scholars' as they were called) "one servant, butter at breakfast and liquid blacking".

The terms, as said, were attractive for the time and there were many applications for posts and places. Lawrence Renehan was appointed to the Chair of Scripture and Hebrew in 1827; he had been a Junior Dean and obtained his new assignment by public concursus. It was to the Chair vacated by Dr. Browne who had gone to Kilmore as Bishop. In 1828 Robert fFrench Whitehead was appointed to the Chair of English Literature, according to O'Beirne because he was "respectably born", being related to one of the lay Trustees. There may be something in it, for he remained in the chair for one year only. O'Beirne maintained that "no man ever supposed that Mr. Whitehead possessed a spark of talent" yet admitted that "his appearance and address are those of a gentleman". During the year 1827 the Reverend C. H. Boylan went to the Chair of English Elocution, which had been vacant since 1818, as well as to that of French, vacant since 1820. He was later to go to Rome as President of the Irish College there, after Dean Dowley had declined to do so. This was in succession to Dr. Blake. Boylan, the typical academic, would not go until after he had corrected the proofs of Dr. McHale's *The Evidence and Doctrines of the Catholic Church,* which McHale is to dedicate to Leo XIII: it is something that "will not offend the most rigid Roman Theologian": McHale always disclaimed being affected by Gallicanism in spite of being the disciple of Delahogue. In fact by May, 1828, Boylan had not yet set out for Rome and was hoping for a quarter of his salary, which he normally would not get until June., A number of young men were to accompany him to the Roman College as students and a young priest had been recommended as its Secretary, none other than the Reverend Michael Collins of Cloyne, expelled from Maynooth after the troubles of 1803, and ordained elsewhere. He was eventually to become Bishop of Cloyne. O'Beirne describes Boylan as "an exemplary ecclesiastic and a gentleman", He was also financially aware, unusual in such a person. In 1828 he wrote to Blake to say that Maynooth is more expensive than Rome yet he will not compare the Colleges: "Maynooth will never be more prosperous nor esteemed than I heartily wish it";

During the same year of 1827 Dr. Anglade received a certificate, the equivalent of the modern passport, from the Clerk of Aliens Office, in respect of a visit abroad. In it he declares that he is an alien who intends to reside at the "Roman Catholic College, Maynooth, Ireland," It describes him as being of five feet, five inches in height, of age thirty seven, of grey hair and dark eyes, with regular nose and dark eyebrows — typically French, one might say, but note the prematurely grey hair. Who could fail to understand the reason why? This certificate was to remain in force until January, 1828. Dr. Anglade was to hold office in Maynooth until 1828, when he resigned. He is buried in the College Cemetery.*Requiescat in pace.*

In the College developments continued. So rapidly were they taking place that in 1828 the Trustees found it necessary to proceed with the erection of additional buildings for the students. Yet some of the College's most able products were turning to other things. That year the Limerick priest, E. J. O'Reilly, was already opting to join the Jesuits. He wrote to his former Professor, Charles McNally, to explain his new-found vocation. The following year Whitehead transferred to the Chair of Logic; he was a rolling stone, while Chavalier Francesco Romeo had it explained to him by the Trustees that it was not their intention to establish a

239

Chair of Italian at Maynooth, to which he had hoped he would be appointed. Then came the strange interlude devoted to Dr. Foran of the Diocese of Waterford. It began in 1831, the year in which McHale journeyed to Rome, being attacked by *banditti* on the way. Foran apparently was appointed to the new See (formerly Wardenship) of Galway that year but, even though he said he received the Bull, resigned the See — having consulted God, friends, etc. If so, it is peculiar that, on the resignation of Dr. Slattery as President of Maynooth in January, 1834, the Reverend Nicholas Foran was elected in his place and the Secretary ordered to inform him of this officially. At the time he was Parish Priest of Dungarvan. Everybody concerned with the College was disappointed as Dr. Montague had been expected to be chosen. They need not have been. Once more Dr. Foran vacillated. Dr. Murray wrote to Cullen in Rome to tell him that he feared Foran would not accept. And he did not, but he put off making a decision until 25 June when eventually he resigned. The then Vice-President, Dr. Michael Montague, was appointed President and Dr. Dowley Vice-President. Charles McNally of Clogher became Prefect of the Dunboyne. It was a very prestigious position at the time. In that year eleven Senior Students sustained their theses, including John Kenyon of Killaloe, of later Young Ireland fame. McNally had been preparing for his advancement for quite some time. He had studied hard and had a fine private collection of books as the Library of the College could show afterwards. In 1827 some other Chairs became vacant. Dr. Anglade died. The Chair of Scripture and Hebrew also fell vacant and was filled in September by Dr. Dixon after a public "examination". He succeeded Dr. Renehan who became Vice-President of the College in succession to Dr. Dowley. Thereby hangs another tale. It was small consolation to Dixon that, on the same 17 September that he was appointed, the Trustees resolved "that, as the statutes are not sufficiently explicit regarding the course of examination to be gone through by a Candidate for the Chair of Sacred Scripture and Hebrew, no Person shall hereafter be approved to that Situation without undergoing an examination in Scripture and the Hebrew language in addition to the matter of examination explicitly prescribed by the Statutes". Dixon, however, survived the implication and went on eventually to be Primate of All Ireland.

In 1835 Patrick J. Carew, Prof. of Divinity in the College, produced his *Ecclesiastical History of Ireland* and by 1837 was being recommended by Dr. Crotty of Cloyne as a possible candidate for the Diocese of Waterford. In the College that year the Reverend W. Lee was appointed Junior Dean, Fr. Cussen of Limerick having already been appointed. It had been a struggle to get a second Dean but now it had been accomplished. There were two almost distinct colleges at Maynooth, the Senior with 310 students, the Junior with 150. The Professors, as always, were on the warpath as regards their salaries and, as always too, the Trustees were dilatory. In June 1837 they resolved "that recognising the reasonableness of their application for an increase of salary in proportion to their time of service, we regret that the present state of the College funds will not allow

us to grant any increase of salary but that in the event of obtaining an increased grant from Parliament, which it is our intention to seize the first favourable opportunity to solicit, we shall not be unmindful of the application''. The following September they decreed that "the Memorial of the Professors of the College to the Trustees respecting an increase of salary in proportion to their time and service, having been read, it is resolved that the consideration of it be deferred to the next Board". The Professors were not the only ones to make petitions that year. In June "the Petition of the Senior Students having been presented to the Board for exemption from sustaining the thesis appointed for this time, it ordered that the Secretary be directed to inform them that the Board received their application with pain, and have conceded to it with reluctance even on the present very peculiar occasion, but with the distinct understanding that no such application is to be made by the present or any future class of the Senior Students". A chair of Theology was to be filled and, on 3 September and succeeding days in 1838 a Concursus was held. Whitehead was now a candidate for Theology but was taken ill before the Concursus was completed. In the end Dr. O'Reilly of Limerick got it, though he was to quit it after a time for the Jesuits. In another competition Mr. Gunn got the Junior Deanship.

The years 1827 to 1838 were also marked by decisions of the Trustees relating to the fabric of the College. In 1827 they sold £742 Royal Canal Stock and "rested" it with the interest due thereon in 3½% Government Stock. They seemingly foresaw the end of the short canal era. January, 1831 saw them submitting estimates for certain additions (one extra Bursar and one Music Master and Secretary) to Government, (c.f. *Official Papers 1824-'31)* the cook and kitchen boy having disappeared from the list! The following June they were resolving that a petition be presented to Parliament for an additional grant of £5,000 for the erection of new buildings, this petition to be forwarded through his Excellency the Marquis of Anglesea. But to more domestic matters; In June, 1828 they ordered "that the Bursar shall procure from time to time a few pieces of black stuff of a better quality than is generally procured by the students for their College Cloaks and that each student shall purchase the materials of his Cloak from the Bursar on his entering the College and whenever the President or Dean shall deem a renewal of the Cloak necessary at such a price as will merely indemnify the College for the money thus advanced". (This measure was to have some repercussions, for a few years after a certain Mr. Downings of Kerry was reprimanded for taking a cloak belonging to one of his companions). That same June it was ordered "that four Rooms in the Infirmary be furnished and supplied with beds and all other articles necessary for the accommodation of the sick". In August the Trustees declared themselves perfectly satisfied with the Hypocausts erected by Dr. Meyler for heating the Library, Lecture and Study Halls. In June, 1829 an alteration to the roof of the "Lay College" was prescribed. It was clear that health matters were beginning to loom large, even if that June also Colonel Keatinge was thanked for "the splendid Painting and the very valuable books" which he had presented to the College — whatever either may be. In the same June too it had been prescribed "that after the expiration of two years from this date no scholar shall be admitted into the College of Maynooth who shall not be found capable of answering in Murray's abridgement of English Grammer, a short system of Geography and the elements of Arithmetic for entrance into the Class of Humanity; in the aforesaid elementary branches, together with Grecian and Roman history and Algebra as far as quadratic equations included, for entrance into Rhetoric; and for entrance into Logic besides the above two courses in English and Irish History with six books of Euclid".

This was admirable but the health question now loomed over all. It was not good at Maynooth. In February, 1832 a Board of Health was established in the College, consisting of the Medical officers, the President, Vice-President and Deans and the Prefect of the Dunboyne and Professor of Sacred Scripture (the latter probably as a representative of the general staff) with the special remit to pay particular attention to the general cleanliness of the College. It was not before its time. In May, John McCann wrote from Carlow College to Dr. Cullen in Rome that Maynooth was closed owing to cholera; it had broken up earlier in the year because of it. This reflected in the June, 1833 report of the aforesaid Board of Health. The Report has been found on a loose leaf inserted in, of all places, the *Liber Poenarum* in the President's Archives. It stressed the need for washing and white-washing in many areas. In other quarters while "generally speaking the rooms were cleanly and well ventilated, on some of the corridors either from accident or the bad condition of the night buckets the floor was wet and noisome; here therefore we would suggest the propriety of having all those night affairs removed at an early hour and by careful and efficient Persons; and here also we must call the attention of the authorities of the College to a practice which seems to have grown into a general habit, of the most abominably disgusting nature — that is the emptying of night vessels out of the Windows". Twiss would seem to have been still in use; the Georgian period was not yet over. But the cholera was not appreciative of epochs. In January Eliza Gifford wrote to Anglade about her recent conversion to Catholicism. She notes that from what she has seen from the newspapers the dreaded disease has again broken out in parts of Ireland: "I begin to fear it will never be totally eradicated". The Trustees did their utmost to ensure that their College at least was preserved. Their resolution of 19 June, 1834 may have been in the interests of hygiene as much as discipline: "That the locks of the Students' Doors be repaired and duly arranged, so that the Master Keys of the Dean and Vice-Deans shall open them; and further that Any student who shall in future alter his lock, and thus render it impervious to the Master Key, shall pay the expenses of restoring it to its former state". More positively, in the same month they directed that the following communication should be forwarded to the Lord Lieutenant:

> "The Trustees of the R.C. College having, agreeably to the power vested in them by the act of Parliament the 35th George the third, Chap. 21, Sec.1, erected ball courts in the College which they deemed essentially necessary, and the expense of which was disallowed by the Commissioners of Accounts, pray that your Excellency may be graciously pleased to order the allowance of the aforesaid item . . . ."

Such facilities were badly needed, judging from what Dr. Crotty had to tell the Inquiry of 1826. At that time the students had little opportunity for real exercise or recreation. They could, he said, play "prison bars". They had "formerly" been allowed to play at foot-ball but that "was considered dangerous and not very decorous". They had only one ball court then. Dr. Crotty had admitted that recreation space was very cramped. They played games in the corridors of the houses and sat generally "in the windows". While they generally enjoyed good health, he said "pulmonary affections" were common. Others testified to the same thing. That it had something to do with improvement of health is known because in September, 1834 the Trustees decided to empower the Infirmary Committee "to contract for the erection of a Brewery for the supply of Beer to the College and to apply to the Directors of the Royal Canal Co. for a supply of water from the Canal". They were not going to be short . . . It would be great to have had Brendan Behan's comment on it. The local convent was now thriving also and must have helped the students as well as the townspeople. The foundation stone of a public school in the town had been laid in 1826 by the Marquis of Kildare. The convent provided another school, monetary help having come from Drs. Anglade and Crotty. Dr. Anglade was a great friend of the convent. In 1833 he was instrumental in its giving breakfast to the poor children who were attending the school. Then, in 1828, the convent opened an industrial school at the request of the Duchess of Leinster, the College professors again patronizing the work, this time especially Dr. Callan the Professor of what later came to be called Experimental Physics, then known as Natural Philosophy. When, in 1830, the daughter of Dr. Edward Talbot O'Kelly, first medical attendant at the College — and followed in that position by his son and his grandson — entered that convent, the unity between town and gown was cemented.

TRAVELLER'S TALES

Between 1820 and 1838 Maynooth must have been the most visited place in Ireland. The first to come was J. N. Brewer, Esq. from England, whose *Beauties of Ireland* came out in two volumes in 1826. As in the case of the others, it is best to let him speak for himself:

"The College of Maynooth is a building on a frugal scale, and has few of the architectural characteristics of a structure devoted to purposes of study. It presents, in its principal facade, a square central pile with spacious wings, the whole front extending to a length of 400 ft. The central structure was originally of a private house, built by the steward of the Duke of Leinster, by whom it was sold to the trustees of this institution. According to the first intention, this principal range of building was to form one side of a square, with a subordinate but spacious quadrangle towards the rear. It was, however, found necessary to relinquish the magnitude of such a design; and, besides the front, there has chiefly been completed one other side, and part of a second side, of the projected quadrangle on the rear. These latter buildings comprise the dormitories of the college, which open from galleries nearly 300 ft. in length, serving as ambulatories during inclement seasons.

"With the exception of the library, the whole of the public buildings are contained in the principal front. The Chapel is sufficiently capacious, and is moderately ornamented, but without any decisive architectural character or striking beauty. The chief Lecture-room and the refectory are of ample proportions, and appear to be well adapted to their respective purposes. The Library, which is properly placed in a retired part of the additional buildings, is a neat and eligible, but not extensive, apartment, containing numerous theological works, but at present lamentably defective in other classes of literature . . . . . .

"The mansion of Carton, distant about one mile from Maynooth, is a spacious and magnificent structure, worthy of its destination in constituting the principal residence of the premier peer of Ireland. This fine seat was erected in the latter part of the eighteenth century, after the designs of Richard Cassels, whom we have already mentioned as the architect of Leinster-house, formerly the town residence of the Duke of Leinster, but now the house of the Dublin Society. The plan comprehends a central edifice, of august proportions, with two projecting pavilions, united to the principal building by a fine and graceful corridor. Few Ornaments are introduced in the design of the exterior. The elevation is lightened at the top by an open balustrade. The entrance is by portico, having the family arms in the tympanum of the pediment. The pavilions are entirely destitute of external embellishment.

"The interior is arranged with a degree of splendour suited to the noble family which excercises within these walls the hospitality of ancient Ireland, refined by the habits of more intellectual ages. The whole of the principal apartments are of large dimensions, and are richly adorned. The dining-room, recently completed under the direction of Richard Morrison, Esq. architect, is fifty-two feet long; twenty-two feet wide; and twenty-four feet high. This is believed to be the finest apartment in Ireland, appropriated to the same use . . . . . .

"The park which surrounds this mansion is of great extent, and has every charm which can be imparted by abundance of wood and judicious disposal. The surface is agreeably varied by gentle swells; but none of the bold features of nature, which characterise by far the greater number of Irish demesnes, and render them magnificent and enchanting, even when of limited size, are here found. Those softer beauties which afford repose to the eye, and which, perhaps, yield the most permanent gratification, are, however, seen in captivating variety. A stream, which winds through the principal parts of this spacious park, has been expanded by art into a river of ample width, and assists in forming much picturesque scenery, as it pursues its course amidst verdant swells of land, peculiarly soft and graceful, or approaches the sheltering masses of wood which dignify the demesne. Scenery so tranquil would appear to invite the introduction of artificial objects; and such we find to have been, accordingly, carried into execution on one of the most elevated parts of the park is placed a well-designed prospect-tower; and from another division of the grounds rises a pillar, which is conspicious through a long tract of the surrounding country. This latter erection is in itself a handsome object, when viewed from the mansion, and acquires additional interest from the circumstance of having afforded employment to the poor in a time of great scarcity and privation. The whole demense is encompassed by plantations, and the house is approached from Maynooth through a long and fine avenue of trees".

Travellers from not so far away came, as well as strangers. An article in *the Clongowinian* (1867) about Francis Sylvester Mahony ('Fr. Prout') tells of another visit to the College:

"It was a pleasant Autumn day in November, 1825. Rhetoric year, about twelve in all, were first in charge of the Rhetoric Master and set off (from Clongowes) to course across country to Maynooth, where they were to have dinner at two o'clock in the hotel; then they were to course home again arriving back in the college by nightfall, breaking the journey at Celbridge. At Maynooth each boy had a glass of whiskey-punch with his dinner, and at Celbridge each was given a good tea . . . but with the tea, we are told came a wide host of decanters, with bowls of sugar and jugs of hot water continually required. John Sheahan, in whose house in Celbridge this latter tea party took place, describes the scene: 'I don't know how many songs we sang, how many patriotic toasts and personal healths we proposed, how many speeches we made, how many decanters we emptied' ''. The Rhetoric Master was Mahony. The P.P. of Celbridge sat at one end of the table — He made an impassioned speech of praise in honour of O'Connell. As the night wore on Mahony spoke up and claimed that the real cause of Catholic Emancipation was the advance of time — its time had come. This caused quite a row but peace was restored by a song from the P.P. They left to walk back — in the rain — met a procession of turf carts, and Mahony made a bargain to get them all a ride home to the College — Clongowes — in time. The outcome was that soon after he was relieved of his duties and departed to the Continent. What a tale lies thereby . . . !

To come back to Bremer. He was critical of the traffic of the town which, he thought, "approaches too close to a building devoted to scholastic uses", the kind of building that is "well placed only when in the shades". The traffic comment was often to be repeated afterwards. But he was satisfied with the lands, "attached" to the College which he found "laid out in retired walks, adorned with plantations, and admirably adapted to the uninterupted exercise of the Students". He gave a short history of the foundation of the College, referred to as "University", and reproduced the horarium from Whitelaw and Walsh's *History of Dublin.* It was a benevolent account, unlike the article headed 'Maynooth' which appeared in March, 1828 in *The Quarterly Review.* As might be expected from that respectable journal, the criticism was clever, not overdone. But it was critical. The discipline of the College is said to be too rigid, especially in the matter of what might be read by the students. The courses are too narrow. It says that the 1826 Commissioners had suppressed some portion of the evidence they received. To counter that kind of thing a Catholic reporter visited the College in October, 1831, although he did not publish his material until 1835 in *The London and Dublin Orthodox Journal of Useful Knowledge:*

"We proceeded through the park, one mile from Dublin Castle, by the Viceregal lodge to Castleknock . . . . we next arrived at Blanchardstown,

246

about five miles from Dublin . . . . (Next) we directed our course to the left, towards the village of Lucan, about six miles from Dublin. There is not, perhaps, a more delightful drive than what are called the strawberry beds to the town of Lucan . . . . As you start you have a fine view of Chapelizod; and from the hills above you can behold the mountains which overhang the metropolis. The woods of Celbridge and Luttrelstown add much beauty to the scene. There is nothing in the town itself to excite wonder, except Vesey's demesne, which opens before it. At a little distance is the far-famed Spa-house, a great retreat for such of the nobility as wish to mend their broken constitutions . . . . Before you enter the town is the beautiful salmon-leap . . . . About three miles from Leixlip lies Maynooth, eleven miles from Dublin . . . . Maynooth presents a miserable spectacle of fallen greatness. The houses are empty, and the inhabitants are without wealth, trade or commerce. But for the College, there would be nothing for workmen of any kind; and the limited means and economic habits of the students leave little in what is necessary to be expended in the town . . . . As you enter Maynooth, the palace and domain of the duke of Leinster border the town to the east, whilst the College and magnificent ruins of the ancient castle of the Fitzgeralds appear before you to the West . . . . There is a beautiful convent to the right as you enter the town, where the religious ladies are most laudably employed in the exercise of every work of piety. In the school attached, several hundred children receive religious instruction on the most improved principles''.

From 19 to 22 July, 1831 there was a Synod of the Dublin clergy in the College. Over a hundred priests attended. It was opened with a solemn procession from the theology hall to the chapel, with cross bearers, curates, parish priests, superiors of religious orders, canons, officials of the Synod, the Archbishop and his deacons — in that order. About this time too J.K.L. dined in the College. As ever he was difficult. Fitzpatrick relates: "That evening in an argument with Dr. Montague, the Bursar, it was observed that he did not seem familiar with a Bull of (pope) Urban quoted by Dr. Doyle, who said — 'It strikes me Mr. Montague, that you know more about bullocks than bulls'. A Loud laugh being raised, M. muttered — 'Indulge your merriment, gentlemen; it is not often that Dr. Doyle makes you laugh' ''. Indeed, indeed. In 1833 *The Dublin Penny Journal* for October contained reference to Maynooth in an article about a traveller to Connaught. He went West via Carton and Maynooth. Of the latter he has to say that, although it has no business, it is not deformed with mud cabins as were so many Irish towns then.

The College is "daily enlarging itself", although resembling a barrack:
We entered Maynooth after passing Carton Demesne — it looks neat like all Irish towns without a stir of business; unlike most, as not deformed

with mud cabins. It was almost certainly rebuilt by the aforesaid Duke of Leinster, who desired to make it somewhat like an English market town; but alas, it is easier to build houses than to change the spirit and liability of a people. It is indeed celebrated as containing the great Roman Catholic College, which stands fronting you as you draw down the street.

"The centre building was erected by a butler of the late Duke of Leinster, who out of his savings erected it as a private mansion; he little thought of all the latin and logic and dogmatic theology it would subsequently contain. This college is daily enlarging itself; and so it should if it is meant to supply the immense and rapidly increasing Catholic population of Ireland with clergymen. To me it seemed to extend itself without any view towards uniformity and to be straggling in its largeness more like a large barrack than a college. It does not want for discipline as I am told, but it wants venerability — it may have academic seclusion, and no doubt it has, but it is deficient in the air, the unction, in that scholastic, grey sobriety that characterises Oxford and Cambridge in England or Padua or Salamanca on the continent. I prefer casting my eyes and feasting it on yonder old castle. I remember well in my younger days driving under yonder archway tower that led into the ballium of this Geraldine fortress — the highway ran under it then and what a grim gloomy prison — like pile is this keep; was it ever inhabited since the traitor — of Silken Thomas betrayed it to the Lord Deputy?"

The old castle was now a coal hole and part of it a ball court, so we are told by the *Orhodox Journal,* which also confirms that Edmund Burke died a Catholic, being attended in his last illness by Dr. Hussey, who was then in London. Its description of the College is exhaustive: "The College is certainly an extensive edifice. The whole forms a neat chapel, schools, halls, lodging rooms for the students, apartments for the president, vice-president, bursar, two deans, librarian, prefect of the Dunboyne establishment, ten professors, tradesmen, as butcher, baker, brewer, essential to the house, and servants and suitable kitchens." It does complain about the damp, which is caused by the proximity of the canal. Stoves — these must have been the 'hypocausts' mentioned earlier — have been erected in the library and halls but should have been better constructed so as to remove a bad smell and to convey warm air to the students' rooms. Yet because of exercise and regularity of life, there is much less disease than in places half the size. A new edifice, or left wing, is commodious. It houses the "junior lads", under Dean Gaffney, "whose manners are peculiarly adapted to them". The President, Dr. Montague, has constructed an "immense and almost impregnable" wall around the lands. "At the outer gates is a small lodge, not remarkable for anything but its economy which seems so essential a part of the establishment. On the walls are the figures of two lions, apparently, sphinxes in fact — forbidding the approach of strangers. The lawn before the house is chaste

248

and simple; having, as far as we could see, neither fruits nor flowers. You ascend the centre of the college by a neat set of stone stairs. The part of the present establishment at first formed the residence of the agent of the late duke of Leinster. His grace, we were informed, made sale of it to the original trustees of the college. Sometime after two spacious wings were added, extending the facade to the length of about 400 feet. If we add the length of the new or juvenile wing, as you turn by the left of the extreme end, it may be, perhaps, 600 feet. The centre projects about 50 feet beyond the front line of the wings, and is carried through three stories furnished with an attic. This house contains the dining and sitting rooms and separate apartments of the president and professors. The deans of the college have apartments in opposite directions, that they may be more convenient to all the students; and the prefect of the Dunboyne establishment resides in the midst of those more immediately under his care . . . . The dormitories of the students communicate with the corridors in the principal building to the extent of some hundred feet. These are converted into ambulatoris, when the severity of the weather forbids exercise in the open air. Before the entrance of the door which leads to the rear in the front house, is a large bell . . . . The dining hall is large but very plain. During meals a pious book is read and the usual grace given from a small pulpit". Our visitors also notes something often mentioned by others, namely, the "men" on the walls of the kitchen, turning spits by machine and reading at the same time also, an admonition written above the main chimney exhorting cleanliness and frugality. He does not appear to have visited the Chapel which, according to the *First Report of the Commissioners of Public Instruction Ireland* (London, 1835) "is almost entirely confined to members of the Roman Catholic College. No other person is allowed to attend the services without permission, which has not been obtained by more than five or six individuals".

Another visitor of the same period was the Reverend G. N. Wright, whose account of the College is contained in his *Scenes in Ireland,* published in 1834. It has nothing much to add to the piece just given. Of greater interest is the visit by Earl Mulgrave, the Lord Lieutenant, on 19 December 1835. It was to be the occasion of a celebrated incident. The *Journal of the Trustees* informs us that the Earl — later the Marquis of Normandy — came thither from Carton, where the President had dined with him a few days before. He came in the Duke of Leinster's carriage, accompanied by the Duke and Aid de Camps (sic.). "The students lined the walk to the gate and as soon as he entered warmly welcomed him with hearty and repeated cheers; the Superiors received him with every demonstration of Joy, confidence and respect at the Hall door and after having been successively presented to His Excellency in the parlour, conducted him to the Distribution of Prayer Hall. Here after acknowledging the long continued cheers of the assembled students, his Excellency was graciously pleased to receive and reply to the full address, read by Rev. Mr. Carey, 1st Professor of Theology". Amongst other things, Mr. Carew said that respect for the representatives of Royalty is only the homage which a subject owes his sovereign but that it was something well owed to this person in his own right. In reply the Earl declared himself most satisfied to hear from them how they inculcate doctrines so worthy of the ministers of peace. After the ceremony, on being joined by Lord Leitrim and Mr. Clements, Mulgrave retired to the parlour for refreshments. The refreshments were undoubtedly good and strong and not stinted, and the students, as is their wont, were not slow to take advantage of their chance. A deputation came to see the Lord Lieutenant and was received. They were seeking exemption from the January examinations. Why not? The Earl was in good mood; the professors? . . . . Why not? The students' petition was granted by the Lord Lieutenant and some wine ordered for them by him also. He departed the College at 3 p.m. to cheers. It had been a great day, enjoyed by one and all. In fact it was not yet over. Days like that need to be prolonged, especially when the wine is flowing. At the Inquiry of 1855 the Reverend J. O'Callaghan, who had been a student at the time, tells of the evening's proceedings. "Three bottles were, accordingly, served to every mess. The students at meals are divided into messes — every mess consists of eight persons. We clubbed, and made up some money to send to Dublin for confectionery and other things; the College supplied us with hot water, and we had a feast. There was a great deal of joviality on the occasion. In the course of the evening some of the professors paid us a visit; then they came in, there was a rush of the students towards them, and they soon formed a circle around them". The professors were assuredly in good form; it has not been unknown. But in all likelihood amongst both professors and students there were some who, despite the good cheer of the day in general and Mulgrave's own personal popularity, were harbouring lowering misgivings about the extent of the loyal manifestation which had been so marked a feature of the occasion. Now patriotic sentiments came to the fore. Even Mr. Whitehead, who is supposed — although the matter is inclear — to have changed his name from the Irish Canavan ('Ceann Ban' or 'White Head') partook of them. In that year of the second Emancipation Act, O'Connell was something of a hero, whether or not generally liked at Maynooth. So "O'Connell's health was proposed and the Professor of Logic, Mr. Whitehead, spoke to the toast". He urged "that, as we were bound by every principle to support and defend those who would fight our battle, and seek liberty and entire emancipation for us; so, on the other hand, there was no law, human or divine, natural or revealed that prevented us from seeking, by all legitimate means, to humble a nation that would grind us, trample upon us, enact penal laws against us, and set the same value upon the head of a priest that it had set upon the head of a wolf". These words, said O'Callaghan were Whitehead's *ipsissima verba*. And fighting words they were, plainly directed to the pro-violence party in Ireland as against the pro-conciliation approach of O'Connell. "That sentiment was applauded for four or five minutes". Dr. Renehen (a good Tipperary man) sang and there were a great many toasts and a great many songs from the students. The feast went on from five p.m. until 11 or 12 at night, the students being "excited, some but slightly, and some a good deal".

At the sequence in October, 1853, when Dr. Whitehead was examined by the Commissioners, he played things down a lot: "I was then only twenty-eight years of age . . . . I did not a thing which I would not do now, that is, I spoke in the presence of the students without any previous preparation". This was not giving away much. The wine, he said, had been supplied by the President, though he does not say at whose orders. He argued that the students must have gone to bed by 10 because that was their custom!! Dr. Gaffney, the Dean, was more forthcoming. He told the Commissioners that a Mr. O'Sullivan was "Chairman" that night and that he had been refused orders at the end of the year and left the College afterwards, "or, to speak more correctly, he was obliged to leave it". Whatever of this, the events alarmed the Commissioners of 1853 into inquiring of O'Callaghan whether "a hatred of England and of Protestantism" was a common sentiment among the students. His reply "was the strongest and most predominant feeling among the students at Maynooth". "Oh what occasions?" "On the occasion on which the walk-days were wet; for instance every Wednesday was an idle day, and when it happened to be wet, the students assembled together, as they had nothing to do after a certain time of the day; I recollect one student, who I was informed and believe (for I was not in the College at the time) was arrested in the College for seditious language made use of at meetings which took place in some parts of Ireland. He was (as I was told) bailed before the Duke of Leinster; and I heard this person myself frequently give specimens of the ovations that he had delivered; and I could swear solemnly that if he had made use of half the same abusive language against any Roman Catholic saint that he did against the Queen and Her Government, he would have been expelled immediately. I never heard that he received the slightest reprimand; on the contrary, I know that he was a great favourite with the professors and students in general". But now he was speaking of Victoria even though he had entered the College in 1835 or 1836 and had left at the beginning of his third year. In the College in June, 1836 the Trustees thought it better to lay down that in no instance should there be an extraordinary "vacant day" allowed to the students except on the express desire of the Lord Lieutenant on the occasion of his visit and enjoined on the staff to see to it that they attend at the students' sermons. In their absence who knows what might be preached!

1836 also saw a visit from Baptist Wriothesley Noel, whose version of things at the College is to be found in *Notes of a Short Tour through the Midland Counties of Ireland in the Summer of 1836.* He had called at Maynooth because of what he had heard about it, a place that had been designated as in a litany — a "hot-bed of bigotry", "nurse of discord", "source of sedition" and "grand curse of Ireland". He was thorough in his recounting of the length of time spent at and nature of the studies there, having reservations about the first year course in Mathematics: "I can remember my freshman's year at Trinity College, Cambridge, and believe that the majority of these students must know about as much on these subjects at the end of the year as at the beginning, and no more''. ''The course on theology . . . . seems very Romish''. ''The students of every class are freely permitted to read the Scriptures in their hours of leisure . . . . I have seen Maynooth severely blamed for its neglect of Scriptures; but to be just, I must confess that to this day there is not, I believe, even in the University of Cambridge, though there is much religion there, an equal attention given to the public exposition of the Bible. With the habits of Oxford I am less acquainted''. As for recreation, ''behind the College is a square space, and beyond this a gravel walk for a quarter of a mile. Here they make their melancholy promenade, unless they play at ball or at prison bars''. As for the Deans: ''By night and day too the Deans have the right of entering every apartment''. On the students there is much, even though it was vacation time when he made his visit. There were forty or fifty of them in the College when he came. ''They were generally athletic youths, with good countenances, and with all the appearance of robust health. Several were dressed as priests. Their caps and gowns are very like those of the smaller colleges at Cambridge . . . . Occasionally I observed a yawning rent at the knee . . . . At the tables each student still wore his cap. The substantial and excellent dinner was served in the simplest style, on a coarse table cloth, adorned with pewter plates and with knives and forks having black bone handles. Amidst the clatter of the knives, and the rapid movement of the hungry operators, a young man, with a sonorous voice, read from a pulpit, according to their custom, a chapter from the Old Testament . . . . As I departed the college . . . . I could not but reflect with melancholy interest on the prodigious moral power lodged within the walls of that mean, rough-cast and white-washed range of buildings, standing without one architectural recommendation, on that dull and gloomy flat. What a vomitory of fiery zeal . . . . !'' Dear Noel — how 'melancholy' he must have been himself: *''Si le jour est triste, c'est parceque nous sommes tristes nous mêmes''* (Sartre), Not ever but nearly ever!

About 1837 Lewis of the great *Topographical Dictionary* came. He was down to earth and accurate in his delineation of the buildings, staff, students and Trustees. In 1838 he was followed by Henry D. Inglis, who gives a long account of the College in is *Journey through Ireland.* But again there is nothing very new — the road down through the strawberry beds, breakfast at Mrs. Collin's inn at Leixlip and then Maynooth, with an account of the student's day. Sometime after that the College was visited by William Makepiece Thackerary who did a vitriolic diatribe on it. But he smacks of the Victorian period and we leave him to it.

EMANCIPATION

The passing of the Emancipation Act of 1829 put the Maynooth students' tails up. Many of them may have been looking for much more but here at least was something, whether or not they liked O'Connell. Many of them preferred a more forceful political stance and did not believe much in what would be done through parliamentary methods, an outlook apparently shared by the *Freeman's Journal* which, on 12 February, 1834 had announced: "The talking nuisance has set in for its six months. What a pest is the parliament!". The *Freeman* .... At times it seemed very loyal. In 1827, for example, on 28 August, it had reported that it was the intention of the Admiralty to build six steam ships of the largest size, for otherwise "by steam the United States may cripple our navy, although successful invasion from that quarter is out of the quesion". The extent to which Catholic emancipation had been hoped for in the College comes through in a letter of 1828 from Anglade, then still in Maynooth, to Boylan, gone to Rome. It is expected urgently, says Anglade, but much opposed. There has been a Protestant petition in favour of it, however, with the *"duc de Lynster's"* name at the head. The newspapers that are opposed are beginning to make an outcry against the administration but Peel is favourable towards the measure. There is much agitation in the North! — the same old story there as always. The patriotic interest of the College is evident too from Anglade's noting that amongst new positions to be filled there was the chair *"d'Irlandois",* by a Mr. Tully, an *"Irlandois".*

The influence of Maynooth on the country was beginning to be felt. The *Creevy Papers* tell of a visit by Creevy to the College in 1828, where he found "three hundred and eighty precious blackguards . . . . the men that are to guide and control the whole Catholic population of Ireland". Whether blackguards or not, the products of Maynooth had, as Wyse said in his *Sketch of the Catholic Association* (1829), "begun to be felt". In 1829 also the then Lord Lieutenant, the Duke of Northumberland, wrote to Peel saying that the Maynooth seminarians went back to their parishes "with the bitterest feeling of the Partizan and the grossest habits of a Peasant". That they had bitter feelings seems sure, In his evidence before the Commission of 1853, the Reverend J. O'Callaghan, already quoted, speaks of the way in which they treated the oath of loyalty in the 1830's. The oath, he says, was administered in open court before an Assistent Barrister by a Clerk of the Peace who read from a parchment. "He would read two or three words to the students, who, in one voice repeated the same. Then he repeated one or two more words, and those the students again repeated, all speaking at the same time, so that nothing could be heard but a confused hum of voices". During the 1826 Inquiry it had emerged that the oath was taken by the students in the Court House of the town of Maynooth. It was in a sort of loft, which the students occupied on two sides, the Barrister being in the lower part facing them. He prefaced the solemnities "by a kind of compliment" to them, saying that they were not to take the oath to His Majesty from any distrust that His Majesty had of their loyal principles but for positive reasons. It had emerged in 1826 that this was a *charade* for many of them. Moloney in his evidence at that time told of their returning to College with a feeling of having been conned: "Some said it was a queer way to be brought to the Court-house to take the oath without knowing someting more about it before they went out; they considered that it was dealing unfairly with them to be called upon to take an oath that they did not see before. I know there was a great bustle about it after they returned home, some saying that they did not know what the oath was, and others saying that they did not know how they could take it in conscience". O'Callaghan remembered that in the 1830's he overheard one student say: "I take this oath with equivocation and mental reservation". It would have been impossible for the officials to detect any such deviation, for the students were sworn in batches; "5 or 6 would stand holding the book . . . . and another batch had another book and so on". 'It all ended together, and we all then, headed by the dean, proceeded to a room in Nolan's hotel, in the town of Maynooth, and every person came up and signed his name to a paper, as having taken the oath of allegiance".

By the mid-1830's the students must really have begun to kick against this goad. The student referred to in his evidence by O'Callaghan as having made seditious speeches (his name was Hawkes and he came from Kerry) was frequently cheered for same, "just as if he had been making a speech at a public meeting". if for no other reason than to inhibit this kind of thing, reading was imperative at dinner even if, as O'Callaghan remarks and students of a much later era had the same experience, it was impossible to hear because of "noise and confusion of servants bringing in dishes and hurrying to and fro". for which reason the reader "husbanded" his voice. He recalled Lingard's *History of England* being read after portion of the Martyrology. This was in the 1830's . . . . Whenever the name of 'Jesus' was spoken, "the students who always wear their caps at dinner, all took them off, and to take them off had to throw down their knives and forks, the clashing of so many knives and forks falling upon the large pewter plates made a great noise". They also wore their caps in the hall while studying but not while being examined! It would seem that, for all their devotion, the students of the earlier 1830's were a difficult enough lot, emancipating themselves at times to the point of being unruly. The *Journal of the Trustees* records this by implication. Thus in February, 1830, they received a report on discipline from the President, at which they declared themseves gratified, but went on to insist on the need for the professors to sign in the presence of the President the same declaration as was prescribed for the students on their admission to the house. The following June they were ordering that a clerical collar be worn by the students from "the next commencement of studies" as a part of the College dress and that "the President be instructed to inform them henceforward to apply themselves with assiduity to the study and practice of the Gregorian note". Let the people sing! Some of the 'people' were obstreperous. In 1835 a student of the Archdiocese of Armagh was reprimanded before the Vice-President and Deans for insolent and disrespectful conduct to the Junior Dean, whose office had been created in 1833 in view of the increased number of students. This student had aggravated his transgression by defending its propriety and calling the conduct of the Dean unjust and unwarranted. On the same day a student from Tuam was reprimanded for severely striking a companion with his fist on one occasion and attempting to strike him with a book on another occasions and calling him a coward.

Whether politics was involved we do not know. We do know that the students engaged in political discussion as they always had done. Earlier, around 1798 and 1803, this had been great so. The Rev. John Cousins, at the 1826 Inquiry, had told how, when he entered Maynooth in 1799,

> "the great body of students . . . . used to talk of the rebellion of 1798, and dwell with pleasure on the bravery with which the rebels fought; we used to regret the failure of former rebellions in Ireland, and also converse about the possibility of Ireland existing as an independent country, whether she could supply herself with coal, salt and other things which were brought from England, and those conversations were frequent; but I must observe that there were some in the house, particularly from the north of Ireland, not many certainly, but there were some that showed a very loyal feeling".

In 1853 the Commissioners reminded the Rev. John O'Callaghen of an incident which was supposed to have taken place — probably around 1835 — when O'Connell was going to Dublin westwards and a number of students collected on top of a haystack and cheered him. He did not remember it but Dr. Whitehead did, admitting that there was cheering "but whether it was on top of a haystack I do not know". In or about the same time the College was illuminated and a feast given to the students to mark the celebration of Emancipation. The College was beginning to go over to the offensive. After a meeting at Exeter Hall on 11 March, 1836, when Mr. J. C. Colquohon criticised it for its part in the rebellion of 1798, saying that Dr. Hussey "was removed from the sedentary mischief of his station at Maynooth to the more active post of Bishop of Waterford" (!), a public meeting was held at Bath on 20 March, for the purpose of petitioning Parliament to continue the grant to Maynooth College. The speeches on the occasion were published under the heading *Equal Laws for Ireland*. The equality would eventually be achieved.

INGENIOUS EXPERIMENTS

If there was one man in the College over whose head all this political turmoil is likely to have passed unnoticed, it is the Reverend Nicholas Callan, Professor of Mathematics and Natural Philosophy. He was a saintly man as well as a scholar; he translated some of the works of St. Alphonsus Liguori into English. He had come up to College in 1817 and become Professor in 1826. Within six years he had made a mark with the appearance of *An Abstract of a Course of Lectures on Electricity and Galvanism,* published in Dublin by Coyne. It was made up of the lectures which he gave at Maynooth. Illustrated, it dealt with questions such as: "What effect has a negative body on the electrical state of a contiguous unelectrified body to which a spark will not pass?" It demonstrates how electricity was capable of breaking and perforating imperfect conductors. Thus: "Into a glass bottle containing salad oil, introduce a pointed wire, so that the point will be under the surface of the oil, and in contact with the side of the bottle. Connect the wire with either conductor of the machine, and present the knuckle to the point; sparks will pass from the point to the knuckle and, in a few seconds, the glass will be perforated". The experiments were primitive. Callan writes: "any of the substances in the following list becomes positive, when rubbed by any of those that follow it, and negative when rubbed by any of those that precede it — the back of a Cat, Smooth Glass, Woollen Cloth, Feathers, Wood, Paper". One could reasonably suppose that the cats at Maynooth tried to make themselves as scarce as possible. During the Victorian period, when his experiments grew more

ABSTRACT

OF A

COURSE OF LECTURES

ON

ELECTRICITY

AND

GALVANISM,

DELIVERED IN THE R. C. COLLEGE, MAYNOOTH

BY THE REV. N. J. CALLAN,

PROFESSOR OF MATHEMATICS AND NATURAL PHILOSOPHY.

DUBLIN
PRINTED BY JOHN COYNE,
24, COOKE-STREET.

1832.

daring, he was to test the voltage of his batteries by electrocuting chickens and one famous occasion, when he had students touch his wires for proof of current, nearly finished the career of William Walsh, the future Archbishop of Dublin. For 1832 we should be content with learning from him that "the electricity of excited glass is different from that of excited sealing wax". It was all very unusual, not only for an Irish Catholic academy but anywhere at that time.

These experiments and those that he was to conduct over the following twenty years were to make Callan's name and make Maynooth very proud of him. He was to come to be cited in such places as Sturgeon's *Annals of Electricity* in 1838, Puggendorf's *Annalen der Chymik,* the *Comptes Rendus* and the *Philosophical Magazine.* This was yet to come. It was quite a performance on the part of one who had had no great training in his chosen field of study. But then the founders of subjects were never trained in them. Callan, after his doctorate in Divinity in Rome in 1825 (he had been ordained priest at Maynooth in 1823), was invited by the President of the College to be a candidate for the chair vacated by the retirement of the Reverend Cornelius Denvir. There was no other candidate at the public examination so Callan got it easily. At the Inquiry of 1826 he caused some surprise by implying that he had never read Euclid but knew enough about it from other treatises. His considerable private fortune helped him with his experiments. These were to prove extraordinary especially during his later period. Not all his fortune went in them. It was he and Dr. Anglade who defrayed much of the cost of the chapel for the local convent, the foundation stone of which was laid by Anglade in 1832. Yet for all his achievements, Callan appears to have been a gawkish man and there are many references in College sources to his ungainly manners. Writing from Rome in 1827, the Rector of the Irish College complained that the hopes of that College getting many students from Ireland appeared to have been jeopardised by the animosity of Maynooth to the idea, something which — he regretted - was only helped by Dr. Callan's presence there because "it appeared, awkwardly enough, that poor Dr. Callan appeared to many to have lost instead of gaining any great information or polish by his tour . . . . ". The 'grand tour' of the 18th century was not yet dead so long as a sojourn in Rome could be thus termed.

Callan was to soldier on. As a scholar, he was undoubtedly pleased when in 1833, the College bought Dr. Boylan's library (for the sum of just £300 by the way) even though it is pretty certain that it contained no scientific works. He would have been more pleased, one fears, when in June of that year, the Trustees ordered fifty guineas for the repair of "the Hypocaust" and set up "a Gazometer". These things were more in his line. In January, 1834 approval was given for the erection of the Hypocaust "or other apparatus for the airing of linens and other underclothing of the members of the College. The Sub-Committee responsible for this success were "also prayed to ascertain for the information of the Board at its next meeting whether any and what mode of heating the Halls and apartments of the College be desirable." And was he delighted when the next item was passed on the same occasion: "That the Professor of Natural Philosophy be empowered, under the direction of the President, to purchase an electro-magnetic apparatus, and to order such repairs of the Air Pump and of every other physical apparatus used in his Class, as he deems necessary". he had got a *carte blanche*, something seldom handed out by the Trustees. It was a break through. He would soon be making his own apparatus.

It may have been Callan's growing fame that caused W. Beaufoy, in 1835, to present to the College his work on hydraulic and nautical experiments, for which the Trustees thanked him in June. In 1837 a model of Callan's induction coil was exhibited at the Electrical Exhibition. In its construction he had been influenced by Bacchoffner and others but made his own special contribution which is

DARRE'S ELEMENTS

OF

GEOMETRY,

WITH BOTH

PLANE AND SPHERICAL

TRIGONOMETRY.

DESIGNED

FOR THE USE OF THE STUDENTS OF THE R. C. COLLEGE, MAYNOOTH.

REVISED AND IMPROVED

BY THE REV. N. J. CALLAN.

PROFESSOR OF PHILOSOPHY IN THAT COLLEGE.

DUBLIN:

PRINTED BY RICHARD COYNE,

4, CAPEL-STREET,

PRINTER AND BOOKSELLER TO THE ROYAL COLLEGE OF ST. PATRICK, AND PUBLISHER TO THE R. C. BISHOPS IN IRELAND.

1832.

recognised in Fleming's *The Alternate Current Transformer*. By then too, in fact by 1836, he had constructed a moving machine, the wheels of which were turned by electro-magnets. For a while he thought of pioneering electro-magnetic engineering to the point of replacing steam by electro-magnetism. An admiring successor of his of the 20th century spoke of "the startling sight witnessed by the young students of Maynooth, who see a machine of Callan's move itself along the floor of the Science Hall, fifty years before the event of the automobile outside". Maynooth had produced an inventor of stature.

FIRST THINGS LAST

For all its wrangling, its political posturing, its academic intriguing and scientific experiments, the College never forgot its basic *raison d'etre*. The preaching of the Gospel was its first reason for being and so merits being the last to be dealt with also. It is a question of first things retaining their priority to the extent that, while remaining first, they are also last. The abiding concern of Maynooth College for the foreign missions bears eloquent witness to this. As a matter of course it provided priests for the home mission, men whose unshakable faith, pastoral zeal and general interest in their people were to pay a large part in the transformation of 19th century Ireland. One might say that the College's part in producing these was taken for granted. It is different in the case of those who went abroad, bringing Christ's message to peoples in far off lands, like St. Paul hazarding all in that intent. These were the men who were to set afoot a Maynooth Mission in India and, much much later, missions to China and Africa, as well as innumerable missions to English-speaking colonies, to say nothing of North America, Scotland and England itself. Indeed it is an irony of fate that Maynooth's position in the world of the Victorian Empire was such as to create an Irish spiritual empire within it.

In Georgian times efforts of a missionary nature were modest but important. As early as 1813, an *"ancien"* Chinese missionary — a Frenchman called Denis Chaumont — wrote from London to De la Hogue trying to sell some of his writings in Sacred Scripture to the College of "Menouth". In his letter he launches into a long description of the state of religion in China, especially in the Province of Sutchwan. He elaborates on the work of the Mission Etrangeres de Paris, giving statistics, etc. The letter can be found in the Clogher Archives among Delahogue's papers. It is fascinating to think that he was writing to the place which was to produce a mission to China over a century later. Chaumont asks Delahogue whether he thinks the work is worth continuing? *"Croyez vous qu'il puis etre avantageux pour les missions de le continuer?"* It was to be continued — later. In 1817 Nicholas Slevin, future Maynooth Professor, wrote from Trieste to James McCormick, O.F.M., Superior of St. Isidore's in Rome, upset because Propaganda had refused him a "patent" to go on the American Missions, on the grounds that he had not been nominated for this by the Irish Bishops: "Yet the call for missionaries is general in the U.S.''. At that time Slevin was ''disgusted at Ireland'' and had ''formed the opinion of never going there. If I should change it, it shall be only to prove to the Propaganda that I am not afraid or ashamed to show my face there''. He hopes that he might get a post in Malta, with the English soldiers or in the Ionian Islands, e.g., Corfu. He asks McCormick to do what he can for him with Galeazzi, the private Secretary to Cardinal Fontana. His journey from Naples to Brindisium was fraught with more incidents than Horace's from Rome to there. If he — Horace — had the good fortune to have fallen into the hands of robbers, his epistle would be more interesting. ''Mine enables me only to say I was left nearly naked''. He wishes to be remembered to, amongst others, Mr. Taylor, thought to be the Dominican priest who, acccording to Lord Cloncurry, had married George IV to Mrs. Fitzherbert. Slevin, within a few years, was Prefect of the Dunboyne, although he did not remain at Maynooth for the rest of his life. Despite his able and ready defence of the College in 1826, he never seems to have really settled down in Maynooth, when, in 1825, we find Edward Maginn, a student for the Diocese of Derry, in the Irish College, Paris, visiting Slevin, who was his uncle at the College, having left Paris for health reasons, we need not be surprised to find the latter trying — unsuccessfully — to resume his studies not at Maynooth but in Paris again, where he might well contest a chair. Maginn was later to become Bishop of Derry.

The first great missionary from Maynooth was possibly John McEncroe (1795 - 1868), who went to Australia. He was born in Cashel and entered Maynooth in 1813. McEncroe met Fr. John Joseph Therry — the great Australian pioneering priest — when he said Mass in Maynooth College Chapel in 1815. Therry was recruiting men for an Australian venture. He set out from Cork towards the end of 1819 or the beginning of 1820 in an old windjammer, bound for the convict settlement of Australia. Writing from New Holland some months later, he urged McEncroe to join him as there was a desperate need for priests. The latter went to New South Wales in 1822. It was the beginning of quite a Maynooth connection with Australia. In 1820 Philip Conolly (1786 - 1839) from Co. Monaghan, also educated at Maynooth, had preceded him by answering the call for volunteer missionaries when the British Government consented to have Roman Catholic chaplains stationed at Derwent and Botany Bay. Earlier, in 1817, Fr. Jeremiah Francis O'Flynn had landed in Van Dieman's Land after seven month's sailing. He did not come from Maynooth. Conolly was accepted by Governor Macquarrie on the latter's being assured by both a Protestant magistrate and the Archbishop of Dublin that the priest was a ''truly loyal man'' and ''of exemplary religious and moral habits''. He and Therry arrived in Sydney in the *Janus* in May, 1820. After a year there Conolly was to go to Hobart where he ministered for fourteen years.

At home the big news was the foundation from Maynooth of the Irish Province of the Vincentian Fathers, the Congregation of the Mission. In 1832 four

Maynooth students, James Lynch, Peter Kenrick (already come across by us) Anthony Reynolds and Michael Burke — all of Dublin — planned the formation of a missionary society. The missions must have been in Kenrick's blood, for he was the brother of the Bishop of Philadelphia, later Archbishop of Baltimore, and himself — following his time with the Vincentians — ended up as Archbishop of St. Louis. That was some way off in 1832. The four were encouraged by Drs. Carew and Dowley (Carew was to become a missionary himself later and Dowley was to join the Vincentians). These told them to contact a Fr. Meagher, who had already tried to introduce the Vincentians into Ireland, only to find that he had abandoned the idea. Again they turned to their professor advisers and also to Dr. Crotty and Dr. Anglade (when Anglade died he left them a £200 bequest). Hope dawned when Dowley announced he was joining them. Kenrick and Reynolds were ordained and went on the Dunboyne. Lynch had one and a half years to go to ordination. He was made a Monitor in the Junior House, during his time as which he enlisted in the 'missionaries' his fellow-monitor Thomas MacNamara of Meath. All that was in 1832. In June, 1833, Lynch and Burke were ordained. The project was about to blast off. Dr. Dowley would be the man to lead it. He remained on at Maynooth for another year, however, being made Vice-President by the Bishops with an increased salary. There is a story to be found in a manuscript in the *Archives of the Irish College, Paris,* that he was offered the Presidency in June, 1834, or at least approached about it by the Archbishop of Dublin, but all to no avail. He left the College in 1835 to set up the first Vincentian group in Ireland. From this small band was to come the great colleges of All Hallows and Castleknock. Others of the group were John McGowan also of Dublin, a student in 1835, who that year spent his vacation in visiting interesting places and monuments throughout Ireland. He was to travel farther afterwards. There was also Mr. Hand, who was assistant to the Bursar and got himself into quite a rumpus in that capacity. He left Maynooth in June, 1835 for Castleknock, where he was ordained the following December. His biographer tells us:

"The Commissariat Department in Maynooth was always an affair of magnitude. At the time of which we are writing, it was administered by only one officer, called the Bursar, but the work was too much for him. In these circumstances, Dr. Montague, the President, resolved to appoint an Assistant, or Under Bursar . . . . who should keep the accounts, and superintend the weighing-out of the daily supplies for the College Dining Hall and Servants' Hall. He was turning over this plan in his mind, and casting about for a fit and proper person to fill the office, when Dr. Cantwell called. The Bishop, from his long experience as College Dean, was in a position to give valuable advice, in reference to the over-worked Department of the Commissariat. Dr. Montague, therefore, very wisely submitted the plan to his distinguished visitor, and the Bishop, after approving it, moved by a supernatural impulse, and wit the vision of Mr.

Hand distinctly before his mind, exclaimed:— "Dr. Montague you have created the hour, and I have the man". His Lordship went on to describe Mr. Hand's aptitudes; to relate the history of his remarkable success and severe trials. "Perhaps" he added with evident emotion, "this fortunate occasion will smooth the way of a truly deserving young man to the services of the altar. Thus, my dear Mr. Montague, you will "be doing an act well-pleasing to God, who loves Mr. Hand, and the salary attached will ease his father of what would certainly be to him a pressing difficulty . . . ."

"Mr. Hand, on entering Maynooth in the August of 1831, encountered the sting of defeat. Most of the men with whom he sat on the same form in the seminary, being intern students, went up to College in the beginning of last session. At their entrance-examination they were weighed and found wanting, and relegated to wander in the mazes of philosophy for another year. They, therefore, considered it a censure, that Mr. Hand now, though a year after them in College, should be allowed to leap on to their bench. It was given out that Dr. Montague had already conceived so profound an esteem for the Assistant Bursar that he registered his name on the roll of the first year's divinity. They felt this and showed their feelings by making ungenerous allusions to Mr. Hand's struggle with poverty, and did not hesitate to characterize the office he had taken to meet the expenses of his College, as an indignity offered to the Diocese of Meath.

"This demonstration of a hostile spirit culminated in a conspiracy to disown Mr. Hand, and scrape him when he entered the class. Now, scraping is the strongest expression of discontent, disapproval, and veiled rebellion on the part of the students of Maynooth, and is happily of rare occurrence. Poor Mr. Hand was, however, subjected to its ignominy, and no one ever more undeservedly. His appearance in the divinity class was greeted with a fierce burst of scraping by the malcontents. Startled by the grating noise, he quailed, but in a moment recovered his balance. He quietly took his seat and was soon deep in noting the Professor's lecture, as if he had been all the time breathing freely under a serene sky. The storm thus ushered in by loud thunder claps, lingered in faint echoes for a short time when it died far away from the hallowed walls of the College . . . .

'The man, who in 1833 started the revival of the missions in Ireland, was the late lamented and devoted servant of God, known from the office he held in Maynooth at the time, as Dean Dowley. In the history of that College no one can be found to have adorned the important office of Dean as Father Dowley, for no other turned his tenure of that office to the same account for the glory of God. Of him it may be truly said that the zeal for saving souls burned in his heart as the oil is consumed in the lamp! Now, since good priests are the great factor in saving souls, he

262

literally spent himself in making the students, who passed through his hands in College, good priests . . . ."

"Dean Dowley's burning zeal for saving souls was not satisfied with the training of good pastors. Though he had a keen relish for the intellectual luxuries of Maynooth, and a singular aptitude for his official duties there, yet he was not happy. He reflected on the many earnest priests he sent forth, and that while intellectually they may be his inferiors, they were giants compared to him in gathering in the harvest of Jesus Christ. 'What', he used to say, 'men without letters rise up and take heaven by violence, and I, with all my learning, have hardly put in my sickle though the harvest is come'. . . ."

"From all this it is easy to see how Dean Dowley became the centre of a circle of fervent students, who, during their last year in College, were striving to form a plan for reviving the missions of St. Vincent de Paul in Ireland. In their secret deliberations they were met at every step by formidable difficulties which were springing under their feet. At last Dean Dowley impatient of their delay, one day after their admission to priests' orders, quickened them into immediate action by words to this effect: 'Why stand here all day idle? go at once into the vineyard, and the Lord of the vineyard will reward your generous sacrifice by maturing your rule and plan of life in His own good time'. And immediately they departed from Maynooth. The Dean followed some time after, and they adopted the rule of St. Vincent of Paul under the name of 'The Fathers of the Congregation of the Mission', who from that day have grown in usefulness, and to be "the good odour of Christ unto God."

'The man, who in 1833 started the revival of the missions in Ireland, was the late lamented and devoted servant of God, known from the office he held in Maynooth at the time, as Dean Dowley. In the history of that College no one can be found to have adorned the important office of Dean as Father Dowley, for no other turned his tenure of that office to the same account for the glory of God. Of him it may be truly said that the zeal for saving souls burned in his heart as the oil is consumed in the lamp! Now, since good priests are the great factor in saving souls, he literally spent himself in making the students, who passed through his hands in College, good priests . . . ."

"Dean Dowley's burning zeal for saving souls was not satisfied with the training of good pastors. Though he had a keen relish for the intellectual luxuries of Maynooth, and a singular aptitude for his official duties there, yet he was not happy. He reflected on the many earnest priests he sent forth, and that while intellectually they may be his inferiors, they were giants compared to him in gathering in the harvest of Jesus Christ. 'What', he used to say, 'men without letters rise up and take heaven by violence, and I, with all my learning, have hardly put in my sickle though the harvest is come'. . . ."

"From all this it is easy to see how Dean Dowley became the centre of a circle of fervent students, who, during their last year in College, were striving to form a plan for reviving the missions of St. Vincent de Paul in Ireland. In their secret deliberations they were met at every step by formidable difficulties which were springing under their feet. At last Dean Dowley impatient of their delay, one day after their admission to priests' orders, quickened them into immediate action by words to this effect: 'Why stand here all day idle? go at once into the vineyard, and the Lord of the vineyard will reward your generous sacrifice by maturing your rule and plan of life in His own good time'. And immediately they departed from Maynooth. The Dean followed some time after, and they adopted the rule of St. Vincent of Paul under the name of 'The Fathers of the Congregation of the Mission', who from that day have grown in usefulness, and to be "the good odour of Christ unto God."

"This company of fervent priests directly on retiring from Maynooth, took a house on Usher's Quay, and with the sanction of Dr. Murray, the venerated Archbishop of Dublin, they opened a day school there, in addition to their special work of giving Missions through the country, which they were not able to begin for some time later on. They fixed their residence in Dublin in 1833, and in due course Castleknock, with its fine demesne, on the border of the Phoenix Park, fell into their hands."

There were other stirrings too. In 1837 a young man called Eugene O'Connell came up to Maynooth from the Meath Diocesan Seminary at Navan. This was the man who, later in the century, was to become the Pioneer Bishop of Northern California, about whose enterprises in Indian country, around places with names like 'Rough and Ready', have since crystallised into a saga. But to get back to the Australian mission, because it was not until the turn of the century that the American mission by Maynooth men really got going, in 1838, as the *College Records* enshrine, seven students "renounced their prospects and exiled themselves from friends and country to the propagation of the Gospel of Our Lord in New South Wales". They came to be known as 'The Men of 38'. One of them, Fr. John J. Lynch of Dublin, had been of "the flower of Maynooth" who had followed Ullathorne for Australia in January, 1837. All reached Sydney in the barque *Cecilia* on 15 July, 1838. They evangelized the upper reaches of the Hunter River. All were excellent horsemen. We are told that they baptized at the rate of one hundred and seventy a year, very good for a sparsely inhabited territory of mainly Anglo-Saxon and Protestant heritage. They lived in shepherd's huts and ate salt junk, said Mass in barns, settlers' huts, pubs and under the open sky. So did another, Fr. O'Reilly, across the Blue Mountains, journeying on his "hacke" 'Shamrock', scouring 'No man's Land', for that was the name of some

of his area. He found time too though for his racehorse, 'Ajax', which later got him into difficulties.

Ullathorne, O.S.B., Vicar General of Sydney, afterwards Archbishop of Westminster during Australia's Benedictine period was well accepted at Maynooth. Were it not for this it is doubtful if the Benedictines could have done much at all in Australia. His right hand man in the College was Francis Murphy — later to be Bishop of Adelaide — who was highly esteemed by the Professors and students. He secured a hearty welcome and fine response for Ullathorne when the latter went to the College in 1837 to seek vocations for Australia. Two Dublin students immediately wished to join him. One who volunteered for the Sydney mission was the Reverend Edward MacCabe, then a Senior Student. He was later to be Cardinal Arcbishop of Dublin — he never made Sydney. The reason is interesting. Both he and a Fr. Fitzpatrick, also of Dublin, had gone together to their Bishop, Dr. Murray, to ask permission to go abroad. Fitzpatrick went in to him first and got it. When MacCabe went in "the Archbishop asked what was to become of Dublin if all his students were to set out for the antipodes". Nevertheless, another Irish-Australian priest who in a different way became a Cardinal back in Ireland — Patrick Francis Moran, historian of the Australian Church — says that so great was the enthusiasm for missionary enterprize at this time among the Maynooth students and so many were volunteering for Australia that the design was formed of instituting a Foreign Missionary College, and soon the beginnings were made by Fr. Hand, which eventually took place in the College of All Hallows on 1 November 1842.

Among those who went to Australia with Ullathorne in 1838 were seven newly ordained priests. As well as Fr. Fitzpatrick, there was also Fr. Lynch and Fr. Rigney, Brennan, Mahoney, O'Reilly and Slattery (a native of Limerick). Rigney later became Archdeacon and Fitzpatrick Vicar General of Melbourne. With them too went Francis Murphy, ordained in 1825 — afterwards to become the first Bishop of Adelaide. The while McEnroe was on the convict Norfolk Island (near Pitcairn Island). He was to remain there from 1838 or 1839 to about 1842. He went there at the request of another Benedictine, Bishop Polding. It was a hard assignment. Amongst those held there between 1801 and 1807 were two Irish priests, Peter O'Neil of Cloyne and James Harold of Dublin, who had been convicted after the rebellion of 1798. It was a very brutal colony. Possibly with a view to distracting himself somewhat, while on norfolk Island McEncroe wrote a book, *The Wanderings of the Human Mind in Searching the Scriptures*. It was printed in Sydney in 1841 and, says Moran, is probably the only work ever written in that penal settlement. It gives a concise history of the origin and growth and condemnation of the principal heresies that had arisen in the Church in the course of the centuries, which the author traced to the unauthorised and perverse interpretation of the Scriptures. And note well: it is dedicated to the students of the Royal College of St. Patrick, Maynooth. He was thinking of old times: "What a current of ideas rushes through my mind when I think of writing from the ends of the earth to you, my reverend brethren, who are now diligently engaged in acquiring useful and sacred knowledge . . . . I beg most earnestly to recommend myself, and about nine hundred unfortunate prisoners under my spiritual care, to your pious prayers and remembrance" — Preface, dated Norfolk Island, 19 July, 1840. Maynooth's involvement with the Australian Church was to continue well after Georgian times.

To conclude with a word concerning other missions. In May, 1838, three Limerick students went off to labour on the Scotch mission. They were countering the bad work that had been done there for a few years before then by Michael Crotty who had been expelled from Maynooth and later ordained in France but who had conformed and lectured again Catholicism in the chief towns of Scotland under the auspices of the Protestant Association. June, 1838, saw the consecration in Maynooth of the former Professor, Dr. Patrick Carew, as Bishop of Philadelphia *(in partibus)* and Coadjuter to the Vicar Apostolic of Madras. In September he left the College for London to prepare for Madras, to be followed within a few days by five priests — all of them ex-Maynooth — including the Professor of English Elocution, Mr. Kelly. The Maynooth Mission to India had been launched. It was destined to be of short duration yet has left behind it an indelible memory. Finally, in that same year, the brothers embarked "for the mission of Trinidad". George Butler was later to become Bishop of Limerick. It was far from the end of Maynooth College but the Maynooth of Georgian Ireland had passed.

The Royal Catholic College of Maynooth.